Chartwell

View of the Main Site at Klasies River Mouth

The Middle Stone Age at Klasies River Mouth in South Africa

Ronald Singer and
John Wymer

With contributions by
K. W. Butzer,
N. J. Shackleton, and
E. Voigt

The University of Chicago Press • Chicago and London

RONALD SINGER is the Robert R. Bensley Professor of Biology and Medical Sciences and professor of anatomy and of anthropology, with joint appointments in the Committee on Evolutionary Biology, Committee on Genetics, and Committee on African Studies, at the University of Chicago.

JOHN WYMER, formerly archeologist for the Museum and Art Gallery, Reading, United Kingdom, was a research associate in anatomy at the University of Chicago from 1965 to 1979. He is the author of several works in prehistory, including *Lower Palaeolithic Archaeology in Britain*.

THE UNIVERSITY OF CHICAGO PRESS, CHICAGO 60637
THE UNIVERSITY OF CHICAGO PRESS, LTD., LONDON

The University of Chicago Press gratefully acknowledges a subvention from the National Science Foundation in partial support of the costs of production of this volume.

LIBRARY OF CONGRESS CATALOGING IN PUBLICATION DATA
Singer, Ronald.
    The Middle Stone Age at Klasies River mouth in South Africa.
    Bibliography: p.
    Includes index.
    1. Mesolithic period—South Africa—Kaapsedrifrivier Valley.   2. Kaapsedrifrivier Valley (South Africa)—Antiquities.   3. South Africa—Antiquities.   I. Wymer, John.   II. Title.
GN774.42.S6S56   968.02   81–16081
ISBN 0–226–76103–7   AACR2

Contents

Acknowledgments

Many individuals have assisted, in different ways and in varying degrees, in either the field operations or the subsequent analyses and completion of this report. All have been important to us, for, without their cooperation or help, this operation could not have been successfully concluded.

We are especially grateful to our collaborators and to those who furnished us with reports on various aspects of the investigation: Mrs. Elizabeth Voigt (née Speed), Transvaal Museum; Dr. Nickolas Shackleton, Cambridge University; Professor Karl Butzer, University of Chicago; Mr. Jalmar Rudner, Cape Town; Dr. John Vogel, National Physical Research Laboratory, Council for Scientific and Industrial Research, Pretoria; Professor Philip Rightmire, State University of New York at Binghamton; Dr. Patricia Smith, University of Tel Aviv; Professor Richard Klein, University of Chicago; and Mr. C. Poggenpoel, South African Museum.

Right of access and permission to excavate Caves 1 and 2 and associated shelters were given by the landowner at that time, Mr. A. B. Potgieter, and by Mr. P. Du Preez for the remaining caves. Storage, working space, and laboratory facilities were kindly provided by the South African Museum, and thanks are due to Dr. T. Barry (director) for making these available, also to members of his staff for assistance in numerous ways, especially Miss M. Shaw and Mrs. Ione Rudner. Help was also received from Dr. John Grindley (then director) and his staff at the Port Elizabeth Museum.

The late Mr. W. Gess of Port Elizabeth visited and worked at the site on several occasions, and generously made available his wide knowledge of the area as well as opened his home to us with unlimited hospitality. Of the many other people in Port Elizabeth who extended their hospitality and kindness to the team of excavators, Mr. and Mrs. D. Organ, Mr. and Mrs. E. Attwell, Mr. and Mrs. L. Abel, and Mr. and Mrs. B. Playdon have our special appreciation. Messrs. D. Scarr, D. V. Spindler, and A. Mann kindly allowed us the use of their beach hut, and special thanks are also due to Mr. David Henderson, who organized the building of the temporary wooden bridge leading into Cave 2 (without which access to the deposits there would have been impossible). Much generosity and help were also received from local people at Klasies River Mouth, especially Mr. and Mrs. R. P. Terblanche at Palmietvlei, Mrs. Waite at Kaapsedrif Post Office, and Mr. James Melville at Humansdorp. Messrs. J. Sutherland (editor), Charles Morgan, and Jack Cooper of the *Port Elizabeth Evening Post* are thanked for their cooperation on publicity, and Mr. Clive Burton of the Port Elizabeth Historical Society for his interest in the site.

Several volunteers worked at the site and did much to expedite the progress of the excavations, some giving days and others weeks of their time. Among those from the University of Cape Town were Messrs. G. Voigt, G. Avery, and Frank Schweitzer and Misses Susan Liebermann and Margaret Denholm. Among those from Port Elizabeth were Messrs. John Knight, M. Turner, K. Edwards, and John Abel. Thanks are also due to Mr. Ivan O'Reilly and Mr. M. Jacobs (South African Museum) of Cape Town, as well as the late Mr. Dieter Hamann, who spent two periods at the site, one with his son and daughter, who both helped. Mr. Hamann also helped in many ways during our stay in Cape Town. In particular, we thank Dr. and Mrs. Barney Hirschson of Cape Town, who helped in diverse ways, including the taking of x-rays of specimens and extending generous hospitality.

The continued interest and advice of Mr. Berry Malan, then secretary of the Historical Monuments Commission, were greatly appreciated, both in Cape Town and at the site, which he visited with Mrs. Malan. Hilary and Janette Deacon visited the site on two occasions and provided valuable discussions. Because of their positions at the Albany Museum, Grahamstown, at the time, they assisted in other ways, and Mrs. Deacon kindly allowed an examination of the material excavated by her from the Howieson's Poort type site, prior to her publication. Dr. Oliver Davies also visited the site on two occasions and made important comments concerning the relationship of the occupational deposits to the chronology of the sea levels. Mr. C. Garth Sampson (now at Southern Methodist University, Dallas) made available his doctoral thesis on the Middle Stone Age in South Africa and also contributed to this report by discussing many points with one of us (J. W.) while working in England.

Last (and certainly not least) our grateful thanks go to the members of our "permanent" field staff—Messrs. Peter Saunders, Andrew Lawson, David Parish, and Jeremy Adams, all of whom reside in the UK. They and the local people who worked with the team often excavated under considerable difficulties and personal sacrifice. Only with their sustained effort could the excavations have been continued to the stage which warrants this report. Mrs. Jane Gilpin did the typing.

The investigations were carried out under grants to one of us (R. S.) from the United States National Science Foundation (GS-1658); USPHS grant 5-RO1-GM-10113; the Wenner-Gren Foundation for Anthropological Research, Inc., New York; the Boise Fund of Oxford University; and the Dr. Wallace C. and Clara A. Abbott Memorial Fund and the Lichtstern Fund (Department of Anthropology) of the University of Chicago.

1 Location and Setting

The caves or rock shelters we investigated all lie within a linear distance of 3 km east of the Klasies River Mouth in the Eastern Cape Province of the Republic of South Africa. Klasies River, otherwise known as the Kaapsedrifrivier, debouches into the Indian Ocean 40 km west of Cape St. Francis (34°6'S, 24°24'E). Humansdorp, the nearest town, is a similar distance away measured directly, and Port Elizabeth is a further 80 km along the coast (fig. 1.1). The Klasies River is small and only drains about 24 km of the coastal plain, unlike the nearby

Tzitzikama[1] River and Krom River, which are fed by waters directly from the Tzitzikama Mountains that dominate the northern skyline. The Klasies River descends in a series of falls and is never dry. The area lies between the Mediterranean climatic zone of the Western Cape and the subtropical zone of Natal. There is rain all year long, with a slightly greater amount in the winter months. At Port Elizabeth an average of 57.66 cm

1. Sometimes spelled "Tsitsikama" or "Tsitsikamma."

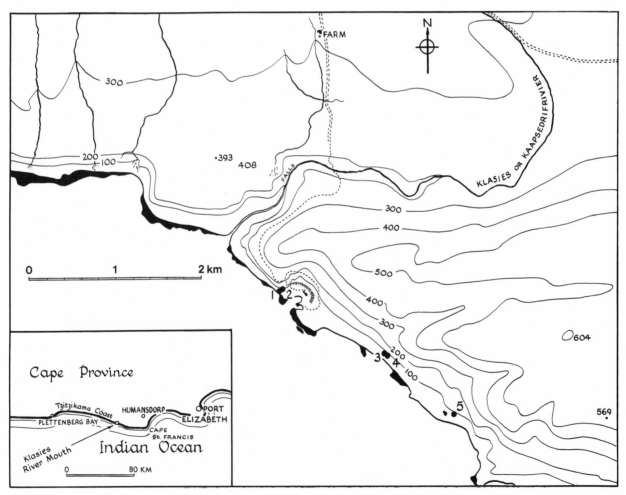

FIG. 1.1. Location map. The contours are at 100 ft. intervals. Nos. 1 through 5 indicate the locations of the caves and rock shelters.

(22.70 in.) of rain is recorded and a mean daily temperature of 62.4° F (see also chap. 4). The coastline is often referred to as the Tzitzikama Coast (pl. 1); although its center is around Storms River Mouth, the eastern and western limits of this coastline are inconsistently described and include sometimes more, sometimes less of the coastline between Plettenberg Bay and Cape St. Francis. It is a wild, rugged coast with steeply dipping quartzitic sandstone, bared and broken along the beaches, and with steep cliffs rarely lower than 60 m. The rock is mapped as Table Mountain sandstone and Bokkeveld shale. There are locally auriferous quartz veins in the sandstone and secondary ferricrete in cracks. The area has not been geologically mapped in detail, and it is possible that the formations predate the Table Mountain Series.

A few caves are known along the coast east of Plettenberg Bay and of the huge rock shelter at the mouth of the Matjes River at Keurboomstrand, but there are no adequate records of any investigations in them. The Klasies River Mouth caves (referred to hereafter as KRM) have been numbered from 1 to 5, although they really constitute three separate but nearby sites: 1–2, 3–4, and 5 (fig. 1.2). At the first site, the main one for the current excavations, there are associated rock shelters adjacent to the caves, and excavation has revealed the existence of another cave completely buried by occupational deposits. Other caves and rock shelters may well exist along this part of the coast, concealed by talus from the cliffs. The caves have evidently been cut by wave action along planes of weakness in the quartzite, and the level of their floors thus relates to high sea levels of the Upper Pleistocene period. The floor of Cave 1 is about 8 m above the present sea level; all the others are at about 20 m.

Caves 3 and 4 are adjacent and actually connected by a low, narrow tunnel through which it is possible to crawl from one to the other (a distance of about 18 m). Cave 3 is very much the larger one and has an impressive high antechamber and a long gallery at right angles to it roughly parallel to the cliff line and extending back about 110 m. It is also called the ''Bat Cave'' because so many bats inhabit it. Cave 5 is in the form of a large tunnel running back into the rock for about 90 m along a fault line. All these caves contain calcite formations, mainly in the form of stalagmites and stalactites. They are most developed in Caves 1 and 5, and in the latter the process is still active, for some signatures penciled about 50 years ago are now beneath a thin film of calcite. The presence of this calcite in predominantly acid rock formations is explained by the thick calcrete deposits which cover parts of the overlying cliff tops. These deposits are probably Pleistocene consolidated dunes and the source of the lime which is carried in solution by all the drainage water in this area flanking the sea.

All the caves at KRM display the obvious signs of use as habitation sites by Stone Age people. Thick accumulations of occupational soil and refuse now partially fill their entrances, and food debris and stone artifacts lie on the surface or have eroded out of these accumulations. Recent interference with these archeological deposits is negligible, and restricted to a few scrapings by fishermen and the curious. A slightly deeper hole about 0.75 m deep inside Cave 5 behind the 10 m high pile of midden deposits that blocks its entrance produced a human parietal fragment, found in 1957 by John Abel of Port Elizabeth in the disturbed soil around this hole. A crude core-like object in Cave 3, found on the surface by Jalmar Rudner, who believed it to date from the Early Stone Age, is in the South African Museum, Cape Town. Everything else naturally exposed in this cave appears to belong to the Later Stone Age (LSA), including some well-burnished black sherds of pottery.

The great mound at the entrance of Cave 5 is a shell midden, or at least the upper part is, but behind it, further inside the cave, Middle Stone Age (MSA) artifacts lie on the surface or are cemented by calcite onto the cave wall just above the present floor. This part of Cave 5 is now very dark, but before the mound at the entrance had accumulated, it would have been well illuminated.

Apart from the caves, other evidence for Upper Pleistocene sea levels is the raised beaches, or (more accurately) the wave-cut platforms, which survive along the coast between the Klasies River and the Point 2 km east (fig. 1.2). Immediately east of Caves 1 and 2 there is a particularly well preserved remnant of the 6–8 m platform (pl. 2). Between here and the caves, in the natural amphitheater used by us as a campsite, the surface is about 3 m above present sea level. Less well preserved platforms at about 6–8 m and higher exist east of Cave 5.

Immediately above Cave 1 is Cave 2 (pls. 3–5); this cave, with its floor at about 18 m, has changed much since it was occupied by Stone Age people: the floor near its original entrance has disappeared and, with it, those archeological deposits that formerly lay on it. Some of the overhang may also have collapsed. All this occupational debris and these rock fragments must have rolled or been washed down to the beach and ground up or dispersed by the sea. At present, on a continuous scree slope from beneath Shelter 1A to the degraded 6–8 m platform are exposed numerous MSA and Howieson's Poort artifacts, together with shells and a few animal bones. Cave 2 is no longer accessible save by a precarious climb. Inside, it extends back some 9 m, and the occupational deposits are clearly truncated by the present erosional slope, although they are also for the most part cemented into a hard limestone breccia. Stone artifacts, bones, and shells cemented to the cave walls up to 2 m above the present floor indicate former levels of the occupational deposits.

Excavation has shown that Shelter 1A and Cave 2 at one time shared a common floor. Archeological and faunal material is also cemented to the rock face beneath Shelter 1A, up to 7 m above the present floor, showing that the deposits once reached up to the overhang itself (pl. 4). At this level, a platelike formation of calcite attached to the rock must have built up on the surface of these deposits which filled the shelter before erosion commenced. It remains as a cast of the original surface.

A slight rock overhang immediately to the west of Cave 1 had a talus slope apparently banked against it, but, on excavation, this slope proved to be another series of occupational deposits severely truncated by later erosion. This shelter is termed Shelter 1B. On the other side of Cave 1 is the cave which was completely buried by deposits. Almost as large as Cave 1, this is Cave 1C. On the east side of our campsite is another small rock shelter, with a slight slope of the ground beneath it to the level of the 3–4 m beach. This is Shelter 1D.

Fresh water would never have been a problem to the occupants of these caves and shelters. In addition to the Klasies River itself, numerous springs emerge from beneath the calcreted dunes overlying the cliffs, and water drips down the cliffs at various places. This water, mainly because of its high lime content, does not taste pleasant but is quite drinkable. Festoons of calcite dipping from the overhang above Caves 1 and 2 indicate that limerich water previously dripped over the edge; a little still does, but whether this is sufficient to account for such formations seems unlikely. More likely is a diversion of the water or the blocking of an original spring. However, excavation demonstrated that a considerable amount of subterranean water is still flowing through the lower part of the occu-

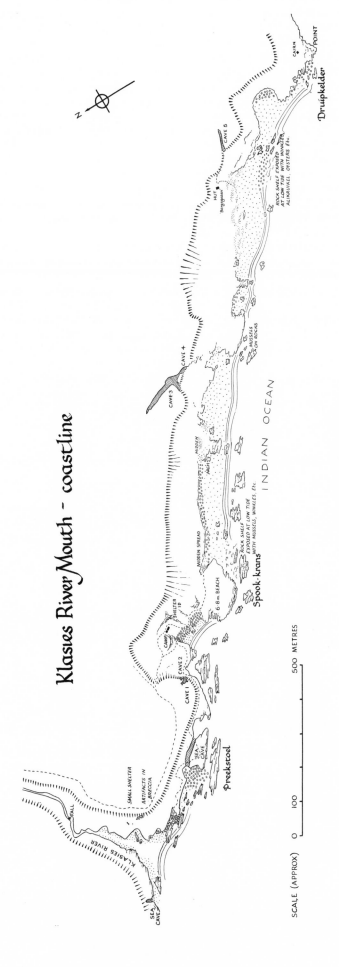

FIG. 1.2. Map of KRM coastline.

pational deposits beneath Shelter 1A (layers 34–36) and has affected their composition as well as the condition of the bones and shells within them. At present, there is plenty of water dripping from the cliffs on each side of Shelter 1D, and this water was used at our excavation camp. A gully on the west side of the campsite partially filled with soil and rock scree suggests the presence of a much more considerable flow of water up to the times of the 3–4 m beach. Even after heavy rain, no more than a trickle of water was ever observed flowing down this gully.

Apart from the middens in the caves, LSA Strandloper[2] activity in the area is shown by the remains of other middens along the beach between Caves 1 and 5 and beyond. They make little in the way of mounds, but form spreads of shells, crude flakes and cores, burnt stones, and a few bleached bones. Potsherds occur on at least two of them. Inland there are few artifacts to be seen on the ploughed fields or wherever else the ground is broken up, except for a remarkable dune site about 3 km east of Cave 1, about 1.5 km from the sea, south of the Tzitzikama River. The site takes its name from the farm it lies on, Geelhoutboom, or Geelhout, and has been described by Laidler (1947). Quartzite artifacts abound on the surface of deflated, ferruginous sands in patches over an area of at least 3

sq km. Well-made handaxes and cleavers are common as well as all the types of MSA artifacts found at KRM. Although there is also some Howieson's Poort material from the site in the Albany Museum, it is not common.

The present-day vegetation of this part of the Eastern Cape Province is varied. The coastal plain is about 9 km wide and for the most part used as arable or pasture land. Behind are the Karreedouw Mountains, being the eastern extension of the Tzitzikama Mountains, rising 1,000 m and more. About 50 km to the west and beyond Storms River is the Tzitzikama Forest Reserve, the remains of one of the largest indigenous forests in South Africa. The Tzitzikama River and Krom River have cut deep valleys in the coastal plain, and these valleys widen considerably toward the sea. Patches of deflated dune sands, as at Geelhoutboom, also occur nearer and at Cape St. Francis, and the coast itself varies from rocky wave-battered cliffs to sandy beaches and bays. Names such as "Palmietvlei" attest to the presence of temporary lakes at high water tables. In Upper Pleistocene times, with none of the recent exploitation of the forest and development of the land, one can be sure that this varied environment attracted an equally rich and varied fauna, which must have been one of the major factors attracting MSA hunters to this part of the Tzitzikama Coast (see chap. 12 and *A Guide to the Vertebrate Fauna of the Eastern Cape Province, Part I: Mammals and Birds* [Grahamstown: Albany Museum, 1931]).

2. Formerly spelled "strandlooper," this word refers to beach-combers in coastal areas.

2 Investigations along the Tzitzikama Coast, and the Discovery of the KRM Caves

The pioneer work in this area was done by F. W. FitzSimons, formerly director of the Port Elizabeth Museum, who claimed to have explored by 1923 all the known sites between Coldstream and Groot Rivier. He refers particularly to Whitcher's Cave and a cave in the "Groot Rivier Gorge," but it is likely that a few other caves or shelters were involved and it is not at all clear from his publications (FitzSimons 1921, 1923, 1926) just what was found where. The problem is accentuated by FitzSimons's (1926) vague reference to the Tzitzikama Coast as including every place between Knysna and Port Elizabeth. A map in the Port Elizabeth Museum gives the approximate positions of the caves that he investigated along the west part of the Tzitzikama Coast but does not help in associating finds with them. Some of the famous painted gravestones may have come from Whitcher's Cave, but as with much of the other spectacular LSA material, it is difficult to be sure. Clark (1959) cautiously cites finds from these explorations as "Tzitzikama Caves," although some more recent research by Schauder (1963) and Turner (1970) has clarified to some extent the whereabouts of Whitcher's Cave and the Groot Rivier Cave. The former is about 19 km inland in the Outeniqua Mountains near Coldstream, but should not be confused with the Coldstream Cave excavated by Peringuey (1911) several years earlier which was near the mouth of the Lottering River. The exact position of the Groot Rivier Cave is not known, but according to Schauder, it may have been on the promontory overlooking Plettenberg Bay at the mouth of the Groot Rivier near the village of Nature's Valley. However, Turner refers to this as the Nature's Valley Cave. Obviously, the confusion is not settled.

These early investigations revealed many aspects of LSA culture in South Africa: elaborate burials, personal ornaments, well-executed paintings on rock slabs, and other equipment indicative of a vital society in contrast to the dreary evidence left in the coastal shell middens. The human burials have provided anthropological material of limited value (Gear 1926; Wells 1952). Unfortunately the excavations have been published with insufficient detail to produce any useful chronological information. One early paper (Kingston 1900) even published a plate of MSA flake-blades from the "Knysna Caves."

Prior to 1966, when one of us (R. S.) was formulating a project designed to try and solve some of the problems concerning human physical and cultural evolution in South Africa during the Pleistocene and Recent periods, the only large excavation that had ever been attempted in the area under consideration was at Matjes River. This great rock shelter, overlooking

the sea and about a mile east of Keurboomstrand, protected by the Historical Monuments Commission, was first dug by the late T. F. Dreyer in 1928. His work was continued by the late A. C. Hoffman of the National Museum, Bloemfontein, in 1952. Dreyer (1933) describes a section with 8 ft. (2.5 m) of midden, mainly mussel shells, containing a stone industry referred to as Smithfield C, overlying 2 ft. (.8 m) of black loam with wooden artifacts.[1] The stone industry in the latter layer is described as Wilton. Beneath this, his layers D and E yielded an industry comparable to that from the Cape St. Blaize Cave at Mossel Bay. Later, more intensive excavations were made by Louw (1960). He cut through the rear part of the rock shelter where the occupational deposits thickened to over 30 ft. (9 m). A similar industrial sequence was recognized in the upper 16 ft. (5 m), but a different interpretation was given for the 20 ft. (6 m) of midden below: the Mossel Bay type artifacts were thought to have been collected and used by people at a much later period.

Many human remains were found at Matjes River, but it is not clear whether they are contemporary with particular layers or intruded into them. Thus it is unfortunately impossible to relate the burials to their correct cultural levels or to place them into any sequence (Singer 1961).

Apart from some trial excavations in Fisherman's Cave on the Robberg Peninsula in 1965 (Hoffman 1967), only one serious investigation of archeological sites in the Tzitzikama region had commenced: work by R. R. Inskeep, then of the University of Cape Town. This was also in a cave on the Robberg Peninsula known as Nelson Bay Cave, and was to prove a valuable site.

Thus, in 1966, not one Late Pleistocene site in the area had been adequately excavated or published. The situation was little different in the whole of the Cape Province, and with some rare exceptions in the rest of South Africa. Only in the north had there been any work of consequence (e.g., Cave of Hearths, Kalkbank, Mwulu's Cave, Bushman Rock, Rose Cottage, Border Cave, Holley Shelter, Olieboompoort), and none of these sites had been published in sufficient detail. This is perhaps not surprising: Inskeep (1961) despairingly considered "the provision, in terms of trained, professional archaeologists, that exists in the Union. Only one museum south of Rhodesia has a university-trained archaeologist on its staff, and only one university in South Africa offers proper instruc-

---

1. All conversions to and from the metric system are approximations.

5

tion in the subject." This was in response to the publication of Louw's (1960) work at Matjes River. Happily, signs of change were coming; in the Cape, the Deacons were digging methodically at Scott's Cave in 1963, and Keller was at Montagu Cave in 1964.

At this time, the terminology in use was that recommended at the Third Pan-African Congress on Prehistory in 1955: Earlier, Middle, and Later Stone Ages with First and Second Intermediate periods (stages) between them. These main divisions were subdivided into various stone industries or regional variants. Already, by 1965, this was seen to be unsatisfactory, and other recommendations were made at a symposium held at Burg Wartenstein, Austria. These were that cultural-stratigraphic terms should be separated from those with connotations of time and that cultural-stratigraphic units should only be used for type sites that had been carefully excavated and well documented (Kleindienst 1967). These recommendations were accepted by the Pan-African Congress at Dakar in 1967. In the meantime, Clark et al. (1966) had published a plea for similar precision and definition in terminology. The difficulty of applying rigid rules in South Africa is immediately apparent when it is realized that all the MSA regional variants were based on type sites that were either surface scatters, selected samples, or virtually unrecorded excavations. Terminology will be discussed further in chapter 15, when the results of the KRM excavations are considered against the rather different situation of 1979, over 10 years later. The same applies to the sites in South Africa which typified the First Intermediate period (Howieson's Poort—inadequately published) and the LSA (Smithfield—surface collection; Wilton—inadequately excavated and published).

The state of knowledge in 1966 concerning the human occupation of the Cape Province during the Late Pleistocene period was extremely vague. The MSA was represented by stone industries dominated by flakes and blades with prepared striking platforms (Levallois technique) and various forms of points. There was also an industry from Howieson's Poort with small, backed crescents and bifacial points which was placed in the Second Intermediate period. The LSA consisted of Smithfield and Wilton complexes, regarded as broadly contemporary. Finally, so-called Strandloper sites, usually with pottery, were a feature of the Cape coastline. For the MSA in the Cape, the only excavated sites were Mossel Bay and some caves in the Fish Hoek-Kalk Bay area near Cape Town, the most important of which was Skildergat (otherwise known as Peers' Cave). There were also the upper levels of the recently excavated cave at Montagu, and Howieson's Poort itself, dug in 1927–28 (Stapleton and Hewitt 1927, 1928) and reinvestigated by Deacon in 1965. Nothing was known with any certainty of the dating of these MSA and Howieson's Poort industries other than that the former were broadly Late Pleistocene. As for the Howieson's Poort, Clark (1959) included this industry with the Magosian complex and estimated that it fell within the limits of 6,000 and 10,000 B.C. A radiocarbon date from this site of 16,790 B.C. ± 320 (I-1844) resulted from Deacon's reinvestigations and seemed rather early. Other radiocarbon dates (Deacon 1966) for MSA sites in South Africa outside the Cape varied from about 10,000 B.C. to greater than 44,000 years.

It was this period of the Late Pleistocene that was chosen as the one which should be given priority for the project envisaged. The distribution of MSA material provided sufficient evidence that there had been plenty of human activity in the southern and eastern Cape, so this area was considered to be very likely to produce a suitable site. What was required was a single site that had been occupied for a long period of the Late Pleistocene, even if intermittently, and preferably one that had not been disturbed or partly destroyed by any recent diggings, either commercial or otherwise. Skildergat Cave would have been a good choice, but most of the deposits had been dug away. Similarly with Mossel Bay (Goodwin and Malan 1935). The Late Pleistocene is such a critical period for the development of *Homo sapiens sapiens* that it was considered this would be the most useful period upon which to concentrate. At that time it was impossible to interpret the evidence already known from the Cape itself, let alone make comparisons with human events of the Late Pleistocene elsewhere in Africa or the world. This situation is no reflection upon the excellent work of such South African archeologists as Goodwin, Malan, and others, who had established order and laid the foundations for the prehistory of the country. Well-excavated and well-documented sites spanning the Late Pleistocene in the Cape were just not known, and it was impossible to do more. This state of affairs was preventing any adequate understanding of the general cultural development in this important area of southern Africa during this period and was an underlying factor in the search for a suitable site. The emphasis in 1966 was on the need to produce a long stratigraphical succession to which past discoveries might be related and a local sequence established.

A few human fragments had been discovered which qualified for a Late Pleistocene date, particularly the Fish Hoek skull from Skildergat Cave. There was some doubt as to the precise horizon from which this skull came, and whether it was associated with a Howieson's Poort industry or a slightly later one referred to as "coarse Stillbay." In either case it still qualified as Late Pleistocene. The Cape Flats skull (found below dune sands) had been related to an MSA Stillbay Industry, but on the extremely tenuous evidence of some Stillbay type artifacts found nearby! Outside the Cape, there were a few other scanty human remains found in South Africa, the most important of which were the cranium from Florisbad, Orange Free State, and an adult and infant burial from the Border Cave, Natal. Radiocarbon dating appeared to support a Late Pleistocene date of c. 50,000 years for the former, and the Border Cave burials were associated with what was described as either an "Epi-Pietersburg" or "Normal Pietersburg" Industry. In the Transvaal, the Tuinplaats skeleton was thought to be at the same level as Pietersburg artifacts. The stated associations of the Boskop remains, found in 1913, are one MSA flake-blade encrusted with ferricrete, as was the skull. Any further human remains with precise cultural associations and dating would obviously be of great use in assessing human physical evolution in the Late Pleistocene.

It was therefore essential that, besides fulfilling the requirements mentioned above, the site chosen have deposits of a suitable nature to ensure the preservation of bone. In an area of predominantly Paleozoic quartzitic sandstone this requirement was not easy to satisfy. There were no known sites along the Tzitzikama Coast where MSA industries had been found under stratified conditions, but a considerable number of surface finds had been reported. Concentrations of surface material have already been mentioned from Geelhoutboom, a dune area 3–4 km east of KRM, and there is a series of surface sites on and near the coast at Slang or Oyster Bay near Cape St. Francis, about 32 km from KRM (W. Gess, personal communication). At the latter sites, MSA artifacts have been found in association with middens and faunal remains, and collections have been made by J. Rudner for the South African Museum and by the late W. Gess for the Port Elizabeth Museum. Similar sites have since been reported from Saldanha Bay, north of Cape Town (Volman 1978). Surface sites are also at Maitland River Mouth near Port Elizabeth (unpublished, communicated by W. Gess at the annual conference of the South African Association for the Advancement of Science, Stellenbosch, 1966), and many more probably exist.

Attention was first drawn to the caves at Klasies River Mouth by Ludwig Abel of the Port Elizabeth Mountain Club in 1955. The club organized a joint excursion to the site with the local branch of the South African Archaeological Society. A member of the latter, W. Gess, then honorary curator of archaeology at Port Elizabeth Museum, observed the mounds in the cave entrances and artifacts on the scree slope beneath Shelter 1A, and through his son, employed as entomologist at the South African Museum, the site came to the notice of archeologists in Cape Town and visits were made by Jalmar Rudner, Ray Inskeep, and one of us (R. S.). In 1962, on the occasion of the annual meeting of the South African Association for the Advancement of Science at Port Elizabeth, a further excursion was made to the site and B. D. Malan, secretary of the Historical Monument Commission, was among the party.

The decision to excavate was made by one of us (R.S.) as part of a project designed to solve some of the problems con-

cerning human physical and cultural evolution in South Africa during the Pleistocene and Recent periods. The caves at Klasies River Mouth were chosen because (i) cultural material exposed on scree slopes showed that archeological deposits certainly existed; (ii) calcareous conditions made it likely that skeletal remains would be preserved; (iii) the proximity of the sea made correlations with former sea levels likely; (iv) samples for radiocarbon dating were likely to be obtained; (v) the association of preserved faunal remains made it likely that human material might be found; and (vi) there were no signs of previous disturbance, whether by guano diggers or treasure hunters.

The project was organized by R. S., and work in the field was directed by J. W. Excavation took place during two seasons: December 1966 to August 1967, and February 1968 to July 1968, under license from the Historical Monuments Commission. The excavation team also comprised David A. Parish, Jeremy M. Adams (first season only), Peter R. J. Saunders, and A. J. Lawson (second season only). An average of four local men were employed as laborers.

The whole complex was divided horizontally into convenient areas for investigation and recording (see site plan, fig. 2.1). All excavated material was recorded in relation to these areas by each vertical layer, as defined in the numerous meas-

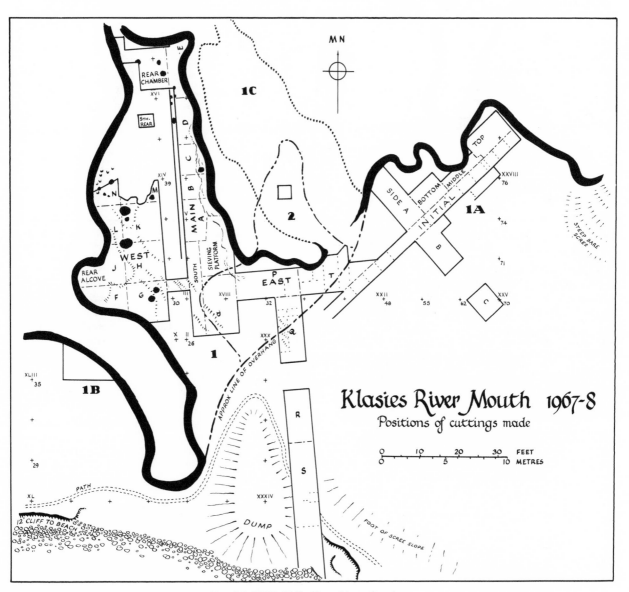

Fig. 2.1. KRM, 1967–68: positions of cuttings.

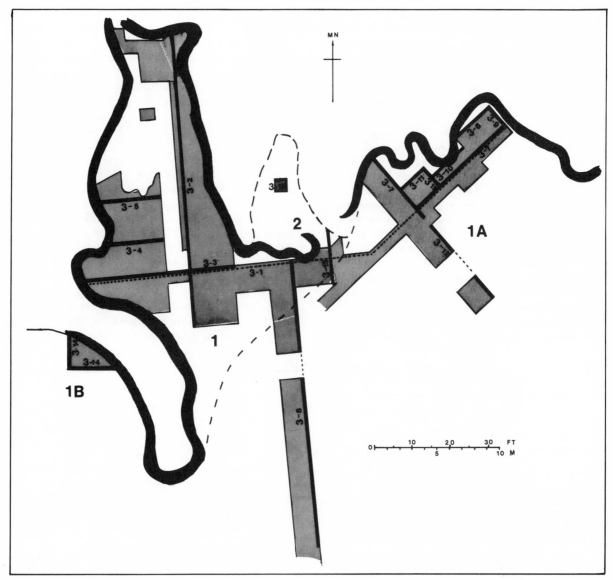

FIG. 2.2. Plan of KRM Main Site. The areas excavated are shaded. Thick lines indicate drawn sections illustrated in chap. 3, with the figure numbers beside them.

ured sections shown in figure 2.2. All the layers were examined by hand troweling and subsequent sieving of the residue. This was done in ½ in. mesh sieves, except in the case of the Howieson's Poort layers, which were wet-sieved through ¼ in. mesh. All archeological and faunal material was recorded in this manner, and catalog numbers were given to all categories except undiagnosable bone fragments and unretouched flakes and flake-blades. The latter were conserved within bags denoting their horizontal and vertical provenances. Detailed photographic records were maintained throughout the investigation.

All the excavated material and field records have been presented to the South African Museum, Cape Town.

3 Archeological Stratigraphy of the Main Site

The complex of caves and rock shelters referred to as Caves 1, 1C, and 2 and Shelters 1A and 1B as shown on the plan (fig. 2.1) constituted the Main Site. Excavation has shown that the deposits which filled these various caves or shelters are all part of the same buildup commencing with MSA habitation on the sandy beach of the 6–8 m sea. The gradual accumulation of occupational deposits under Shelter 1B, and inside and outside Cave 1, gradually blocked them, but the great mound which resulted eventually allowed easy access to Cave 2 and Shelter 1A. Cave 1C, too wet for habitation, also became completely blocked in the process and was not visible again until revealed by excavation. A great mass of the original deposits, possibly the majority, has been eroded away; a brief glance at any of the sections that are drawn along axes toward the sea shows the truncated nature of the layers caused by this erosion. Extrapolation of bedding planes and the continuation of the occupational deposits revealed in the side cuttings from Shelter 1A indicate the enormous quantity of archeological material that must still remain in the lee of the cliff face on the east side.

The figures accompanying this chapter show sections from the different parts of the site. The full history of the long occupation can be read from the composite and isometric sections (figs. 3.1 and 3.1A), which show the total accumulation from the bedrock and shingle of the 6–8 m beach to the truncated top of the deposits beneath Shelter 1A. They also indicate the presence of stone artifacts, shells, and bones which adhere to the cliff wall above and beside Shelter 1A, proving the previous existence of deposits which extended their accumulation at least 6 m above the present surface of the ground and suggesting how Shelter 1A and Cave 2 were linked. For ease of reference, figure 2.2 shows the positions of all the sections illustrated in this report, with their figure numbers.

The evidence for LSA occupation inside Cave 1 is considered separately, in detail, in chapter 9, as is that from Shelter 1D.

Horizontal plotting of the occupational deposits beneath Shelters 1A and 1B is of no consequence, as erosion and lack of total excavation prevent their former spread from being estimated. However, inside Cave 1, their complete preservation and total excavation, save for a central witness section, show how successive phases of occupation were gradually pushed toward the cave mouth as the interior became choked. Their former extent outside the cave along the old beach can only be inferred. (For plans of the horizontal distributions of the various archeological layers in Cave 1, see figs. 3.19–3.26 at the end of this chapter and figs. 9.2 and 9.3.) The detailed descrip-

tion of the sections will be followed by some notes on the general stratigraphy which explain how it is used as a basis for subdividing the stone industries found throughout the sequence. Only general reference will be made to the quantity of artifacts, bones, etc., recorded in the various layers of the deposits. Numerical details are given in the chapters dealing with the industries, e.g., chapters 5, 6, and 7 (tables 7.1 and 7.2).

Cave 1 (Figures 3.2–3.6, Plates 7–15)

Two sections are shown, one along the major axis of the cave from front to rear on the east side of the witness section (fig. 3.2), and another at right angles to it near the mouth (fig. 3.3). Two further sections also at right angles to the major axis show the vertical distribution of the layers deeper inside the cave (figs. 3.4 and 3.5). Figure 3.6 shows the relationship of the lower deposits on the rock platform outside the cave.

Before proceeding to a detailed discussion of each of the layers, we should make a remark on the layer numbering of Cave 1 and Shelter 1A at Klasies River Mouth. The discovery that the occupation deposits of Cave 1 and Shelter 1A constitute one continuous sequence, and the necessity to subdivide certain layers as work progressed, made renumbering of some of the layers necessary in order to prevent confusion. Table 3.1 is for the use of those referring to material from KRM at the South African Museum, which is marked with the layer number as excavated.

Layers + and 4 to 12. Surface soil and LSA middens, described in chapter 9.

Layer 13. Soft sand with lenses of silt and clay.[1] The sand was pale yellow (Munsell 5Y 7/3) and the silt and clay mainly an olive gray (Munsell 5Y 5/2). The sand was cross-bedded, and the thin lenses of silt and clay followed these bedding planes. This layer was continuous over all the earlier deposits in the cave and attained a maximum thickness of nearly a meter on the west side. Silts and clays were much thicker close to the cave wall on the same side. The upper part was cemented in patches to a depth of up to 15 cm with a near-continuous crust a few centimeters thick at the top which formed the surface for the initial LSA occupation.

1. Consistencies and other soil features are described to conform with recommendations contained in Jennings and Brink (1961).

10

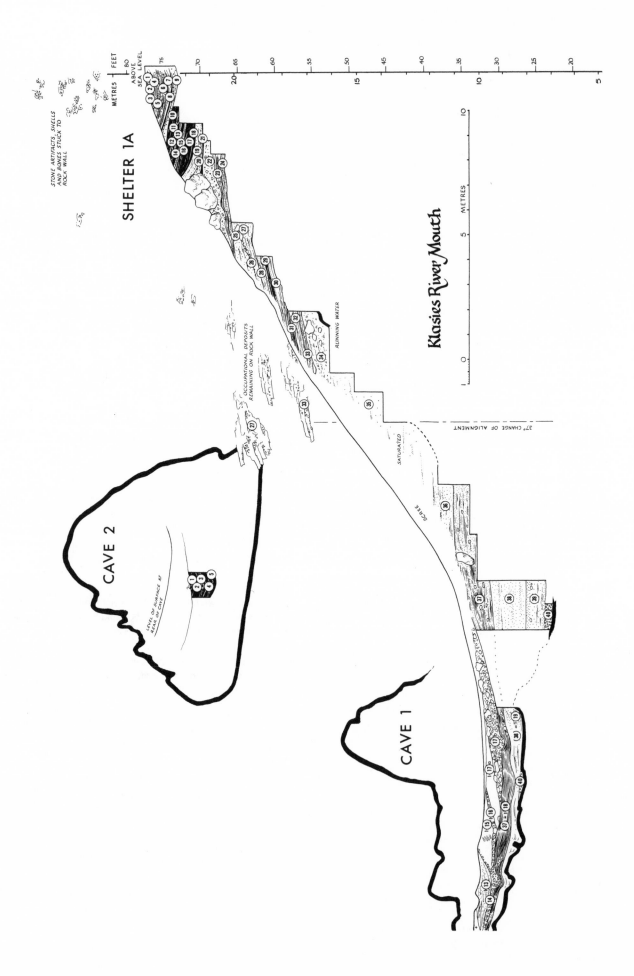

SHELTER 1A

STONE ARTIFACTS, SHELLS AND BONES STUCK TO ROCK WALL

Klasies River Mouth

OCCUPATIONAL DEPOSITS REMAINING ON ROCK WALL

CAVE 2

CAVE 1

LEVEL OF SURFACE AT REAR OF CAVE

RUNNING WATER

SATURATED

SCREE

37° CHANGE OF ALIGNMENT

METRES FEET ABOVE SEA LEVEL

METRES

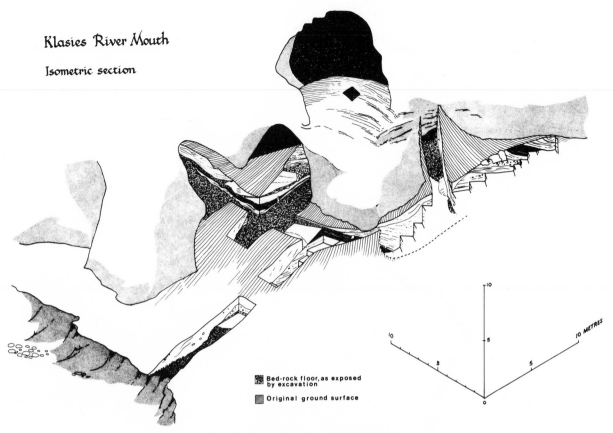

Klasies River Mouth

Isometric section

Bed-rock floor, as exposed by excavation

Original ground surface

10 METRES

FIG. 3.1A. Isometric section of KRM Main Site.

FIG. 3.1. General section from Cave 1 to Shelter 1A, based on contiguous cuttings made in 1966–68. The stratigraphy has been used to divide the MSA industries into four stages. These are represented by the following deposits:

MSA I	Cave 1, Layers 37 to 38
	Shelter 1A, Layers 37 to 39
MSA II	Cave 1, Layers 13 to 17, 17a, 17b
	Shelter 1A, Layers 22 to 36
Howieson's Poort	Shelter 1A, Layers 10 to 21
	Cave 2, Layers 1 to 5
MSA III	Shelter 1A, Layers 1 to 9
MSA IV	Cave 1, Layer 13

(N.B. Shelter 1B, not shown on this figure, contained MSA I in layers 1 to 15. Cave 1C, also not shown, only contained occupational deposits near its entrance; none was more recent than MSA II.)

12

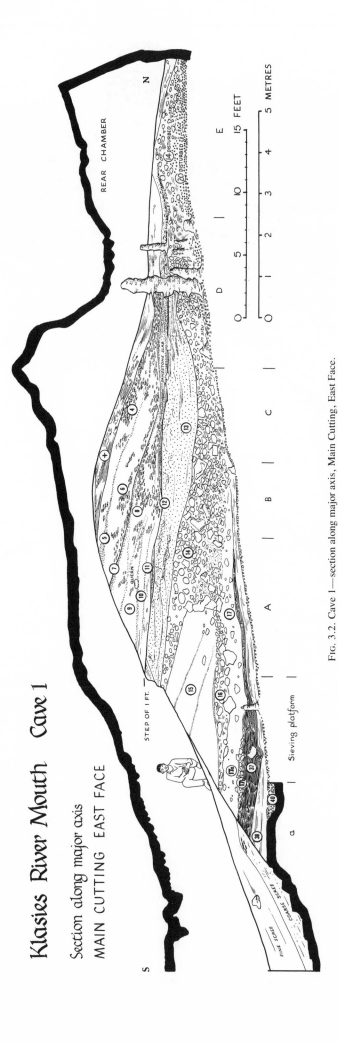

Klasies River Mouth   Cave 1

Section along major axis
MAIN CUTTING   EAST FACE

REAR CHAMBER

STEP OF 1 FT.

Sieving platform

FINE SCREE
COARSE SCREE

0   5   10   15   FEET

0   1   2   3   4   5   METRES

FIG. 3.2. Cave 1—section along major axis, Main Cutting, East Face.

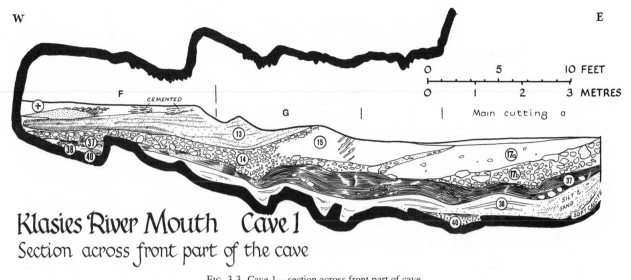

W   E

Klasies River Mouth   Cave 1
Section across front part of the cave

FIG. 3.3. Cave 1—section across front part of cave.

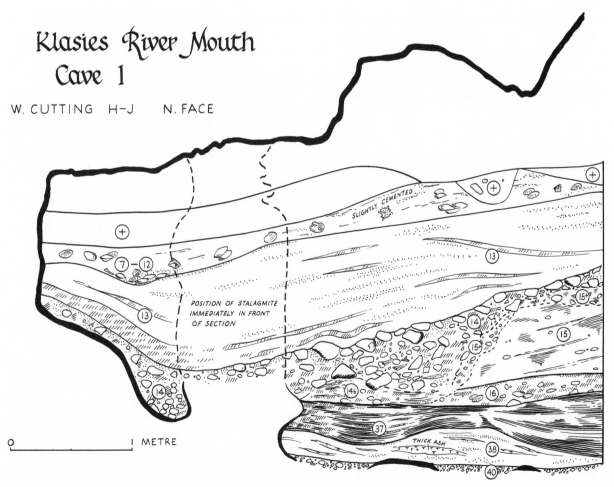

Klasies River Mouth Cave 1

W. CUTTING H–J   N. FACE

FIG. 3.4. Cave 1—West Cutting H–J, North Face.

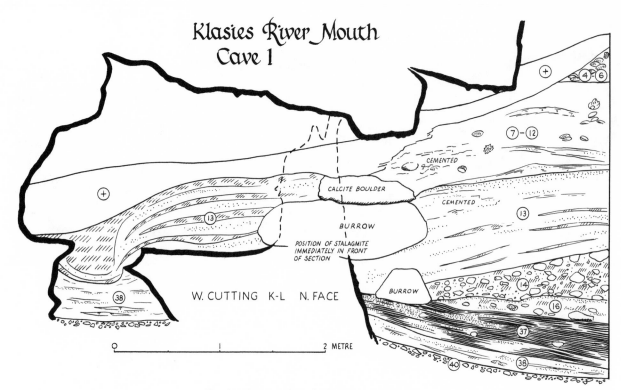

FIG. 3.5. Cave 1—West Cutting K–L, North Face.

No hearths were found in this layer, nor were there any soils that might have formed through the activities of occupants over a lengthy period. The only possible exception was a pocket of darker brown sand about 1 m wide and 12 cm thick on the east side (in Main Cutting A) that contained several shells and flakes. Otherwise, bone fragments, shells, and stone artifacts were distributed throughout the sand somewhat scantily. Nothing was found in the silt or clay.

Layer 14. A dirty, dark grayish brown (Munsell 2.5Y 4/2) sand and silt forming a matrix to a rubble of beach pebbles and boulders, lumps of calcite, broken stalagmites or stalactites, and fragments of the rock wall. This was thickest on the east side of the cave, where it was banked against the mound of the underlying layer 15. Here it was nearly a meter thick, but it thinned out to less than half this thickness on the west side and toward the rear of the cave, where it was much less coarse. Pebbles were more numerous toward the rear of the cave, but, as shown in the sections, this area appears to have suffered so much disturbance that it is referred to as layer 14+. Similarly, it had become mixed with the upper part of the underlying layer 15 on the west side, and this is referred to as layer 14b. On the extreme west side of the cave the harder elements of the layer were firmly cemented to the wall. Nowhere did the matrix or the rubble show any signs of bedding.

This was one of the richest layers for archeological material, both faunal and cultural. Bones and stone artifacts formed a considerable proportion of the rubble, as the numerical tables of finds indicate (see chap. 7). No hearths occurred, but occasional small lumps of charcoal and numerous flecks were recovered. The only articulated skeleton, that of a leopard, was found on the west side, on the edge of the mound of layer 15. It was complete but slightly disturbed, perhaps by natural movement within the layer sometime after it had been covered.

Layer 15. A soft to firm, compact occupational soil, dark grayish brown in color (Munsell 2.5Y 4/2), which contained numerous thin lines of ash and was flecked with charcoal. The layer formed a mound resting on the near-horizontal layer 16 below, with the upper part partially cemented into a crust by lime. A few small stalagmites had also formed prior to the formation of layer 14. Intermittently dripping water in one small, restricted area had also formed a series of calcite crusts one above the other as the soil developed in thickness. This shows in the section across the front part of the cave (fig. 3.3) and emphasizes the steep dip of the mound.

Toward the east side of the cave the soil was looser and, close to the wall, mixed with calcite and soft, calcareous clay. A large broken stalagmite shows in the section (fig. 3.2) along the major axis of the cave toward the rear, and the soil of this layer was banked up against it but very mixed with the rubble of layer 14 on its other side. The top of this mound of soil was 1.2 m above its base.

Bone fragments were plentiful and fairly well preserved, but shells were mainly fragmentary and highly decalcified. Both were distributed throughout the layer. Stone artifacts were very numerous (see chap. 5).

Layer 16. The composition of this thin layer differed considerably from one end of the cave to the other: dirty sand and clay at the front increased to a thickness of 24 cm further inside, where it contained a thick rubble of pebbles, angular rock fragments, large lumps of soft and hard calcite, broken stalagmites, and many large and small bones in good condition, as well as a prolific stone industry. A small patch near the cave mouth contained a jumble of burnt stones and bones. Shells occurred throughout, mainly decalcified in the clayey front part but better preserved in the rubble. Near the east wall of the cave the layer thickened to about 30 cm and merged into a soft, sticky calcareous clay. Traces of clean sand were sealed by this layer in niches or on ledges along the cave wall. Where it outcropped beyond the mound of layer 15 and met the rubble of layer 14, it was indistinguishable from that layer. However, as shown on the plan (fig. 3.22), it did not appear to extend

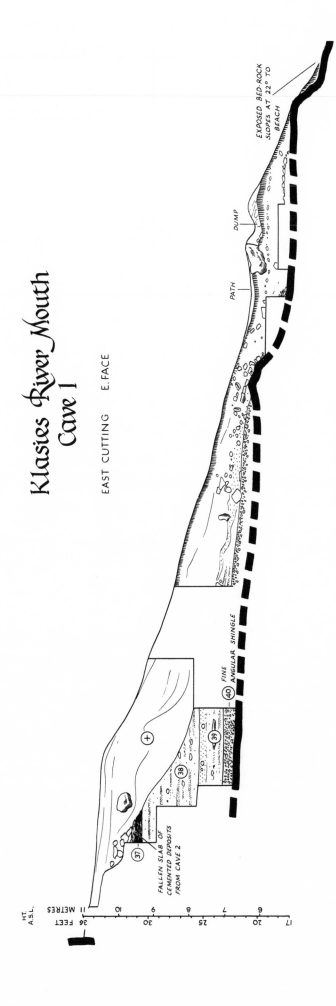

Klasies River Mouth
Cave 1

EAST CUTTING   E. FACE

FIG. 3.6. Cave 1—East Cutting, East Face.

Table 3.1. LAYER NUMBERING OF CAVE 1 AND SHELTER 1A AT KLASIES RIVER MOUTH

Shelter 1A		Cave 1	
As Excavated	As Published	As Excavated	As Published
1	1	1	1
2	2	2	2
3	3	3	3
4	4	4	4
5	5	5	5
6	6	6	6
7a	7	7	7
7b	8	8	8
7c	9	9	9
8a	10	10	10
8b	11	11	11
8c	12	12	12
9a	13	13	13
9b	14	14	14
9c	15	15	15
9d	16	16	16
10a	17	17a	17a
10b	18	17b	17b
10c	19	18	37
10d	20	19a	38
10e	21	19b	39
11	22	20	40
12a	23		
12b	24	? 16-17	
13	25	East Cutting	36
14	26		
15	27		
16a	28		
16b	29		
17	30		
18	31		
19a	32		
19b	33		
20	34		
?	35		

beyond Main Cutting B, about halfway back from the cave mouth. Where there was doubt, faunal and cultural material were attributed to layer 14.

Layer 17. In the rear part, this layer was originally dug as one unit, a dark, grayish brown occupational soil with a small amount of pebbles, calcite fragments, and other rubble. Nearer the front of the cave, however, the rubble content increased and an upper occupational soil (17a) could be differentiated from a lower rubble (17b).

Layer 17a. This dirty occupational soil showed no signs of bedding and merged into clay toward the east wall of the cave. Flecks of charcoal occurred throughout. Bones were fairly plentiful and in good condition, but much of the shell was decomposed. Stone artifacts were very numerous.

Layer 17b. The matrix of the rubble was soil and clay identical to that of layer 17a. Much of the rubble consisted of blocks of

soft calcite. It was very rich in bones and stone artifacts, which were lying, as with the other rubble layers, at all angles. Shells were mainly decomposed, but occasional ones occurred in near-perfect condition. The large rubble was largely confined to the very front of the cave mouth on the east side.

Layer 37 (see table 3.1). A black, greasy occupational soil (Munsell 10YR 2/1) which extended over both sides of the cave from the mouth to halfway to the rear. It was no more than .5 m thick at any point and thinned to nothing on the west side. The color and texture of this soil contrasted greatly with the overlying layers, but no signs of any weathering between them could be detected. The soil was highly carbonaceous and flecked with charcoal, but it was not possible to isolate individual hearths. Pebbles and small stones occurred throughout, but there were very few large lumps of calcite or wall fragments. Bedding was clear and even, but with several undulations due to the nature of the soil and the underlying irregularities. On the west side it was a little mixed with overlying and underlying layers. Bones and stone artifacts were plentiful, shells being mainly decomposed.

Layer 38. Silty sand and occupational soil which extended over both sides of the cave halfway toward the rear and varied from 15 to 45 cm in thickness. A palimpsest of laminated ash hearths occurred throughout most of the layer, especially toward the cave mouth, although one of the thickest accumulations of ash was well inside the cave on the west side (fig. 3.25). This layer rested directly on the beach shingle, filling up any hollows that existed in the underlying bedrock. Toward the cave mouth the layer was much sandier, and further in the cave on the same side it merged into clay against the wall.

Bone was well preserved and plentiful in this layer, as were stone artifacts. Shells were also found in large numbers, although very crushed for the most part.

Layer 40. A thin spread of clean beach gravel and shingle was found over much of the cave floor. Near the front of the cave the upper few centimeters was generally cemented into a crust. The positions of the major stalagmites which had formed on this surface are shown on the plan (fig. 3.26). Some of these may have been growing during the time of the cave's occupation, but it seems most likely that they were already nearly in their present form beforehand. Some calcite was certainly being formed around their bases during the period of occupation, for lateral projections must represent growth around new floor levels. Intensity of growth could also reflect climatic changes. The large stalagmite between the main cave and the rear chamber has a marked growth of calcite around the level of the top of layer 13 and just above it, and another between the top of the upper midden and the most recent soil accumulation.

Bedrock. The bedrock is hard quartzite mapped as Table Mountain sandstone but possibly of a different formation.

Interpretation of Cave 1 Stratigraphy

The stratification of the MSA deposits shows occupational soils alternating with rubble layers, the total complex being covered by sand. The occupational soils with their hearths or contained faunal and cultural remains clearly indicate habitation of the cave, commencing at some unknown time after the cutting of Cave 1 by the 6–8 m sea. Enough time had elapsed since the cutting of the cave for substantial stalagmites to form on the bedrock or beach gravel before the initial occupation. The earliest occupants were able to take advantage of the excellent shelter offered by the west side of the cave, where the roof was a convenient 2–3 m height above the floor. Their litter and resulting soils constitute layers 37 and 38. By the time the upper part of layer 37 had accumulated, the roof was uncomfortably close, and later occupants needed to move closer to the east side, where the roof was some 8 m high.

The section across the front part of the cave (fig. 3.3) shows that all the later layers up to layer 14 rest unconformably on the top of layer 37. These layers can be understood only in relation to the accumulation beneath Shelter 1A. It would seem that a vast buildup of occupational deposits took place outside the cave mouth toward Shelter 1A and that the three rubble layers 1-17b, 1-16, and 1-14² were formed by material rolling down the slope of the resulting mound. Their horizontal distribution supports this, especially the presence of larger rubble in the

2. Reference to a specific layer in a particular cave or shelter will be made in the order cave or shelter-layer, e.g., 1-17b refers to Cave 1, layer 17b.

front of the cave and the manner in which the mounds of true occupational soils, 1-17 and 1-15, acted as barriers. These two soils indicate further habitation of the cave mouth. The presence of numerous beach pebbles in the rubble layers, particularly layer 1-14, at first suggested some marine action and the possibility of storm beaches, but this interpretation is no longer considered likely: it requires invoking some catastrophic tidal wave, the evidence for which has never been reported from other sites along the Tzitzikama Coast, and explaining the complete lack of bedding. Tumble from a slope outside the cave mouth explains all the observed features. However, Butzer (chap. 4) favors the former interpretation.

The sand of layer 1-13 is considered to be windborne. This is supported by the cross-bedding and examination of the sand grains. The lenses of silt and clay suggest moderately wet conditions, whereas blown sand suggests dry conditions. However, blown sand, without further evidence, is not necessarily a reflection of climate, for dune activity can still be seen in parts of the Cape Peninsula, as at Hout Bay and Fish Hoek, in spite of an average rainfall of about 53 cm (21 in.).

The uneven accumulations on the sides of the major stalagmites were noted. The thick formation around the top of the windblown sand seen on the stalagmite in front of the rear chamber may indicate a considerable time interval, but there was nothing pronouncedly like it on the other stalagmites. Similarly, the platelike projection on the same stalagmite at the level of the top of the upper midden may indicate a long time interval between it and the deposition of the topmost, mainly windborne soil. Although the body of this soil is considerably cemented together, no calcite has formed on the present surface.

The horizontal distributions of the various layers within Cave 1 are illustrated in figures 3.19–3.26.

Shelter 1A (Figures 3.7–3.11, Plates 6 and 16–23)

The full sequence that remains of the great thickness of occupational deposits that accumulated between the mouth of Cave 1 and under the rock overhang referred to as Shelter 1A is demonstrated in the composite section (fig. 3.1). The upper part, as revealed by the Initial Cutting, is given on a larger scale, and there are also detailed sections of the Middle and Bottom Cuttings (see plan, fig. 2.1). The profile of an interrupted cutting at right angles to the Initial Cutting gives some indication of the bulk of deposits that have not been investigated (Side Cuttings A–C, figs. 2.1, 3.12), and one from below Cave 2 to the present beach (East Cutting P–S, fig. 2.1) emphasizes the erosion that has taken place since and possibly during the MSA occupation of the site.

The buildup commences on the 6–8 m beach, and these lower levels are continuous with layers inside Cave 1. However, above layer 37 erosion has isolated the sequence beneath Shelter 1A. There are alternations of sandy and carbonaceous soils, ash hearths, and minor spreads of rubble from the walls up to the top, with two significant horizons: a major rockfall associated with layer 22, and a series of intensely carbonaceous soils and concentrations of laminated hearths that constitute layers 10 to 21. It is the latter which contain a Howieson's Poort Industry and also make a stratigraphical division between two stages of the Middle Stone Age Industry.

Numbering of the layers beneath Shelter 1A as shown on the sections is not the same as that used during excavation, but has been revised in order to make a continuity from the lower to the upper part (see table 3.1).

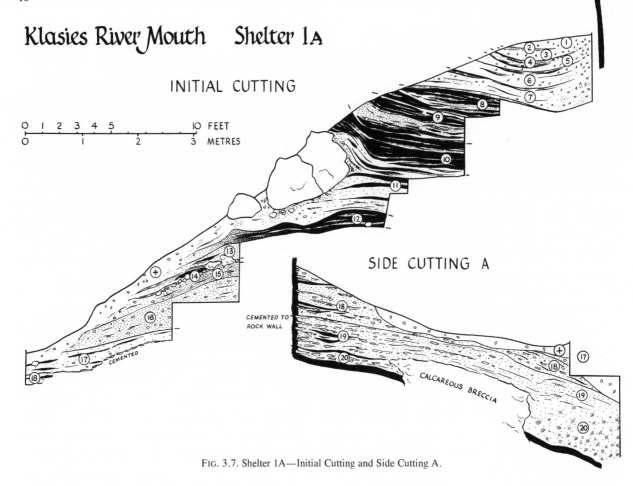

FIG. 3.7. Shelter 1A—Initial Cutting and Side Cutting A.

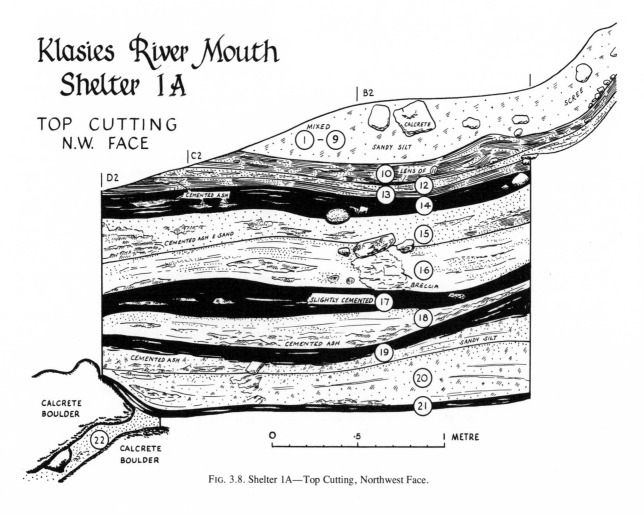

FIG. 3.8. Shelter 1A—Top Cutting, Northwest Face.

Klasies River Mouth Shelter 1A

|B2   TOP CUTTING   N.E. FACE

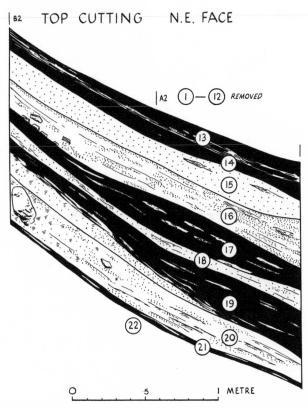

FIG. 3.9. Shelter 1A—Top Cutting, Northeast Face.

Klasies River Mouth Shelter 1A

MIDDLE CUTTING   N.W. FACE

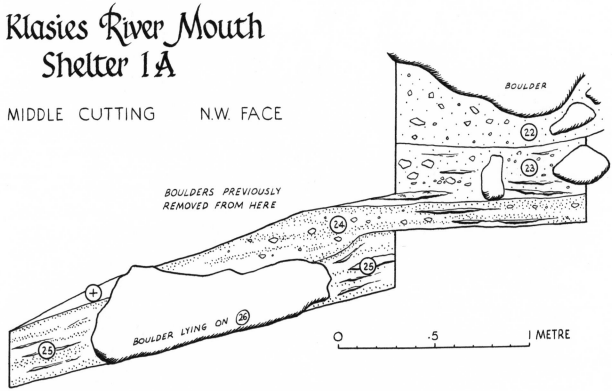

FIG. 3.10. Shelter 1A—Middle Cutting.

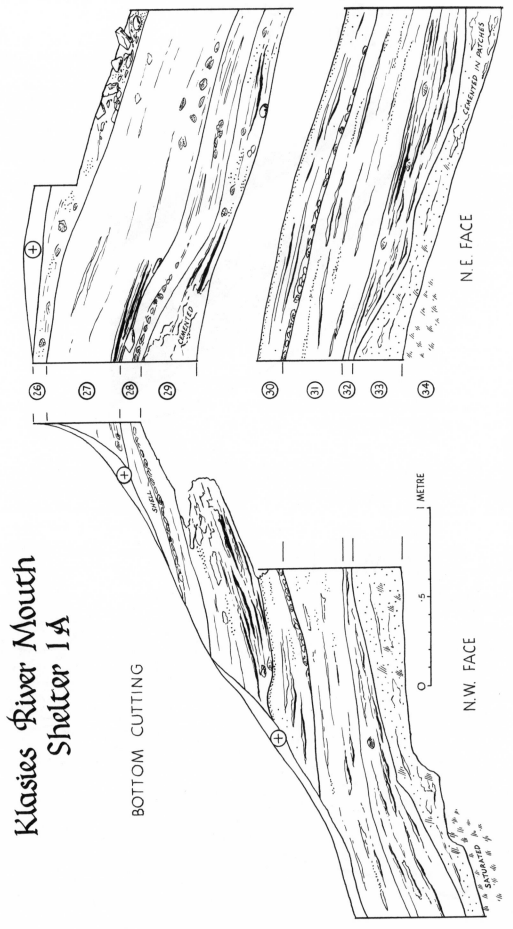

Fig. 3.11. Shelter 1A—Bottom Cutting.

Residual deposits on the rock wall above the present surface at the top of layer 1 denoting the former existence of at least another 6 m of occupational soils are indicated on the composite section (fig. 3.1) and are illustrated by plate 4. A feature which confirms this former buildup is a flat lid of calcite close to and under the actual overhang. This must have formed over the uppermost layers before they were eroded away, leaving it suspended to the shelter wall 6 m above the present surface (pl. 6). It also indicates that the deposits were originally sloping down toward the back of the shelter, so that an even greater thickness than 6 m has probably disappeared from a little in front of the shelter. The connection between the layers of Shelter 1A and Cave 2 is considered when the latter cave is discussed. The deposits of Shelter 1A are subdivided and described in what follows.

Layer 1. Soft, sandy soil which contained numerous small scree fragments (mainly < 2 cm) of the local quartzite.

Layer 2. A thin lens of sandy, carbonaceous soil.

Layer 3. Sandy scree with numerous small, angular rock fragments. This had come from the east side of the shelter, where a steep, naturally formed scree slope from the cliff above still exists, and was consequently sandier toward this side and contained more soil toward the shelter wall.

These top three layers may best be considered as one unit, because layer 2 was found to be a discontinuous lens. Bone in good condition was present throughout, and microfauna was plentiful. Shell was also in good condition. Artifacts were numerous. (See inventories in chaps. 5 and 6.)

Layer 4. Laminated ash, sand, and carbonaceous soil. Stone artifacts were numerous, but bone was mainly in small fragments and in poor condition. Many of the bone fragments were burnt. No shells were found.

Layer 5. Mainly sandy scree with some laminated carbonaceous layers. Artifacts were numerous. Bone was mainly in small pieces, burnt or in poor condition. Microfauna was plentiful and in good condition. There were few shells, but they were well preserved.

Layer 6. Laminations of dark soil, ash, charcoal, and fine sandy scree. The lower part of this layer was mainly sandy scree. The layer was disturbed near the rock wall, apparently by burrows. Material from this disturbed area was kept separate from that used to describe the contents of the layer. Disturbed areas, particularly close to the rock wall, were similarly treated in other layers.

Bone was plentiful and in good condition, although mainly broken or burnt. Microfauna was present in large quantities, particularly in the sandy scree. Shells were present in good condition. Artifacts were numerous, mainly in the upper part.

Layer 7. Black, compressed carbonaceous soil and sand. Bone was plentiful but mainly very fragmented, and much was burnt. A few shells were found in fair condition. Artifacts were prolific.

Layer 8. A thin (c. 2 cm) layer of dark occupational soil above 6–10 cm of buff, sandy scree containing much microfauna. Little bone and shell was found, but it was in good condition. Artifacts were not very numerous in the Top Cutting, but were plentiful in the continuation of the same layer exposed in the Initial Cutting. Bone fragments were also more plentiful there. Little shell was recovered, but it was in good condition.

Layer 9. Fine, buff sandy scree with layers of carbonaceous soil at the top and in the middle. Bone, including microfauna, was plentiful, also fragmentary shell. Artifacts were numerous.

Layers 10 to 21. These layers represent a distinct unit and are best considered with reference to the drawn sections. Laminations of ash, black carbonaceous soil, and silty sand were superimposed throughout. Carbonaceous soil and ash predominated toward the Initial Cutting, whereas toward the shelter wall the deposits became sandier, included more rubble, and were locally cemented into a hard breccia.

Bone was prolific throughout, but almost entirely in the form of small fragments and much was burnt. Microfauna was mainly in the sandier layers. Shells were also present throughout but not in great quantity, and their condition of preservation varied from one layer to another. Stone artifacts were very prolific in every layer.

Divisions between these layers are only arbitrary ones, taken along particularly clear surfaces at 15–20 cm intervals. However, the lowest one, layer 21, did represent a distinct stratigraphical break. It was a continuous layer of carbonaceous soil and ash, and overlay the irregular surface of the massive rockfall of the underlying layer 22. It was banked up against some of the large fallen rocks at a very steep angle, almost vertically in places. Hearths could not have formed in this manner on such a slope, and it is clear that there has been considerable distortion of these layers by the pressure of the overlying deposits (figs. 3.7, 3.9).

Layer 22. Laminations of sand and soil, with two thicker carbonaceous layers. The layer thickened away from the shelter wall. Several large boulders of calcite and rock had fallen on this layer, locally compressing it into marked undulations. Some rubble was within the layer as well. Bone was not plentiful save for microfauna. Shells, in good condition, were present in fair quantity in the carbonaceous layers. Artifacts were numerous.

Layer 23. Charcoal, ash, occupational soil, and sand sloping down from the shelter wall. Bone and shell were well preserved. Artifacts were numerous. Microfauna was plentiful.

Layer 24. Similar to the layer above, but the carbonaceous soils were more developed away from the shelter wall. Artifacts were prolific. Bone was well preserved but mainly fragmentary. Shells were numerous and in fair condition.

Layer 25. Sandy occupational soils with diffused ash and charcoal and thin laminations from hearths. Shell and bone were in fair condition, but mainly fragmentary. Artifacts were numerous.

Layer 26. A thin but continuous spread of small rubble, with an irregular filling of sand, soil, and occupational refuse between the lumps of calcite and rock fragments. Bone was present in good condition but in little quantity. There was much shell, although mainly in fragments. Artifacts were numerous.

Layer 27. Laminations of gray soil and shells which sloped up toward the shelter wall. No hearths were visible, but the soil was flecked with charcoal. A large quantity of bone was found in good condition, also many shells. Artifacts were prolific.

Layer 28. Laminations of dark sand, carbonaceous soil, and ash hearths. Large quantities of bones and shells were preserved in good condition. Artifacts were prolific. The lower part was consistently sandy.

Layer 29. The same as the above layer but with less bone and fewer artifacts. Shells, however, were still present in large quantities. Toward the shelter wall part of this layer was found to be cemented by lime.

Layer 30. Mainly a sandy layer with a few laminated carbonaceous lenses. The upper part was clean sand broken only by the traces of small rodent burrows filled with darker sand. The layer was cemented by lime toward the shelter wall. Not much bone was found but plenty of microfauna and shell. Artifacts were numerous.

Layer 31. Partly cemented laminations of sand, carbonaceous soil, ash, and shell. Little bone was present, but shell was prolific. Artifacts were numerous.

Layer 32. Laminations of sand, soil, and ash, blacker than the overlying layers. Cemented patchily by lime. Much bone was found in poor condition, but little shell. Artifacts were numerous.

Layer 33. Similar to the layer above but graded into a dirty brown cemented soil and silt at the base. Little bone was found, and it was in poor condition; but microfauna was plentiful. Many shells, mainly fragmentary, were present in fair condition. Artifacts were numerous.

Layer 34. Saturated sand and silt with faint traces of carbonaceous lenses. Several boulders of calcite were contained in this layer. In part, it was banked against the steeply sloping bedrock. The sand also contained several beach pebbles. The instability of the deposits and the presence of running water made it impossible to dig by normal archeological methods. A little bone was found in good condition, but shells were absent. Artifacts appeared to be numerous.

Layer 35. This thick layer, a continuation of the layer above, was similarly saturated by underground water. Normal archeological methods of excavation were impossible, but a continuous vertical section was recorded (fig. 3.1, pl. 27). The wet sand and silt presented an almost uniform appearance until cleaned with a trowel. Faint bedding planes of darker soils and hearths could then be discerned, and several white lenses of decomposed shell. Bone, however, was in very good condition and occurred throughout. Artifacts were also numerous, but conditions were such that only a selection could be made.

The scree deposits which postdate the truncated occupational deposits beneath Shelter 1A are thick at this point and almost as saturated as the layer itself. In a few places, slabs of cemented layers apparently derived from Cave 2 were found resting on the slope actually between the scree deposits and the saturated occupational soils. Similar slabs in the same position were found above the underlying layers 36 and 37.

Layer 36. This was a similar deposit to the layer above but not so wet, and it could be dug normally in places. There was nothing to indicate any break between them. Shells were mainly dissolved away, but bone was well preserved. Artifacts were numerous.

Toward the rock wall near the mouth of Cave 1 this layer was found to dip steeply into what proved to be the mouth of Cave 1C, completely blocked by the accumulation (fig. 3.15).

Layer 37. Dark, sandy occupational soil with lines of carbonaceous soil and a few lumps of calcite. It was found to have a greater clay content toward Cave 1, where it continued as a black greasy soil beneath layers 13 to 17 of that cave. Bones and artifacts were numerous. Few shells were present.

Layer 38. A sandy soil, clayey in places, which had horizontal bands of carbonaceous soil and a few ash hearths. This was a continuation of the same layer in Cave 1, but greater in thickness and sandier. Bone was plentiful and in good condition, but fragmentary. There was much shell in good condition, and artifacts were numerous.

Layer 39. Clean beach sand with a few pebbles. A few artifacts were in the upper part of this sand. Beneath the sand, in the lower part of this layer, was a series of interdigitated natural and disturbed sands, the latter containing traces of hearths and a few bones and artifacts. There were also a few shells in poor condition.

This layer was only exposed in East Cutting Q and was not present under layer 38 in Cave 1 where the bedrock was higher.

Layer 40. Beach shingle, similar to that at the base of Cave 1 but containing a large proportion of small, angular rock fragments. It was very ocherous, particularly in the exposures toward the present beach, where it was covered by scree deposits (fig. 3.6). Only two stone artifacts were found in this shingle.

Bedrock. Quartzite, mapped as Table Mountain sandstone.

Profile across Slope Southeast from Shelter 1A
(Side Cutting A–C, Figure 3.12)

The layers exposed in Side Cutting A (layers 30 to 34) show their continuation toward the rock wall in this lower part of the shelter. They become more cemented nearer to the wall and intensely so against it. Plate 18 shows more clearly than the section how the layers cemented to the wall above the present surface of the deposits merge into those below it. At this point all the layers are dipping steeply downward, and it was surprising to discover that in Side Cutting B they were nearly horizontal. This localized dip is probably associated with the saturation of the deposits between them. The layers exposed were a continuation of layers 32 and 33 but varied considerably in aspect, being softer and a uniform pale gray. The horizontal bedding of darker soils and lines of shells could be discerned only by troweling. To some extent this change must be due to the effect of running water. Bone was in very good condition, and some shells were preserved intact. Artifacts were numerous.

At Side Cutting C, the existence of the same, still nearly horizontal accumulation of occupational deposits was proved beneath 3 m of brown silty scree, 15 m from the face of the shelter wall. Bones and artifacts were present. There seemed reason to think that the ridge on the slope 40 m from the rock wall might reflect the position of the underlying bedrock, which was exposed at this point a little higher up the scree slope—in which case, occupational deposits might be expected as far as this point. However, a test section dug to nearly 2 m revealed only dark brown silty scree.

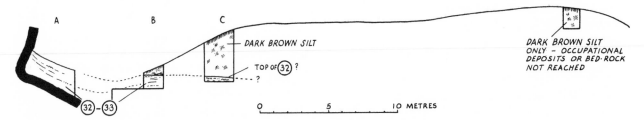

N.W.   S.E.

A   B   C
— DARK BROWN SILT
TOP OF ③② ?
?

DARK BROWN SILT
ONLY - OCCUPATIONAL
DEPOSITS OR BED·ROCK
NOT REACHED

0   5   1O METRES

③②-③③

Klasies River Mouth ~ profile from wall of Shelter 1A to ridge of hillside - with Side Cuttings

FIG. 3.12. Profile from wall of Shelter 1A to ridge of hillside, with Side Cuttings.

Interpretation of Shelter 1A Stratigraphy

The stratification of the occupational deposits beneath Shelter 1A is straightforward, as the layers present an unbroken sequence from a bedrock platform 6 m above the present sea level to a point 24 m above it. Artifacts, shells, and bones stuck to the rock wall above this extend the accumulation to a height of at least 30 m above present sea level, making a total thickness of deposits of 24 m.

The erosion of these layers has been severe, not only from the top 6 m but to the front and side of the shelter. The former lateral extent of these layers was at least 15 m from the wall and probably much more.

Occupation commenced at the time when the sea level was at 6–8 m above its present level, for hearths and occupational remains are found interdigitating with natural beach sands in layer 39. Initial occupation on a bare, sandy beach explains the clean, sandy nature of the lowermost deposits, layers 38 to 39. Layer 17 of Cave 1 rests uncomfortably on layer 37 and cannot be directly related to the Shelter 1A sequence. Alternating layers of sand, carbonaceous or dark soils, crushed shell, and ash hearths continue upward. Sandy layers may indicate temporary absence of occupation, but they are never sterile, so it could merely mean that the concentration of human activity at that particular time was elsewhere on the site. No signs were detected of ancient weathering of soils, or of their erosion prior to further accumulation, indicating virtual unbroken occupation for a very long period.

Lumps of calcite, pebbles, and rock fragments occur sporadically throughout the layers, with a more marked accumulation of rubble in layer 26. Only during the time of layer 22 is there any sign of a major rockfall. This could perhaps relate to climatic change or even intentional human removal of dangerous growths of coarse calcite that were precariously situated against the rock wall above the living surface. It may not be fortuitous that both the nature of occupational deposit and the stone industry change radically immediately after this rockfall. Microfauna appears more plentiful near the time of this rockfall, and after the occupation represented by layers 10 to 21.

The topmost layers, 1 to 9, are similar in character to those below layer 21, as is the stone industry. There is thus a good stratigraphical reason for differentiating between these two phases of a similar industry. A major difference in the composition of these layers is that they contain a much larger proportion of small, angular rock fragments. This also may have a climatic interpretation but, alternatively, could be connected with the proximity of the upper face of the cliff, which is more subject to weathering.

Cave 2 (Figure 3.13, Plate 24)

The front of these truncated occupational layers, at the mouth of the cave and beneath the drip-line, was cemented by lime into a hard breccia. However, inside the cave near the rear the layers were unconsolidated. A meter-square test section was dug to ascertain this and produce artifacts for comparison with the sequence beneath Shelter 1A.

The section revealed intensely black carbonaceous soil from top to bottom with lines of white or yellow ash and a little sand.

Klasies River Mouth Cave 2

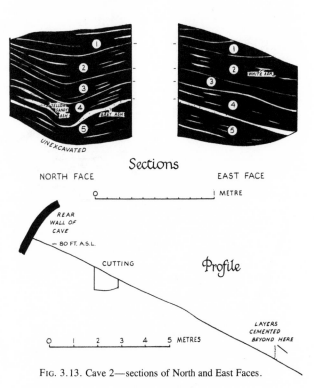

Sections

NORTH FACE   EAST FACE

0   1 METRE

REAR
WALL OF
CAVE

— 80 FT. A.S.L.

CUTTING

Profile

0   1   2   3   4   5 METRES

LAYERS
CEMENTED
BEYOND HERE

FIG. 3.13. Cave 2—sections of North and East Faces.

It was divided into five layers along bedding planes for convenience and not because of any significant changes between one layer and another. Bedrock was not reached. Stone artifacts were very prolific throughout, but bone and shell were poorly represented and very fragmentary.

Interpretation of Cave 2 Stratigraphy

The nature of the deposits and the stone industry allow a correlation to be made with layers 10 to 21 of Shelter 1A. There can be little doubt that they were originally contemporary and probably continuous upon a common floor before erosion isolated the accumulation in Cave 2. The residual deposits adhering to the rock wall between Cave 2 and Shelter 1A are not sufficiently preserved to establish a direct linkup, but, as indicated on the composite section (fig. 3.1), it seems that by the time layer 27 had built up, entrance into the cave would have been safe and simple. This may have some connection with the small rubble layer that overlies layer 27 under Shelter 1A.

Shelter 1B (Figure 3.14, Plates 25 and 26)

An Initial Cutting made at the rear of this small rock shelter exposed just over a meter of finely stratified deposits sloping upward toward the sea, resting on beach shingle and bedrock at 10 m above the present sea level. Animal or root disturbance had confused the front part of the section, but it is clear that this is only the rear part of a former thick accumulation, for the upper layers are truncated by the present erosion slope. Further excavation would be necessary to determine whether the rise of ground immediately to the west consists of higher occupational levels or is merely a scree cover: the former seems more likely.

Layer 1. Sandy soil with some ash and small rock fragments. Artifacts were numerous, but only a small part of this layer remained and they were mixed inadvertently with the underlying layer.

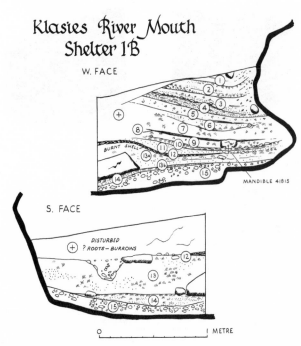

FIG. 3.14. Shelter 1B—plans of West and South Faces.

Layer 2. Buff sand which contained small rock chips and rubble. The layer was silty in patches. Bones and artifacts were numerous.

Layer 3. This was a black carbonaceous soil with ash laminations and a spread of small, angular rock fragments at the base. Shells were decomposed to white flecks, but bone was in fair condition. Artifacts were numerous.

Layer 4. Same as the layer above without the rock fragments at the base.

Layer 5. Buff sand and small rock fragments which thinned toward the shelter wall. The base was marked by a thin layer of carbonaceous soil. Artifacts were numerous, but only a few fragmentary bones and shells were present.

Layer 6. A gravelly to silty occupational soil with smears of ash hearths. Artifacts and bones were numerous, but the latter were in poor condition and very fragmentary. Shells were scarce.

Layer 7. Buff sand and silty soil with many small, angular rock fragments. The numerous artifacts and many bones were in better condition than those in the layer above. Shells were scarce.

Layer 8. The surface of a thin (1–2 cm) but continuous hearth spread. There were several artifacts and bones, the latter in good condition. No shell was found.

Layer 9. Buff sand and silty soil with small, angular rock fragments. Several bone fragments were found in good condition, also shell fragments. Artifacts were numerous.

Layer 10. A dark gray clayey soil which had many small, angular rock fragments at its base and one large block of soft calcite. It was flecked with charcoal but had no clear hearth spreads. Several bone fragments in good condition were recovered, including a near-complete human mandible (no. 41815). Artifacts were numerous.

Layer 11. A firm buff sandy silt which contained many small, angular rock fragments. A few bone fragments and several shells in good condition, as well as numerous artifacts, were found.

Layer 12. A thin, soft silty layer with a spread of loose, mainly burnt shell. Several bones in good condition and numerous artifacts were found.

Layer 13a. Brown sand that appeared to be a weathered horizon of the underlying layer. A few bone fragments, shells, and artifacts were recovered.

Layer 13b. Yellow sand and silt. Many bone fragments in a good, semimineralized condition, a few shells in poor condition, and numerous artifacts were found.

Layer 14. A thin (2–4 cm) spread of carbonaceous soil with small fragments of shell. On the south side lay two large fallen blocks of the rock wall or overhang: one is featured in the drawn section. Several bones were found in good mineralized condition. Artifacts were numerous.

Layer 15. Clean, angular, sandy beach gravel. Artifacts were numerous in the upper part, and there were a few bone fragments but no shells.

Bedrock. Same as in the above caves.

Interpretation of Shelter 1B Stratigraphy

These layers constitute a straightforward succession of occupational deposits commencing on the shingle of the 6–8 m raised beach and thus almost certainly relate to the lowest levels of Cave 1, layers 37 to 40. The apparently weathered sandy soil of layer 13b may represent a time interval, but otherwise there was probably a near-continuous occupation of the shelter. Erosion has removed all but the bottom and rear of a larger accumulation, although a greater amount may remain in the unexcavated area immediately to the west.

Cave 1C (Figures 3.15 and 3.16, Plates 27 and 28)

The section (fig. 3.15, pl. 27) made in East Cutting T shows the dip of the layers (36 and 37) into the mouth of Cave 1C, indicating that the cave was blocked before layer 35 accumulated. The main internal features are shown on the sketch plan (fig. 3.16, pl. 28). Archeological deposits were restricted to the talus of occupational soil and debris which came through the cave mouth as the deposits outside built up higher. The mouth was 5 m wide, and the final blocking deposits had come in three fans through the highest parts of the roof on each side and in the middle, extending back 8 m into the cave.

The rear of the cave is 22 m from the mouth, although the last 5–8 m is much narrower. Dripping water and the formation of stalagmites, stalactites, and other calcitic phenomena before and since the blocking of the cave suggest that it has always been wet and therefore unsuitable for occupation. The present floor, between the stalagmites, is a very soft, calcareous mud, and it was probably the same in MSA times. Occasional bones and stone artifacts were dropped or thrown inside, but there was nothing in the way of deposits or structures. The most striking indication of human activity was a destructive one: several stalagmites had been broken down and a veritable path made through the center of them toward the rear, probably to explore the back of the cave.

Some of the fallen stalagmites were of a peculiar pointed and ribbed kind, and two of these were found in the Rear Chamber of Cave 1, so this was probably their source. These, and others in the cave, were somewhat dirty in contrast to the pristine freshness of the calcitic formations that had grown since the blocking of the cave, and they are still forming with the constant dripping of water. Plate 28 shows their great variety and spectacular appearance: most unusual are those which hang in filaments of fragile delicacy, so thin that to brush against them would destroy in an instant the growth of thousands of years. Such stalactites could form only where there was not the slightest movement of air, a condition prevailing since the cave was blocked during the MSA.

Parts of the walls of Cave 1C are pale and smooth and would have made excellent surfaces for rock paintings. A search was made, but not a trace could be found to suggest that the hunters of this time applied pigment to the walls in any form whatsoever. However, pieces of red ocher, some smoothed and scratched from use, were found in all the MSA levels (pl. 51). Paintings in this cave could be expected to survive for a long period, unlike paintings in any exposed position, so the inference is that the ocher was used only for personal or artifactual adornment.

Apart from our own footmarks on the clay floor, this cave has not been interfered with in any way. It has been resealed behind wooden boards and a dump of soil.

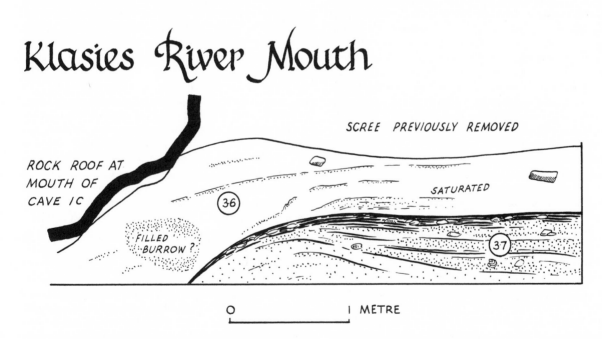

Klasies River Mouth

SCREE PREVIOUSLY REMOVED

ROCK ROOF AT MOUTH OF CAVE 1C

SATURATED

36

FILLED BURROW ?

37

O   1 METRE

East Cutting T ~ section across mouth of Cave 1C

FIG. 3.15. Cave 1C—East Cutting T, section across mouth of cave.

Klasies River Mouth Cave 1C

SKETCH PLAN

BEACH GRAVEL

PATH THROUGH BROKEN STALAGMITES

HIPPO TUSK

STALAGMITES

N

TALUS

EAST CUTTING T

0   1   2   3   4   5 METRES (Approx)

FIG. 3.16. Cave 1C—sketch plan.

General Interpretation of the Stratigraphy of the Main Site

There are 18 m of occupational deposits below Shelter 1A, and traces on the rock wall above show that another 6 m originally covered this accumulation. No other prehistoric site in southern Africa has produced such a thickness of deposits resulting from human activity, and yet, in spite of this thickness, the stratification is relatively simple. There are no signs whatsoever that the occupants dug pits or created structures which would have complicated the gradual buildup of the deposits. The main difficulty with the interpretation is that enormous quantities of the occupational deposits have been eroded away since their original formation. Freak conditions have preserved remnants of these vanished layers on the rock walls of the shelter and thus facilitated their reconstruction.

The drawn sections (especially figs. 3.1, 3.2, 3.6, and 3.14) and their descriptions show the main elements of the stratification.

Bedrock is of the local quartzite, which, although mapped as Table Mountain sandstone, may be a different formation. A platform has been cut in this solid rock in front of Cave 1, sloping gently upward from 6 to 8 m and extending back into the cave itself. This shelf is covered for the most part by a thin deposit of clean, sandy beach gravel. At the mouth of the cave the upper few centimeters of this gravel is partially cemented by lime, but outside in East Cutting Q (see plan, fig. 2.1) it is not so. Here the gravel is covered by marine sand which interdigitates with hearths and archeological material. The same beach gravel covers the bedrock at Shelter 1B.

The lowermost occupational layers (37 to 39) accumulated on the beach gravel and extended over most of the inside of the cave. They are thickest just outside the cave mouth, as exposed in the East Cutting. The lower layers (38 and 39) are very sandy

and contrast markedly with layer 37, which is a black, greasy soil containing a few large calcite boulders.

Toward Shelter 1A the deposits build up in a series of laminations to the very top of the sequence. They vary in composition, some being sandier than others, some with more or less evidence of fires, some with more calcite rubble, and so on, but it is only between layers 10 and 21 that there is a really significant change in the type of deposit. At the bottom, on layer 21, there is a mass of fallen rock, mainly large boulders of calcite. Some of these boulders are over a meter in thickness and weigh several tons. Immediately over them come occupational layers of intensely black carbonaceous soil and hundreds of laminated, interleaved hearths. These are regarded as layers of intense occupation. They are 1.5 m thick, and above them is a similar thickness of more normal, sandier deposits.

Above layer 37, the sections clearly show how the layers have been truncated by erosion. It is most marked in the uppermost layers. Some idea of their former extent can be assessed by the lime-cemented residual deposits on the rock wall immediately east of the mouth of Cave 2. They do not remain in a completely unbroken chain, and it is possible to link them to the deposits as exposed by excavation. Careful study of the rock wall enables at least two of the larger areas to be related to layers 27 and 33 with confidence, as shown on figure 3.1. Their angle of dip conforms to that exposed in the cuttings, and it is not difficult to visualize their continuation.

The floor of Cave 2 is at 19–20 m above present sea level. Bedrock was met behind layer 34 at 17 m sloping steeply upward. The size of the cutting did not allow this bedrock to be followed to the rock wall at the back of Shelter 1A, but it appeared that it slopes upward to form a shelf at about the same height as the floor of Cave 2. This would explain the saturation of the deposits below layer 34, for the impervious bedrock would trap all the ground water and cause it to flow over the edge through the soft, permeable occupational deposits. There has been some change in the saturated deposits through this continuous flow of water: shells have almost been dissolved away, yet the bone is highly mineralized. If water has been flowing in this manner for a long period of time, it is surprising that it has not caused greater change. The probability is that the water is a relatively recent flow (in terms of the total time which has elapsed since the deposits were accumulated), for there is some evidence that the drainage off the plateau above the site and along the nearby coast is subject to changes. For example, there is no continuous dripping of water now over the drip-line of Shelter 1A, yet the thick incrustations of nodular calcite which have formed around it and in other places further along the cliff show that it must have been very wet at one time in this particular place. As large lumps of calcite are mixed with the occupational soils, it seems likely that this period predated the occupation. Similarly, about 50 m east of Shelter 1A close to where the footpath descends, a dry gully marks the former passage of a flow of water from the cliff top. At the present time, water drips and flows off the cliffs on the east side of the natural amphitheater in which the site of KRM is located.

The thick deposits of layer 36 conceal and drop into a small cave (1C). It is possible that other caves, or at least shelters, exist further back at the same level, and the same may apply to the rear wall of Shelter 1A at the higher level.

In Cave 1 there are a series of deposits which lie unconformably on layer 37. They alternate between occupational soils (layers 17b and 15) and tumble layers (17a, 16, and 14). They are sealed beneath a clean sand with silt lenses on top of which are LSA middens. It is impossible to prove, but the tumble layers appear to be the continuation of the lower levels of Shelter 1A. The sand (layer 13) is partly eolian (see chap. 4), and its absence from the sequence below 1A implies that it is more recent than any of the deposits there.

Along the drip-line of Cave 2 the deposits are cemented into a breccia that can only be broken with a heavy hammer. Inside the cave, however, a small excavation proved what was apparent from surface indications. The occupational layers were identical in aspect to those described as layers of intense occupation at 1A. In the front of the cave they are severely truncated, and the cave is now inaccessible except by a dangerous climb; but before the lower deposits at 1A were eroded away they would have extended to the lip of the cave and given easy access. Residual deposits remain cemented to the walls of Cave 2, above the height of existing deposits, and prove their former greater thickness.

The occupational layers beneath Shelter 1B are severely truncated and must represent only a minor portion of the original accumulation. They lie conformably on the bedrock and beach gravel and appear to relate to the lowermost layers at Cave 1.

Not one of the deposits is without stone artifacts, and on the basis of the stratigraphy alone, the following divisions of the stone industries have been made:

Industry	Stage	Site Where Represented
Later Stone Age	. . .	Cave 1, Layers 1 to 12
Middle Stone Age	IV	Cave 1, Layer 13
Middle Stone Age	III	Shelter 1A, Layers 1 to 9
Howieson's Poort	. . .	Shelter 1A, Layers 10 to 21
		Cave 2, Layers 1 to 5
Middle Stone Age	II	Cave 1, Layers 14 to 17b
		Shelter 1A, Layers 22 to 36
Middle Stone Age	I	Cave 1, Layers 37 to 40
		Shelter 1B, Layers 1 to 15

The favored interpretation is that the initial occupation of the site (MSA I) was on the beach shingle of the 6–8 m raised beach, in and outside the mouth of Cave 1, and also beneath Shelter 1B. By the time of MSA II, occupational deposits had accumulated to such an extent beneath Shelter 1B that it no longer afforded much protection and was therefore abandoned. A substantial accumulation had also formed within Cave 1, but it was still accessible and in use. However, the buildup of deposits both inside and immediately outside the cave mouth rendered the cave uninhabitable toward the end of MSA II. The occupation of the site was now centered to the east of the cave mouth, Cave 1C was already blocked, and deposits accumulated beneath Cave 2 and toward Shelter 1A. By the end of MSA II the midden was so large that it reached to the level of Cave 2, so that people of the Howieson's Poort period were able to use this cave to advantage as well as Shelter 1A. Cave 2 appears to have been blocked by the time of MSA III, the deposits of which built up under Shelter 1A until they reached the very overhang of the shelter. The further history of the site is obscure. It may or may not have been abandoned. The former is most likely, and the recession of the coastline would be a good reason for it. Subaerial erosion of the occupational deposits commenced, and in this respect it is very significant that there is no evidence for any such erosion prior to this time. None of the occupational deposits lie unconformably on any other truncated deposits. It is this which demonstrates the permanent or semipermanent nature of the occupation. It is clear that a great quantity of the deposits has been eroded away, to such an extent that most of the MSA III deposits have disap-

peared and Cave 2 is half-emptied and once more inaccessible. At some time prior to or during this erosional phase, blown sand accumulated in Cave 1. Most probably, this was after erosion had removed at least some of the deposits that were in front of the cave mouth. MSA IV is associated with this sand. There is thus a hiatus of unknown duration in the occupation of KRM between MSA III and MSA IV, and another one before the earliest LSA midden, which lies conformably on the blown sand. As will be seen in the discussion on dating (chap. 14), the hiatus between MSA IV and the LSA may be on the order of 50,000 years. It is certainly to be measured in tens of thousands of years.

Comments on the Stratigraphical Division of the Stone Industries

There is no stratigraphical proof that the industries at Shelter 1B and the lowermost layers of Cave 1 are the same. However, both lie directly on the beach gravel, and this, taken with their typological similarities makes it seem reasonable to include them both in MSA I. In case future work at Klasies River Mouth or at other sites should question this correlation, it might be useful to describe this industry (as well as the others) per location and layer.

The problem with MSA II is to know the precise relationship between the industry as found in Cave 1 and that found beneath Shelter 1A. The evidence from the lowermost layers of 1A gives nothing to indicate any break between MSA I and MSA II, but the unconformable position of layers 14 to 17b in Cave 1 justifies a division. In spite of the strong evidence that these layers in Cave 1 are a continuation of deposits which once sloped down from Shelter 1A, there is no actual proof through a stratigraphical linkup. A convincing corroboration, however, is that there is a complete lack of the small, distinctive artifacts characteristic of the Howieson's Poort Industry. If the deposits in Cave 1 did postdate this industry, some derived material would almost certainly have been included in the tumble layers at least, in the same way as there are a few typical Howieson's Poort crescents in the MSA III industry above it, and both Howieson's Poort crescents and MSA material in the LSA middens.

The position of the Howieson's Poort Industry in between MSA II and III is unequivocal. The slight traces of residual layers between Shelter 1A and Cave 2, and the similarity of the type of deposit and the industry itself are adequate grounds for grouping them together.

The position of MSA IV is not so straightforward, but if the interpretation of the sand which contains it as dune sand is correct, there can be little doubt that it is more recent than the MSA III industry. Apart from this consideration it is directly overlain by the LSA middens. The considerable time interval between the MSA IV industry and the middens is substantiated by the upper part of the sand being firmly cemented by lime to a depth of 15 cm and more.

There are reasons for dividing the midden accumulation into two periods, and these are described in the relevant chapter (9).

The massive calcite boulders on the surface of layer 22 immediately below Howieson's Poort levels represent either a catastrophic collapse from the rock walls above or the possible intentional dislodgment of precarious lumps of calcite and rock face by people who intended to make use of this part of the shelter. It is possible that much of this material rolled down the slope onto the beach below or contributed to the rubble in layer 14 in Cave 1.

The Probable Sequence of Events at Klasies River Mouth
(Figures 3.17 and 3.18)

A series of diagrams has been drawn to represent the probable stratigraphical evolution at KRM, and the following descriptions explain each stage depicted.

1. The numbering of the caves and shelters is shown, with the lower ones already cut by the 6–8 m sea. Cave 2 may have been cut by the much earlier 18–20 m sea and was already isolated at the top of a low but vertical rock face.

2. There was a sufficient recession of the sea to prevent any further cutting of the lower caves, and a sandy beach formed in front of them. The first people to occupy the site, with an MSA I industry, lived on the beach, inside Cave 1, and beneath Shelter 1B. Cave 1C was too wet for habitation and Cave 2 inaccessible. The proximity of an almost inexhaustible supply

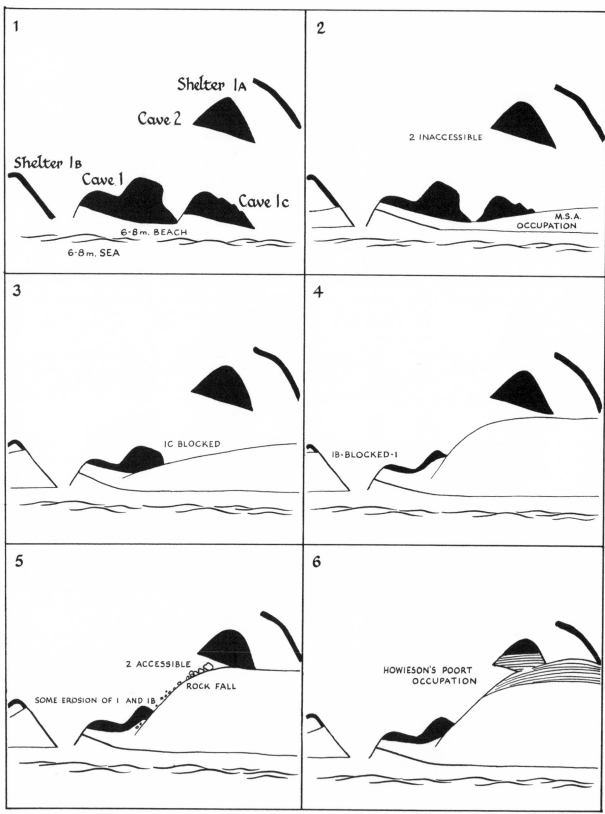

FIG. 3.17. Diagrammatic representation of the probable sequence of events at KRM.

of shellfish, marine birds, and plentiful small and large game prompted permanent or near-permanent, continuous occupation. Soil, food remains, and industrial litter accumulated.

3. Continued occupation produced the deposits which eventually blocked Shelter 1B and most of the entrance of Cave 1C.

4. The buildup of occupational deposits was continued by people with an MSA II industry. Cave 1C became completely blocked, and there was sufficient living space only on the higher, east side of Cave 1. An alternation of occupational soils and rubble layers formed in Cave 1. The rubble had rolled down the steep slope of the deposits which had formed outside the cave mouth, and presumably represents the activity of people living on top of it at times when Cave 1 was uninhabited. Large lumps of calcite appear to have been deliberately pushed down the slope, possibly being knocked from the walls

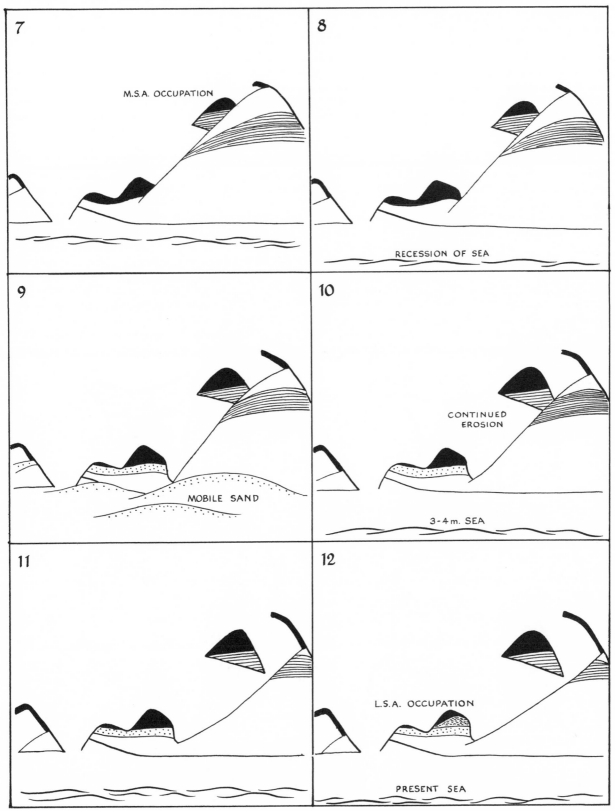

FIG. 3.18. Continuation of sequence shown in fig. 3.17.

in order to extend the living space in the most sheltered parts. It seems most unlikely that anyone would have lived in the cave while these rubble layers were forming.

5. The occupational deposits outside Cave 1 built up to such an extent that the top of them reached the level of the floor of Cave 2. Probably at this time some erosion of earlier deposits, particularly at Shelter 1B, may have occurred through normal subaerial processes. The MSA II industry continued.

6. Large rockfalls and sandier layers at the top of the MSA II deposits beneath Shelter 1A may indicate a break in the occupation, but the lack of weathered soils suggests it was not a long one. The site was reoccupied by people with a Howieson's Poort Industry. They settled beneath Shelter 1A and in Cave 2, and the black carbonaceous soils and numerous hearths resulting from their occupation may indicate a greater number of people living on the site at one time. Cave 2 and Shelter 1A were connected by a common floor, and deposits formed continuously across it. Cave 1 was not occupied: it was either choked with MSA II deposits or buried by scree.

7. Following the Howieson's Poort occupation, the site was again occupied by people with an MSA III industry. Living space was restricted to Shelter 1A, as Cave 2 was mainly, if not entirely, choked with Howieson's Poort deposits. Soils accumulated to a height of at least 6 m above the present surface of the ground beneath Shelter 1A.

8, 9. Following the MSA III occupation a recession of the sea is postulated, for during this period, which may have been of considerable duration, subaerial erosion of the uppermost deposits in all the caves and shelters preceded the blowing of a thick layer of sand into Cave 1. Possibly much of the site was buried by this sand, but it has since blown away again, except where it was protected inside Cave 1. This sand would be consistent with the exposure of the 6–8 m wave-cut platform at the time of a low sea level. The shoreline may have receded several miles, and evidence of the coast at this time probably now lies buried beneath the sea. Silt lenses within the sand may indicate a wetter period, but local factors in the drainage could also account for it. People with an MSA IV industry frequented the cave, but, as hearths were absent and their litter scanty, apparently did not live in it. Its inland situation at this time may have made it an unfavorable habitat, apart from the discomfort residents would have experienced whenever the wind was strong enough to blow the sand.

10. Erosion of the deposits, particularly those beneath Shelter 1A, continued slowly during this period, and it is thought that this might have been the time when a rising sea level cut the 3–4 m platform (as seen at Shelter 1D) and once more transformed the site into a coastal one.

11. The continued effect of erosion was to remove almost all of the MSA III deposits beneath Shelter 1A and to isolate Cave 2, leaving its Howieson's Poort deposits inside truncated.

12. LSA people moved into Cave 1, and their middens formed on the partly cemented surface of the blown sand. By this time it would seem that most of the earlier deposits had been worn down to an angle of rest, and erosion has subsequently been much slower. The topography of the site appears to have changed little since the LSA people arrived.

Two groups of people are concerned, as two major midden accumulations were found separated in time, according to radiocarbon dates, by about 2,000 years. The latest occupation of the site was away from the main complex of caves and shelters shown in the diagrams, beneath Shelter 1D nearby. Pottery from here indicates another long period of abandonment of the site, at least for 1,500 years, probably longer. These intervals may well be represented by the massive LSA middens in the entrance of Cave 5, and possibly Caves 3 and 4.

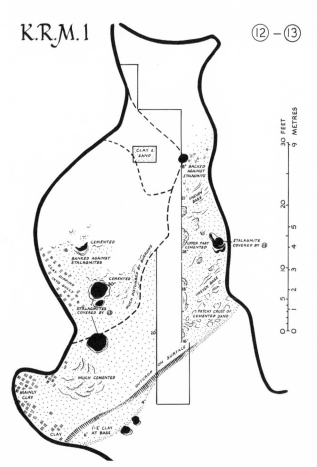

FIG. 3.19. Cave 1—plan of layers 12 to 13.

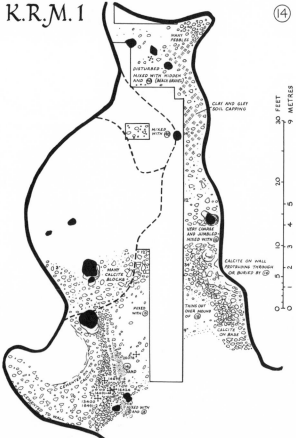

FIG. 3.20. Cave 1—plan of layer 14. The positions of human remains discovered are indicated by crosses and the relevant catalog numbers.

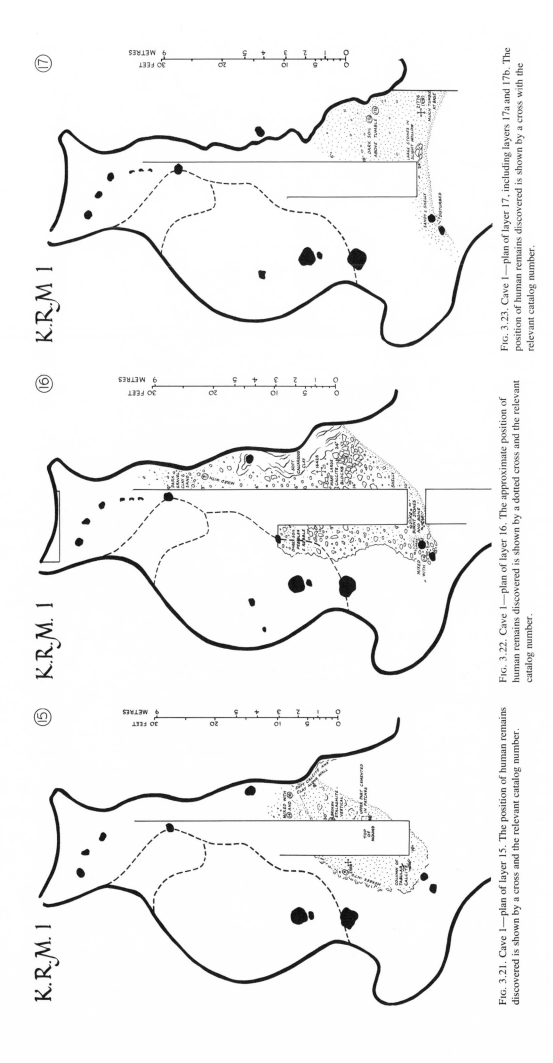

FIG. 3.23. Cave 1—plan of layer 17, including layers 17a and 17b. The position of human remains discovered is shown by a cross with the relevant catalog number.

FIG. 3.22. Cave 1—plan of layer 16. The approximate position of human remains discovered is shown by a dotted cross and the relevant catalog number.

FIG. 3.21. Cave 1—plan of layer 15. The position of human remains discovered is shown by a cross and the relevant catalog number.

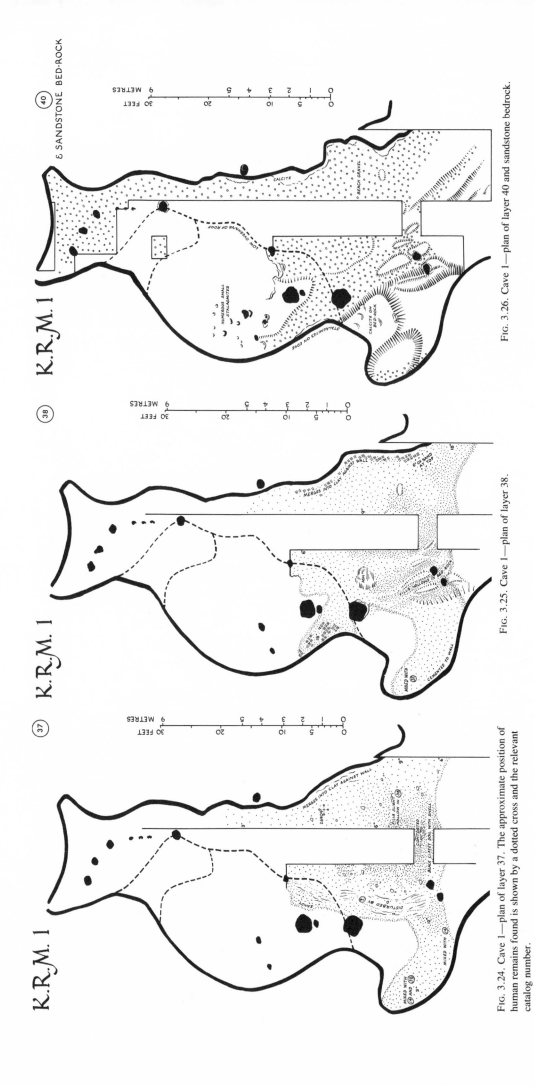

FIG. 3.26. Cave 1—plan of layer 40 and sandstone bedrock.

FIG. 3.25. Cave 1—plan of layer 38.

FIG. 3.24. Cave 1—plan of layer 37. The approximate position of human remains found is shown by a dotted cross and the relevant catalog number.

4 Geomorphology and Sediment Stratigraphy
Karl W. Butzer*

The Environmental Setting

The KRM caves today lie near the watermark, at the foot of 60–100 m cliffs that rise abruptly to a coastal upland, here some 8–10 km wide (fig. 4.1). The seaward margin of this tabular upland is veneered with patches of dune sand that thicken and grow more extensive from west to east. These sand ridges at KRM attain a maximum elevation of 200 m and a presumed thickness of up to 120 m. The coastal upland rises in three steps—the first at 90–120 m elevation, the second at 140–60 m, and the third at 200–250 m—to the foot of the coastal range, locally formed by the Kareedouwberge of the Tzitzikama range. The Kareedouwberge have an average crestline elevation of 500–700 m, and the highest peak, Wolfkop, attains 739 m.

On the basis of the station data (see *Climate of South Africa,* part 2, 1954), rainfall decreases rapidly across the coastal upland from west to east, from about 1,100 mm at 24°E to 975 mm at 24°20′E and under 700 mm beyond 24°45′E. There also is a noticeable but far less marked increase of rainfall from the coast to the crest of the coastal range, with increasingly accentuated rainshadow effects in the transverse valleys of the Cape Folded Ranges, e.g., north of the Kareedouwberge. Therefore, average precipitation at KRM is estimated at about 750 mm; it is distributed relatively evenly throughout the year, with a late autumn maximum. Temperatures can be inferred from Cape St. Francis, where the coldest month (July) has a mean temperature of 14.2° C, a mean daily minimum of 10° C, a mean lowest monthly temperature of 5.7° C, and a record low of +2.2° C (70 year average; see *Climate of South Africa,* part 1, 1954). Significantly, frost is unknown at sea level. The warmest months are January and February with means of 20° C and a mean daily maximum of 22.9° C. Thus, KRM belongs to the humid mesothermal, *Cfb* climate of Koeppen and the subhumid mesothermal C_2B_2r climatic type (with little or no water deficit) of Thornthwaite.

* Mr. Butzer is at the Univeristy of Chicago.

Field and laboratory work was supported in part by a Wenner-Gren grant-in-aid (no. 2344) and NSF grants GS-3013 and GS-39625 (to R. G. Klein and K. W Butzer) as well as BNS74-12223 (K. W. Butzer). Substantial assistance was provided by D. M. Helgren (University of California, Davis), and the illustrations were drawn by C. Mueller-Wille. Helpful discussion was provided by R. G. Klein, T. P. Volman, and R. Singer (Chicago); N. J. Shackleton (Cambridge); Minze Stuiver (Seattle); L. Jacobson (Windhoek); and, last but not least, John Wymer.

This chapter has been published in the *South African Archaeological Bulletin* 33 (1978): 141–51.

The "natural" vegetation of the coastal upland near KRM is "forest and scrubforest" of Knysna type, i.e., broad-leaved and evergreen, according to Acocks (1975). However, the actual vegetation of the area includes (i) evergreen scrubforest of the "dry" type on the western slopes of the adjacent Kaapsedrif valley; (ii) sclerophyllous macchia (fynbos) and scrub on the sand ridges and coastal cliffs; (iii) a broad expanse of grazed grassland, interspersed with the xerophytic rhenoster bush (*Elytropappus rhinocerotis*) or patches of planted conifers and eucalyptus, across the coastal upland; and (iv) mountain macchia and scrub along the flanks of the coastal range, relatively dense in the valleys but sparse on stony ridges. Although this vegetation pattern reflects drastic modification by deforestation and overgrazing, it is nonetheless improbable that closed evergreen forest dominated the area in late prehistoric times. Instead, there probably was a mosaic of vegetation types, including macchia, scrub, and parkland, with forest restricted to entrenched gorges or kloofs, much like on the western fringes of the Knysna Forest (see Martin 1968).

Soil distributions are equally fragmentary, and complicated by extensive areas of relict soils. Steeper slopes (the coastal ranges, most valley walls, and the coastal cliffs) have bare rock, scree lithosols, or thin, humic A-horizons, locally grading into dark, humic podsolic profiles on the colluvial or alluvial surfaces of the lower slopes. Similar humic, podsolized soils appear to be dominant on the sandy veneers that overlie the 90–160 m surfaces of the coastal upland, while deep, reddish ferruginous soils, often with reworked or *in situ* lateritic plinthite, are found on the sands that mantle most of the 200–250 m surface. Finally, wherever stable, the coastal sand ridges have humic A-horizons, although relict reddish soils or soil sediments are locally exposed on older substrates.

Regional Lithology and Geomorphology

Folded and metamorphosed rocks of the mid-Paleozoic Cape System form the cliffs, upland, and ranges of the KRM area. These strike west-northwest to east-southeast, and consist of Table Mountain quartzite with slate/shale interbeds and synclinical occurrences of Bokkeveld metashales. The steep-sided coastal ranges with their angular crests and subangular footslopes are of structural and erosional origin. The tabular coastal upland, on the other hand, cuts smoothly across lithological variations and structural grain, and clearly is erosional. Nonetheless, the drainage lines have trellis organization

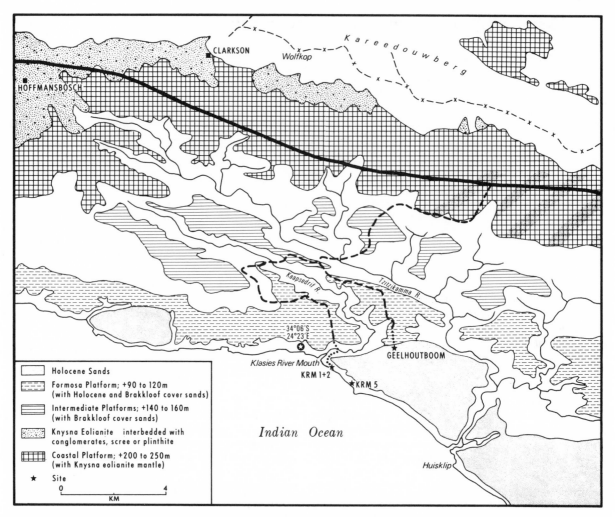

FIG. 4.1. Geomorphic setting of Klasies River Mouth.

(fig. 4.1) and the deeply incised, major valleys follow the weaker shales in close conformity with structural lineaments. Thus, the longer stream segments are oriented N 60–75°W, parallel to the coastal ranges, while shorter sections strike N 10–30°E. Although somewhat obscured by entrenched meanders, the stream segments intersect at near-right angles. The coast itself is poorly articulated and compartmentalized into long, rectilinear units (fig. 4.1) that follow the general structural pattern.

The dominant feature of the coastal upland is the early Tertiary planation surface at 200–250 m (fig. 4.1) (see Butzer and Helgren 1972, Helgren and Butzer 1977). No coeval deposits are preserved on this oldest portion of the Coastal Platform, although the gently undulating surface is covered by 3–8 m of overlying, intensely weathered, quartzose sands. These ancient eolian sands typically have 3–5 m deep, red oxic or argillic B-horizons, comparable to the early Pleistocene Knysna Soil of Helgren and Butzer (1977). *In situ* ferricretes (plinthite) may locally be observed at depth. More common are near-surface colluvia of reworked lateritic concretions, commonly found on the shoulders of drainage lines. Near the foot of the Kareedouwberge there are thicker eolianites (up to 30 m) that merge with coarse alluvial fans or interfinger with stream conglomerates or talus breccias. Relict, reddish B-horizons of 3–5 m thickness are generally present under shallow Holocene humic horizons. In addition, there are patches of younger eolianite as well as alluvial cones with yellowish ultisols that

recall the Middle Pleistocene Brakkloof Soil of Helgren and Butzer (1977).

At least some of the weathered eolianites on the 200–250 m platform are younger than the lower marine platforms cut by relative sea levels at 140–60 m and 100–120 m (fig. 4.1). The last level appears to represent the early Pleistocene Formosa beach of Butzer and Helgren (1972), and along the road to Hengelaarskroonstrand (34°04′S, 24°14′E), Davies (1971) found beach cobbles at +107 m near a possible marine nip. Cover eolianites on the lower platforms are generally obscured by younger sands, but Brakkloof plinthite profiles can be observed along the valley shoulders. An informative sequence is also preserved at the Acheulian site of Geelhoutboom. (34°6′05″S, 24°25′15″E). Here the upper part of the eolianite complex includes vestiges of late Pleistocene to Holocene paleosols, namely, the Brenton and Beacon Island Soils as defined in the Knysna–Plettenberg Bay area (Helgren and Butzer 1977). These marker soils indicate the presence of late Middle and Upper Pleistocene transgressive eolianites beneath unconsolidated, later Holocene sands.

Since the formation of these extensive abrasional platforms, the dominant geomorphic trend of the study area has been bedrock dissection, with selective incision into metashales. So, for example, the Tzitzikama River, which enters the sea via a drowned gorge, with a relief of over 120 m, still follows a canyon that is 60 m deep some 20 km (via channel trace) upstream (fig. 4.1). Similarly, the smaller Kaapsedrif River descends rapidly over a series of nicks to an overdeepened embouchure, locally designated as Klasies River Mouth. It is probable that this incision was accelerated and made possible by Pleistocene glacial-eustatic regressions. Entrenched meanders are restricted to the lower valleys (fig. 4.1), suggesting that the middle and upper stream courses were incised in the course of progressive headward erosion. This in-turning confirms the impression that regional drainage developed along structural lines only after the cutting and subsequent emergence of the several platforms of the coastal upland. Thus, the gross articulation of the coast and its drowned river mouths may be no older than mid-Pleistocene.

Younger glacial-eustatic fluctuations of sea level have left few traces along the steep cliffs, and although there are fragmentary wave-cut platforms, sea caves, and notches, these are inadequate to establish an independent sequence of marine stages. At KRM 1 the archeological cave is obviously wave cut in quartzites that dip steeply at 22–28°; there is a notch at 9 m above mean sea level (m.s.l.) or 7 m above the modern storm beach; the upper cave, KRM 2, is also marine, and has its major notch at +23 m (m.s.l.); 200 m to the east there is a conspicuous wave-cut platform reflecting a m.s.l. of about +11 m. The cave at KRM 5, on the other hand, is not a clear wave-cut feature (D. M. Helgren, personal communication), although Singer and Wymer (chap. 10) found beach shingle on the floor at +19 m. Further east, Krige (1927) and Davies (1972) were able to verify a 24 m marine cave at Huisklip (34°08′S, 24°27′E), while to the west there are 6 m and 9 m platform fragments at Hengelaarskroonstrand and Oubosstrand (34°04′S, 24°12′E). The writer predicts that a variety of minor platforms at 1–4 m are too small to distinguish on account of (a) the bizarre structural-lithological relief of the various "reefs," and (b) the complexities of a 1.6 m tidal amplitude, combined with effective storm-wave sculpture to at least 1 m above spring high-tide level.

Only in view of the more compelling evidence from complex depositional sequences studied in the Cape area, at Swartklip, Melkbosstrand, and Saldanha Bay (Butzer, in preparation), as well as along the Coega River (Butzer and Helgren 1972), can the writer suggest that the +6 to +9 m shoreline features of the KRM coastal sector generally pertain to a sea level stage associated with the maximum of the last, Pleistocene interglacial (deep-sea isotopic stage 5e). Relative elevations corresponding to the high sea levels of the late Last Interglacial (deep-sea stages 5a, 5c; see Butzer 1975, Shackleton 1975) were near or only a few meters higher than modern watermark along the Cape coasts. This information implies that the 9 m sea cave known as KRM 1 was created, or at least significantly remodeled, by marine action at the very beginning of the Upper Pleistocene, c. 125,000 B.P. This provides a critical datum for the archeological cave fills. Other, higher sea caves in the region are substantially older, i.e., Middle Pleistocene, at least in terms of their marine origin.

Sedimentological Procedures

The writer removed sediment samples at KRM 1 in 1970 and again in 1973. Additional samples from KRM 1A, collected during the archeological excavations, were searched out in the South African Museum by R. G. Klein in 1972 and shipped to Chicago. The total of 38 samples selected for full analysis represent the entire stratigraphic sequence.

The procedural routine followed during study in the Paleo-Ecology Laboratory of the University of Chicago is as follows:

(1) Decalcify the samples in 25 percent hydrochloric acid after removing shell or bone fragments coarser than the 2 mm sieve. (2) Do hydrometer analyses, using a 5 percent solution of sodium pyrophosphate as peptizing agent, to determine the 2, 6, 20, and 60μ fractions. (3) Sift the sand (wet), using standard sieves (37, 63, 210, and 595μ, 2.0 and 6.4 mm). (4) Carry out textural classification according to Link (1966), with sand percentages defined as the 60μ–2 mm fraction. (5) Determine textural parameters for the 37μ–6.4 mm fraction by the indices of Folk and Ward (see Folk 1966): mean (Mz), sorting (So), skewness (Ski), and kurtosis (Kg). (6) Calculate the calcium carbonate equivalent (C.C.E.) on the basis of mass loss during application of HCl to bulk samples finer than 2 mm. (7) Determine the pH, electrometrically, in distilled water. (8) Perform semiquantitative estimates of sand-grain micromorphology and composition, including degree of rounding and frosting. (9) Color, dry, by the *Munsell Soil Color Charts*.

In addition to these quantitative studies, all samples as well as several trench faces in KRM 1 were qualitatively examined, in the field, in terms of structure, consolidation, stratification, calcification or oxidation, humus and other organic forms. Two gravel samples were analyzed morphometrically by the modified Lüttig method (outlined in Butzer 1971, p. 166f., and applied by Butzer 1973a).

The more significant data are synthesized in figure 4.2. The schematic profile is based on the writer's sections for KRM 1 as well as on the archeological profiles (figs. 3.3–3.6). Unless otherwise reported, all samples are moderately sorted (So 0.7–1.0), slightly negatively skewed (Ski 0 to −0.2), with intermediate Kg values (0.8–1.2), representing matrices that are well stratified, horizontal, of fine granular to medium subrounded blocky structure, and loose or unconsolidated. Except for traces of glauconite in four samples (KRM 1, levels 40, 17, 16, and 13) and hematite in one (KRM 1A-38), no heavy minerals were noted. The remainder of the sands and fine gravel consists of quartz, quartzite, "fused" quartz of quartzite derivation, and occasional pegmatite.

Sediment Stratigraphy

The representative sedimentary sequence of KRM 1/1A can be described as follows, from base to top, as resting on quartzitic bedrock with some ancient knobs of stalagmite. Organization follows the broad archeological horizons and specific layers as described in chapter 3 (especially with respect to "Major Cutting East Face").

Middle Stone Age I

(KRM 1-40) *20–25 cm*. Grades from a basal, angular gravelly sand of white or pink quartzite, to a poorly sorted, silty sand with abundant quartzite grit. The gravel is subrounded on the average but ranges from angular to well rounded (index of rounding ρ, 24 percent; coefficient of variation of ρ, 59.3 percent); the pebbles are relatively flat (ratio of breadth to major axis E/L, 30.7 percent, breadth to minor axis, E/l, 45.4 percent) and coarse in grade (mean length L, 4.44 cm, with coefficient of variation 33 percent). Once this was a typical beach gravel, moved mainly by sliding motions, but post-depositional alteration has led to partial disintegration: most pebbles are brittle and some appear freshly fractured. Whereas the gravel matrix has few quartzite-derived sands that show mechanical wear or rounded quartz grains, these may account for as much as 30 percent of the coarse sand (200–600μ frac-

36

KRM 1/1A

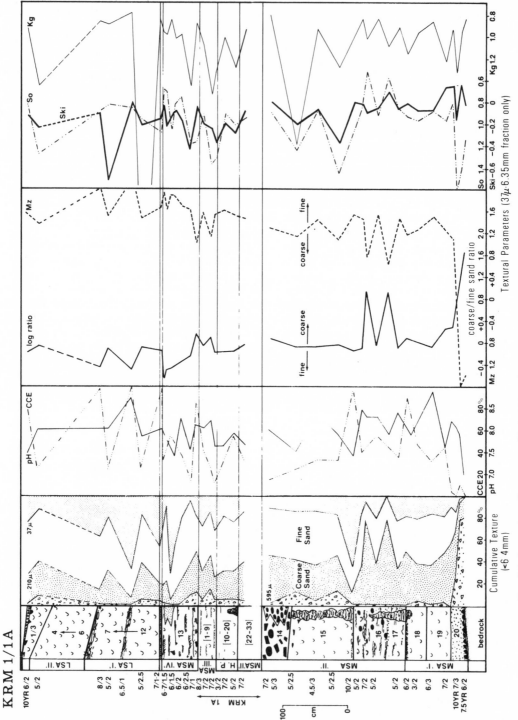

Fig. 4.2. Composite sedimentary profile for KRM 1/1A. Sediment thickness in Shelter 1A shown at half-scale. Basic stratigraphy based on description in chapter 3. Note that the layers for MSA I (col. 2) are numbered *as excavated*. For equating with layers in the text, see chapter 3. Thus, in Cave 1, layers 18 to 20 = 37 to 40.

tion) in the upper, finer facies. Although there is some microbone, this level has been largely decalcified and most of the localized carbonates appear to be secondary. Limited artifacts, a little bone, and some shell fragments. Broken, reworked fragments of dripstone verify at least one generation of older stalagmites or stalactites in the cave.

(KRM 1-38) *35 cm*. Basic matrix of very pale brown sand, mainly modified by organic residues and cultural components to a pale brown, light gray, or dark grayish brown silty sand. Compact, with coarse, angular blocky structure. Some 25–50 percent of the coarse sand is worn quartzite or subangular to subrounded polished quartz not immediately derived from the cave bedrock. Inclined 2° to the back of the cave, where the dip is reversed. Artifacts, debitage, bone, partly decalcified or fragmented marine shell, nacre, and some small land snails are generally related to thin hearths with humus and ash, or reddish oxidation.

(KRM 1-37) *30 cm*. Very dark grayish brown, highly organic silty sand. Up to 25 percent worn quartzite in coarse sand fraction. Artifactual materials, ash and charcoal, as well as partly decalcified or fragmented shell are present.

Middle Stone Age II

(KRM 1-17) *40 cm*. Grayish brown, organic silty sand; up to 25 percent worn quartzite in coarse sand fraction. Shell partly decalcified at base, intact at top; active stalagmite accumulation, leading to cementation of top of level 17, and subsequent creation of local calcrete lenticles. Diffuse archeological debris.

(KRM 1-16) *15–40 cm*. Grayish brown, organic silty sand with dispersed, well-rounded marine pebbles, probably introduced by man, as was the abundant marine shell debris. Interbedded with several lenticles of primary, eolian sand (coarse, well sorted, in part positively skewed, no cultural debris) derived from adjacent beaches. However, coarse sands from layer 16 are highly variable in terms of rounding. The terminal deposits, including discontinuous flowstone lenticles, comprise markedly finer sands. Stalagmites developed locally, with extensive, irregular zones of cementation. Diffuse archeological materials.

(KRM 1-15) *50–170 cm*. Brown to grayish brown, organic silty sand, poorly sorted and leptokurtic. Includes the back debris-slope (12–18° dips) of a midden accumulating fairly rapidly just in front of the cave, whereas the interior deposits suggest intensive, primary occupation, possibly a stone workshop. Up to 50 percent of coarse sands worn. Stalagmites resumed development, but in different locations.

(KRM 1-14) *30–50 cm*. Brown, organic silty sand, as matrix to chaotic rubble of battered eolianite and dripstone-cemented sediment, intermixed with well-rounded, spheroidal beach cobbles. The rubble is not in primary context but reworked, probably from older deposits near the cave entrance.

At the back of the cave (Rear Chamber) layer 14 intergrades with 50 cm of well-stratified, mainly undisturbed gravel to +9.5 m m.s.l., and that is partly sealed under younger deposits (KRM 1-13). Morphometric analysis gave an index of rounding of 52.9 percent, with a coefficient of variation of 48.9 percent, E/L and E/l ratios of 29.2 and 47.8 percent, respectively, and a mean length of 2.84 cm. Descriptively, this is a homogeneously rounded, medium-grade gravel, very flat in shape because of a dominance of sliding motions. Some 28 percent of the pebbles were mechanically fractured before final rounding. There is next to no fine matrix other than a little coarse sand. This typical beach deposit rests on older stalagmites, probably pertaining to KRM 1-15 to 17. Since the layer 14 deposits of

the main cave are as much as 1 m lower than the gravel lens in the Rear Chamber, effective sea level was somewhat lower than +9.5 m. The beach gravel presumably was laid down by a funneled swash, and the main cave deposits were probably reworked by wave action. An alternative explanation is proposed in chapter 3, viz., rubble rolling down the steep slope next to the cave. However, I contend that the original field designation of layer 14 as a "storm beach" may be correct.

The next two depositional complexes, MSA III and Howieson's Poort, are absent from KRM 1, either because the cave entrance was partly blocked by existing middens or because occupation shifted to the talus piedmont in front of the cave or because KRM 1 was abandoned at about the time of storm-wave ingression (KRM 1-14) in favor of a higher and drier site on the slope. It is possible that part of the MSA II sequence of KRM 1A (layers 22 to 33) is unique. Unfortunately, this possible sedimentary gap in our composite profile was not apparent during the field visits nor at the time that samples were selected during excavations. In any event only one sample from the topmost layer (KRM 1A-22) was available for analysis.

(KRM 1A-22 to 33) *330 cm*. Alternating well-stratified hearth zones and light gray silty sand. Local development of a stalagmite knob (30 cm) on top of this final MSA II bed suggests a protracted period with little or no detrital sedimentation.

Howieson's Poort

(KRM 1A-10 to 21) *100 cm*. Alternating beds of light gray and dark grayish brown silty sand, positively skewed, with color variation reflecting organic and other cultural admixture. Coarse sands are of subordinate importance, and include up to 30 percent worn quartzite. Marine shell rare in upper half of horizon; relatively abundant microbone. An abri deposit with little evidence of scree slope admixture.

Middle Stone Age III

(KRM 1A-1 to 9) *90 cm*. Alternating beds of light gray and very dark grayish brown silty sand, reflecting variable cultural admixture, including abundant artifactual debris and bone. Basal unit includes up to 50 percent worn quartzite and exotic quartz in the coarse sand fraction, whereas the middle and upper parts consist predominantly of unworn, locally derived sands. Despite the presence of secondary carbonate aggregates, increasing from bottom to top, the shell is in poor condition. The lower, culturally modified deposits are poorly sorted, negatively skewed, and leptokurtic because of the fine "tail." The characteristic fine sands of the Howieson's Poort deposit continue into the lowest part of the MSA III unit.

Bone, shell, and artifacts are cemented to the cliff face behind KRM 1A as much as 5 m above the extant MSA III midden, indicating major subsequent erosion. Undercutting by high post-Pleistocene sea levels may have been responsible, but the edge of a cone of crude slope rubble, incorporating angular quartzite spall, rests against the edge of the eroded MSA III deposits (Wymer, personal communication). Such rubble mantles are characteristic of the late Pleistocene of the southern Cape coast (Butzer and Helgren 1972) and suggest an alternative explanation of Pleistocene slope wash erosion.

Middle Stone Age IV

(KRM 1-13) *40–85 cm*. Mainly light gray sand or silty sand, with planar, laminated bedding and traces of adhesion ripples;

dips as much as 8° to cave interior. Basal unit is poorly sorted and negatively skewed, with traces of angular gravel, macroshell, and glauconite; increasingly well sorted and finer in upper part. Coarse sand fraction consists mainly of worn quartzite with some exotic quartz. Laterally, layer 13 grades (Rear Alcove and Rear Chamber) into a prismatic, light gray or grayish brown (10YR 6-7/1-2) sandy clay-silt, with over 50 percent C.C.E., i.e., a marl; includes terrestrial snails and some plant stem impressions. Scanty and diffuse archeological residues, mainly near base.

In the main cave, layer 13 represents a typical, fine-grade, regressional eolianite; it was accompanied by deposition of calcareous suspended material in pools of standing water near the cave rear. The cementation of the now-eroded MSA III deposits above KRM 1A may have taken place at this time.

Post–Middle Stone Age

A long hiatus, with next to no detrital accumulation, followed. There was some accumulation of thin, discontinuous flowstones with a small residue (2.5 percent) of silty sand-clay that includes abundant amorphous silica and oxides. These light gray flowstones are related to development of a great stalagmite boss with a relief of 1.3 m below a joint fissure in the ceiling at the entrance to the Rear Chamber. In a quartzite cave with limited travertine development such a stalagmite almost certainly requires tens of thousands of years to develop. During this time the cave appears to have been essentially sealed off from detrital sediment sources. Subsequent reopening of KRM 1 can best be explained by wave erosion of a blocking eolianite or shell midden, when sea level returned to its present position in mid-Holocene times. At any rate the next detrital deposits of KRM 1 are all younger than 5,000 years.

Later Stone Age

(KRM 1-7 to 12) *50–120 cm.* Shell debris with a limited soil matrix of grayish brown, organic silty sand, including thin ash laminae and very rare beach cobbles. The stratification is at least partly cultural in origin, with dips of 8–12° to the interior once again suggesting the back slope of a midden. A degree of moisture is suggested by local development (Rear Alcove) of incomplete flowstone laminae, both midway and near the top of this unit (10–25 cm thick). The limited sand fraction is generally fine grained, presumably because the midden at the entrance reached almost to the roof of the cave, so allowing only culturally filtered sediment to enter. An approximate time range of 4850–4500 B.P. can be inferred from the sigma ranges of two radiocarbon dates (see Singer and Wymer 1969); a third relevant date from KRM 5 may extend this sedimentary complex to as late as 4000 B.P.

(KRM 1-4 to 6) *60–90 cm.* Loose shell rubble with negligible soil matrix, inadequate for representative sampling. Well-stratified and dipping 8–15° into the cave. A ^{14}C range of c. 2850–2450 B.P. is indicated.

(KRM 1-1 to 3) *35 cm.* Grayish brown silty sand, poorly sorted and leptokurtic, with traces of angular rubble. These uncompacted beds are foreset (at 20–45°) near the cave entrance, where they rest against the truncated slope of layers 12 to 4; further inside, they are backset (at 10–25°) and conformable. This demonstrates substantial erosion of the earlier middens, prior to accumulation of layers 3 to 1. A temporary rise of sea level to a maximum of as much as +4 m is suggested, not too long after 2450 B.P. The coarse sand fraction consists mainly of worn quartzite of beach origin. There is some shell and evidence of occupation.

Capping Flowstone

0–5 cm. Cemented, banded to laminated, light grayish brown impure flowstone, with a 25 percent residue of organic silty sand. Probably was forming more actively in the recent past than today, since there now is dry dust on the flowstone. Predominantly worn quartzite and exotic quartz in sand fractions.

Interpretation of the Sedimentary Facies
Coarse Rubble

Perhaps the most striking aspect of the KRM sedimentary column is the absence of incontrovertible roof spall. Coarse clasts are prominent in several horizons, but detailed study suggests better alternative explanations. The one important exception is the angular scree that abuts the eroded edge of the MSA III deposits (Wymer, personal communication); this rubble, which includes spall from the walls above, probably dates to the major hiatus between KRM 1-13 and 12.

The clasts of basal, gravelly sand, or grit (KRM 1/1A-40) originally were a typical flat, sandy-beach gravel. The post-depositional disintegration of beach gravel abandoned on the cave floor as the sea recede from its +7 m stand may have been favored by salt hydration, provided that the cave microenvironment was sufficiently dry. Frost-weathering is unlikely since the pebbles are highly brittle and have evidently been subject to a degree of decomposition.

The coarse clasts of KRM 1-15 to 19 and 4 to 12 include dispersed marine cobbles in a matrix of low-energy cultural deposits, or fractured pebbles with evidence of stone-working. These pebbles and cobbles must have been brought into the cave, from an adjacent high-energy beach, by human agency. Even the grit component is largely a matter of débitage when examined under the microscope. Other apparent clasts in these levels are calcrete aggregates of sand or cultural residue representing dripstone formation.

The dispersed cobbles, the battered dripstone rubble, and a lens of primary beach gravel in layer 14 have already been attributed to storm-wave activity in the cave. The basal angular gravel of layer 13 may represent roof spall, but there was not enough for systematic morphometric analysis without destroying a large block of the witness section; some pieces clearly are débitage, however, and the possibility of derivation from layer 14 must be considered. Even in KRM 1A, where spall would be likely (below a cliff), most coarse material can be identified as débitage.

It is therefore apparent that mechanical weathering of all kinds has been ineffectual in enlarging the KRM 1 cavern since its inception. This is in striking contrast to Nelson Bay Cave (Robberg), where frost-shattered clasts are often very prominent in an identical microclimatic context (see Butzer 1973*a*, *b*). The difference is that KRM is cut into Table Mountain quartzite, whereas Nelson Bay Cave is developed in Cretaceous breccias, with a friable matrix and crude quartzite rubble evidently predisposed to fracturing by lines of weakness. Evaluation of the sand residues in the two caves also shows substantial differences. Roof matrix sands are prominent at Nelson Bay Cave but are probably absent at KRM, where two major sedimentary breaks, coincident with human abandonment, failed to produce any detrital sediment. As discussed further below, almost all the sand in KRM is primary eolian or re-worked beach sand. As a consequence, the KRM sequence fails to provide information on mechanical weathering and, by implication, on thermal fluctuations of the cave microenvironment. This does not imply an absence of Pleistocene frost-weathering; instead it reflects on a geomorphic threshold too high to provide a sensitive record of those changes that have occurred.

Sea Level Changes

The cave record is particularly informative as to sea level changes. (1) KRM 1-40 represents a regressional cave deposit that is only slightly younger than a long-term sea level of about +7 m. (2) Layers 17 and 16 include lenticles of typical foreshore eolian sand, and artificially introduced beach cobbles are common in 16; this argues for a relatively high, or oscillating, sea level, with a sandy beach initially exposed on the platform, then an adjacent shingle beach as the watermark once again approached the cave entrance. (3) Layer 14 coincided with a rising sea level that brought storm-wave action directly into the cave. Estimating the maximum sea level responsible for layer 14 is difficult; the modern storm beach is 2 m above m.s.l., but storm surges can be doubly effective in a confined space such as an elongated cave; it is unlikely that the responsible level was more than 4 or 5 m above that of the present. If the storm beach reflected once-a-year events (e.g., spring-tide storm swash), or even one-in-ten-year storms, no more than a few millennia would be required to generate these deposits. (4) Layer 13 is a typical regressional eolianite, recording a falling sea level that was initially near the cave but ultimately quite distant. A major glacial-eustatic regression is indicated. (5) The temporary high sea level between layers 4 and 3 served to destroy much of the MSA deposit (in part now found as rolled cobbles in the modern beach) as well as the substantial LSA middens. Storm surges were effective to about +6 m, implying a m.s.l. at least 1 m and more probably 2 m above the present.

These direct records of marine activity in and adjacent to KRM 1 are complemented by the faunal record. Marine shells of the littoral or sublittoral zone are abundant in most KRM 1 horizons, except layer 40 (due to partial decalcification) and middle and upper layer 13 (where there are land snails but no marine shells). In KRM 1A, shell generally is poorly preserved, but absolute shell quantities also are relatively low between layers 1 and 16, i.e., above the lower third of the Howieson's Poort unit (see also Voigt 1975). Marine mammals (Cape fur seal, rare dolphins) are found in all layers except the upper MSA III unit and the middle and upper part of KRM 1-13 (Klein 1976a); the less complete record of marine birds appears to be much the same (R. G. Klein and G. Avery, personal communication, and see also chap. 12). These data demonstrate that most but not quite all of the KRM 1/1A deposits record coastal occupations. The important exception is middle and upper KRM 1-13.

The cliffs of this coastal sector continue offshore as an initially steep submarine slope. Consequently, the littoral environment would have been less than 5 km distant with a relative regression of 50 m, but 78 km distant with a regression of 125 m (see Dingle and Rogers 1972; also World Nautical Chart no. 3838, U.S. Naval Oceanographic Office 1963). In relation to the offshore topography, the sedimentological criteria argue that all of the primary eolian or secondary beach deposits within KRM, even the regressional eolianite, were predicated on a littoral zone within 5 km of the cave. In effect, all deposits

other than travertines are related to *relatively* high sea levels—from 7 m above to several tens of meters below—as opposed to glacial-eustatic sea level minima.

The sand component of the sedimentary column is remarkably sensitive to sea level proximity, or at least to littoral sediment supply and cave aperture. This can be inferred from scanning of the mean size (Mz) of the 37μ–6.4 mm fraction (fig. 4.2), which is broadly proportional to the sea level trends inferred from the direct evidence discussed above. An additional parameter was devised to gauge the details of sand availability and transport: the ratio of coarse sands (200–2000 μ) to those less coarse (60–200 μ). This ratio is shown in figure 4.2 as a log function. It demonstrates a reduced supply of, or access for, coarser sand at the bottom of KRM 1-15, through most of the Howieson's Poort unit and the basal MSA IV, and again in the middle and upper segments of KRM 1-13. Since none of the sedimentary units prior to the final deposition of KRM 1-13 was affected by limited access, most of the MSA deposits should be diagnostic of periods of relatively lower or higher sea level. Accordingly, the sea level inferences are summarized in table 4.1.

Travertines

Calcareous precipitates are incidental in KRM 1, and dripstone and flowstone formation was local and sporadic. All of the dissolved carbonates appear to have entered via joints and fissures in the roof, the loci of deposition shifting repeatedly as some cracks were sealed with lime. Since carbonates are absent in the quartzitic bedrock, the various laminated travertines must be attributed to percolating soil waters coming from high up, above the cliffs, in response to leaching of eolian sands rich in ground-up marine shell. Leaching within the cave sediments of KRM 1 is either incomplete or absent, except in layer 20, judging from the preservation of marine shell or land snails; the sediments themselves appear to have contributed little to the solubles represented by the flowstones and other calcareous concretions. It is probable that, under these circumstances, active travertine formation reflects on active leaching among the dune sands above the cliffs, and vice versa. In other words, travertine development in KRM 1 was probably proportional to the intensity of external pedogenesis.

Coeval dripstones are rare or absent only in KRM 1-37 and 38 or 1 to 6 and during the KRM 1 hiatus spanned by KRM 1A-1 to 33. On the other hand, the cave environment of KRM 1 experienced an abundance of water during the accumulation of layer 40 (late) (decalcification), layers 16 to 17 (widespread cementation), layer 13 (ponding in back), and layers 7 to 12 (local cementation). Except for layer 13—a regressional eolianite—sea spray and dew may have contributed substantially to the cave moisture indicated.

On these criteria of external leaching and cave dampness, KRM-1 layers 37 and 38 and 1 to 6 as well as most of the break between 14 and 13 suggest drier conditions than the mean of the last two millennia. KRM 1-13 and 17 argue for a substantially wetter climate; all other levels infer conditions comparable to those of the recent past or perhaps just a little wetter.

More specific inferences would be possible only by gauging the relative bulk of travertines developed in relation to mean sedimentation rates and cave ventilation. Nonetheless, the variability evident argues for significant changes in external pedogenesis and, by implication, both soil moisture budget and vegetative cover. Such changes are amply verified for the southern Cape coast by the complex nature of the paleosol

Table 4.1. RELATIVE SEA LEVELS, ENVIRONMENTAL INTERPRETATION, AND EXTERNAL STRATIGRAPHIC INFERENCES

KRM 1

(Capping travertine) Sea near present. Some external pedogenesis. No occupation.

(Layers 1 to 3) Sea near present. Cave dry. LSA II(?).

(Storm-wave erosion) Sea about +1 to 2 m. Postdates 2500 B.P.

(Layers 4 to 6) Sea probably near present. Cave dry. LSA II. C. 2850-2450 B.P.

(Layers 7 to 12) Sea near present. External pedogenesis, cave damp. LSA I. C. 4850-4000 B.P.

(Major stalagmite) in part, sea near present. In part, wash erosion of KRM 1A, followed by accumulation of angular slope screes. In part, external pedogenesis. No occupation. Interpolated dates, c. 65,000-5,000 B.P. (Includes span of Rubble Horizon; Gray, Yellow, and Brown Stony Loams; Oxidation Horizons 2 and 3; as well as most of the midden sequence at NBC.)

(Layer 13) Sea at first near or slightly above present, then dropping rapidly to well below modern level. Cave wet, major external pedogenesis, e.g., Brenton Soil. MSA IV. Deep-sea stage 4 (c. 70,000 B.P.). (Correlates with major ferricretion [Oxidation Horizon 1] at NBC.)

KRM 1A

(Layers 1 to 9) Sea rising from slightly below to slightly above present, then falling again. Cave dry. MSA III. Deep-sea substage 5a (c. 80,000 B.P.) (Hiatus at NBC.)

(Layers 10 to 21) Sea initially near present, then somewhat below. Cave dry. Howieson's Poort. Deep-sea substage 5b (cool waters in littoral zone) (c. 95,000 B.P.). (Major frost-weathering and Black Loam at NBC.)

(Local stalagmite) External pedogenesis (Brenton Soil).

(Layers 22 to 33) Sea near present at end, no information for earlier segments. Cave dry. MSA II (late). ? Deep-sea substage 5c, late.

KRM 1

(Layer 14) Sea rising to maximum of about +4 to +5 m, reworking cave deposits during rare storms. MSA II (middle). Deep-sea substage 5c (middle) (c. 105,000 B.P.). (Marine incursion at back of NBC.)

(Layer 15) Sea initially slightly below, then near or a little above present. External pedogenesis. MSA II (Middle). Deep-sea substage 5c (early) (c. 110,000). (Pale Brown Loam at NBC.)

(Layer 16/17) Sea rising from somewhat below to about present level. Cave increasingly damp, major external pedogenesis (early Brenton Soil). MSA II (early). Deep-sea substage 5d (late). (c. 115,000 B.P.). (Basal Loam at NBC.)

(Layers 37 to 40) Sea falling from somewaht above to slightly below present, then rising again. Cave initially wet, then dry. MSA I. Deep-sea substage 5e (late) to 5d (early). (c. 120,000 B.P.).

(Cave eroded or remodeled) Maximum transgression +7 m. Deep-sea substage 5e (early). (c. 125,000 B.P.).

Note. Correlations with Nelson Bay Cave (NBC) refer to units of Butzer (1973a), with appropriate stratigraphic revision.

record, which indicates that intervals of moderate or high intensity pedogenesis represent only a modest proportion of later Pleistocene time (Butzer and Helgren 1972; Helgren and Butzer 1977). Significant changes of the Holocene vegetation communities in the Knysna Forest are also verified palynologically (Martin 1968). It is therefore possible to infer a range of variation in the upland and kloof vegetation between drier formations, such as sclerophyllous parkland, on one hand, and wetter formations, such as closed scrubforest, on the other.

We can suggest that later Pleistocene pedogenesis was most effective contemporaneous with KRM 1-17 and 13, at which time it is most probable that the Brenton Soil was actively forming; scrubforest may have been dominant at this time. Pedogenesis was least effective at the time KRM 1-37 to 39 was deposited and during the hiatus between layers 14 and 13; parkland with sclerophyllous elements may have been characteristic, with only small tracts of kloof scrubforest. The remainder of the time, pedogenesis and the vegetation mosaic probably resembled that just prior to the contact period beginning A.D. c. 1750. These deductions are basically compatible with those of Klein's (1976a) faunal analyses. He has browsing mammals (*Cephalophus, Raphicerus, Tragelaphus*) increasing in number immediately after deposition of KRM 1-38 and 39, then becoming characteristic and remaining so through KRM 1-14; the limited fauna of KRM 1A-22 to 33 is inconclusive, but open-country equids and alcelaphines are prominent in the remaining MSA levels, through the base of KRM 1-13. The apparent contradiction for the MSA IV may be a result of the limited sample, entirely derived from the lower part of the deposit and in identical state of fossilization as bone of the underlying unit (R. G. Klein, personal communication); it may also reflect a colder environment accompanying a glacial-eustatic regression.

These suggestions in regard to the cave or external, pedogenetic environment are included in table 4.1.

Cultural Components

All the evidence indicates that there is a close relationship between prehistoric occupation and sedimentation at KRM. This is best illustrated by the lack of sediment accumulation in KRM 1 at times of cave abandonment or the absence of further sediment on top of the MSA III levels at KRM 1A. Only a few units or lenses are primarily of nonhuman origin: the various travertines, small eolian lenticles, the eolianite of KRM 1, the gritty facies of KRM 1-20, and the marine components of KRM 1-14. All others, while consisting to one degree or other of mineral components, owe their accumulation to human agencies:

a) Lithic raw material. A great deal of quartzite, in the form of pebbles, or flakes detached from pebbles, was introduced from adjacent beaches and subsequently worked within the cave or on top of middens situated near the entrance. Mesocrystalline quartz, probably derived from veins and other ancient shear and tension zones within the Table Mountain quartzite, was also introduced in limited quantity, probably from no great distance. Finally, several of the archeological levels include small amounts of exotic lithic material, mainly cryptocrystalline siliceous ("silcrete," jasper, agates, also lydianite) of uncertain derivation, probably from well inland. The sum total of such artifactual rock, much of it in the form of fine débitage or partially flaked chunks or hammerstones, accounts for most of the rubble coarser than 2 mm.

b) In a moist littoral environment (tidal, spray, and mist zone), wet sand and soil are readily introduced into a cave or midden on people's feet, on the hide and fur of game, and on or in shells.

c) Plants, fiber, and food were inevitably introduced as food, fuel, dress, and bedding or construction material. In the long run, feces and wood ash would be the principal components, adding organic colloids, amino acids, lignin, nitrates, resins, phosphates, manganese, and potash to the sediment. Plant materials would also be introduced through the digestive tract of slain herbivores or by temporary animal occupants of the cave—mammals or birds.

d) Animal products were also introduced in great quantity and ultimately added to the cultural midden as shell and bone refuse or fecal residues, producing quasi-intact macrorubble as well as decomposition products, e.g., phosphate, nitrogen compounds, organic acids, carbonates, and silica colloids. For example, a good part of the 5 percent median value of clay-size particles consists of colloids released during acid reduction of shell fragments in the fine sediment residue (under 2 mm) during laboratory preparation.

In these various ways the prehistoric occupants of KRM 1/1A, directly or indirectly, contributed substantial amounts of rock, mineral soil, and organic colloids or ions during the course of repeated and protracted occupation. These built up the sand and grit component and augmented the clay-humus fraction by adding specific, soluble mineral compounds and generally increasing the proportion of organic carbon. The great bulk of the clay and finer silt (under 37 μ) fraction shown in figure 4.2 is of such "cultural" origin. These fine residues consequently have no direct environmental significance, e.g., in regard to biochemical weathering processes or rates. Their generally good preservation can be attributed to a relatively dry cave microenvironment, maintained at an alkaline pH by the abundance of shell debris and other carbonates.

The various archeological levels can be informally classified in geoarcheological terms as "primary," "secondary," and "incidental." The *in situ*, minimally disturbed occupation residues would be primary, midden debris-slopes or reworked deposits would be secondary, while strata with limited cultural components would be incidental. Primary cultural deposits include most of KRM 1-16 to 38 and part of 15, KRM 1A-1 to 33, and parts of the LSA levels. Secondary cultural deposits include KRM 1-14 and parts of 15 and 17, and much of the LSA midden debris. Incidental cultural deposits would include KRM 1-40 and 13, as well as most of the key travertines.

Chronostratigraphic Interpretation

The sedimentary sequence recorded in KRM 1 and 1A provides no direct information on regional or global temperature changes, and the moisture inferences derived above are qualitative and difficult to relate to long-term, extraregional climatic anomalies. However, the sea level stratigraphy established for the MSA sequence (table 4.1) is reasonably firm and does allow a measure of correlation with worldwide glacial-eustatic fluctuations. Particular reference can be made to the Mediterranean sea level trace based on interdigitated marine-littoral and continental deposits on Mallorca, as approximately dated by a suite of mainly consistent thorium-uranium dates (Butzer 1975). This Mallorcan trace was established independently of, but correlates satisfactorily with, Shackleton's (1975) deep-sea core microzonation of oxygen isotope composition.

Table 4.1 proposes a suite of correlations between the sea level record at KRM and the deep-sea isotope stratigraphy. The very approximate dates suggested are consonant with the best available estimates for the duration and chronometric subdivision of the Upper Pleistocene. They place the KRM MSA I within a span of perhaps five millennia about or shortly after 120,000 B.P., while intermittent MSA II occupation followed until about 95,000 B.P. The Howieson's Poort would coincide with the cool horizon (Orgnac interval; see Butzer 1975, 1976), c. 95,000 B.P., while the MSA III occupations continued until c. 80,000 B.P. The KRM MSA IV begins at the end of the Last Interglacial complex and extends well into the major regression at the beginning of the Last Glacial, c. 70,000 B.P. As the cave was ultimately separated from the coast by a broad emergent shelf, the site was abandoned, presumably in favor of locations along the new littoral zone. It was not reoccupied until some 65,000 years later.

Intermittent Middle Stone Age occupation at KRM between 120,000 and 70,000 B.P. is compatible with contemporary thinking that most MSA levels are substantially older than 50,000 B.P. (Beaumont and Vogel 1972; Klein 1977). It is also compatible with other lines of independent investigation at KRM:

a) The MSA and Howieson's Poort levels at KRM have a large suite of radiocarbon dates on shell (chap. 14) that are generally infinite (in excess of 33,000 B.P.), but that do include some apparently finite assays (27,500 B.P. and older) with very large stated ranges of error (implying very small samples). These samples were run by a commercial laboratory where pretreatment and date calibration may not have been totally satisfactory. Furthermore, even shell aragonite, under the best of circumstances, represents an open system to the degree that any date greater than 27,000 years may well be infinite (M. Stuiver, personal communication). In effect, therefore, there are no finite radiocarbon dates for the KRM Middle Stone Age.

b) Aspartic acid racemization has also been applied to certain levels at KRM 1. Bone from layers 38, 37, 16, and 13 gave apparent ages of 110,000, 85,000, 84,000, and 61,000 B.P., respectively, using radiocarbon dated bone from Nelson Bay Cave as a reference (Bada and Deems 1975). However, racemization dating is still fraught with difficulties, ranging from the exact nature of the organic components being dated to the paleotemperature assumptions made in assessing the thermal history of the specimen. The very fact that these dates are of an order of magnitude similar to our sea level inferences should be viewed as gratifying to all concerned.

c) Some 200 oxygen isotopic determinations were carried out on a suite of shells from the MSA I (five shells, including KRM 1-38 and samples from KRM 1B and 5), the MSA II (seven shells, KRM 1-15), the Howieson's Poort (one shell only, KRM 1A-40), and the LSA midden (two shells, as reference) (Shackleton, chap. 14). The MSA I shells indicate an isotopic composition essentially identical to that of the LSA reference material and are firmly assigned by Shackleton to isotope substage 5e. The level 15 shell indicates a sea slightly heavier isotopically than it is today; correlation with either substage 5c or substage 5a is proposed. Finally, the single unrecrystallized shell from the lower Howieson's Poort level indicates isotopic conditions intermediate between a full glacial and a full interglacial. Shackleton concludes that this "would be consistent with deposition within stage 3 although a cooler part of stage 5 cannot be excluded." In effect, Shackleton's inferences independently confirm the sedimentological interpretation proposed here.

The cool period about or shortly after 95,000 B.P. is of considerable interest. Regionally, it is noteworthy that the major episode of Upper Pleistocene frost-weathering in South African caves coincides with Howieson's Poort contexts, e.g., the Black Loam units of Nelson Bay Cave (Butzer 1973a; T. P. Volman, personal communication) (see table 4.1) or the antepenultimate éboulis horizon ("Third Brown Sand, Lower" and "Third White Ash") of Border Cave (Butzer, Beaumont, and Vogel 1978; Beaumont 1973a). Globally, this interval was marked by distinct cooling and replacement of thermophile woodlands with steppe or forest-steppe in the Mediterranean Basin (Butzer 1975) and central Europe (Kukla 1975). Mörner (1975) suggests considerable expansion of high-latitude glaciers c. 90,000 B.P., a point borne out by sea level and oxygen isotopic evidence; cooler conditions at this same time are verified from the isotopic record of both the Greenland and Devon Island ice sheets (Paterson et al. 1977).

By way of conclusion, it can be argued that the KRM sediment sequence is one of the most informative in South Africa, providing a substantial chronostratigraphic context for one of the longest and most complete Middle Stone Age successions anywhere. It shows that the earliest MSA is no younger than 120,000 B.P. and therefore implies that even earlier contexts can be expected elsewhere, as indeed they can be verified at Border Cave (Butzer, Beaumont, and Vogel 1978). The KRM sequence places the so-called Howieson's Poort Industry (which may or may not be identical with the essentially unpublished collection from the type site) in isotopic substage 5b, over 90,000 years ago, identifying it as a remarkably precocious lithic entity. It is further apparent that most of the MSA at KRM predates 65,000 B.P., a surprising fact that could not have been anticipated a decade ago.

5 The MSA Stages I–IV

The MSA at KRM was subdivided into four stages on the basis of the stratigraphy discussed in chapter 3. The Howieson's Poort Industry intervened between MSA II and III, and is treated separately in chapter 6.

It is emphasized that these four stratigraphical subdivisions refer to the MSA at this site only, and are not meant as some new typological sequence for application at other sites (see footnote 1, chap. 6).

The four stages are described and compared by dealing separately with individual artifact categories, viz., cores, core preparation and rejuvenation flakes, flake-blades, pointed flake-blades, broken flake-blade segments, worked points, worked flakes, handaxes, hammerstones, flakes, and nonlocal rock artifacts. A summary is presented at the end of each category, wherein comparisons are made between the four stages. (A summary of the total sequence, including the Howieson's Poort Industry, is given in chap. 7.)

Since the preliminary preparation of this report, Sampson (1972) has published a typological classification of MSA artifacts and, although the terms used in this report are descriptive, the following table relates them:

Terminology in This Report	Equivalent Term in Sampson (1972)
Single platform core	Single platform blade core
Double platform core	Opposed platform blade core
Irregular and undeveloped core	Irregular and adjacent platform core
Other core	Miscellaneous core
Core preparation flake	. . .
Core rejuvenation flake	. . .
Flake	Untrimmed flake
Flake-blade	Untrimmed blade
Pointed flake-blade	Untrimmed blade
Broken flake-blade segment	Untrimmed blade fragment
Bulbous segment	Butt fragment
Middle segment	Body fragment
Nonbulbous segment	Tip fragment
Worked point	Trimmed point
Worked flake	Trimmed/utilized blade or flake
Scraper	Scraper
Graver	Burin
Borer	Borer
Denticulate	. . .

Terminology in This Report	Equivalent Term in Sampson (1972)
Notched	. . .
Unspecialized	. . .
Backed all along one edge	Backed blade
Backed flake-blade	Backed piece
Crescent	Crescent
Trapeze	Trapeze
Triangle	. . .
Obliquely blunted point	. . .
Outil écaillé	Outil écaillé
Hammerstone	Pebble hammer

Cores

The main element of the MSA industries at KRM is the production of flake-blades (see below), either parallel-sided or purposely converging to a point, and this is clearly reflected in the core types. Basically there are two types, single platform cores and double platform cores, with variations of each, but between the selection of a suitable piece of raw material and the blocked-out core ready for flake-blade production there are a multitude of transitional stages. These give a valuable insight into knapping methods but do not justify classification into types. There are a few cores which have nothing to do with flake-blade production, and these do justify separate classification, such as tortoise cores, pebble chopper-cores, biconical and discoidal cores.

Any analysis of the cores for flake-blade production is beset with two series of difficulties: (a) The examiner has the difficulty of dealing with either cores that have gone wrong in the blocking-out process and have been discarded, or cores that have been worked down to a state beyond which no more suitable flake-blades could be obtained. It is rare that a core is found at a stage neatly prepared in all respects for the removal of a number of flake-blades, for the obvious reason that no person desiring to produce them would abandon the core unless he was interrupted in his work; he would continue to strike off flake-blades until either the core was whittled down to an inconveniently small size or, much more likely, a series of accidents rendered systematic knapping impossible. The remaining piece may give little impression of the former carefully prepared core. This is very evident when a comparison is made between the length of the flake-blades found at the site and the average size of the cores; in fact, no cores even approach the size of the larger flake-blades. Yet, sufficient material remains to show the methods used for flake-blade production, and the details are recorded below. (*b*) The second series of difficulties is interrelated, but is more directly the difficulty experienced by the knapper. Apart from the degree of personal skill, the quartzite raw material to which he had ready access, although abundant, was a coarse, intractible rock with numerous flaws and incipient fractures that would only reveal themselves as it was flaked. No two rocks would initially be exactly the same shape or texture. Every piece had to be judged on its own merit and worked accordingly, so it would be surprising if any two cores were ever prepared in exactly the same way. Frequently the blocking-out process would go wrong and what had been intended as a core for large flake-blades became suitable only for small ones, or it became just an irregular piece from which one or two useful flakes may have been retrieved for an immediate purpose. That several cores were clearly abandoned after some preliminary blocking out is indicated by obvious signs such as plunged flakes, shattering and striking platforms exceeding the critical angle, or signs which were apparent only to the knapper. These are considered as undeveloped cores.

At KRM the source of raw material was the almost unlimited supply of beach cobbles. These may have existed in greater or lesser numbers on the 6–8 m beach than they do on the present beach, but if they were as numerous as they are now, there would never have been any problem in finding suitable stone. As mentioned above, none of the local quartzite is a good material for careful knapping: some is better than other, and a relatively fine-grained brownish quartzite was favored. The quality of the quartzite is not apparent when it is in the state of a beach cobble, and many cobbles must have been smashed just to determine this. The beach cobbles are derived from the quartzite of the cliffs, and it would have been unnecessary to quarry rock as so much was naturally available. Remaining cortex on the cores or flakes shows conclusively that beach cobbles were the source of raw material.

The elements of the technology and terminology of the cores are shown in figure 5.1, and it is convenient to consider the cores under the following headings: (i) primary splitting, (ii) single platform cores, (iii) double platform cores, (iv) irregular and undeveloped cores, and (v) other cores. Experiments by one of us (J. W.) with beach cobbles showed that the primary splitting could be easily achieved by throwing a selected cobble forcefully onto another on the ground. Once a platform had been created, further flaking was simplified. If the shape of the pebble and the resulting platform was suitable, the core could be dressed by unidirectional flaking from it; if not, one edge was trimmed by lateral flaking (as in the "trial" specimen in fig. 5.1), a platform was struck across one end, and the flake-blades were removed. The first flake-blade from a core trimmed in this manner is a distinctive core-preparation flake (see below).

Primary Splitting

The first task in taking a beach cobble is to split it and see whether the quality of the quartzite is suitable. If the cobble is of an irregular shape, with a flattish surface or projection, it may be easy to strike off a flake or flakes and discover this within a few seconds, but it is much less easy to remove pieces from a spherical cobble. This is best achieved by a violent blow upon its surface, and if a hammerstone held in the hand is used, there is every chance that the force will smash the hammerstone

instead of the cobble, which is dangerous as well as useless. The safest and most effective method is to hurl one cobble at another. Eventually, if not at first, it will split across, leaving a good, flat surface from which the initial blocking out or trial flaking can commence. More than one fracture may occur, or the cobble it hits may be split itself. If the stone seems suitable after a few flakes have been detached it may be put on one side, and if unsuitable it would be discarded.

The beach was not only the source of raw material but also the obvious place to break up the cobbles and do the initial or primary flaking. The evidence from the various MSA occupational deposits is in accordance with this, for there is a marked lack of flakes with 100 percent cortex on their reverses (or dorsal surfaces) or of beach cobbles that have been split unsuccessfully. There are a few cobbles or pebbles with a half dozen or less flakes removed haphazardly that appear to be trial pieces, probably brought to the living site to serve some purpose. During the occupation, the beach must have been littered with smashed and partially flaked cobbles, now ground to sand by the constant rolling of the sea.

A beach cobble hurled against another may split across the middle or, more likely, at one end so that a smaller and larger segment result. Respectively, these could serve as cores for small or large flake-blades. A beach cobble split across at both ends would be ideal for a double platform core. Once the knapper was satisfied with both the fracture and initial flaking of the stone, and its quality, at least some of the further blocking out and the actual striking of flake-blades was probably conducted on the living site. This would explain the large quantities of primary flakes and cores of all types found in the various layers; alternatively, it could be argued that both flakes and cores were brought there from outside. There is some support for the latter interpretation when one considers the enormous accumulations of waste flakes that occur on factory sites, for it does not take a long period of knapping on one place before an actual layer of waste flakes several centimeters thick occurs. In spite of the great numbers of artifacts found during the course of the excavations there were no actual layers of flakes; they were always admixed with the occupational soil. Neither were nests of flakes found which could be reconstructed into parts of the raw material used. Most probably, much of the flaking was done on the beach or outside the living area, yet at the same time some was done within.

Single Platform Cores (Plate 29)

There are two different types of single platform cores, one for roughly parallel-sided flake-blades, the other for pointed flake-blades. There are distinctive examples of both types but so much grading from one type to the other that, for the purposes of numerical analysis, it was found misleading to make any subdivisions beyond "single platform cores."

The method of flaking in the primary stages was the same for most of these cores: one side of a split beach cobble or pebble was flaked until the cortex was removed. If no difficulties or irregularities of shape were met, all this flaking may have been from the same platform, i.e., the facet produced by the initial splitting. To ensure that the face of the core was clean, it was essential to get at least most of these primary flakes to run down the whole length of the core and this might entail some preparation of the striking platform and one or more of the edges. The use of beach cobbles meant that, in plan view, the striking platform was at first oval or circular. The primary flaking would generally be confined to about half of the circumference, and at this stage the knapper would employ

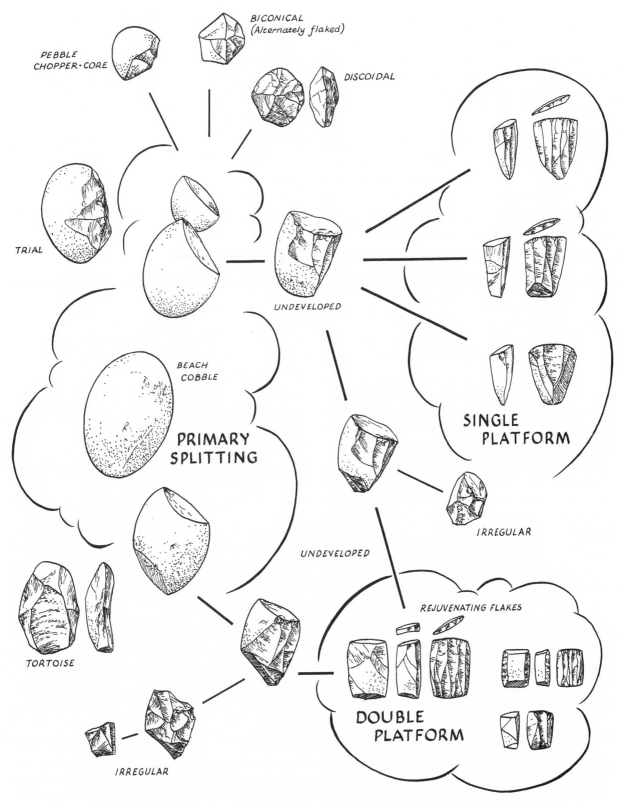

FIG. 5.1. Diagram to illustrate the technology and terminology of MSA cores at KRM.

a different technique, depending on whether he intended to produce parallel-sided or pointed flake-blades. If the former, the platform was carefully prepared and flake-blades were struck downward all round the dressed side of the core. Another batch could be detached behind these and so on, until an irreparable accident made the core useless or it became too small. Minor flaking failures could be made good by further dressing. The striking platform would need constant attention, and so, as the flaking angle decreased or the edge of the core

became too irregular, rejuvenation flakes would need to be removed skillfully along it.

If the core was worked around its entire circumference and the flaking was regular, the inevitable result would be a conical core. Such cores are virtually nonexistent in this MSA industry. A few approach this form (pl. 29, nos. 1, 3, 5), and a particularly good example is illustrated (pl. 37, no. 7), one of the rare finds of cores that seem to have been abandoned before being whittled down to something smaller or irregular. Many others of the cruder end-products may have passed through this stage, but most of the single platform cores have cortex or fracture surfaces which indicate that only half or less of the circumference was used. A practical reason for this is that dressing of the face of the core to remedy minor flaking failures could often be done more conveniently from the sides. The typical end-product of such a single platform core is shown at the top right of figure 5.1.

Many single platform cores are flattish at the end opposite the striking platform. This may be part of an original fracture from the primary splitting, caused by flaking during the blocking-out process or in dressing irregularities from flake-blade mis-strikings, or done with the intention of making another striking platform. In the latter case this is a stage toward the production of a double platform core (described below), but unless flake-blades have actually been struck from this new platform such cores have been classified as single platform ones. One is diagrammatically represented in the middle of the group of single platform cores shown in figure 5.1.

The type of core designed for making flake-blades is no more than a specialized form of tortoise core: instead of the core being prepared by radial flaking, two or more large flakes are struck from each side of the striking platform so that a central ridge is formed. The upper part of this ridge is removed by a small flake struck from immediately behind it. After a final preparation of the striking platform, another flake is removed from behind this one and, if the force of the blow has been judged correctly, the result will be a pointed flake-blade. Most cores of this form appear to have been made just for the one pointed flake-blade, but, depending on the size of the remaining core, yet another can be struck from it, or even more. Each one would be successively larger, and there would be a corresponding decrease in the chance of getting one with the central ridge running clean to the point, an essential feature for strength if intended for use as a projectile point. This type of core is described as a convergently flaked single platform core. It is found in all South African MSA industries, but especially in what has been described as the Mossel Bay variant or wherever quartzite has been the main source of raw material, for example, in the Cave of Hearths at Makapansgat in the Transvaal. It is an ingenious manner of solving the problem of creating strong points from an essentially brittle rock. One such core is illustrated diagrammatically at the bottom of the group of single platform cores in figure 5.1. This technique for producing pointed flake-blades is, of course, that normally referred to as "Levallois," as is the process of preparing striking platforms. The resulting pointed flake-blade is identical to the "Levallois point" of European terminology (Bordes 1961)

Double Platform Cores (Plate 30)

Double platform cores were intended solely for the production of parallel-sided flake-blades. There are several variations, some showing regular, systematic method, others apparently influenced by the exigencies of the material or by chance strikings. The most systematic and probably successful type of double platform core is one where the two platforms oppose each other and flake-blades are struck from both ends. This gives the maximum opportunity for keeping the face of the core clean, as the scars from faulty strikings can be removed from either end. Constant preparation of the platforms kept the flaking angle correct, and this was also maintained by the occasional removal of rejuvenation flakes, generally along the edge of the platform or, much less commonly, across the whole platform. Core preparation flakes are useful indicators of the original size of

some of the cores and are described separately below. The efficiency of this type of core depends considerably on the care with which the opposing platforms are made: they need to be reasonably parallel to each other, flat, and at the correct flaking angle to the face of the core (c. 75°–85° being ideal), so that the core is the shape of a trapezoidal prism. "Double platformed prismatic core" is a more precise name. One is shown diagrammatically on the left side of the group in figure 5.1. Plate 30 shows some cores of this type. Generally they are worked down until they become small and irregular.

To maintain the shape of the core, it may be dressed across the face from the sides. A particularly methodical type has the sides trimmed along their entire edges, but only very small cores, often less than 5 cm from platform to platform, are found like this. It appears to have been a special refinement when small flake-blades or micro–flake-blades were required, and it is significant that exactly the same type of core occurs in the Howieson's Poort levels.

A common variation of the double platformed prismatic core (with flake-blades struck from both directions on the same face) is one with the flake-blades struck on alternate faces. In side view, this form of core is the shape of a parallelogram and not a trapezium. Other cores have series of flake-blades removed from any other convenient platform on either face. Sometimes the scars of one series of flake-blades form a platform so that the second series is at right angles. As the core was reduced in size by the repeated removal of flake-blades, the knapping tended to become less systematic. The random choice of striking platforms sometimes resulted in cores with more than two platforms; but such multiplatformed cores have little to suggest that they were purposeful types, and they grade insensibly into irregular cores.

Irregular and Undeveloped Cores (Plate 31)

There seems little or nothing to be gained by a detailed typological breakdown of these crude pieces, for, as described above, they represent for the most part knapping failures or cores whittled down to such an extent that signs of any former systematic flaking have been obliterated. Figure 5.1 shows the stages between the primary splitting of beach cobbles and the development of single or double platform cores, when, if not carried further, the cores would justify classification as undeveloped or irregular. Many of the single platform cores are undeveloped, in the sense that attempts to produce a second, opposed platform so that the core could have developed into a double platform one had been unsuccessful. For convenience, these cores are classified as single platform cores. It is often impossible to know whether the small irregular cores are failures from faulty blocking out, or have passed through a stage during which they could have been classified differently. Many, of course, may have produced numbers of useful flakes; in fact they owe their existence to nothing more than a sudden exigency being met by a few sharp blows on the nearest available piece of quartzite of suitable size. Whether any of these crude cores served a purpose in themselves can only be speculated: many may have been used for chopping or pounding soft materials, and the very small ones may have been missiles.

Other Cores (Plate 32)

Pebble and biconical chopper cores. These occur occasionally, the former being a clear type but the latter merging imperceptibly into an irregular category. The pebble chopper-cores were probably tools, some definitely so judging from the signs of use along the sharp edge, but the biconical chopper-cores are less determinate. Both are identical to the primitive cores that are found in industries ranging from the Oldowan of East Africa to various handax industries of the late Middle Pleistocene, in fact almost wherever man has resorted to stone for toolmaking. No other continuity is implied.

Discoidal cores. A few rare cores show radial flaking on both surfaces and a distinct intention of making a continuous or near-continuous straight edge. It seems likely that they are tools or weapons of some sort and not just residual pieces from flake manufacture. About half a kilogram is a typical weight, and it is suggested that they were missiles.

Tortoise cores. Tortoise cores, in the sense used to describe these characteristic cores of Levalloisian industries in the Northern Hemisphere, are extremely rare at KRM, as at other South African sites. The two or three that do occur merely show that the technique could be employed but was not part of the industrial tradition.

Summary of MSA I–IV Cores

The numerical analyses shown in table 5.1 show no clear trends in technological development through the four stages, in spite of the long period involved. There *are* differences in the relative proportions of core types within different layers, but it could be argued that these reflect various exigencies and personal elements and not industrial traditions. The main differences justify consideration because, in common with other elements of these industries, comparison with sequences obtained from future excavations of contemporary MSA sites may well amplify the present interpretation.

Table 5.1. THE NUMBER AND DISTRIBUTION OF THE VARIOUS CORES ACCORDING TO MSA STAGES

MSA IV (Pl. 34)

Only represented at CAVE 1, layer 13

Single platform	13
Double platform	9
Irregular and/or undeveloped	26 - includes 1 trial piece
Others: Pebble chopper-core	8
	TOTAL = 56

MSA III (Pl. 35)

SHELTER 1A	1	2	3	1-3	4	5	6	7	8	9	undiff 7-9
Single platform				1			3	1			
Double platform		2		3		1	7	6	1		13
" " micro								2			
Irregular and/or undeveloped				3	2	2	2	1		4	
Others:											
Discoidal							5				
Tortoise							1				
Small (less than 5 cm) or micro (less than 3.5 cm) of:											
Quartz							1		1	1	
Fine silcrete										4	
Indurated shale								1			

TOTAL = 68

Table 5.1 Continued

MSA II (Pl. 29-33)

CAVE 1	Layer 14 incl. 14+ & 14b	15 incl. 15+	16	17	17a	17b
Single platform	102	16	32	13	6	42
Double platform	119	22	35	25	4	46
Irregular and/or undeveloped	416	90	172	47	16	153
Others:						
Discoidal	6	2			1	4
Biconical	3	20				2
Pebble chopper-core			3	1		4
Tortoise	2			2		
Tribrach			1			
Small or micro-cores of:						
Quartz	28	5			1	
Fine silcrete	3.			1		
Coarse silcrete	'1					
Indurated shale	34	17	7			
Chalcedony	2	1				
Biconical core of coarse silcrete	1					

TOTAL = 1508

Several cores from layer 14 could perhaps be classified as pebble chopper-cores but because of their general crudity they have been included with the irregular and/or undeveloped category.

The tribrach from layer 16 is a small, crude piece that probably owes its shape to chance.

There is a slight increase in the proportion of single platform cores to double ones in the MSA I industry, and, coupled with the more subjective observation that these MSA single platform cores (particularly from 1-37 and 38) are more systematically struck, this could be significant. Similarly there seems to be a rise in the numbers of irregular and/or undeveloped cores throughout MSA II. The increase in the numbers of double platform cores during MSA III does appear to reflect some continuation from the traditions of the underlying Howieson's Poort Industry, but there is little in the enigmatical MSA IV to support any continuation of this trend.

The use of fine-grained rocks for small or microcores occurs spasmodically throughout MSA I and II. The few found in MSA III are in the lowermost layers and may, of course, be derived from Howieson's Poort surfaces nearby, at this time still partly uncovered by later occupational rubbish. This could also be applicable to the apparent increase of double platform cores in MSA III mentioned above. There are none of these fine-grained cores in MSA IV, and there is also a noticeable lack in the MSA II sequence as represented at Shelter 1A,

except for a few at the bottom. Conversely there are none at the bottom of the MSA II sequence in Cave 1, but a high proportion at the top.

Other types of cores occur intermittently in small numbers throughout the four MSA stages. Broadly, throughout this long MSA sequence, it can be concluded that the tradition of flake-blade and pointed flake-blade production continued with only minor variations, resulting in similar cores throughout the entire sequence.

Core Preparation and Rejuvenation Flakes (Figures 5.1 and 5.2)

In order to ensure relatively straight flake-blades it is essential that the first one to be struck be detached successfully. This can only be achieved with any certainty by having a straight edge on the blocked-out core along which the first flake is struck. This straight edge will form a medial ridge along the dorsal side of the flake. In many cases (probably the majority), the initial

Table 5.1 Continued

MSA II (Pl. 36)

SHELTER 1A	Layer 22	23, 24	25	26	27	28, 29	30	31	32, 33	34	35	36
Single platform		11	3	5	18	34	1	2	16	4		20
Double platform		11	6	6	11	17			11	11		4
" " micro	1	5	3									
Irregular and/or undeveloped	9	21	2	4	20	25		1	9	9	1	41
Others:												
Discoidal	1	1			2					1		
Biconical				1						1		
Tortoise	1								1			
Small or micro-cores of:												
Quartz	11	1										4
Fine silcrete	1											1
Indurated shale										1		
Chalcedony												1

TOTAL = 295

Layer 36 is represented by material from East Cutting T of Cave 1 and the Initial Cutting of 1C. Material from Side Cuttings B and C of 1A are not included.

MSA I (Pl. 37)

CAVE 1	Layer 37	38	39	40
Single platform	94	52	1	1
" " micro	2			
Double platform	86	37		
" " micro	3			
Irregular and/or undeveloped	110	57		
Others:				
Discoidal	2	1		
Pebble chopper		1		
Tortoise		1		
Small or micro-cores of:				
Quartz	4	2		
Quartz crystal	1			
Fine silcrete	1			
Indurated shale	1	1		

TOTAL = 358

Table 5.1 Continued

SHELTER 1B	Layer 1	2	3	4	5	6	7	8	9	10	11	12	13	14	15
Single platform		3	1		3	1	2		1	1			2	1	1
Double platform			2	3	4	1	2	2	1	2		1	2	1	
" " micro				1											
Irregular and/or undeveloped			2	1	3		1		1	2			1		
Small core of quartz			1												

TOTAL = 50

smashing of the beach cobbles produced such a suitable straight edge, but where the core was too curved or irregular it was necessary to remove flakes along an edge and create one. These flakes would be at right angles to the first flake intended to be struck from the striking platform. The latter flake would thus have a very distinctive pattern of facets on one side of its dorsal surface and a smooth surface on the other. It would also be triangular in section. They are referred to as core preparation flakes, as they merely prepare the core for the striking of the second flake from the same striking platform which, if successful, will be a flake-blade. In French terminology they are *lames à crête;* otherwise, ''crested ridge flakes.'' It is significant that the MSA technique at KRM did not often involve the production of a straight edge along a core by flaking alternately from both sides, as commonly used in the production of true blades in European Upper Paleolithic industries (Bordes and Crabtree 1969). This may have been due to the nature of the material and the inevitable presence of at least one smooth surface from the initial smashing of the beach cobbles. There are a few rare examples of such double crested ridge flakes (e.g., fig. 5.2, no. 2).

Occasionally, the striking platform of a core became too irregular or the wrong angle to the surface from which flake-blades were being struck. This was rectified by the removal of a flake across the core; in this way the old platform was sliced off and a new one created (e.g., fig. 5.2, nos. 1, 3, and 4). These constitute true core platform rejuvenation flakes.

Some of the larger core preparation flakes are readily adaptable as chisel or picklike tools without further trimming and may have been so utilized: their high proportion in some of the layers almost suggests that they may have been collected from the knapping area for some purpose. They rarely show any secondary working, and the few that do are included with the descriptions of worked flakes.

Summary of MSA I–IV Core Preparation and Rejuvenation Flakes

The flakes occur in most of the layers of all four stages with the exception of the upper part of MSA III, but this is not thought to reflect anything but chance distribution (table 5.2). No variation can be detected throughout this long sequence, and the only unusual thing is the high proportion of them in MSA II at Shelter 1A throughout layers 27, 28, 29, 32, and 33.

Flake-Blades

This term describes those flakes which have been struck from prismatic cores so that their sides are roughly parallel. They are devoid of cortex, save for an occasional small patch on their reverse sides (dorsal surfaces), which does not impair the efficiency of their cutting edges. The striking platforms, except in rare instances, bear the marks of careful preparation of the core and thus are faceted. They are at least twice as long as they are broad.

Such flakes are found in stone industries throughout the Old and New Worlds, from the time of the Levalloisian industries of Europe, throughout the Upper Paleolithic, and in many later industries. The more elegant examples may be called blades; this term is not used in this account, however, as it would exclude too many others which, although somewhat coarser and less regular, still satisfy the above criteria. The most obvious use for flake-blades is as knives, and as such, with no further trimming, they were presumably regarded as an end-product of the industry. Larger flake-blades possibly served different functions from smaller ones: whether size-proportion throughout the vertical sequence reflects economic requirements, personal whim, or stone-working tradition is debatable, but flake-blade lengths are presented below in tables for reasons of both description and comparison. The rare flake-blades of fine-grained or nonlocal quartzitic rocks are not included in the tables since the nature and size of the raw material would dictate the length more than any other factor.

The division between flake-blades and flakes remains a subjective one, especially with the smaller artifacts, but the number of problematical ones for classification is very small in relation to the total. A more serious consideration is the larger number of flakes that satisfy all the criteria for flake-blades except that they are less than twice as long as they are broad. These flakes undoubtedly would have served many purposes equally as well as the flake-blades, and to exclude them from this category creates an artificial division that would not have been apparent to their makers and users. However, a separate category would complicate rather than clarify, so these serviceable flakes are relegated to the plain flake category. Some notes on their numbers are included in that section below.

It is difficult to justify any general statements on the varying elegance of the flake-blades in one layer or another, except in the case of those in the MSA I stage. The observations noted

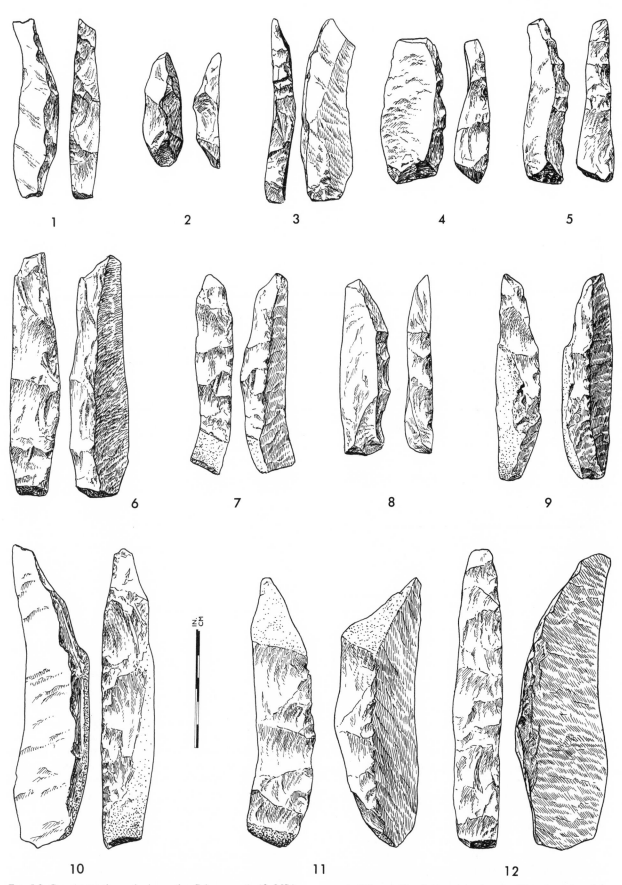

FIG. 5.2. Core preparation and rejuvenation flakes: nos. 1–12. MSA IV: 2, 7–9; MSA III: 3, 4; MSA II: 1, 5, 6, 10–12. All are shown with the bulbar side face downward and the bulb at the bottom (except 4, 5, 8) so that the flat surface is that part remaining on the flake of the striking platform on the core. It is generally unprepared, but the large example 12 has shallow flaking along the edge. The preparation of the platform for the removal of the actual rejuvenation flake shows clearly on 5. The pointed ends of 7 and 9 show slight signs of retouch and use. Large examples such as 10–12 are considerably longer than the width of the striking platforms of any cores found.

Table 5.2. THE NUMBER AND DISTRIBUTION OF CORE PREPARATION AND REJUVENATION FLAKES ACCORDING TO MSA STAGES

MSA IV

Only represented at CAVE 1, layer 13   TOTAL = 19

MSA III

SHELTER 1A	Layer 1	2	3	4	5	6	7	8	9	7-9
						14	9			6

TOTAL = 29

MSA II

CAVE 1	Layer 14 incl. 14+ & 14b	15 incl. 15+	16	17	17a	17b
	23	5	21	11	13	37

TOTAL = 110

SHELTER 1A	Layer 22	23, 24	25	26	27	28, 29	30	31	32, 33	34	35	36
	6	20	12	1	40	69	2	1	62	13	1	19

TOTAL = 246

MSA I

CAVE 1	Layer 37	38	39	40
	77	61	2	

TOTAL = 140

SHELTER 1B	Layer 1	2	3	4	5	6	7	8	9	10	11	12	13	14	15
		1	9	2		1	1		1			2		2	

TOTAL = 19

below relate to table 5.3 and are discussed in the summary that follows.

Many flake-blades have blunting or chipping of their edges consistent with heavy use. Sometimes an inconvenient projection or irregularity has been removed by a few slight blows with a hammerstone. These are not included in the separate category "flakes with secondary working" unless there has been an obvious intention to alter the edge or shape of the tool.

Despite the relatively small number of artifacts found in 1-13, the absence of any flake-blades longer than 4 in. is significant (table 5.3). There may have been an environmental reason for this (see the discussion below in the general summary of the MSA stages). The striking platforms of the flake-blades in MSA IV tend to be thick, with no attempt to reduce them either before or after removal from the core (fig. 5.3). For the most part the flake-blades in MSA III are a little crude, with thick and irregular striking platforms. However, several, par-

ticularly in 1A-6, have carefully prepared, thin and somewhat rounded platforms, some of which are slightly battered. Such small, near-microlithic flake-blades as those shown in figure 5.4, as numbers 5 and 6 made of silcrete and shale, respectively, and both from layer 6 are much more characteristic of the Howieson's Poort Industry below. It is possible that they are derived from these earlier levels.

The flake-blades of MSA II are, like those above it, often thick and rather irregular (e.g., fig. 5.5, nos. 13 and 14), but very elegant, large examples occasionally occur, such as figure 5.5, number 18. Rarely has any attempt been made to reduce the thickness or irregularity of the striking platform. However, there is great diversity in size and form, with some of the small flake-blades approaching the microlithic form of those from the Howieson's Poort levels (e.g., fig. 5.5, nos. 5-9). Fine-grained nonlocal rock, when used, has also tended to result in small, thin, delicate flake-blades. Cones and bulbs of percus-

Table 5.3. THE NUMBER AND DISTRIBUTION OF FLAKE-BLADES ACCORDING TO MSA STAGES

MSA IV (Fig. 5.3)

Only represented at CAVE 1, layer 13

Length (in.)	No.
3 - 4	14
2 - 3	58
1 - 2	98
	TOTAL = 170

MSA III (Fig. 5.4)

SHELTER 1A	Layer 1 - 3	4	5	6	7	8	9	undiff 7 - 9
Length (cm)								
14 - 16	1	1						
12 - 14		1	2	1				
10 - 12	4	2	6	7	1			3
8 - 10	2	4	3	18	4			2
6 - 8	8	7	12	51	9	2	2	8
4 - 6	5	7	9	109	37	5	14	45
2 - 4	3	1	3	94	41	4	7	32
	23	23	35	280	92	11	23	90

TOTAL = 577

MSA II (Fig. 5.5)

CAVE 1	Layer 14 incl. 14+ & 14b	15 incl. 15+	16	undiff 17	17a	17b	total 17
Length (in.)							
7 - 8	2	2		1		1	2
6 - 7	10	5	3	2		2	4
5 - 6	61	11	21	14	3	22	39
4 - 5	331	120	172	34	11	77	122
3 - 4	1120	530	591	157	46	433	636
2 - 3	2517	1304	1462	467	139	1315	1921
1 - 2	683	661	520	241	91	228	560
	4724	2633	2769				3284

TOTAL = 13,410

Table 5.3 Continued

SHELTER 1A	22	Layer undiff 23-24	23	24	25	26	27	28	29	30	31	32	33	36
Length (cm)														
16 - 18														1
14 - 16				3			1					1		2
12 - 14				1			2					1	1	11
10 - 12		9	1	3	1		3		6	1		2	2	30
8 - 10		22	2	10	4	3	12	17	10	6	1	4	2	125
6 - 8	2	86	8	31	12	8	52	92	23	32	11	26	8	273
4 - 6	10	157	22	29	25	15	142	232	42	72	26	74	10	286
2 - 4	9	72	7	15	9	7	87	64	12	21	6	27	2	32
	21	346	40	92	51	33	299	405	93	132	44	135	25	760

N.B. Flake-blades from the initial cutting of 1A are not included except for layers 23-24 and 26.

TOTAL = 2,476

MSA   I   (Fig. 5.6)

CAVE 1	Layer 37	38
Length (in.)		
7 - 8		1
6 - 7	4	10
5 - 6	34	40
4 - 5	193	164
3 - 4	693	731
2 - 3	1924	1334
1 - 2	837	407
	3685	2687

TOTAL = 6,372

Table 5.3 Continued

SHELTER	1B	Layer 2	3	4	5	6	7	8	9	10	11	12	13a	13b	14	15
Length (cm)																
14 - 16												1				
12 - 14			2	4					1			2				
10 - 12			4	8	1		1	1		7	1	3		2	2	2
8 - 10		2	23	18	9	5	12	5	6	3	2	4		8	4	6
6 - 8		7	61	54	17	8	26	14	17	15	4	12	5	6	10	17
4 - 6		10	123	78	24	11	27	11	13	20	7	11	3	13	10	11
2 - 4		6	50	22	11	7	6	1	4	2				1	4	1
		25	263	184	62	31	72	32	41	47	14	33	8	30	30	37

TOTAL = 909

Note. It is regretted that these tables are in both British and metric units but the decision to change to metric was taken during the course of the work, when the amount of future excavation was unknown. Remeasurements have been made where necessary to render each table consistent in itself. However, the histograms in fig. 7-3 clearly show virtually identical patterns whether measurements are in inches or centimeters. This militates against an artificial posthoc conversion of inches to metric.

The lengths of the flake-blades and the pointed flake-blades have been measured from the cone of percussion at the striking platform along the major axis. When this measurement is exactly a category size, the flake-blade in the larger one, i.e., a flake-blade 4 in. long is placed in the category 4-5 in.

sion are usually well developed, indicating the heavy use of a hard hammerstone, presumably a quartzite beach pebble. Intermediate punches of slightly softer pebbles may have been used for striking the smaller, thinner flake-blades which have soft, diffused bulbs.

An unusual feature of the flake-blades in 1A-24 is that there were five examples with the thinned and battered striking platform so characteristic of the flake-blades from MSA I described below. Six of the bulbous end segments of broken flake-blades also had this feature, and several other flake-blades and segments showed slight battering of the platform. Apart from one other broken bulbous segment in layer 25 immediately below, no other flake-blades with battered striking platforms were noticed in MSA II.

The flake-blades of MSA I, particularly those in the lowermost layers (38 and 39) of Cave 1, include a higher proportion of elegant examples than those in the stages situated above it. The most distinctive feature is the attention frequently given to the butt of the flake-blade so that it is thin and neatly rounded. A special knapping or abrasion technique was used which imparted a bruised, battered appearance to the reverse edge of the striking platform. This was seen only in the lowermost layers, which rest on bedrock or beach shingle and thus represent the first occupation of the site. The layer immediately above (layer 37) only yielded three flake-blades with this feature, and in a

position toward the back of Cave 1 (West Cutting K) where the occupational soil of this period was thin and some contamination with material from the layer beneath was likely. Mention has been made above of a few odd flake-blades with the same battered striking platforms in the MSA II stage of 1A-24 and 25; otherwise the technique is restricted to the early part of MSA I. It occurs at 1B-13b and below to the beach shingle, also in layers 38 and 39 at the cave mouth (East Cutting Q). In the beach shingle at the latter spot, a flake with this feature was found in contact with the bedrock. Its slightly rolled appearance suggests that it is contemporary with the raised beach.

The battering or abrasion of the edge of the striking platform was probably a method of producing slight concavities on the platform which acted as "rests" for a bone punch. The technique is explained by Bordes and Crabtree (1969) on the basis of their experiments in blade production. The greater precision in directing the final blow gave much better control over the thickness of the striking platform and the regularity of the flake-blade.

This butt-thinning technique is more in evidence on the pointed flake-blades from the MSA I layers, and it seems likely that it evolved in order to produce thinner butts to facilitate hafting into cleft sticks. If the interpretation of pointed flake-blades, with or without secondary working, as spearheads is correct, this would be a distinct advantage. The surprising thing

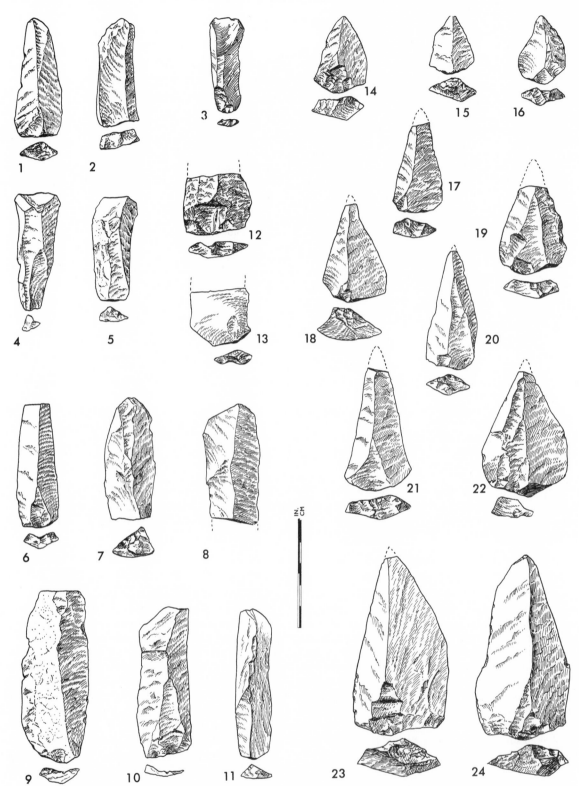

Fig. 5.3. Flake-blades and pointed flake-blades: nos. 1–24. MSA IV. 1–11: flake-blades. No. 9 is included although the remaining cortex strictly excludes it from this category. No. 3 is of black indurated shale and exemplifies the more microlithic nature of the industry when finer-grained rock was available. Striking platforms are mainly wide and show little or no preparation beyond the production of a suitable flaking angle. 12–13: bulbous segments of broken flake-blades. 14–24: pointed flake-blades. No. 19 has one edge trimmed; a few of the others show slight signs of blunting or minute chipping along their edges, particularly near the striking platforms, and this may have been caused by their insertion into spear-shafts: the lengths of such broken pointed flake-blades for the metrical analyses have been based on the estimated original length as shown by dotted line in the figure. This can be done with reasonable confidence, which is not the case with flake-blades. Broken flake-blades, such as 7, have been measured along their present length. Striking platforms of these pointed flake-blades are generally wide with no attempt made to round them prior to or after striking.

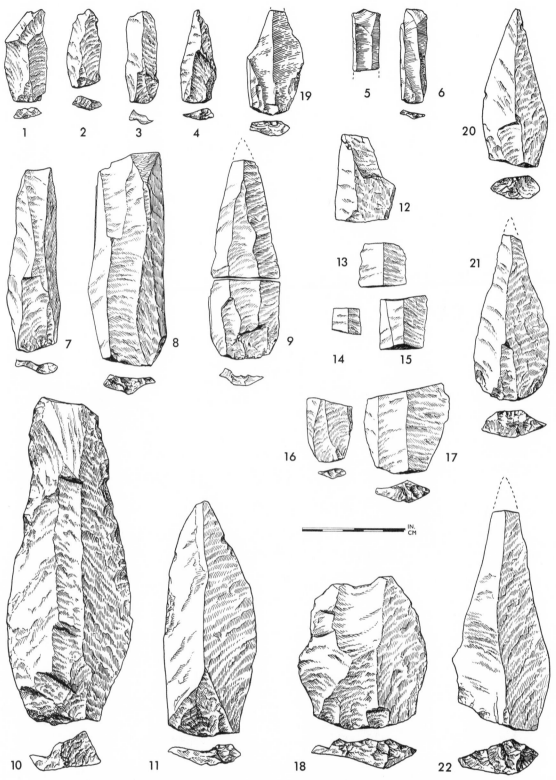

FIG. 5.4. Flake-blades, pointed flake-blades, flake-blade segments, and flake: nos. 1–22. MSA III. 1–11: flake-blades. Striking platforms have been carefully prepared but little attempt made to reduce their thickness or make them more regular. No. 3 has a plain platform. No. 5 is of fine red silcrete and 6 of black indurated shale. No. 9 was found separately in two pieces. 12–17: segments of flake-blades. Bulbous ends, 16–17; middle segments, 13–15; nonbulbous end, 12. 18: flake. Struck from a prepared core with a well-prepared platform. Such flakes are not classified as flake-blades, as their length is not at least double their width. It would presumably have been a serviceable cutting or scraping tool, equal to most of the flake-blades. Such flakes, however, merge into the irregular flakes presumably struck in the preparation and dressing of cores, misstrikings, and other general knapping. The separation of these well-struck squat flakes is so beset with subjective criteria that they are included in the general category of flakes. They occur in very small numbers in comparison with flake-blades. 19–22: pointed flake-blades. No. 19 of a pale, coarse quartzite.

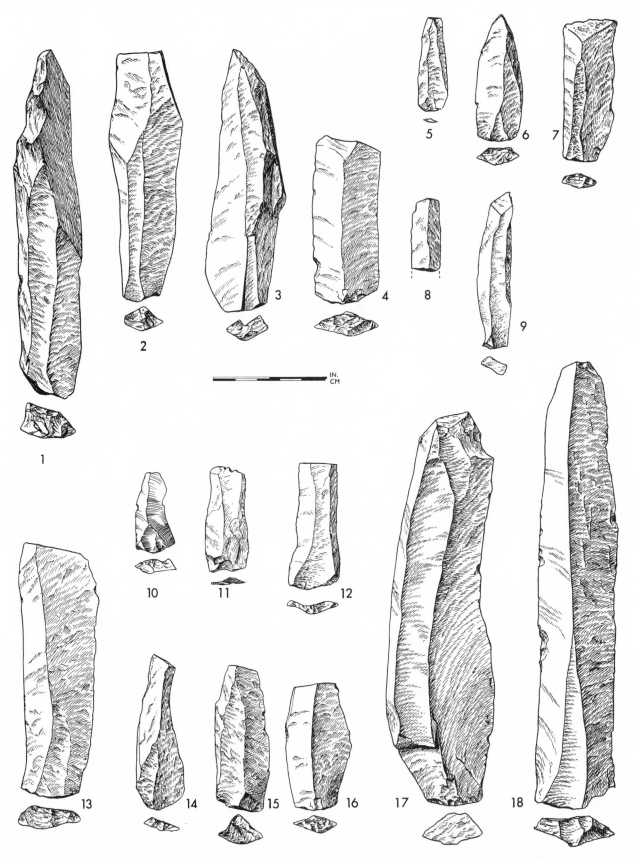

FIG. 5.5. Flake-blades: nos. 1–18. MSA II. No. 9 is of a pale coarse silcrete, 10 of dark chalcedony, 11 of indurated shale, and 12 of pale coarse silcrete. No. 18 is the most elegant of all the long flake-blades.

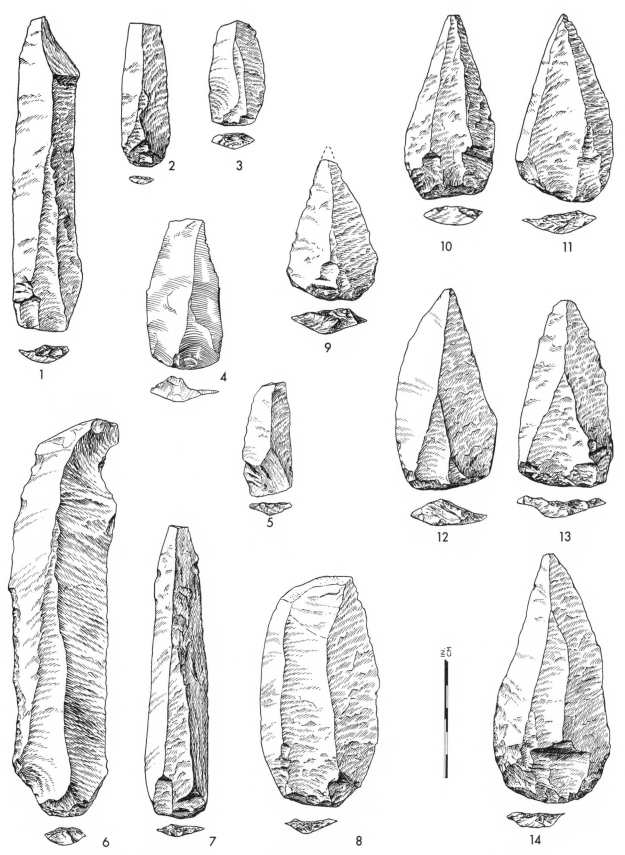

Fɪɢ. 5.6. Flake-blades and pointed flake-blades: nos. 1–14. MSA I. 1–8: flake-blades, 4 of chalcedony. 9–14: pointed flake-blades.

is the virtual unconcern with which pointed flake-blades with crude, thick butts were produced in the later stages. Flake-blades were sometimes treated in the same way, especially those in the larger size categories. The following analysis of the flake-blades from layer 38, well inside Cave 1 (West Cutting H), gives typical proportions of those with battered striking platforms. Several of the flake-blades are elegant, and the striking platforms are often small and rounded without any battering.

Length (in.)	No.	Comment
7–8	1	The striking platform is not battered, but this flake-blade had "plunged" slightly into the core and signs of battering along the edge remain on the thick nonbulbous end
6–7	2	1 with battered striking platform
5–6	5	2 as above
4–5	46	5 as above
3–4	169	17 as above
2–3	210	4 as above
1–2	42	1 as above; but this is a broken flake-blade and originally was probably 3–4 in.

Similarly, several of the bulbous ends of broken flake-blades show the same preparation and battering.

The flake-blades of this section are summarized together with the pointed flake-blades at the end of the section which follows.

Pointed Flake-Blades

Pointed flake-blades are interpreted as projectile points, although it is not suggested that they all saw service as such. The simple but ingenious manner by which they were made allowed large numbers to be produced (table 5.4), from which could be selected those of the most suitable form and size. They were struck from specially prepared single platform convergent cores as described in the section on cores above. Each core was intended to produce just one pointed flake-blade, although sometimes it may have been possible to obtain another one or two from the same core. It is a wasteful method, but this would be of no consequence where the raw material for knapping was unlimited.

Apart from producing a symmetrical point, the MSA knapper aimed at having a single, central ridge on the dorsal surface of the flake meeting exactly at the point. This was not an aesthetic whim but a means of getting the maximum strength at the tip. With such brittle rock as the local quartzite this was essential if any weapon was to be dependable. Finer-grained rocks such as silcrete could be thinned down with neat, shallow flaking and still be strong, but not the local quartzite. There are a few rare examples of worked points (see below) with shallow flaking entirely over one or both faces, but secondary working is generally confined to some rounding or thinning of the butt, or strengthening of the edges. Pointed flake-blades are such a distinctive feature of all the MSA stages at KRM (as well as most other South African MSA sites where coarse quartzite was

Table 5.4. THE NUMBER AND DISTRIBUTION OF POINTED FLAKE-BLADES ACCORDING TO MSA STAGES

MSA   IV   (Fig. 5.3)

Only represented at CAVE 1, layer 13

Length (in.)	No.
3 - 4	2
2 - 3	20
1 - 2	69
	TOTAL = 91

MSA   III   (Fig. 5.4)

SHELTER 1A	Layer 1-3	4	5	6	7	8	9	undiff 7-9
Length (cm)								
8 - 10	1			1				
6 - 8			2	3				
4 - 6	2	1	2	5	1		1	2
2 - 4	1			1	4			1
	4	1	4	10	5	-	1	3

TOTAL = 28

Table 5.4 Continued

MSA II (Fig. 5.7)

CAVE 1	Layer						
	14 incl. 14+ & 14b	15 incl. 15+	16	undiff 17	17a	17b	total 17
Length (in.)							
5 - 6		1		1			1
4 - 5	7	6	16	1		8	9
3 - 4	102	59	78	15	5	41	61
2 - 3	338	311	312	73	40	141	254
1 - 2	92	133	106	32	15	35	82
	539	510	512				407

TOTAL = 1,968

SHELTER 1A *	Layer													
	22	undiff 23-24	23	24	25	26	27	28	29	30	31	32	33	36
Length (cm)														
10 - 12														1
8 - 10	1	4		1				6	3			. 4		15
6 - 8	3	3		2	3			16	14	2	1	14	3	42
4 - 6	3	5		6	14			51	42	17	5	32	10	54
2 - 4		1	2		4			16	5	4	5	8		11
	7	13	2	9	21	-	-	89	64	23	11	58	13	123

TOTAL = 433

* As with the flake-blades, layers 34 and 35 of Shelter 1A are excluded as only small quantities of material were recovered from the saturated deposits.

MSA I (Fig. 5.6)

CAVE 1	Layer	
	37	38
Length (in.)		
4 - 5	7	10
3 - 4	39	57
2 - 3	175	101
1 - 2	69	22
	290	190

TOTAL = 480

Table 5.4 Continued

SHELTER 1B	Layer 2	3	4	5	6	7	8	9	10	11	12	13a	13b	14	15*
Length (cm)															
8 - 10		1						1							
6 - 8		6		4	2		1	2	3		1			1	
4 - 6	3	8	1	2	2	3	1	7					2		1
2 - 4	1	2		1		1		1							
	4	17	1	7	4	4	2	11	3	-	1	-	2	1	1

TOTAL = 58

* The specimen from layer 15, disturbed beach gravel, is rolled.

the main source of raw material) that they probably are a response to the continual need for spearheads in an area where only this brittle rock was available. This adaptation of knapping techniques to suit the raw material is a major factor to consider when making comparisons with other South African MSA industries.

Retouched pointed flake-blades, here included in the term "worked points," are few in number. Although several have slight signs of notching along one or both edges, or a few minute flakes removed to smooth some irregularity, the great majority are otherwise unretouched; in fact many of the worked points can be regarded as nothing more than the trimming up of imperfectly struck, pointed flake-blades. Most of the pointed flake-blades from the earliest stage of the MSA at KRM have well-thinned, rounded butts, the efforts expended in obtaining this resulted in the battered nature of the reverse edge of the striking platform, as described above for the flake-blades from MSA I. A thin butt seems such an obvious advantage for efficient hafting that it is hard to explain the apparent indifference to this in later stages, when attempts to produce a really thin butt are virtually unknown. A knifelike edge would obviously be too brittle, but the average thickness of the striking platforms must have made for a very clumsy hafting.

Except for very rare instances the striking platforms are well faceted from careful core preparation. Only flakes from convergent cores with a ridge meeting at the point are classified as pointed flake-blades; chance flakes which simulate them are excluded, as are mis-strikings. Lengths have been measured from their point of percussion to the tip (table 5.4). Where a small part of the tip is missing, the original length has been estimated. It has sometimes been difficult to draw a line between some flake-blades which converge to a point. A note is made of these doubtful examples, but they have not been measured.

Despite the low number of pointed flake-blades from 1-13, the proportion of small ones in the 1–2 in. category is probably significant. In figure 5.3, very few show even the slightest trimming of the butt, edges, or point, and, correspondingly, there is only one example of a worked point.

There are fewer pointed flake-blades in MSA III in proportion to flake-blades. Numbers 20 and 21 of figure 5.4 are

typical examples, with thick striking platforms. There are no examples with carefully rounded and thinned butts, but the sample is a small one.

Elegant symmetrical pointed flake-blades do occur in MSA II but are uncommon. The average specimen is rather crude and irregular but would nevertheless have made just as lethal a spearhead. The platforms are usually thick and cumbersome. Number 8 of figure 5.7 is a typical example: there is every reason to think it has been hafted as a spearhead, for blunting and notching on the edges have probably been caused by the binding media; yet no attempt has been made to reduce a projecting part of the striking platform. The very small examples such as figure 5.7, number 5, suggest very light spears, if not arrows.

The pointed flake-blades from the lower levels of MSA I, i.e., layer 38 in Cave 1 and in the corresponding levels in Shelter 1B and in the cuttings made at the cave mouth, are considerably more regular and refined (fig. 5.6) than those in the more recent stages above. The most distinctive feature is the crushed and battered aspect of many of the striking platforms, in the same manner as seen on several of the flake-blades. This is the end-product of a process designed to reduce the thickness of the platform, smooth its reverse edge, and also round the butt of the pointed flake-blade. Most, if not all, of this appears to have been done before the flake was struck from the core. Rather less than one-fifth of all the pointed flake-blades have this feature well developed, but several others show some slight battering of the reverse edge of the striking platform.

Summary of MSA I–IV Flake-Blades and Pointed Flake-Blades

The production of flake-blades was the major feature of the MSA stages at KRM. As described below, several were further worked into various specialized and nonspecialized tool forms, but the great mass were not and it seems reasonable to conclude that they were intended for use just as they were. Signs of utilization on many of them confirm this. Generally, flake-blades could be used as knives and pointed flake-blades as spearheads. It is unlikely that all the flake-blades produced

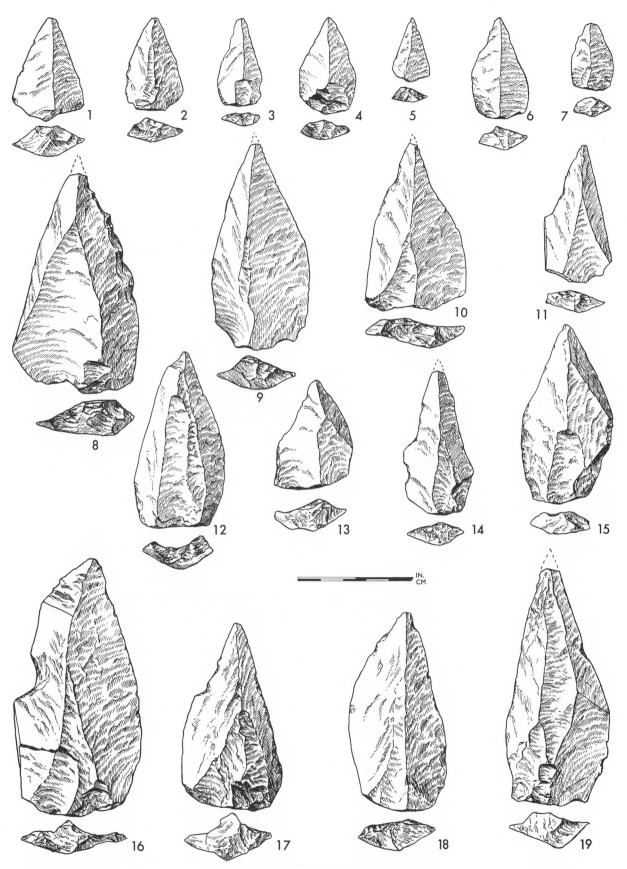

FIG. 5.7. Pointed flake-blades: nos. 1–19. MSA II.

were actually so used: overproduction was probably intentional, so that the tool of one's choice could be selected from a pile. Where raw material was virtually unlimited, this was practical. In the case of pointed flake-blades there would be a great advantage in having a selection, when a spearhead of a certain size was required to replace some preexisting slit or method of attachment in a shaft that had become headless. Rather than work one down to the required size or shape, a pointed flake-blade could be selected that fitted. The making of spearshafts with suitable methods of attachment would certainly have been a much more laborious task than striking off pointed flake-blades, provided the skill to do so had been acquired. It was much easier to fit the stone to the wood than vice versa. This overproduction approach could explain the relatively small number of worked points at KRM; the opposite state of affairs might be found at another living site where stone was scarce.

Details have been tabulated above of the numbers and lengths of these artifacts per each stratigraphical division within the four separate MSA stages, with a few comments concerning their manufacture. It remains to be seen whether there are any features throughout the long sequence represented by these stages which justify any conclusions that can be interpreted as changes in industrial tradition, changes which might indicate cultural development or allow the different stages to be recognized and thus affect local or more distant correlations. There *are* changes, but not very marked ones. They are probably sufficient to enable the MSA stages in the immediate locality (i.e., in the other caves, numbered 3 to 5) to be placed within the sequence, but it is very questionable whether they would have any bearing on more distant MSA sites, especially inland ones. There is certainly nothing to suggest any cultural change throughout, such as is indicated by the drastic reduction in size and the choice of raw material and flaking methods seen in the Howieson's Poort Industry. The size proportions for MSA IV are quite different from those of the earlier stages, but, as discussed later (chap. 15), there may be other reasons for this.

The only significant difference is to be found in the earliest stage, MSA I. There is a slight increase in the size of both ordinary and pointed flake-blades, and a corresponding reduction in the numbers of small ones (1–3 in. categories), but most important is the attention that was given to the striking platform, so that it was neatly rounded and reduced in thickness, making a much more elegant tool that may or may not have had some functional advantage. The technique used to do this imparted a battered and crushed appearance to the reverse side of the striking platform. Not all flake-blades received this treatment, in fact only a minority, but there was a general tendency to keep the platforms as thin as possible. The more elaborate preparation was usually made on flake-blades within the larger size categories, presumably ones which were regarded as most useful. With minor exceptions within MSA II and III, this feature is diagnostic of MSA I, and mainly in the lower levels of that stage.

The proportions of flake-blades and pointed flake-blades, both by layers and stages, are remarkably constant, suggesting a continuity of similar activities.

Broken Flake-Blade Segments

In every layer of all the MSA stages at KRM there occur numerous segments of broken flake-blades. These may only bear one break and be recognizable as the bulbous or nonbulbous ends of flake-blades, or they may be middle segments with breaks at both ends. In every case the break is in the nature of a clean snap across the flake-blade roughly at right angles to the major axis. If these segments are still more than twice as long as they are wide (e.g., fig. 5.5, no. 16), they are classified with the flake-blades. This is necessary because so many of the thin, nonbulbous ends of the smaller flake-blades have broken off, and it would be misleading to put them in a separate category from the rest of the flake-blades. Typical examples of these segments are shown in figure 5.4, numbers 12–17, and number 9, where a bulbous and middle segment that were found close together in the same layer have been rejoined. Similar cases were noticed in other layers.

The numbers and distribution of broken flake-blade segments according to the MSA stages are listed in table 5.5.

Summary of MSA I–IV Broken Flake-Blade Segments

The problem with these pieces is to determine whether they were broken intentionally or accidentally. The local quartzite is brittle, and there can be little doubt that many of the flake-blades broke across as they were struck from the core. Such an accident would produce a bulbous segment and a remainder which might be classified here as a flake-blade or a nonbulbous segment depending upon its proportions. It is most unlikely that the bulbous part would be long enough to be classified as a flake-blade, for the vulnerable section is that section close to where the hammerstone falls. This fact alone could account for there always being a greater number of bulbous segments than others.

Apart from accidental breaking during their production, flake-blades lying on the ground might be snapped in half by a sudden pressure caused just by the movement of the occupants of the cave or shelter, or by compression of the actual layers. Rock clearance or the dropping of heavy stones could do similar damage. Only one instance was noticed of a flake-blade lying *in situ,* snapped in two places apparently by pressure, thus transformed into three segments. However, it is difficult to believe that some of the middle segments, especially from thick flake-blades, were not produced intentionally. Clumsy bulbous segments and thin, fragile nonbulbous segments can almost certainly be regarded as waste pieces, but some of the neat, regular middle segments would have made useful knives or scrapers if mounted in wooden handles, or even just held between thumb and forefinger. Several do show marks of use, but it could also be argued that these are the remains of flake-blades which broke through heavy use. Only one middle segment, from 1A-33, is blunted by secondary working along the whole of its reverse edge, but this could also just be a broken flake-blade with one edge trimmed.

There is nothing special about the flake-blades which are broken into segments: they bear the same features as the unbroken flake-blades from the same layers. Correspondingly, those bulbous segments from the MSA I stage frequently have battered striking platforms characteristic of the flake-blades and pointed flake-blades found in that stage (see above). Usually the proportions of the three different types of flake-blade segments in each layer are the same: a majority of bulbous segments and a minority of nonbulbous (e.g., see fig. 7.2 for Cave 1). This consistency points more to chance and accident than the intentional production of middle segments or the removal of irregular bulbous ends from long flake-blades. There may be some significance in the few instances where nonbulbous segments predominate over middle ones, as in MSA IV and perhaps layer 36 of MSA II, but in other cases the numbers seem too small for any importance to be attached to them.

Table 5.5. THE NUMBER AND DISTRIBUTION OF BROKEN FLAKE-BLADE SEGMENTS ACCORDING TO MSA STAGES

MSA   IV

Only represented at CAVE 1, layer 13

Bulbous segments	84
Middle segments	36
Nonbulbous segments	50

TOTAL = 170

MSA   III

SHELTER 1A	Layer 1-3	4	5	6	undiff 7	7a	7b	7c	total 7
Bulbous segments	10	5	8	101	36	67	16	40	159
Middle segments	2	1	5	77	28	48	7	18	101
Nonbulbous segments	3	-	9	51	36	35	10	15	96
	15	6	22	229					356

TOTAL = 628

MSA   II

CAVE 1	Layer 14 incl. 14+ & 14b	15 incl. 15+	16	undiff 17	17a	17b	total 17
Bulbous segments	904	372	525	170	65	490	725
Middle segments	418	187	213	101	41	217	359
Nonbulbous segments	294	149	142	64	30	167	261
	1616	708	880				1345

TOTAL = 4,549

Table 5.5 Continued

SHELTER 1A	Layer 22	23	24	undiff 23-24	25	26	27	28	29	undiff 28-29	30	31	32	33	undiff 32-33	34	35	36
Bulbous segments	77	13	48	128	42	9	87	68	32	24	70	20	34	18	42	77		201
Middle segments	47	7	45	116	14	4	32	16	9	31	39	10	4	6	11	28		87
Non-bulbous segments	28	9	28	52	14	1	28	18	11	5	27	8	11	7	6	17		101
	152	29	121	296	70	14	147	102	52	60	136	38	49	31	59	122	-	389

TOTAL = 1,867

MSA I

CAVE 1	Layer 37	38	39
Bulbous segments	685	323	2
Middle segments	277	152	1
Nonbulbous segments	251	131	1
	1213	606	4

TOTAL = 1,823

SHELTER 1B	Layer 2	3	4	5	6	7	8	9	10	11	12	13a	13b	14	15
Bulbous segments	6	55	29	27	12	18	9	5	12	2	11	2	9	10	
Middle segments	2	33	16	13	7	22	2	6	3	2	3		7	2	
Nonbulbous segments	3	33	12	12	4	18	4	9	1	3	4		6	7	
	11	121	57	52	23	58	15	20	16	7	18	2	22	19	-

TOTAL = 431

Accident must account for many of these segments, and the likelihood is that some were intentional.

Worked Points

This class of artifact is characteristic of all South African MSA industries which rely on quartzite as the normal raw material. The term "worked points" has been used here in order to distinguish these artifacts from pointed flake-blades which have no secondary working or other pointed flakes, yet it is difficult to conclude that many were not used for the same purpose, i.e., as spearheads. For the most part it would seem that secondary working of pointed flake-blades, flake-blades, or even just flakes was merely directed to increasing the efficiency or usefulness of the intended spearhead: thickening of the edges for strength, thinning of the butt end for easier hafting, increasing the acuteness of the point for greater penetration, and the making of notches for tighter binding to the shaft. Symmetry and other perfections of shape and elegance are more likely to reflect personal expressions of the knapper than the adherence to a deep-rooted industrial tradition. This is the conclusion from our study of the worked points found throughout the long period represented by the MSA stages at KRM.

Such is the great variety of treatment of the worked points that classification into types is not justified, and it is very questionable what an analysis of each or any of the particular aspects of secondary working would signify. With exceptions, almost every worked point warrants description in its own right. The exceptions are a few groups of similar worked points or consistent features that call for some comment. The difficulty of description has been mitigated, it is hoped, by the inclusion of more drawings than for other classes of artifacts. This is because it is felt that these worked points are more important as possible cultural or chronological indices. The differences between one industry and another, as described below and in the drawings (figs. 5.8–5.11), may offer better chances of correlations with other South African MSA industries than do the more general products and less specialized worked flakes.

As with all artifact classes there are border-line cases, with some worked points verging toward possible knives or even scrapers. In these cases the function of the artifact has been taken as a guide: assuming that the majority of worked points were used as spearheads, if the border-line examples would have served as spearheads equally well, they have been included with them. The term "unifacial point" is applied here in the sense of a point with shallow secondary working over half or more of the reverse (i.e., nonbulbar or dorsal) side. Similarly, bifacial points are worked over both faces. Both types are rare in the KRM MSA but are noted where they occur in table 5.6. "Partly bifacial" means that the point is worked from both sides but over less than half of either one or both sides. "Shallow flaking" is used in preference to "pressure flaking" to describe the neat, scalelike flaking produced by delicate platform preparation and percussion, the use of intermediate punches, or the use of some other advanced flaking technique. This, too, is rare, but is noted where it occurs in table 5.6.

In MSA IV there are no worked points with the exception of one small triangular flake (4 cm) that has some slight secondary working along one edge. There is also a small, broken worked piece that may have been a small point.

The absence of worked points from this stage is unlikely to be significant in view of the relatively small number of artifacts found in layer 1-13, the only layer in which this stage is represented.

The unifacial points in MSA III are distinctive (figs. 5.8, 5.9), and there is nothing exactly the same as numbers 1 and 18 in figure 5.8 in the earlier stages, although a few unifacial points in MSA II are very similar and equally symmetrical and well made. All the worked points in table 5.6 are drawn in figures 5.8 and 5.9, and it will be seen that the similarities with the worked points of earlier stages (figs. 5.10, 5.11) are far more marked than any differences, excluding the Howieson's Poort Industry which underlies MSA III.

In MSA II, the unifacial point from 1-17 (fig. 5.10, no. 6) is of the same form as another from 1A-36 (fig. 5.10, no. 5). One of the ?bifacial points from layer 14 is possibly the butt end of an unfinished point, as the flaking is crude. It is slightly rolled so may even be derived from an earlier layer. It was well inside the cave (West Cutting G), and it was unusual that nearly all the worked points from this layer were on this west side. One point from layer 15 is of indurated shale.

In MSA II, the partly bifacial forms from 1A-23 have the bifacial secondary working restricted to the butt end, and in three cases the striking platform has been removed completely so that the end has become thin and rounded. The butt is similarly treated in the elegant example from layer 26. The large flake with a bifacially worked point (fig. 5.15, no. 12) from layer 25 is included, as it may be an unfinished, completely bifacially worked point. That from layers 28 and 29 is unfortunately broken. There are rudimentary tangs of the worked points (one broken) from layers 23 and 24.

In MSA I worked points are more numerous. Secondary working is generally restricted to one edge and part of the butt. The forms are simple, but the workmanship is good.

The small, partly bifacial point from 1B-4 with an incipient tang is the only one of its type found (fig. 5.11, no. 7) and must have tipped an arrow or very small throwing spear. A few of the points have shallow flaking, and one long worked point from layer 37 has a distinct tang. Several have the battered striking platforms described above as being a distinctive feature of flake-blade production in MSA I. Many appear to be made on flake-blades rather than on pointed flake-blades.

Summary of MSA I–IV Worked Points

Worked points are a distinctive feature of all the MSA stages although they do not occur in large numbers. They are regarded as spearheads, although it is quite possible that they may have had other uses. There is a great variety of forms and, especially in view of the small numbers, little apparent justification for separating them into numerous categories. For the most part they are pointed flakes or flake-blades which have been modified by the minimum of secondary working to make them more suitable for their purpose, and this has usually entailed the thickening of one edge toward the point and the slight rounding of the butt. Sometimes the butt has been very neatly rounded and the striking platform completely removed by bifacial flaking. This would seem to offer such advantages for hafting that it is most puzzling it was not done more often. Most of the worked points have rather thick, clumsy butts, similar to the average pointed flake-blade, and the same indifference to the thickness of the striking platform was noted above when describing the pointed flake-blades. However, in the MSA I stage much more attention was given to the thinning of the platform, in the same manner as the flake-blades, pointed or otherwise. This is probably the most significant distinguishing feature for

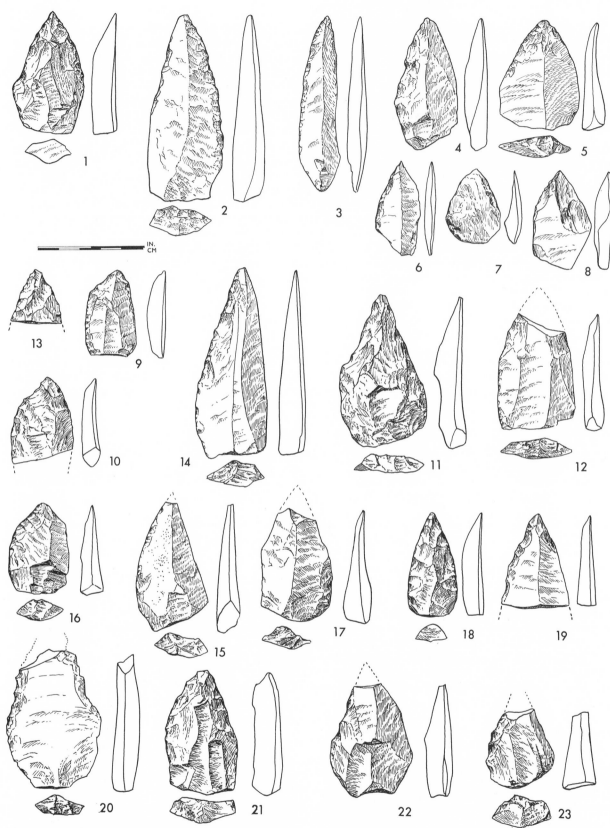

Fig. 5.8. Worked points: nos. 1–23. MSA III. 1, 10, 11, 18: unifacial points. No. 13 tip of ? unifacial point. Nos. 5, 10, 16 with some shallow flaking. There is some inverse thinning of the butt of 7, and one edge of 8 is bifacially worked. There is also some slight inverse retouch on the butt ends of 11, 12, 14, 18, 20.

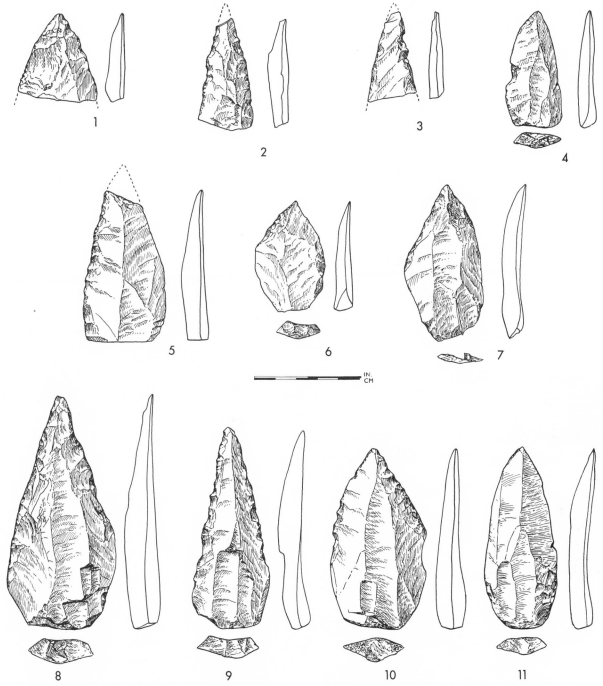

FIG. 5.9. Worked points: nos. 1–11. MSA III. 1: tip of ? unifacial point. Nos. 2, 3, 9 are denticulated. No. 10 shows shallow flaking along part of one edge. No. 2 is snapped across at the butt end but may be complete. There is slight inverse retouch near the butt on 4 and 11. The broken tip of 5 has been rechipped, and 11 is made of coarse silcrete.

this stage, yet it must be noted that occasional examples in the later MSA stages are equally well thinned around the butts.

Unifacial points are not present in the MSA I stage, but occur in small numbers in MSA II and III. A long, slender, leaf-shaped form is typical of the former and (on the weak evidence of two specimens) a wider form of the latter. Nothing can be said about worked points in MSA IV, as only one doubtful example was found.

Shallow flaking on part of the point, generally along one edge toward the point, is a little more common in MSA II and III. Coarse, denticulated edges occur sporadically throughout.

There is not a single example of a completely bifacially worked oval point that would be regarded as typical of the Stillbay Industry, yet a few of the bifacially worked pieces tend toward this shape, particularly when the butts have been thinned and rounded. It is very unfortunate that the only Stillbay-type bifacial point found was a surface find on the scree slope below Shelter 1A (fig. 6.7, no. 2). It was halfway down the slope and could have eroded out of layers containing MSA II or III or the Howieson's Poort Industry. It was actually on the truncated layers of MSA II, but this is no proof that it came from them. However, it does suggest that it is more recent than MSA I. It is made of fine, gray silcrete and is broken in two places.

Another feature which distinguishes the worked points of MSA I from those of the later stages is that the former are more numerous. There is also a drop in the proportion of pointed flake-blades in MSA I, and these two facts may be connected.

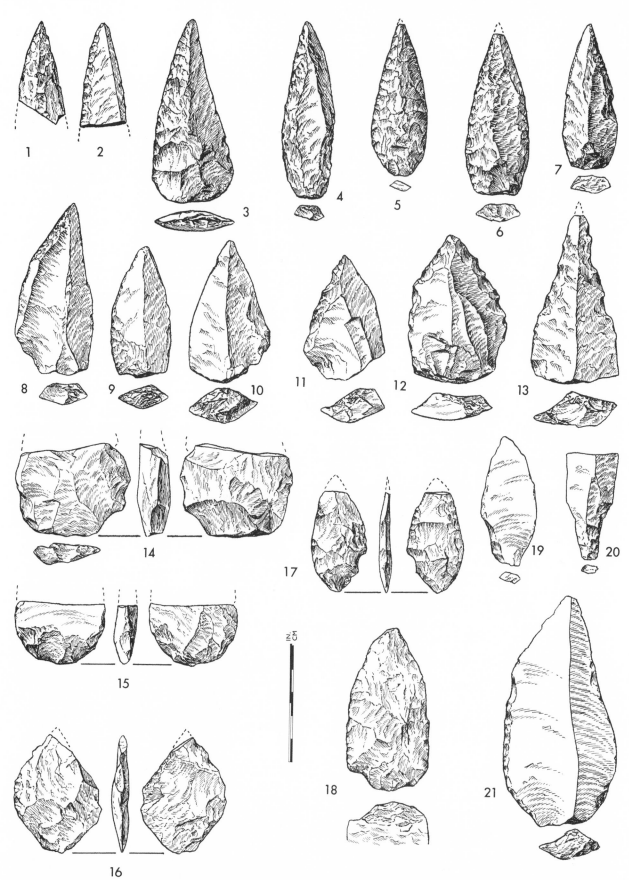

FIG. 5.10. Worked points: nos. 1–21. MSA II. 3, 4, 5, 6, 18: unifacial points. 1: probably tip of another. 12, 13: denticulated. 7, 8, 9, 10, 11, 21: normal type with minimum of secondary working. 19: point with incipient tang worked from reverse side. 20: tang on a broken flake-blade, worked bifacially on one edge. 16: ovoid bifacial point. 17: small, leaf-shaped bifacial point. 14: ? butt of an unfinished bifacial point broken in manufacture. 15: neatly rounded butt of a partly bifacial point. There is slight inverse retouch on the point of 19 and the butt of 21.

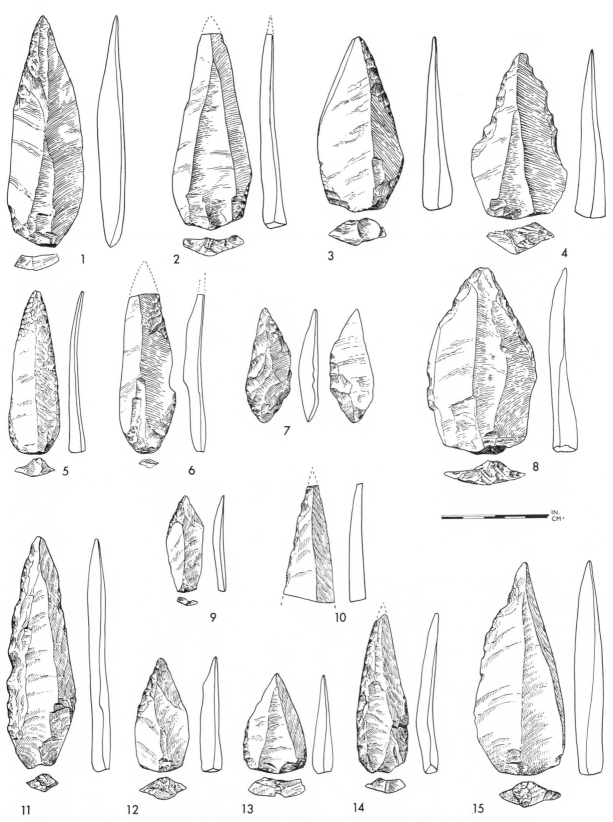

Fig. 5.11. Worked points, Shelter 1B: nos. 1–15. MSA I. No. 1 is of course white silcrete. There is slight inverse retouch on the butt ends of 6 and 15.

Table 5.6. The Number and Distribution of Worked Points in MSA I–III

MSA III (Figs. 5.8, 5.9)

SHELTER 1A	Layer 1-3	4	5	6	7	8	9	undiff 7-9
Total	8	4	3	8	6		1	4
Including:								
Unifacial	1	2	?1*	1				?1*
Denticulated					1			2
With shallow flaking	1	1		1	1			1
Tip fragment only		1	1	1				2

    (* tip only)   TOTAL = 34

MSA II (Fig. 5.10)

CAVE 1	Layer 14 incl. 14+ & 14b	15 incl. 15b	16	17	17a	17b
Total	26	9	5	8		7
Including:						
Denticulated	5		4			
Unifacial				1		
With shallow flaking						1
Bifacial	?2*					

    (* both broken)   TOTAL = 55

MSA II - WORKED POINTS

SHELTER 1A	Layer 22	23	24	undiff 23-24	25	26	27	28	29	undiff 28-29	30	31	32	33	34	35	36
Total		1	14	24	3	1	1	1	1	1	2			1	4		19
Including:																	
Denticulated			1														1
Unifacial		1		4													2
With shallow flaking			1														
Bifacial				1													2
Partly bifacial				5	?1	1				1							1
Tip fragment only			2	6										1			

        TOTAL = 73

Table 5.6 Continued

MSA I (Fig. 5.11) CAVE 1	Layer		SHELTER 1B	Layer			
	37	38		2	3	4	5
Total	76	36		2	12	13	3
Including:							
Denticulate	4	7			1	1	
Partly bifacial	1					1	
With shallow flaking	3					3	1
Tip fragment only					1		

TOTAL = 142

Worked Flakes (Figures 5.12–5.14)

The term "worked flakes" is used in the sense of any flake or flake-blade that has been modified by secondary working. It does not include pieces with crushed or chipped edges that could have resulted from heavy usage, or others with a few random chips that could have been accidental. However, any flake that shows the signs of deliberate, intentional secondary working is included. They occur in small numbers compared with unworked flake-blades, and only about half of them can be classified as specialized tool forms. The remainder are the "tools-of-the-moment" which occur in stone industries of any age, with the secondary working usually confined to one edge either to afford a better grip or to render it more suitable for a particular purpose. These are classified here as unspecialized.

There are four specialized forms, apart from the worked points which have been treated separately above: denticulates, scrapers, borers, and gravers. A few flakes which have distinctive notches or have secondary working entirely down one edge are also noted separately, but both forms tend to merge into the unspecialized category and it is impossible to know where to draw the line between them. The number of these worked flakes per layer within each MSA stage are given in table 5.7, and some comments on the major forms are given below.

Denticulates (Figure 5.12)

The most numerous class of worked flakes, denticulates occur throughout all the MSA stages except MSA IV. These serrated pieces vary from flakes with a few crude notches spaced along one edge to elegant, parallel-sided flake-blades with one or both edges neatly toothed by a series of small, evenly spaced notches that in many cases must have been produced with a punch (fig. 5.12, nos. 3 and 2, respectively). The range of variation is so large that it might seem wrong to include such extremes in the same tool class, but there is every intermediate gradation between them.

With exceptions, the regular, elegant denticulates are confined to the MSA I stage, where the tool occurs in greater numbers than in the later stages. This is particularly so in the

Table 5.7. THE NUMBER AND DISTRIBUTION OF WORKED FLAKES ACCORDING TO MSA STAGES

	MSA IV	MSA III								
	CAVE 1	SHELTER 1A								
Layer	13	1-3	4	5	6	7	8	9	undiff 7-9	
Denticulates		4	2	1	8	4			1	
Scrapers	2	7	3	1	7			2		
Gravers	4				7	4				
Borers					2					
Backed all along one edge		2	2	1	5				1	
Unspecialized	2	7		5	22	8		3	1	
	8	20	7	8	51	16	-	5	3	
	TOTAL = 8	TOTAL = 110								

Table 5.7 Continued

MSA II

CAVE 1	Layer 14 incl. 14+ & 14b	15 incl. 15+	16	17a	17b	undiff 17
Denticulates	54	47	45	6	35	14
Scrapers	42	17	40		47	27
Gravers	24	2	3		2	1
Borers	2		2	1		1
Notched	9	12				
Unspecialized	143	44	85	65	7	25
	274	122	175	72	91	68

TOTAL = 802

MSA II - WORKED FLAKES

SHELTER 1A	Layer 22	23	24	undiff 23-24	25	26	27	28	29	undiff 28-29	30	31	32	33	undiff 32-33	34	35	36
Denticulates	2	1	1	8	1		1	1			1	1			3			7
Scrapers	4		2	4	2	2	3	1	1		1			2				4
Gravers			1	1			1	1				1			2			3
Borers				1	1		1				1							
Backed all along one edge			1	4			1											
Notched		1	3		1		3	2	1		1							2
Unspecialized	3	6	6	11	4	4	2	2	3		4	1			9	10		37
	9	8	14	29	9	6	12	7	5	-	8	3	-	2	14	10	-	53

TOTAL = 189

MSA I - WORKED FLAKES

CAVE 1	Layer 37	38	39	40
Denticulates	48	85	3	
Scrapers	50	13		
Gravers	20	3		
Borers	3	1		
Notched	5			
Unspecialized	101	58		
	227	160	3	-

TOTAL = 63

Table 5.7 Continued

SHELTER 1B	Layer										
	1	2	3	4	5	6	7–11	12	13	14	15
Denticulates			8	6		1		1	1	2	
Scrapers			7	1	4	1					
Gravers			1		1	1					
Borers				1							
Notched				1							
Unspecialized		1	13	6	4				2		
	–	1	29	15	9	3	–	1	3	2	–

TOTAL = 63

lower layers; e.g., layer 38 produced 85 denticulates as opposed to only 13 scrapers and 58 unspecialized worked flakes.

The purpose of these denticulates, whether crude or refined, was probably the same, but it is difficult to know what exactly it was. They make ineffectual saws on wood or bone and seem insufficiently comblike for teasing furs. If they were used on hard substances, some marks of wear would be expected, and these are not evident. It would seem feasible that they may have been used for cutting fish or performing minor butchering activities. Whatever it was, their persistent numbers indicate some constant specialized activity.

Scrapers (Figure 5.13)

These are almost as numerous as denticulates. Rounded scrapers on thick flakes are the commonest form, but large and small end-scrapers occur. Most are crude, but surprisingly elegant examples occur which, out of context, could well be mistaken for the products of much more recent stone industries (fig. 5.13, nos. 5, 6, 7). Hollow scrapers are uncommon, although several of the cruder, unspecialized forms of worked flakes could have been used as such. Fine silcrete was used for two small, rounded scrapers in the MSA II stage, and one is shown (fig. 5.13, no. 15). There were also two unusual double-ended scrapers from the same industry (fig. 5.13, nos. 7, 16), and those from 1-16 were particularly well finished.

Although these tools are termed scrapers, this is more to accord with archeological convention than to describe their use. They probably had a variety of uses of which scraping was just one. It seems unlikely that they were employed for the kind of rigorous scraping required to prepare skins, for an experiment on an antelope skin showed that little more than ten minutes' work reduced the edge of a scraper made of local quartzite to a very distinct dulled and rounded condition. Such signs of use are almost nonexistent on these scrapers, although similar signs of wear can be seen on many of the worked flakes described as unspecialized.

Gravers (Figure 5.14)

Gravers are not common, but occur in all four stages. The examples tabulated and figured have been selected with caution: they are clearly deliberately made tools produced in a variety of systematic ways and are of a type which can be found in many stone industries throughout the world. Particular caution is necessary, as the identification of gravers in South African MSA industries has been questioned and criticized in the past. The evidence from KRM is conclusive, but it is possible that the exercise of such caution has resulted in the relegation of several worked flakes intended by their makers as gravers to a less definite category. The brittle nature of the local quartzite and the simple manner in which a crude graver can be produced sometimes make it very difficult to decide whether the product is intentional or accidental. Where the probability is stronger that it is intentional, the artifact has been classified as "?graver," but even with the addition of these doubtful specimens it is clear that gravers were not produced in large numbers (tables 5.7, 5.8). However, there was an occasional demand for a tool with a strong, narrow edge, and the significant thing is that a tradition of systematic graver production was alive.

There are five main ways of making gravers, and it cannot be said on the basis of the small numbers found that any particular one was favored during the different MSA stages:

Stage	Plain Right Angle	Backed Right Angle	Plain Oblique Angle	Backed Oblique Angle	Simple "Screwdriver"
MSA IV	...	1	...	1	
MSA III	6	1	...	...	
MSA II	4	1	4	2	3
MSA I	3	3	1	...	4

Nonlocal Rock Artifacts

There is an element in all MSA stages of nonlocal rock finer-grained than the quartzite of the cliffs and beach boulders. Neither the term "nonlocal" nor the term "finer-grained" is strictly accurate, for quartz occurs in veins locally, and some of the coarse silcretes are slightly more granular than the finer varieties of local quartzite. Soft shale is also exposed along the beach in a few places and may be the source of the occasional pieces found. Excluding the quartz, however, most of these other rocks have probably been brought to the site from varying

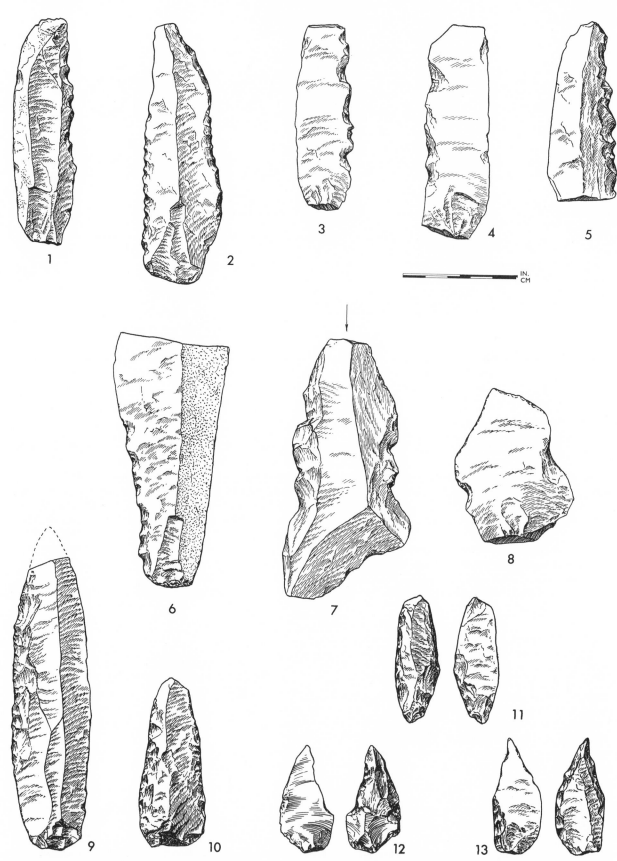

FIG. 5.12. Denticulates and other worked flakes: nos. 1–13. MSA I–III. MSA III: 9; MSA II: 1, 3, 4, 5, 7, 8, 10, 12, 13; MSA I: 2, 6, 12. 1–7: denticulates. 8: notched. 9–10: shallow-flaked knives. The elegant no. 9 has similar shallow flaking on the alternate side on the bulbous face. 11: ? punch or graver. 12, 13: borers. No. 12 is made from a flake of pale brown chalcedony.

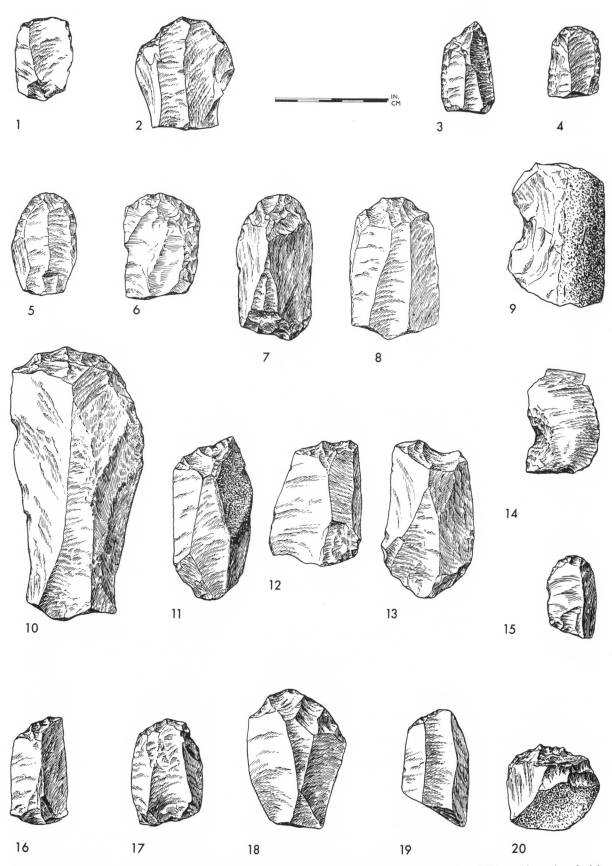

FIG. 5.13. Scrapers: nos. 1–20. MSA I–IV. MSA IV: 1–2; MSA III: 3–4; MSA II: 5–15; MSA I: 16–20. All made of local quartzite except 6 and 15, which are of fine silcrete. No. 7 is a rare double-ended example with some inverse retouch, and 10 has a thin coating of calcite on the right side of the face drawn which may obscure some more secondary working.

distances. Where cortex is present, it can be seen that pebbles have been used. The most likely source for pebbles of fine-grained rock would be the nearby river valleys, particularly the Tzitzikama, and perhaps the old gravels in the region of Kareedouw.

As mentioned, although there is plenty of local quartz in the form of veins, it is mainly exposed in rocks along the beach, and the constant pounding of the sea has shattered it so much that most would be useless for knapping. Because of this, an inland source of the quartz is possible. A few large quartz crystals also occurred in some of the occupational layers, and none of these were ever seen in the rocks nearby.

The quantities of nonlocal rock artifacts in each stage per layer are shown in table 5.9. The numbers are very small compared with artifacts of local rock, and they rank more as curiosities than part of the industrial tradition, in marked con-

trast to their large numbers in the Howieson's Poort Industry. There was certainly no regular demand for these fine-grained rocks. Generally they have been flaked in the same manner as the normal quartzite, with careful preparation of the striking platforms, but the very fineness of the rock and small size of some of the pebbles have resulted in a few very small, near-microlithic pieces. Typical examples from the MSA II stage are shown in figure 5.15, numbers 4–11. Worked pieces have been included with the numbers of worked flakes in table 5.8.

The cores are all small and irregular. Typical ones from the MSA III stage are shown in plate 33. Numbers of cores per stage and layer are given in tables 5.1 and 7.2 with the other nonlocal rock artifacts. In table 5.8 flake-blades and pointed flake-blades are included with the flakes because of their small numbers. There are seven pointed flake-blades of nonlocal rock divided among the MSA stages in Cave 1:

Table 5.8. DISTRIBUTION OF NONLOCAL ROCK ARTIFACTS (MOSTLY SINGLE) ACCORDING TO MSA STAGES

			Cave or Shelter	Layer	
MSA	III	Ground edge on flake-blade of indurated shale	1A	6	
		Worked point of coarse silcrete	1A	7	
MSA	II	Rounded scraper of fine silcrete	1	14	
		Nose scraper of fine silcrete	1	14	
		Unspecialized worked flake of fine silcrete	1	14	
		Worked point of indurated shale	1	15	(Fig. 5.15, no. 5)
		Small scraper of indurated shale	1	15	(Fig. 5.15, no. 4)
		Hollow scraper of fine silcrete	1	15+	
		Unspecialized worked flake of fine silcrete	1	15+	
		Rounded scraper of fine silcrete	1	17	
		Core rejuvenation flake of indurated shale	1A	36	
		Rounded scraper of fine silcrete	1A	36	
		? Graver of fine silcrete	1A	36	
		3 unspecialized worked flakes of indurated shale	1A	36	
		Notched flake of indurated shale 1	1A	36	
MSA	I	Borer of chalcedony	1	37	
		Unspecialized worked flake of coarse silcrete	1	38	
		Worked point of coarse silcrete	1B	4	

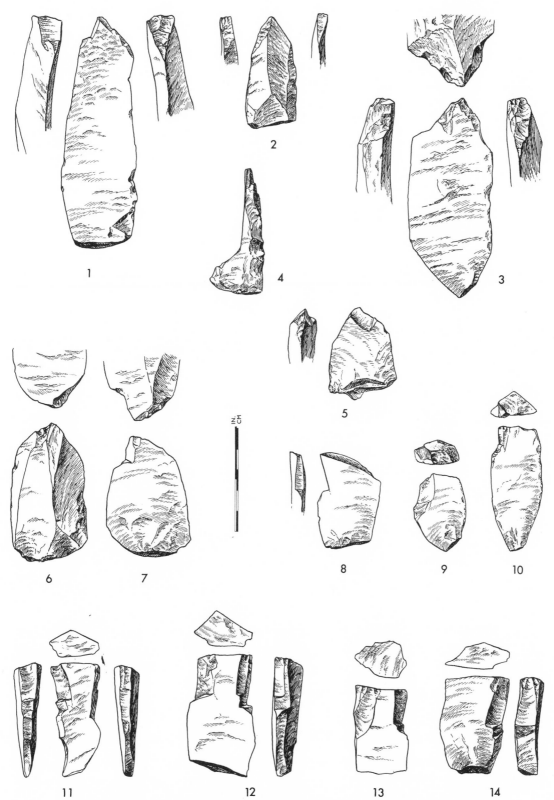

FIG. 5.14. Gravers: nos. 1–14. MSA I–IV. MSA IV: 5, 9; MSA III: 10–12; MSA II: 1, 2, 4, 7, 8, 13, 14; MSA I: 3, 6. All are made of local quartzite. Various methods have been used to produce the graving tip, influenced by the fortuitous shape of the flake selected.

Simple or screwdriver gravers. 1 and 2. In both examples there is a single, plain facet (primary blow) opposite a multiple one (secondary blows to complete the tool).

Oblique angle gravers. (*a*) Plain (i.e., with a snapped or fortuitous surface requiring no primary trimming before the removal of the flake intended to produce the graving edge): 8. (*b*) Backed (i.e., with secondary working from the bulbous side of the flake to form a platform for the removal of the flake or flakes intended to produce the graving edge): 3, 5–7. Nos. 3 and 7 are multifaceted.

Right-angle gravers. (*a*) Plain, single: 14, which is also multifaceted. (*b*) Plain, double: 11–13. (*c*) Backed: 9, 10. No. 10 is multifaceted.

Plunging flake. 4, probably misstruck in the process of resharpening a graver.

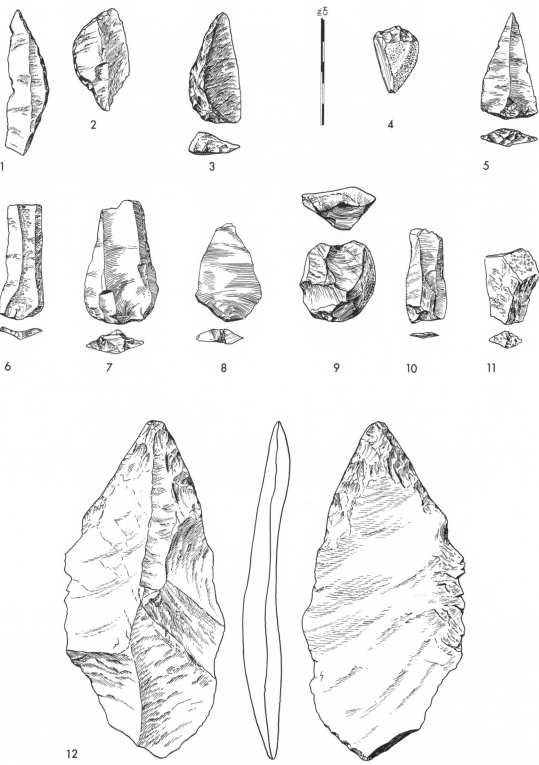

Fig. 5.15. Nonlocal rock and miscellaneous: nos. 1–12. MSA II. 1, 2, 3: crescents. The only crescents found throughout the entire sequence of MSA I and MSA II layers are those shown. Significantly, nos. 1 and 2 came from layers immediately below those containing a Howieson's Poort Industry and these were slightly disturbed by large rockfalls, so it is most likely that these two crescents are derived from above. The thick crescent, no. 3, from an indisputable MSA II provenance, is not typical of Howieson's Poort crescents and probably served a different purpose. 4: small scraper, of reddish gray fine silcrete. 5: pointed flake-blade, of indurated shale, with slight signs of blunting on lower left side. 6: flake-blade, of white coarse silcrete; signs of use. 7: flake-blade, of gray fine silcrete; secondary working on right side. 8: flake, of translucent, brown chalcedony. 9: small core of indurated shale. 10: flake-blade of indurated shale; signs of use. 11: flake of quartz. 12: large flake with point bifacially worked. Possibly an unfinished bifacial point. Depicted with bulbar end upward for clarity.

MSA II
    1 of fine silcrete   Layer 14
    2 of indurated shale   Layer 15
    1 of indurated shale   Layer 16

MSA I
    2 of coarse silcrete   Layer 37
    1 of indurated shale   Layer 38

The frequency of the types of nonlocal rock used in the various MSA stages is given in table 5.9. The quartz used was very intractable, with the result that systematic flaking was rarely possible: in most cases, small pieces of quartz have been hammered until they shattered, and the resulting splinters, rather than flakes, were presumably used if they were of suitable size and sharpness. "Shatter-pieces" would be a better description than flakes for most of them, but it is impossible to draw the line between them.

The fine silcrete is generally a pale red or light gray color, and flakes cleanly. The coarse silcrete is of very variable texture and usually a pale white to cream color. The indurated shale also varies greatly, from a fine, black siliceous rock to a much softer, dull gray green type of shale. A dark gray, intermediate type of shale was most commonly used. All the other types of rocks used were found in much smaller numbers.

Table 5.9. THE USE OF NONLOCAL ROCK IN THE MSA STAGES

| | MSA IV | MSA III | | | | | | | |
| | CAVE 1 | SHELTER 1A | | | | | | | |
Layer	13	1-3	4	5	6	7	8	9	undiff 7-9
Quartz	8	7	1		35	14	18	32	9
Fine silcrete	2	1			36	3		30	2
Coarse silcrete					3	3		2	
Indurated shale	4	3		2	13	2		7	10
Fine quartzite					7	1		3	
Chert					1			1	
Other rocks	1								
	15	11	1	2	95	23	18	75	21
	TOTAL = 15	TOTAL = 246							

MSA II

| CAVE 1 | Layer | | | | | |
	14 incl. 14+ & 14b	15 incl. 15+	16	17a	17b	undiff 17
Quartz	59	75	22	10	9	9
Fine silcrete	62	39	23	1	9	1
Coarse silcrete	30	19	2	1		2
Indurated shale	126	185	80	11	17	6
Chalcedony	3	5	2			1
Shale/sandstone	1	8	2		5	
Fine quartzite	4	9		1		
Chert	1	2				
Other rocks		1				
	286	343	131	24	40	19
		TOTAL = 843				

Table 5.9 Continued

SHELTER 1A	Layer 22	23	24	undiff 23-24	25	26	27	28	29	undiff 28-29	30	31	32	33	undiff 32-33	34	35	36
Quartz	61	19	2	5	3	1	2			5	2	2	1	3		4		12
Fine silcrete	5	11		2			1			1	1		6	2	20	3		6
Coarse silcrete		4	2	4			3	1	1			2	33	8				13
Indurated shale	3	4		5	1	1	3		2	2	4	1	8		1	2	1	16
Chalcedony	2														2			1
Shale/ sandstone									1						1			1
Fine quartzite								1	2									1
Other rocks																		1
	71	38	4	16	4	2	9	2	6	8	7	5	48	13	24	9	1	51

TOTAL = 318

MSA I

CAVE 1	Layer 37	38	39	40
Quartz	25	13		
Fine silcrete	7			
Coarse silcrete	11	6		
Indurated shale	21	11		
Shale/sandstone	2	5		
Chalcedony	9	5		
	75	40	-	-

TOTAL = 115

The higher proportion of nonlocal rock artifacts in the MSA III stage may reflect material from the Howieson's Poort occupation, for most of the pieces are very small.

Miscellaneous Stone Artifacts
Crescents (Figure 5.15, Numbers 1–3)

A few crescents identical in form to those found in the Howieson's Poort occupational layers have come from the MSA III stage and the uppermost part of MSA II beneath Shelter 1A.

The numbers are shown in table 7.1: there are 8 from MSA III and 12 from MSA II. The problem is to know whether these are really products of the MSA stages or have been derived from the levels above containing the Howieson's Poort Industry. The distribution of the few between layers 22 and 24 strongly suggests that these crescents are derived from levels immediately above, for, as has been described, the top of layer 22 represents a time of much collapse when large lumps and boulders of calcite fell onto the surface. Some weighed many tons and sank into the underlying soil, compressing or disturbing it at least as far down as layer 23. Occupation by people with a

Table 5.9 Continued

SHELTER 1B	Layer											
	1	2	3	4	5	6	7	8	9	10	11	12-15
Quartz		1	4	2	6					2	1	
Coarse silcrete								1				
Indurated shale			2		1		3					
Shale/ sandstone			2									
Fine quartzite			1									
	-	1	9	2	7	-	3	1	-	2	1	-

TOTAL = 26

Note. These refer to the number of flakes found per layer, including a few flake-blades (see the section on flake-blades). Cores, worked flakes, and any crescents of non-local rock are not included in these figures. Details of these are in the relevant sections.

Howieson's Poort Industry immediately following this rockfall could have caused small artifacts to slip down to lower levels.

Similarly, the crescents between layers 1 and 9 beneath Shelter 1A may well have been derived from Howieson's Poort levels a little higher up the slope and perhaps not completely covered by more recent occupational soils. Their rarity, and the fact that over half of them come from the lowermost levels, supports this conclusion.

Apart from one obliquely blunted point from 1A-36 there were no other similar forms in this MSA II stage and nothing at all in MSA I.

An interesting small tool from the lower part of the MSA II stage is shown (fig. 5.15, no. 3): a thick, backed asymmetrical crescent. It resembles a small version of the tools found in the LSA middens at KRM described as thick-backed scraper-knives rather than the crescents of the Howieson's Poort, but no connection is suggested. It may just be an aberrant form of worked point.

Handaxes (Figures 5.16 and 5.17)

Another class of tool that may or may not be contemporary with its associated artifacts is the handax. There are three definite handaxes, one from MSA II (1-14), one from MSA I (1A-37), and one from the beach shingle in Cave 1 which may represent Early Stone Age (ESA) activity at the site. As there is no other possible evidence for an ESA Industry at KRM and as it is a matter of importance to know whether handaxes were a part of the MSA tradition, details of these three handaxes are given below.

Figure 5.16, number 3. Cave 1, layer 40, which consists of beach gravel overlying bedrock. This picklike implement, comparable to the products of Sangoan industries, qualifies for a possible ESA date for two reasons: it underlies the earliest MSA occupational layers on the site, and it is rolled, suggesting that it is contemporary with some stage of the 6–8 m sea. Against this interpretation, it must be noted that a few rolled flake-blades typical of MSA I were found in the same beach gravel.

Figure 5.16, number 2. Shelter 1A, layer 36. This is the butt of a large, very worn handax that has been rechipped into a tool resembling a smaller handax. The more recent work, presumably that of the MSA I stage, is crude and devoid of the shallow, skimming flakes characteristic of handax manufacture.

Figure 5.17, number 1. Cave 1, layer 14. This flat-butted cordate handax is slightly smoothed and weathered, unlike the MSA artifacts in mint condition with which it is associated. Almost certainly it was a local surface find brought to the site either for use or as a curiosity. Its condition is identical to that of many of the numerous handaxes which now lie exposed on the surface at Geelhoutboom, 3 km distant.

As can be seen from table 7.1, there are a few doubtful handaxes which might alternatively be classified as irregular cores or choppers. Figure 5.17, number 2, is the more likely of two doubtful specimens from 1-16. Another, figure 5.16, number 1, is from the upper levels of the Howieson's Poort Industry: its blunt, pointed end is not typical of handaxes.

The conclusion is that handaxes were not part of the Klasies River Mouth MSA stone-working tradition, but that occasional cores resembled crude handaxes and that the occupants sometimes picked up the products of earlier industries and brought them back to the site. A similar reuse of handaxes was found at Ohrigstad in the Eastern Transvaal (Louw 1969). There is no evidence to prove an ESA occupation at KRM prior to the MSA.

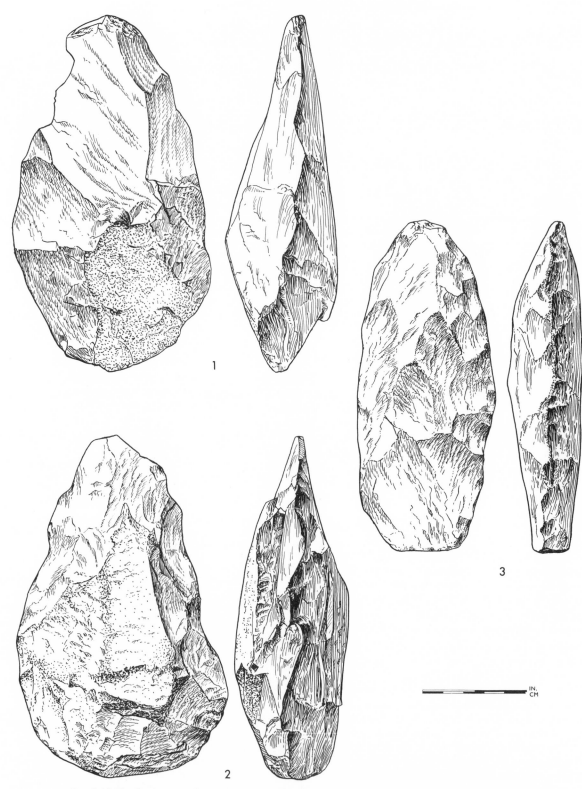

Fig. 5.16. Handaxes: nos. 1–3. 1: a doubtful specimen found in the Howieson's Poort Industry, KRM 1A-12. Probably an aberrant core. The blunting at the pointed end is not characteristic of handaxes. 2: a large, much worn and weathered handax that has been rechipped into a smaller and cruder one. The rechipping is as fresh and sharp as the associated MSA I industry, KRM 1-37. 3: a rolled picklike handax from the beach gravel (layer 40) beneath the MSA I industry at Cave 1.

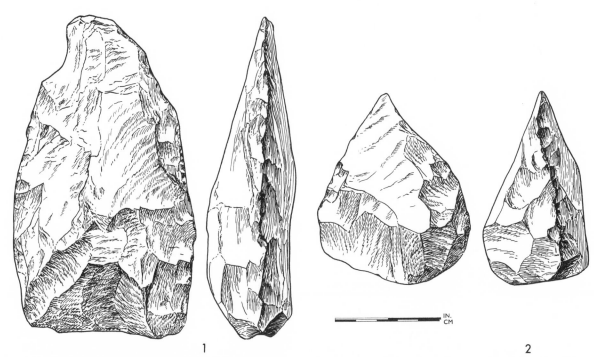

FIG. 5.17. Handaxes: nos. 1–2. 1: flat-butted cordate handax. Slightly smoothed and weathered, so probably found on the surface locally and brought back as a curiosity. MSA II, in 1-14. 2: core tool resembling a handax. MSA II, in 1-16.

Hammerstones

Only two quartzite pebbles were found with sufficiently marked localized battering to warrant their classification as hammerstones. Both were in the MSA II stage, 1-14 and 17b. Considering that many thousands of hammerstones must have been used to account for the large numbers of flakes produced over a long period of time, it is surprising that they are so rare. Assuming that quartzite pebble hammerstones were used for the flaking, the explanation could lie in the virtually unlimited source of suitable pebbles on the nearby beach, where, in any case, much of the primary flaking was probably done. With such a choice of potential hammerstones, there was possibly no need to retain any particular one so that the constant use of it made its purpose readily identifiable. The marks from a few minutes' use are indistinguishable from the natural marks of battering on beach pebbles.

No evidence at all was found for grinding: pounders, rubbers, and quern stones were nonexistent in all the layers. The only possible exception was a long (22 cm), cylindrical pebble of fine-grained sandstone from 1-14. A few small flakes have been removed from the narrow end, and the other end shows slight signs of smoothing, as does one of the flatter faces. It fits in the hand like a small club, and similar pebbles in European coastal Mesolithic sites have been identified as hammers for knocking limpets off rocks.

Flakes

The many thousands of flakes which litter every occupational level at KRM must represent, for the most part, the waste products of flake-blade and pointed flake-blade production. It would be misleading to refer to them as waste flakes. Many of these flakes show signs of use or have been worked into specialized or nonspecialized tool forms. Also, the criteria used here to define flake-blades and pointed flake-blades, simple and broad as they are, relegate many flakes out of those categories, which, as far as the makers were concerned, were just as useful. Our criteria are advantageous merely for descriptive purposes and make no pretense to assess every human whim of the people who created these industries. It is clear that the flake-blades and pointed flake-blades represent an end-product of required tool forms and that many of those flakes which approach those forms may also have had similar uses.

In some of the layers within particular MSA stages, there do appear to be higher proportions of flakes in this category, for example, many with well-prepared striking platforms devoid of cortex, yet too wide to be classified as a flake-blade, or pointed but without the central ridge meeting at the point used to define pointed flake-blades. During the initial classification some attempt was made to describe these as "serviceable" or "near-pointed flake-blades," respectively, but it seemed too subjective or complicated to continue this. Detailed analysis of the flakes, by class factors or measurements, could express the differences, but it is very questionable what these differences would imply. Therefore, no attempt is made to make any subdivisions in table 5.10, which gives the number of flakes in each stage per layer.

There is fairly constant proportion between the number of flakes and other artifacts within each layer, flakes being about 62 percent of the total number of artifacts (fig. 7.1).

Occasionally, the use of a distinctive type of quartzite has made it readily apparent that some of the flakes or flake-blades within one layer fit together. This strongly suggests that some knapping was actually done on the living site, which is not surprising. However, as mentioned when describing the cores, there is a noticeable lack of outer flakes, that is, the initial flakes

Table 5.10. The Number of Flakes Found per Layer (local quartzite only) and Subdivided into Each MSA Stage

	Layer	Number			Layer	Number
MSA IV						
CAVE 1	13	1572			34	1764
					35	16
MSA III					36	1998
SHELTER 1A	1-3	156				25561
	4	47				
	5	141		**MSA I**		
	6	2221		CAVE 1	37	12407
	7	1478			38	5697
	8	105			39	16
	9	219			40	1
	undiff 7-9	452				18121
		4819				
				SHELTER 1B	1	-
MSA II					2	51
CAVE 1	14 incl.				3	686
	14+ &				4	298
	14b	11359			5	239
	15 incl.				6	107
	15+	8912			7	204
	16	8290			8	40
	17a	2690			9	85
	17b	2610			10	116
	undiff 17	6014			11	74
		39875			12	140
					13	91
					14	80
SHELTER 1A	22	783			15	102
	23	391				2313
	24	1415				
	undiff 23-24	3088				
	25	1714		GRAND TOTAL OF ALL FLAKES		
	26	494		= 92,261		
	27	3762				
	28	2093				
	29	926				
	undiff 28-29	2404				
	30	831				
	31	829				
	32	932				
	undiff 32-33	1636				

struck from a beach cobble. These are easily recognizable by the cortex remaining on the major or entire part of their dorsal sides. Presumably, much of this primary flaking was done on the nearby beach, which was also the source of the raw material.

The large numbers of flakes (over 65,000 in the MSA II stage alone) constitute a problem in conservation. As a compromise, every excavated flake has been recorded and a minimum of 2,000 per layer retained for the collections of the South African Museum.

6   The Howieson's Poort Industry

Shelter 1A

The industry described below comes from layers 10 to 21 beneath Shelter 1A. These are the occupation layers, composed, for the most part, of laminated hearths and black carbonaceous soil, suggesting permanent or semipermanent, protracted occupation of the shelter. The stratigraphy has already been described, the main considerations being that these layers lie directly over a massive rockfall on layers containing an industry described as MSA II and are covered by sandier deposits containing MSA III.

The industry contrasts so markedly with those above and below it that, coupled with the different type of occupational deposit which accumulated, it can be concluded that there was a somewhat different pattern of human activity. The typology of the industry is thus described in detail so that comparisons can be made with the other Middle Stone Age stages and the uses for the various tools considered.[1]

Stone artifacts occur in these layers in far greater numbers than in the other MSA occupational layers (see tables 6.1 to 6.6). To some extent, if not wholly, this is because of the nature of the industry. It would be misleading to call it microlithic, although some of the pieces would certainly fit this description, but it is an industry based on the production of small flake-blades and the delicate trimming of many of them into a series of specialized forms. Some of the flake-blade manufacture was done on the spot, for it is possible to rejoin occasional ones found close together, and the small flakes or spalls resulting from the secondary working litter the site. It is the latter which so increase the yield of artifacts. If weight were taken as a comparison, there would be little difference in the yield of the other MSA and the Howieson's Poort material per equal area.

The information given by the Initial Cutting made in 1967

1. The standard terminology of the South African Stone Age places the Howieson's Poort Industry within the Middle Stone Age. In view of the inadmissibility of the use of MSA *variants* (e.g., Mossel Bay, Pietersburg, Stillbay, etc.) by general consensus of those workers currently engaged in this area of research and in view of the lack of adequate excavated data covering these so-called variants (Klein 1970; Sampson 1972, 1974; and others), some term is required to described the industries which are so distinct typologically from the Howieson's Poort Industry. For the purpose of this report, we have preferred to use the stages MSA I–IV, based on stratigraphy, to reinforce this distinction. This does not necessarily imply any temporal considerations. Thus, when we refer to "MSA stages," we mean the industrial tradition typified by the production of flake-blades, worked points, and other tools, as described in the previous chapter, as opposed to the semimicrolithic Howieson's Poort Industry described in this chapter.

determined the method used for the main excavation of these layers in the following season. The area to be dug was divided into square meters, and each one was excavated and recorded separately so that a horizontal control could be maintained of the distribution of all the material found in them—artifacts, bone fragments, shell, charcoal—a technique often referred to as "transect excavation" (fig. 6.1). Arbitrary divisions in the vertical sequence were made at 15–20 cm vertical intervals along the bedding planes of the deposits. These were sloping fairly steeply in two directions and were not of uniform thickness, so that the thickness of each square meter which was dug would vary. No disturbances, marked irregularities, or marked structures existed, so the thicknesses never varied by more than a few centimeters, as can be seen by referring to the sections drawn at right angles to each other (figs. 3.8, 3.9). The three layers originally dug in the Initial Cutting were subdivided into twelve in view of the richness of the occupation. For this reason the material used for description of the industry below is all from the transect excavation: that from the Initial Cutting is recorded in table 7.2 and contains nothing to alter or add to the results.

Between 3,000 and 4,000 artifacts were commonly found in each square meter. This represents the accumulation in a phase of occupation, of course, and not a particular point in time. Evidence for material which would all relate to occupation at any one brief time might be obtained by skimming across the level of one bedding plane, thus exposing a surface as it existed at one stage in the accumulation of deposits beneath the shelter. The division between each vertical layer did just this, but it does not mean that all of the material on it belongs to that very period: some will, but the remainder will be a mixture from the underlying (immediately preceding) occupation and that left by the next one. Stratigraphy can do nothing to unravel this, unless there should be only intermittent occupation with a continuous natural process of accumulation to seal layers in its absence. Such microstratigraphy was not feasible in view of obvious intense occupation of the site.

Deposits close to vertical rock faces are notorious for their disturbed state, and those beneath Shelter 1A were no exception. Animal burrows could be plainly discerned in places, and the remains of rodents were plentiful. Constant disturbance, and some of this may have been human, had reduced some of the layers close to the wall to a homogeneous whole. This was especially noticeable at the rear of the shelter, i.e., the NW face. Where such confused deposits were met in a square meter they were treated separately, being recorded with a "plus"

Table 6.1. Howieson's Poort Industry—Cores and Core Preparation and Rejuvenation Flakes of Local Quartzite from Shelter 1A

	Layer 10	11	12	13	14	15	16	17	18	19	20	21
Single platform	2	1	2			1	3	9	8	6	10	2
Double platform	18	20	10	1	2		1	6	6	10	12	6
Irregular and/or undeveloped	15	9	9	9	2	4	6	26	5	11	27	5
Small (3.5–5 cm max. diam.)	11	4	9	4	3	1	4	8	3	11	4	4
Micro (5 cm max. diam.)	1	1		1	8			3	2	4	3	2
Rejuvenators	12	21	7	1			17	66	16	30	15	6
Choppers				1								1
Choppers resembling handaxes			2							1		
Others								1				
	59	56	39	18	15	6	34	118	42	71	72	24

TOTALS:

Cores = 363
Rejuvenators = 191

suffix to the layer number, and the material is not included in the analyses below. They did not, however, produce anything which would have been out of place in the undisturbed layers. In one instance a square meter produced so much material that it was thought expedient to subdivide the layer, so the material from one square meter in layers 15 and 16 is recorded separately.

Layers 10 to 12 represent eight square meters, and all those below, six square meters. The tables are based on actual numbers of artifacts recovered and not percentages.

Klasies River Mouth   Shelter 1A

Numbering of transects

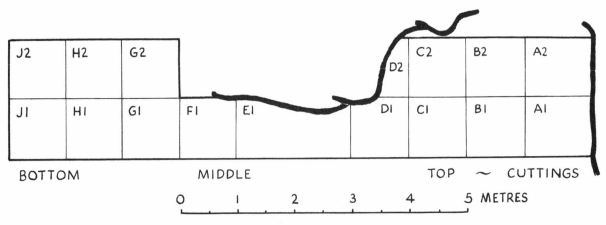

Fig. 6.1. Shelter 1A—numbering of transects.

Table 6.2. Howieson's Poort Industry—Cores and Core Preparation and Rejuvenation Flakes of Nonlocal Rock from Shelter 1A

	Layer											
	10	11	12	13	14	15	16	17	18	19	20	21
Fine silcrete												
Small			1			2	6	6	5	1	2	1
Micro	2	1	1		7	6	9	48	5	4	62	
Rejuvenators						2	5	18		2	3	
Coarse silcrete												
Small	2		3						3	2		
Micro		3	3	6	3	1	1		1	4	2	
Rejuvenators									1			
Indurated shale												
Small	1	1	1			1	3	2				1
Micro	2	2			8	4	16	11				
Rejuvenators	3						3	1				
Quartz												
Small	28	3	7	37	101	3		2	7	1	8	1
Micro		5	2	8			3	9	2	8	13	
Chalcedony												
Small					1							
Micro	3	2			1			1				
Rejuvenators								1				
Others												
Small			2									
	41	19	18	51	121	19	58	97	24	22	90	3

TOTALS:

Cores = 524
Rejuvenators = 39

The horizontal plotting of the different classes of stone artifacts by square meters per layer is disappointing because the mass of material appears to have overwhelmed any possible patterns of distribution. There is an even scattering of all classes over the squares, and for this reason such distribution plans are not included in this report. The information, if required, can be obtained from the site record books held at the South African Museum, Cape Town. The exposure of a larger area might warrant such treatment.

As with the MSA stages, the material is dealt with by artifact classes per layer.

Cores

The main concern of this industry was the production of small, thin flakes and flake-blades, which could either be further worked into specialized forms or used as they were. Even the finer-grained varieties of the local quartzite were not very satisfactory as raw material, for, although the skill of the knappers allowed them to make such flakes and flake-blades from it, the rock was so brittle that they would break across under quite light pressure. Denser, more crystalline rocks such as silcrete and indurated shale were clearly much more satisfactory, being relatively easier to flake and stronger. The difficulty would be to find such rocks. At the present time no beach pebbles are to be found (save of the local quartzite), and a cursory examination of the local riverbeds and plateaus in the vicinity failed to yield any. In most cases smallish pebbles have been used and a source nearer the mountains seems likely. Rock-hunting forays may have been organized, or roaming hunters may have picked them up whenever they saw them. The source of these finer-grained nonlocal rocks was obviously a limited one, and the stone industry had to resort to the local quartzite in spite of its inferiority. The preference for the finer-grained material is

Table 6.3. Howieson's Poort Industry—Flake-Blades and Segments of Nonlocal Rock from Shelter 1A

| | Layer | | | | | | | | | | | | |
	10	11	12	13	14	15	16	17	18	19	20	21	Totals
Fine silcrete													
Flake-blades	11	32	4		20	114	192	336	36	20	122		889
Segments	5	2				50	148	455	111	24	130		925
Coarse silcrete													
Flake-blades	12	10	13		20	3	2	2	23	35	3	7	130
Segments	4	2	2		1			1	24	48	4	6	92
Indurated shale													
Flake-blades	4		6	4	7	41	72	58					192
Segments							18						18
Quartz (incl. crystal and other rocks													
Flake-blades	2			2	8		6	4		9	4		35
Segments							4	1		1	8		14

TOTALS:
Flake-blades = 1,246
Segments = 1,049

shown in the total number of cores: 366 of local quartzite and 524 of nonlocal rock. The total numbers of flakes and flake-blades are not in this proportion, for there are many more of the local quartzite. This is not surprising when the size of the raw material is taken into account: the massive beach boulders of local quartzite would yield many times more flakes than the small pebbles of nonlocal rock. The proportion would probably have been very much higher but for the practice of doing the primary splitting and flaking on the beach itself. In contrast, the knapping of the pebbles of finer-grained rock appears to have been done entirely on the living sites, as outer flakes of these rocks are commonly found.

At certain levels there is a clear preference for particular types of fine-grained rock; in fact, the varying proportions of each type throughout the whole sequence (layers 10 to 21) must reflect some changing aspect of the economy, whether it was a change of hunting areas, the discovery of a rich source of one type of useful rock, or an industrial demand to satisfy some new tool requirement. If future work can ever locate the sources of these rocks, it might give significant information on the wanderings or even migrations of these people.

The main nonlocal rock types used were fine and coarse silcretes, indurated shale, chalcedony, and quartz. The cores and other artifacts are listed separately in the tables so that comparisons can be made between the rock types used in each level.

Quartz occurs in fairly high proportion throughout the whole sequence, although it becomes more common in the upper levels to a point of dominance over all other nonlocal rocks used. The quartz used was either of the type found in

veins, as in the local quartzite cliffs, or in its pure crystal state. The latter is rare, although there are a few cores of this material from which glasslike flakes have been struck. A few unstruck complete crystals 3–5 cm long were also found. No such crystals were ever seen along the cliffs in the vicinity of the site, and so a nonlocal origin is likely. The normal vein quartz is a most intractable rock, and its common use is at first consideration surprising, yet is must have satisfied some requirement. Methodical knapping techniques were hardly possible with the quartz, and small pieces appear to have been hammered until they broke into numerous splinters and fragments, a few of which might fit the precise definition of flakes. "Shatterpieces" is really a better description; yet many of these pieces, in spite of their irregularity, had dangerous, razor-sharp edges, much keener than the edges of flakes of local quartzite, and it is this property which must have been favored. Occasionally, a more tractable piece of quartz or a larger crystal would allow some small flake-blades to be removed from it.

The *silcrete* used varies from a pale, coarse, granular variety to a fine-grained red or gray siliceous rock. The latter was greatly favored and in layers 16 and 17 was used in some abundance. It allowed delicate control of the flaking of the cores, the majority of which are in the microcategory, i.e., less than 3.5 cm across at their greatest diameter. Yellow buff varieties of silcrete were also used and, rarely, a fine-grained bright red jasperlike form. The coarse silcrete did not flake so smoothly and was used in lesser quantities, but in most of the levels. It was virtually ignored in layers 16 and 17, when plenty of the superior fine-grained silcrete was available. Sometimes it has been difficult to decide whether a silcrete was a fine coarse

Table 6.4. HOWIESON'S POORT INDUSTRY—FLAKE-BLADES, SEGMENTS, AND POINTED FLAKE-BLADES OF LOCAL QUARTZITE FROM SHELTER 1A

	Layer											
	10	11	12	13	14	15	16	17	18	19	20	21
Flake-blades												
Length (cm)												
10 - 12	3								2		2	1
8 - 10	5	3	2	1	1		6	13	2	8	8	1
6 - 8	26	20	8	4	2	3	22	89	17	41	47	12
4 - 6	120	92	58	3	13	15	99	297	97	143	208	55
2 - 4	142	217	198	17	26	13	132	330	98	174	258	41
	296	332	266	25	42	31	259	731	214	368	522	109

TOTAL = 3,195

Segments												
Bulbous segments	290	256	215	22	34	21	280	630	282	455	458	92
Middle segments	173	122	102	12	13	19	211	637	167	268	215	66
Nonbulbous segments	90	124	115	13	3	5	103	166	101	124	152	44
	553	502	432	47	50	45	594	1433	550	847	825	202

TOTAL = 5,880

Pointed flake-blades	3	1	-	-	3	-	-	3	-	5	6	-

TOTAL = 21

or a coarse fine one, but generally these varieties form distinct rock types.

The *indurated shale* used was also of a very variable quality, ranging from a very rare jet black siliceous rock to a much softer, dull variety which is just indurated enough to flake with a conchoidal feature. Softer shale or slate that merely splits along its bedding or fracture planes has been relegated to the "other rocks" category. The most common type was a green to dark gray form which contained many imperfections but could sometimes be flaked cleanly into useful flake-blades.

The purest, most siliceous rock used was *chalcedony,* usually a dark brown to black translucent variety. There were only eight cores of this rock and a correspondingly small number of flakes and flake-blades. Presumably this rock was very difficult to find or it would have been used more frequently.

Other rocks constitute only two other cores in the whole Howieson's Poort sequence. The flakes show that quite a variety of other rocks were brought to the site, apparently as odd pebbles with the usual rocks or pieces of shale that were probably picked up along the beach. There are fragments of soft sandstone that could have been of little use for flaking, and flakes of a quartzite similar to the local cliffs and beach boulders but darker and finer-grained. There were also a few rare flakes of granite and chert.

The local quartzite has been used in very much the same way as in the MSA stages. Single platform cores are uncommon in the upper levels, and those in the lower ones are not well-formed examples. The more methodical double platform cores tend to be much smaller than their MSA counterparts, and many are less than 5 cm at their greatest diameter and so are classified in the tables as small cores. A few are smaller still and are classified as microcores. These small and double platform microcores are generally very flat and rectangular with flake-blades struck from both ends on one side only. The shape of the core has been maintained by careful dressing of the sides. Rejuvenation flakes have kept the striking platform at the correct angle or devoid of irregularities, and these flakes are included in the tables. This type of flat, rectangular double platform core is also found made of the nonlocal rocks, and examples of both types are shown in plates 38 and 39.

Another characteristic core form is a flat, discoidal type in the small core or microcore category, made of either local or

Table 6.5. HOWIESON'S POORT INDUSTRY—SIZES OF FLAKE-BLADES OF FINE SILCRETE AND INDURATED SHALE FROM SHELTER 1A

Fine silcrete Length (cm)	10	11	12	13	14	15	16	17	18	19	20	21
7 - 8								2				
6 - 7						1	1	5			2	
5 - 6						3	5	15			6	
4 - 5	1	3	2		3	5	15	39		4	16	
3 - 4	6	17	1		9	41	36	122	12	8	49	
2 - 3	3	10			8	44	99	132	19	6	48	
1 - 2	1	2	1			20	36	21	5	2	1	
	11	32	4		20	114	192	336	36	20	122	

TOTAL = 887

Indurated shale Length (cm)	14	17
6 - 7		3
5 - 6		2
4 - 5	2	7
3 - 4	3	25
2 - 3	2	21
	7	58

TOTAL = 65

Table 6.6. HOWIESON'S POORT INDUSTRY—FLAKES FROM SHELTER 1A

Layer	10	11	12	13	14	15	16	17	18	19	20	21	Total
Local quartzite	390	6264	3929	1178	1302	440	2506	11370	4786	7877	12324	1613	53979
Fine silcrete	207	266	45	7	161	349	1101	3297	338	113	1311	6	7201
Coarse silcrete	88	105	141	39	145	14	6	1	86	161	45	24	855
Indurated shale	67	45	86	36	82	76	547	494	23	9	5		1470
Quartz (incl. crystal)	1764	1625	2455	1017	4189	250	160	1080	1259	442	860	23	15124
Chalcedony	28	79	62	45	38	4	14	5	7	6	1		289
Other rocks	6	14	17	19	51	6	9	4	2	5	2	1	136

TOTAL = 79,054

nonlocal rocks. Small, delicate flakes have been struck from them in their final stages, but they were too broad to be described as flake-blades. Sometimes the scar of a somewhat large final flake makes them resemble miniature tortoise cores, which they may well be.

Most of the small cores and microcores of nonlocal rock have been worked down so small that any previous state at which they might have been typologically classified has been flaked away. Not surprisingly, every flake, however small and irregular, was worth removing from these pebbles. A few still retain the small parallel scars produced by the production of microblades, struck from carefully prepared or any convenient striking platform. The small size of the flakes or flake-blades, the diffused bulbs, and the negligible striking platforms all point to the use of some intermediate punch between the hammerstone and the cores. Nothing was found that was obviously made for this purpose, but any available bone, tooth, or pebble of suitable shape might have been utilized.

Although most of these nonlocal rock cores have been whittled down substantially, some idea of their former size and regularity can be obtained by examining the core rejuvenators of the same rock.

There are only two cores of local quartzite which appear to have been used as choppers, and there are three resembling handaxes (e.g., fig. 5.16, no. 1). One other core from layer 17 is crudely flaked into an axlike shape 8.7 × 4 cm, but this may also be fortuitous.

Flake-Blades

The flake-blades of the Howieson's Poort Industry at KRM vary considerably from those in the MSA stages above and below them. Apart from the far greater use of finer-grained nonlocal rocks, there are differences in the proportions of size ranges and also in subtleties of manufacture. As can be seen from table 6.4, the majority of the flake-blades made from the local quartzite are less than 6 cm long. Those made from nonlocal rocks are even smaller; e.g., as can be seen in table 6.5, the majority of the fine silcrete flake-blades are less than 4 cm in length. The same is true of the flake-blades made from other nonlocal rocks, but their much smaller numbers do not warrant tabulation.

The differences in manufacture are most evident in the forms of the striking platform. The heavy, wide, well-faceted platforms typical of the MSA flake-blades are uncommon in the local quartzite and nonexistent in the nonlocal rock. To consider the use of the local rock first, the platform was reduced in thickness by delicate trimming of the core edge before detachment of the flake-blade and the actual blow was aimed only a few millimeters behind it. The bulbs of percussion invariably are diffused, and this strongly suggests some intermediate punch of a softer material than the quartzite being struck. The quartzite varies so much in texture and hardness that there would be no difficulty in finding pebbles to satisfy this requirement. The use of a punch not only keeps the swelling of the bulbous end of the flake-blade to a minimum, but gives an accurate control over the exact point where the flake is to be detached. Platforms of flake-blades in the 6–8 cm range tend to be about 5 mm wide at their thickest point and are correspondingly less in the smaller ranges. Frequently (as shown in fig. 6.2, nos. 1, 2) the platform is plain. Sometimes it has been reduced so much that it has become negligible and there is a slightly battered aspect to it, probably caused by the trimming or by use of a punch. Not surprisingly, with the thin examples in particular, in the smaller flake-blades made of local quartzite the bulbous end is missing altogether. There tends to be a point

of weakness immediately below the slight swelling of the bulb, and the flake-blade snaps across it. Whether this happened as the flake-blade was struck or was a later, intentional removal of the offending irregularity cannot be shown. The latter presented no technical problem as the thin flake-blades can easily be snapped across between the fingers. In this connection it is interesting to note that in every layer, segments of broken flake-blades made of the local quartzite outnumber actual flake-blades found. Both accident and intent could account for this. Their very high numbers in comparison with the broken flake-blade segments in the MSA stages may only reflect the smaller, and thus weaker, sizes of the flake-blades. On the other hand, it may reflect a need for the neat, small rectangular middle segments. The high number of middle segments, especially in layers 16 and 17, supports this, but the proportions of bulbous, middle, and nonbulbous segments remain generally the same, i.e., a greater number of bulbous and a lesser number of nonbulbous ends in relation to middle segments.

Pointed flake-blades are rare; in fact, nearly all those found (only 21 from all the layers) may be fortuitous. It has already been noted that typical examples of single platform convergent cores are almost nonexistent, so it can be concluded that the tradition of making points in this fashion had little influence, if any, on the Howieson's Poort Industry at this site.

Flake-blades under 5 cm long could well qualify for the description of being microlithic, and the majority of those struck from fine-grained nonlocal rocks are in this category. Striking platforms, as seen either on the flake-blades themselves or on the bulbous segments of broken ones, are nearly all carefully reduced in thickness, often to a point of being negligible. Bulbs of percussion are slight, and, as seen with the smaller flake-blades made of local quartzite, there can be little doubt that a punch technique was used for their detachment. Similarly, there are large numbers of broken flake-blade segments in most of the layers. The same arguments as to whether these were accidental or intentional snappings apply as with those made of the local quartzite. It is perhaps even less easy to decide this with these finer-grained rocks for most of the segments are extremely small (i.e., less than 1 cm long) and narrow, and it has not always been easy to decide where the line is to be drawn between a small flake-blade with one end missing, and a segment. The former, on the criteria previously mentioned, must be at least twice as long as they are broad. However, very slender flake-blades more than four times as long as they are broad might well snap in the middle and be classified as two flake-blades. It is easy to think of several other objections to this and the more subjective elements of the classification, but it is felt that it does not detract seriously from the description of the industry.

Fine silcrete was most highly favored, probably on account of its quality and availability, and there are many more flake-blades and segments of this rock than all the other nonlocal rocks combined. However, it is not the dominant rock in the upper levels and, oddly, does not occur at all in the lowermost layer (layer 21). The matter of the varying proportions of the different types of nonlocal rocks has already been mentioned in the section on the cores. Coarse silcrete was used throughout the whole sequence, and, in spite of its coarseness, there are several thin, delicate flake-blades of this material. The great variety in the quality of the indurated shale has affected the degree of refinement of the flake-blades: those made of the lustrous black siliceous variety are thin and regular; those made of the soft, coarser variety are correspondingly thicker and less regular. The quartz used was rarely fine enough to allow any flake-blades to be struck at all, but an opaque, milky variety occurred in layer 19 and this was more satisfactory. A few

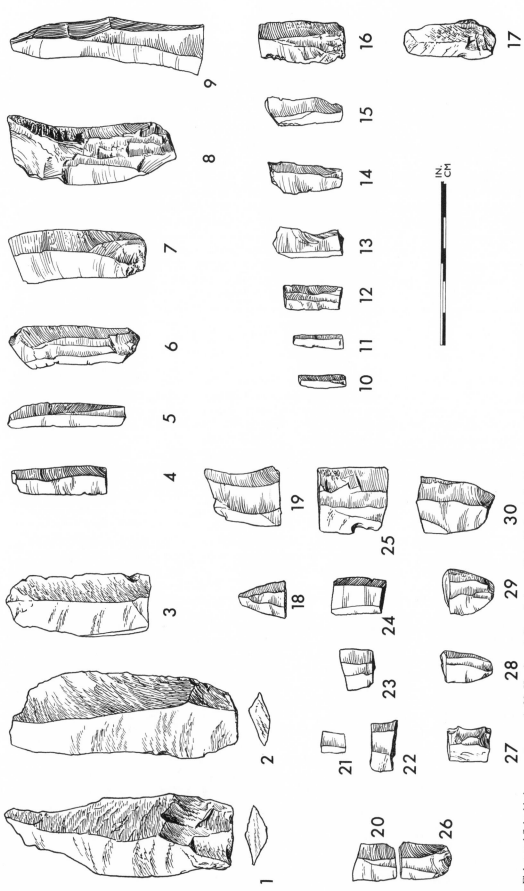

Fig. 6.2. Flakes and flake-blade segments: nos. 1–30. Howieson's Poort Industry. Flake-blades: 1–3 of local quartzite. The striking platforms on the larger ones (e.g., 1, 2) are often unprepared. The extreme bulbous end on many of the thinner ones (e.g., 3) are missing; they were either intentionally removed by snapping or accidentally broken off in the process of knapping. Nos. 4–16 of fine silcrete. The striking platforms are negligible or missing. Several show slight signs of secondary chipping or blunting. No. 17 of quartz. Segments: 18–30 all of fine silcrete. Nos. 18–19 nonbulbous ends; 20–25 middle segments; 26–30 bulbous ends. No. 20

fits 26. Small, thin flake-blades of fine silcrete, quartzite, and most other rocks are brittle, and many were doubtless reduced to segments by accident. However, it does seem almost certain that some were purposely snapped, probably for the neat middle segments. These could have been used as spear-barbs or other composite tools and weapons. Small notches at the point of snapping (e.g., between 20 and 26 and on 19 and 23) suggest a punch technique. All from 1A-15 and 16, transects C1 and C2.

flake-blades were successfully struck from quartz crystals. Chalcedony and other rocks account for very few flake-blades.

Flakes

A large proportion of the flakes found are very small, being less than 2 cm across their greatest width. Most of them, and the larger ones, are probably the waste products from flake-blade manufacture, but it could be misleading to refer to them as waste flakes. The chances are that many, especially of the nonlocal rocks, were selected for various uses which did not require any secondary trimming. Whatever uses the crescents, trapezes, and other small worked pieces were put to, it seems certain that many of the flakes, apart from the flake-blades, could have been used for similar functions. It seems reasonable to think that at least one of the uses was for tipping small spearheads or being inserted as side-barbs. There is adequate ethnographical and archeological evidence that stone barbs along the edges of spears may be nothing more than suitably sized and edged flakes. In fact, snapped pieces of shell, bone splinters, thorns, or even shark's teeth are known to have been used for this purpose from modern Polynesian parallels. If this were so at KRM, excavation was unable to detect it, but the large numbers of small flakes of fine-grained rock may have been produced with this purpose in mind. The use of the quartz strongly supports the suggestion that not all these flakes were necessarily just the waste products of flake-blade manufacture, for little could be done with this intractable rock other than to shatter it into numerous small pieces, from which it may well have been possible to select some useful ones. Correspondingly small flakes of the local quartzite would tend to be very brittle and, as barbs, very vulnerable to breaking off by accident once firmly inserted in any shaft.

The following data indicate the difference in mass between the flakes of local quartzite and nonlocal rocks, layers 15 and 16 serving as examples:

> 440 flakes of local quartzite
> from layer 15 —————— 2.60 kg
> 349 flakes of fine silcrete
> from layer 15 —————— 0.95 kg
> 2,506 flakes of local quartzite
> from layer 16 —————— 11.95 kg
> 1,101 flakes of fine silcrete
> from layer 16 —————— 1.90 kg

These may be compared with flakes of local quartzite from the MSA II layers beneath the Howieson's Poort:

> 761 flakes of local quartzite
> from layer 30 —————— 8.30 kg
> 932 flakes of local quartzite
> from layer 32 —————— 15.90 kg
> 485 flakes of local quartzite
> from layer 33 —————— 7.00 kg

The proportions of different types of nonlocal rocks used follows the same pattern for the cores and the flake-blades, as would be expected. The increase in quartz from layer 14 upward corresponds with a general decrease in the use of fine silcrete and other rocks. The explanation may well be that all the known sources of other fine-grained rocks in the district had been exhausted.

Crescents, Trapezes, and Allied Forms of Backed Flake-Blades
(Figures 6.3 and 6.4)

These specialized forms occur throughout all the layers attributed to the Howieson's Poort Industry at KRM. There were

878 complete examples (including those with just minor damage to tips) found during the 1968 season, and many others during the excavation of the Initial Cutting. As with the other classes of artifacts in this industry, only those found during the 1968 season have been used in tables 6.7 and 6.8, but some of those from the Initial Cutting have also been illustrated. The standard of workmanship is high, and these neat artifacts can be classified confidently into four main groups:

> crescents
> trapezes
> triangles
> obliquely blunted points

Crescents can be further subdivided into those where the blunting extends from one end to the other along the entire edge of the flake-blade (completely blunted) and those where the blunting is confined to the ends and part of the original thin edge of the flake-blade is left between them (partially blunted). The obliquely blunted points can also be subdivided according to whether the blunting, restricted to one end, forms an angle or an arc with the unblunted, thin edge of the flake-blade. Rarely, blunting does continue along the straight edge (fig. 6.3, no. 39). Trapezes, except in rare cases such as number 9 in figure 6.4, have the blunting restricted to each end. There were only seven examples of triangles.

The variation in the proportions of these forms in the various layers may have some traditional significance, particularly the almost total absence of trapezes from the upper layers (10 to 14) and their common occurrence in the lower ones. In all layers, completely blunted crescents dominate partially blunted ones, and obliquely blunted points forming an arc outnumber those blunted to form an angle. Alternatively, the types of rocks available may have been a determining factor in the preferred forms. There is, for instance, a distinct correlation between the numbers of trapezes and the use of fine silcrete. In some of the lower layers, greater use has been made of fine-grained nonlocal rocks than of the local quartzite.

Certain details occur on all forms and must reflect the uses to which they were put. On several of the unblunted edges small notches appear either close to one of the pointed ends or in the center of the edge. These notches appear to have been made in a variety of ways: some are clearly nibbled out by using a pointed fabricator, some look worn out by attrition, and some present a wide, nonconchoidal fracture as if a small, semicircular spall had been pinched out. In most cases these notches are associated with minute chippings and serrations of the edges that would appear to be the result of fairly heavy use and not secondary working. Various examples are illustrated on figure 6.3, numbers 21–27. Number 22 is a good example of the pinched-out type of notch, and numbers 24–26 have double notches. Small notches also sometimes occur on the center of the dorsal, blunted edge, at times opposite a notch on the other edge (e.g., nos. 21, 22, 24, 26).

Another significant detail is that several of the crescents, trapezes, or obliquely blunted points have a delicate, beaked end (e.g., fig. 6.3, nos. 1, 3, 21, 27, 42; fig. 6.4, nos. 1, 4, 8, 31, 32, 37, 41, 44). The other end is generally plainly curved or straight, and double-beaked crescents or trapezes (such as fig. 6.3, no. 24) are rare. This feature may or may not be combined with the notches mentioned above.

At least one piece, an obliquely blunted point (arc) from layer 11, is slightly polished, presumably by use at one end. The edges of the trapeze (fig. 6.4, no. 41) are also ground very smooth, but so are all the flake-bed facets so it is much more likely that this one was left for a while on the beach and became

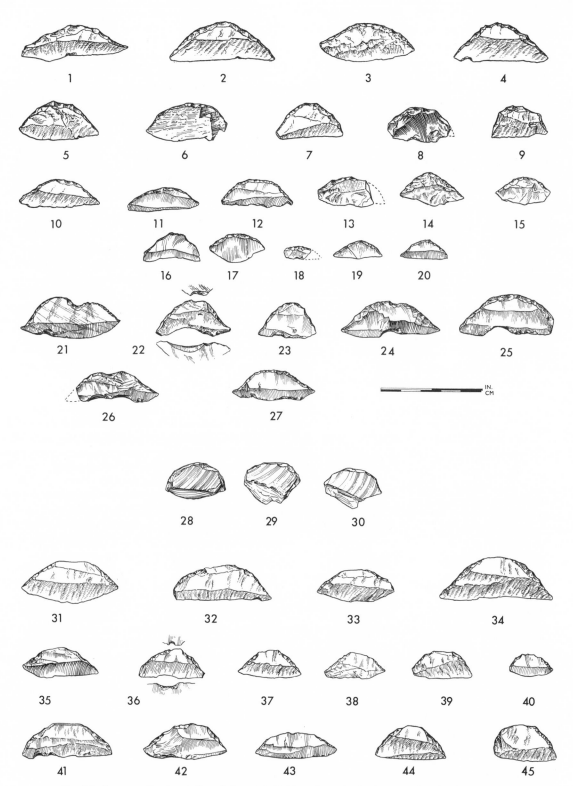

FIG. 6.3. Crescents. Howieson's Poort Industry. 1–30: blunted completely along one edge. 31–45: blunted only at both ends. Those made of other rocks or materials than the local quartzite are 12, 17–20, 22, 24–27, 35, 36, 40–43: fine silcrete; 3, 9: coarse silcrete; 6, 16, 21: indurated shale; 15, 38: quartz; 13, 14: quartz crystal; 8, 23: chalcedony; 11: chert; 28–30: shell. Several of the crescents have notches or signs of use along the unblunted edge (especially 21–27) and sometimes a small notch in the middle of the blunted edge (e.g., nos. 21, 22, 24, 26, 36). The edges and facets of 41 are all considerably smoothed.

worn naturally. Another partially blunted crescent from layer 10 was found to have patches of shiny redeposited silica generally referred to as ''corn gloss.'' Almost identical tools with such gloss, in other contexts, have been recognized as component parts of sickles, and a similar use for some of the crescents and allied forms from KRM cannot be excluded. Such ''corn gloss'' was not seen on any other pieces, however, and this crescent remains unique. The precise use for the majority of these specialized forms can only be guessed: there is much to suggest that they formed barbs or tips of either spearheads or arrowheads or both, for in most cases there has been a concentration on producing an acute, strong point. Notches suggest

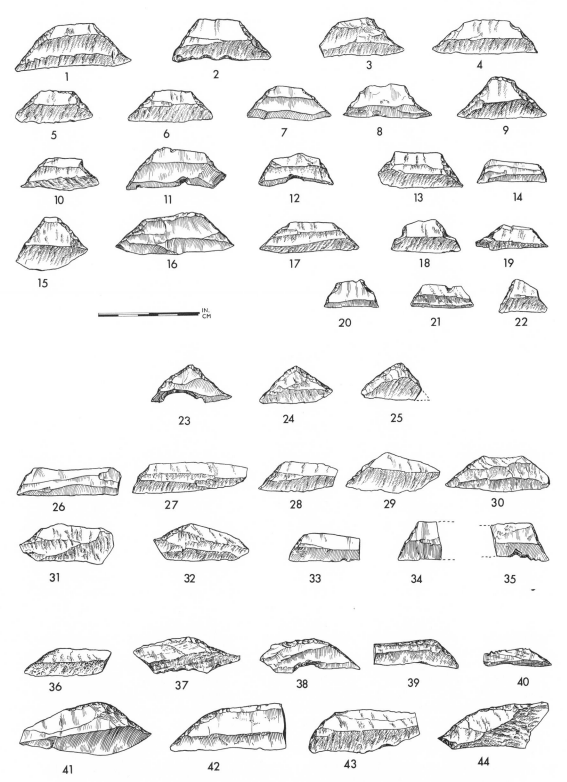

Fig. 6.4. Trapezes, triangles, and obliquely blunted points: nos. 1–44. Howieson's Poort Industry. Those made of rocks other than the local quartzite are 7, 8, 11, 12, 14, 16, 20, 23, 26, 33–35, 38, 39, 41, 42: fine silcrete; 30, 36: coarse silcrete; 21, 37, 40: indurated shale. 1–22: trapezes; 23–25: triangles; 26–35: obliquely blunted points to form an angle; 36–44: obliquely blunted points to form an arc. No. 21 is snapped across at one end and may not be complete. Nos. 34 and 35 could be broken trapezes. There are marks of heavy use or intentional blunting on the straight edge of 42. Notches and other signs of use occur in the same manner as on the crescents.

hafting and binding procedures. However, signs of fairly heavy use along the edges would not be expected on barbs or spearheads, and much remains to be explained.

Blunting across the thick end of a flake-blade resulted in a strong point, and the thickest end of a flake-blade is generally the bulbous end. Thus, one end of a crescent tends to be thicker and hence stronger than the other, and obliquely blunted points usually have the blunting across the bulbous end. However, it is obvious from an examination of these forms that the manner of blunting depended on the shape of the flake-blade, and advantage was taken of whatever happened to be the most suitable end. Blunting of small flake-blades is an easy task, with either

Table 6.7. Howieson's Poort Industry—Crescents, Trapezes, and Allied Forms from Shelter 1A

| | Layer | | | | | | | | | | | | |
	10	11	12	13	14	15	16	17	18	19	20	21	Totals
Crescents: completely blunted	64	55	48	21	14	11	4	23	20	43	92	9	394
Crescents: partially blunted	19	29	12	1	1			15	10	12	19	7	125
Trapezes	1					7	16	21	3	24	9	1	82
Triangles		3							2		1	1	7
Obliquely blunted points: forming angle	15			1	1	2	2	19	5	3	16	4	68
Obliquely blunted points: forming arc	24	45	43	4	5	7	5	25	14	10	18	2	202
Broken indeterminate	69	44	31	5	7	2	19	63	30	19	39	6	334
Unfinished or aberrant forms	3	2	2		1				3			4	15
Notched and snapped rejects	2	5	8	1						2			18
TOTAL	197	183	144	33	29	19	46	166	87	113	194	34	1245

TOTAL = 1,245

a small pebble or another thick flake as a fabricator. The danger is striking or pressing against the flake-blade too hard and causing it to snap across before it is finished. Many of the broken pieces probably represent such failures. Thick parts of the flake-blade by the actual bulb of percussion would be the most difficult parts to chip away, and it is fascinating to see that the KRM craftsmen occasionally tackled this problem in exactly the same way as their counterparts in the much more recent Upper Paleolithic and Mesolithic industries of Europe, that is, by the notch and snap technique. Eighteen examples of the reject parts of such a technique were found; four are perhaps fortuitous, but the remainder are convincing and the two shown (fig. 6.6, nos. 1, 2) are normal microburins, as the developed forms of these reject pieces are usually termed. In most cases, though, it was probably easier to nibble away with a pebble or fabricator, and it cannot be concluded that this notch and snap technique was an essential part of the industry.

Three crescents (fig. 6.3, nos. 28–30) are made of shell, probably limpet. They were all found within the same square meter in layer 11, and their artificial origin is substantiated by our failure to find others elsewhere in the deposits, although broken shell was profuse in almost every occupational horizon.

Worked Flakes and Flake-Blades (Figures 6.5 and 6.6)

These include all flakes and flake-blades with secondary working other than the crescents and allied forms already described. They do not constitute a large part of the industry but include some specialized forms (table 6.9). Heavy tools comprise scrapers, gravers, and some of the unspecialized pieces, but the majority are near-microlithic tools made on flakes or flake-blades of fine-grained nonlocal rocks, especially fine silcrete and indurated shale, and are less than 5 cm long. The classification of the latter is very subjective: secondary working is mainly in the form of microlithic blunting of the edges as with the crescents and trapezes, and many may well be aberrant forms more reasonably associated with them.

The following categories are defined for convenience of description:

scrapers
gravers
notched flakes
other microblunted flakes
outils écaillés
other specialized forms
unspecialized forms

Table 6.10 gives the numbers of these categories per layer and examples are shown in figures 6.5 and 6.6.

Scrapers (figure 6.5). Rounded end-scrapers constitute nearly all those found. The workmanship is neat and regular, and they form a well-specialized group. Of all the scrapers recovered, all but 7 of a total of 57 are made of quartzite. Nonlocal fine-grained rocks constitute the others:

fine silcrete	3
coarse silcrete	3
chert	1

Table 6.8. HOWIESON'S POORT INDUSTRY—TYPES OF ROCKS USED FOR CRESCENTS AND ALLIED FORMS FROM SHELTER 1A

	Layer											
	10	11	12	13	14	15	16	17	18	19	20	21
Local quartzite	170	161	117	22	11	7	4	59	48	87	87	31
Fine silcrete	9	3	6	1	1	9	27	78	20	5	88	
Coarse silcrete	13	3	4	1	7		1	3	10	17	11	2
Indurated shale	3	4	1	3	3	1	13	22	3	1		1
Quartz incl. quartz crystal	1	9	15	4	7	2		11	2	3	8	
Chalcedony	1	3	1	1			1	2	4			
Chert				1				1				
TOTALS of nonlocal rocks used	27	22	27	11	18	12	42	107	39	26	107	3
TOTALS of all rocks used	197	183	144	33	29	19	46	166	87	113	194	34

TOTAL = 1,245

Table 6.9. HOWIESON'S POORT INDUSTRY—WORKED FLAKES FROM SHELTER 1A

	Layer												
	10	11	12	13	14	15	16	17	18	19	20	21	Totals
Scrapers	4	4	4	1	1		3	3	2	1	15	20	58
Gravers	4	2	4					2		1	4	1	18
? Graver spall	1												1
Notched	6	4	6		2	7	32	87	17	12	39	2	214
Microblunted	3	3	3		1		10	6	8	3	2		39
Outils écaillés			1			1	6	5	1		8	1	23
Borers										1	1		2
Broken or unfinished bifacial points?								1			5		6
? Punch	1												1
Denticulated											2	2	4
With shallow flaking							1			2			3
Unspecialized	22	9	9	3	3	2	2	5	16	7	17	5	100
	41	22	26	5	7	10	54	109	44	27	93	31	469

TOTAL = 469

Table 6.10. Howieson's Poort Industry in Cave 2

	Layer 1	2	3	4	5
Cores of local quartzite					
Single platform		1	1	1	
Double platform					1
Irregular and/or undeveloped	1	4	3	9	1
Small or micro	1	6	1	2	7
Rejuvenators	2	8	32	23	16
Cores of nonlocal rock					
Fine silcrete					1
Coarse silcrete				1	1
Rejuvenator					1
Indurated shale			1	1	
Quartz		7	37	6	5
Flake-blades of local quartzite					
Length (cm)					
10 - 12		1			
8 - 10	1	3		18	4
6 - 8	8	28	97	46	22
4 - 6	27	91	148	160	69
2 - 4	30	111	261	4	50
Segments					
Bulbous	63	203	13	69	40
Middle	118	169	99	62	18
Nonbulbous	6	73	22	9	8
Pointed flake-blades	2				
Flake-blades and segments of nonlocal rock					
Fine silcrete					
Flake-blades		10		2	7
Segments				1	
Coarse silcrete					
Flake-blades		7	6	1	2
Segments		7	5	1	7
Indurated shale					
Flake-blades			4	2	2
Segments			1		
Quartz					
Flake-blades		13		2	

Nearly all the end-scrapers are of medium size, in the 3–6 cm category, mainly made on flake-blades, but also on broken flake-blade segments and on outer flakes. One is double-ended (fig. 6.5, no. 25), and there is one freak, diminutive "thumbnail" scraper (no. 22). Some of the edges are slightly smoothed as though by use while others are so sharp it is difficult to believe that they were ever used.

Only one has been classified as a hollow scraper. It could perhaps be included with the notched forms, but the concavity which has been chipped out is on a thick flake and nonmicrolithic in character.

Gravers (figure 6.5). Eighteen tools have been classified as gravers: a few may be suspect, but the remainder are well-made unequivocal examples of standard types, including some small ones of fine silcrete. Two of the latter, both shown (nos. 4, 5),

are simple multifaceted gravers, and one is worn fairly smooth on its chisel edge. There is a double-ended simple graver of local quartzite (no. 1), and the remainder are plain or backed right-angled gravers. One small, fine silcrete flake appears to be a spall from the sharpening of a graver.

Notched flakes (figure 6.6). This forms the largest category of worked flakes and includes flake-blades with one or more small notches worked out along their edges, to near-microlithic tools which might be classified as standard tool forms. The notching varies greatly in its size, position on the edge of the flake-blade, and general arrangement where the notching is multiple. A few recurring features are worthy of comment, and, whatever their purpose, it is significant that about three-quarters of them are made of nonlocal fine-grained rocks:

Table 6.10. Continued

	Layer				
	1	2	3	4	5
Crescents, trapezes, and allied forms					
Crescents	2		7	4	2
Trapezes	4		3	2	6
Broken indeterminate	4				
Rocks used					
Local quartzite	8		8	5	5
Fine silcrete	2				2
Coarse silcrete			1		1
Indurated shale			1	1	
Worked flakes					
Scrapers					
of local quartzite			2	4	2
of fine silcrete					1
of quartz			1		
Notched					
of local quartzite			1		
of indurated shale			1		
Unspecialized					
of local quartzite			3	5	2
of quartz			1		
Flakes					
Local quartzite	1643	2502	2084	1542	478
Fine silcrete					7
Coarse silcrete			4	9	18
Indurated shale		4	17	28	7
Quartz		539	34	61	49
Chalcedony		2			

KRM CAVE 2 ARTIFACT TOTALS	
Cores	39
Core preparation and rejuvenation flakes	81
Cores of nonlocal rock	60
Rejuvenators of nonlocal rock	1
Flake-blades	1,179
Segments	972
Flake-blades of nonlocal rock	58
Segments of nonlocal rock	22
Pointed flake-blades	2
Crescents, trapezes, and allied forms	34
Worked flakes of local quartzite	19
Worked flakes of nonlocal rock	4
Flakes of local quartzite	8,249
Flakes of nonlocal rock	779
TOTAL	11,499

fine silcrete	142
indurated shale	18
local quartzite	52
coarse silcrete	1
milky quartz	1
TOTAL	214

This suggests a delicate use for which a jagged edge of a coarse rock would be unsuitable. There is one group with opposed notches (e.g., fig. 6.6, nos. 33, 34). This could have facilitated binding in some hafting procedure, but why or how remains problematical. Number 28 is distinctive in having elongated concavities that produce a waisted effect, a type sometimes referred to as "strangulated scraper"; and there are a few others of these. Double, adjacent notches are common (e.g., nos. 9, 17). The most elaborate form is one where the notch is near one end of a small flake-blade and blunting of the opposite edge to a rough point has imparted a beaked or sickle shape to the finished tool. Where this is combined with multiple notching, somewhat grotesque forms have been produced (e.g., no. 9). At least 16 of the notched forms can be classified as sickle-

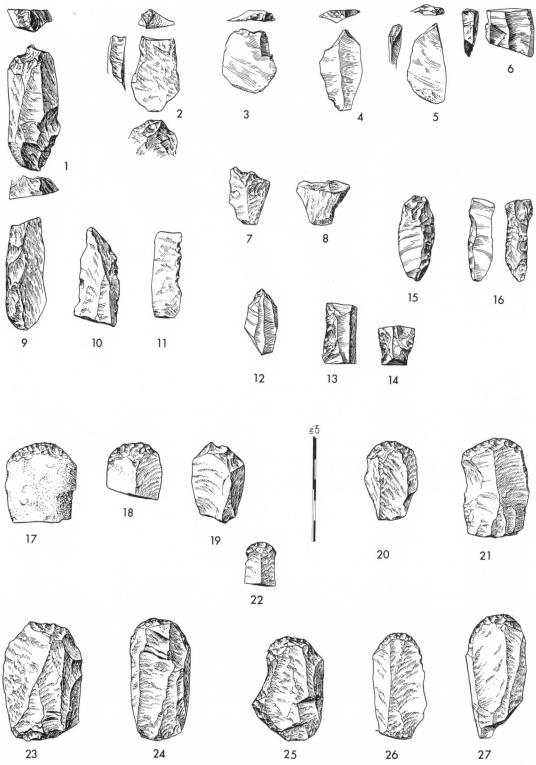

FIG. 6.5. Worked flakes: nos. 1–27. Howieson's Poort Industry.

Gravers. 1: double-ended simple graver. 2: plain right-angled graver with opposing end rounded. 3: backed right-angled graver. 4, 5: simple multifaceted gravers. The working edge of 5 is smoothed. 6: plain right-angled graver.

Scrapers. 7: small notched end-scraper. 17–27: various end-scrapers. No. 22 is unusually diminutive, and 25 is double-ended. Nos. 9, 15 have shallow flaking all along one edge. No. 15 may be an outil écaillé. No. 16 is a shallow-flaking sluglike tool. 13, 14: two thick middle segments steeply trimmed along one or both edges. Both found in layer 17 within the same square meter. 12: small borer. 8, 10, 11: unspecialized. All the tools are of local quartzite except 3–6 and 12–16, which are of fine silcrete.

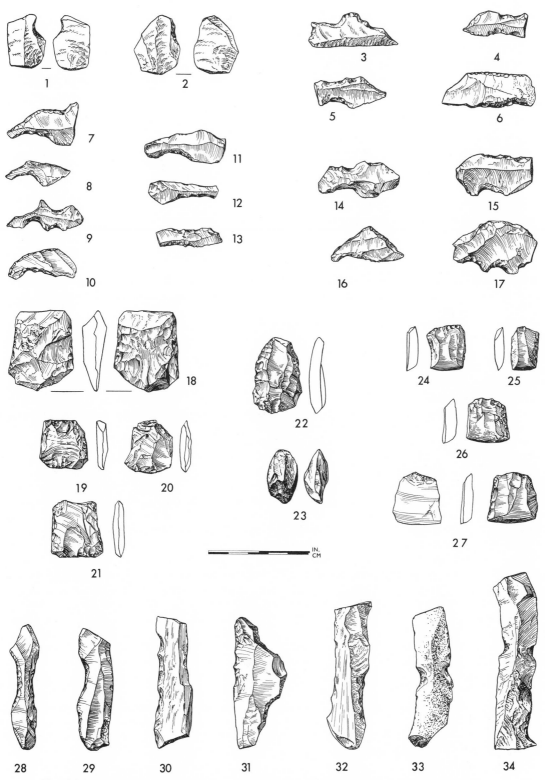

FIG. 6.6. Worked flakes and other pieces: nos. 1–34. Howieson's Poort Industry. 1, 2: microburins. 3: unfinished crescents. 4–17, 28–34: various notched forms. 18–27: outils écaillés of two main types: (i) Rectangular, flat, and bifacial (18–21). (ii) Unifacial except for one end opposed to a reverse hinge fracture (24–27). Nos. 1–3 of local quartzite; 4, 5, 7, 9, 10, 12–14, 16–29, 31, 33, 34 of fine silcrete; 6, 8, 11, 15, 30, 32 of indurated shale.

shaped, and of these, 10 are of fine silcrete and 4 of indurated shale.

Notching was noticed as a feature of several of the crescents, trapezes, and allied forms, and there is a marked similarity between these and some of the notched flake-blades, especially those described as sickle-shaped. Of those figured, numbers 7, 10, and 16 could perhaps be described as obliquely blunted points with notches near their tips, but they grade so insensibly into forms like number 11 that they possibly had different uses. Alternatively, some of them could be unfinished examples of the more standard forms of crescents and obliquely blunted points.

Other microblunted flakes. Several other flake-blades, mainly of fine-grained rocks, have the steep edge-blunting used to produce the crescents, trapezes, and allied forms, but it is of an unspecialized nature. The category is only included in order to distinguish these pieces from the remaining unspecialized worked flakes, where the secondary working is not of a microlithic nature.

Outils écaillés (figure 6.6). This highly specialized tool form is very characteristic of the Howieson's Poort Industry at KRM, being mainly confined to the lower levels (layers 16 to 21). There are 23 well-formed examples, although this number could be increased if all the flakes were included which bore similar marks of use along their edges. Those placed in this category have been unquestionably flaked to a particular shape for a special purpose. "Chisel-adzes" is a term which has been used to describe them, and the marks of use on their cutting edges certainly seem to be consistent with this suggested use. The majority resemble flat, near-rectangular microcores. Some may have been just microcores adapted for a secondary use, but others appear to have been carefully prepared as an intentional tool. Among the latter are two particular forms both of which exhibit a refined degree of delicate flaking exceeding anything else in the industry. All are made of the best quality fine silcrete, generally a reddish color. One form is flat, rectangular and bifacial (nos. 18–21) and the other is flat, rectangular and unifacial (nos. 24–27). The technique used to produce the unifacial form is not understood; apparently they are made on flake segments, and micro flake-blades have been removed from one end in such a way that one has plunged in to produce a smoothed, rounded end, viewed in profile. What remains of the platform is multifaceted and presents a sharp edge against the flake-beds. How the plunging flake was controlled is not understood, nor why it was done at all.

Unspecialized forms (figure 6.5, numbers 8–11). These call for little comment. They are mostly flakes or flake-blades of local quartzite with a little secondary working along one or more edges:

local quartzite	70
fine silcrete	21
coarse silcrete	7
indurated shale	5
quartz	1

There are two flakes from layers 11 and 18 with slight bifacial working, and one of fine silcrete from layer 16 with a smoothed edge.

Other specialized forms (figures 6.5, 6.6, and 6.7). A few other tools merit discussion, although their small numbers do not justify their classification as types.

Borers. Two small flakes worked to a point at one end can be described as borers, from layers 19 and 20. The general absence of this form of tool in such a specialized industry suggests that some of the more pointed crescents or other microlithic pieces may have been used as borers.

Punch. The battered end of a small, picklike bifacially worked piece from layer 10 appears to have been a punch (fig. 6.5, no. 23).

Denticulated. This form, so common in the MSA stages, was virtually absent. Apart from crude, serrated pieces placed in the unspecialized category, only four small, truly denticulated tools were found, in layers 20 and 21. A few of the end-scrapers described had denticulated edges.

Shallow flaking. Signs of this were rare, and there only two examples of flake-blades with shallow flaking along one edge, both from layer 19. An unusual slug-shaped form (fig. 6.6, no. 16) comes from layer 16, with shallow flaking along one bifacially worked edge.

Worked unifacial or bifacial points. There is a complete absence of the typical small triangular unifacial or bifacial points which are characteristic of the Howieson's Poort Industry at the type site. The most likely evidence that these tools were made at KRM is one broken piece from layer 20, the pointed end of a flake of fine, dark red silcrete, slightly worked bifacially along its edges (fig. 6.7, no. 3). The point is actually at the bulbous end. This may be a bifacial point broken in manufacture. A couple of bifacial pieces of quartzite and fine silcrete (fig. 6.7, no. 1) from the same layer may be crude bifacial points, but could equally be unfinished outils écaillés, although one is made of local quartzite. Also from layer 20 comes a quartzite flake-blade obliquely worked across to form a point and a small pointed flake-blade with some very slight bifacial working along one edge (fig. 6.7, no. 5). Another pointed flake-blade with the platform removed by neat bifacial flaking comes from layer 17 (fig. 6.7, no. 6). It remains the only definite worked point in the Howieson's Poort layers that has good reason to be classed as a spearhead, but its resemblance to the worked points from the MSA II layers makes it very possible that it has been derived from these earlier levels. Similarly, a large unifacial point (fig. 6.7, no. 7) found on the surface of the eroded Howieson's Poort levels in Cave 2 may also derive from MSA levels. One well-made but broken bifacial point (fig. 6.7, no. 4) of indurated shale was found in Cave 2, but unfortunately it was cemented to deposits remaining on the cave wall a meter or so above the surface of the Howieson's Poort levels. The only other possible indication of the manufacture of such points is the slightly bifacially worked pieces from layers 11 and 18 already mentioned in the comments on unspecialized worked flakes.

Unless there is some unusual horizontal distribution, which seems most unlikely in the large numbers of actual surfaces exposed, it can be concluded that small bifacial or unifacial points were very rare or unknown to the makers of the Howieson's Poort Industry at KRM.

Miscellaneous Finds

Apart from the pieces of ocher and ostrich egg shell which are considered separately below, a few other objects were found in the occupational layers that have some bearing on the activities of the occupants at this time. Of similar significance is the absence of certain types of artifacts, for example, the total absence of querns or any large slabs of rock worn smooth from any grinding process, and of any pebbles with ground facets.

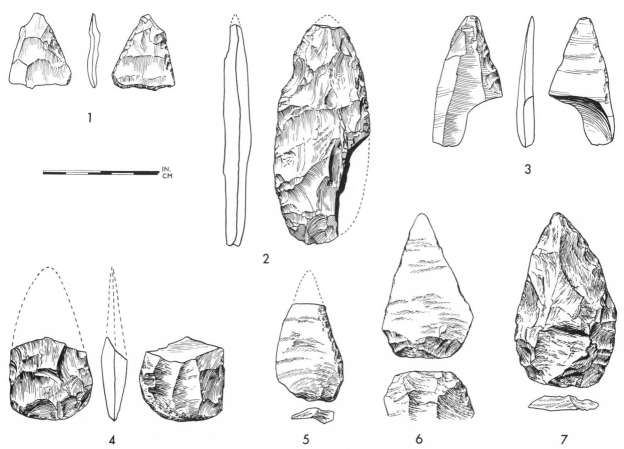

FIG. 6.7. Bifacial and other points: nos. 1–7. The absence of bifacial and small triangular points from the Howieson's Poort Industry at KRM is puzzling, when the industry is so similar in almost every respect to that at the type site. These points may, of course, be absent only from the particular part of the site examined. Those shown include all the artifacts which may belong to this category. Nos. 1, 3, 5 are all from close to the bottom of the Howieson's Poort occupation beneath Shelter 1A. Nos. 1 and 3 are of fine red silcrete, and 3 qualifies best as a possible broken unfinished point. No. 1 is more in the category of an outil écaillé but may be an unfinished small bifacial point. No. 5 is of local quartzite, with one edge blunted and bruised from both sides. No. 6 is a pointed flake-blade of local quartzite with the platform entirely removed from both sides. It is a typical MSA point and may well be derived from earlier MSA II levels, although it was found well up in the Howieson's Poort levels.

2: The only example, nearly complete, of a Stillbay Point, made of fine, gray silcrete. Unfortunately, this was not found in any of the stratified levels, but on the surface of the present scree slope below Shelter 1A. Assuming that its position is genuine and it is not a collector's throw-out, then its distance down the scree slope indicates that it could not have been derived from any layers prior to about layer 30, i.e., the upper part of MSA II.

4: The butt-end of a bifacial point made of black, indurated shale. From the west wall of Cave 2, cemented against the wall about a meter above the present line of truncation of the occupational deposits. Cemented material against this wall indicated the former existence of deposits at this height. The broken point thus appears to have come from one of the upper Howieson's Poort levels.

7: An elegant unifacial point of local quartzite found on the present floor of Cave 2 and thus apparently eroded from Howieson's Poort levels.

The only indication that any rock was brought to the occupational site for purposes other than knapping was the discovery in layer 19 of four pieces of tabular quartzite between 10 and 20 cm long. None was smoothed, but one is battered along one edge apparently in some effort to make it more regular, and bears faint traces of what may be red pigment. All four pieces were found close together in the same square meter.

A pebble in layer 12 is battered on its edges and also has slightly pecked hollows on both faces. Nothing else was found of this nature, although five pebble hammerstones were noted.

In every level were a few quartz or quartzite pebbles about 1–2 cm in diameter. They showed no signs of any use or particular concentration, and it seems most probable that they were brought to the site accidentally, yet these were not noted in the MSA layers.

Cave 2

The position of the deposits in Cave 2 in relation to the rest of the KRM sequence has already been considered in the section on the archeological stratigraphy of the site (chap. 3). It was seen that this cave, with its mouth hanging some 14 m above the surface on which the first MSA people lived, remained inaccessible until occupational rubbish had accumulated to such an extent below it that the floor of the cave and the top of the deposits were the same. Entrance was then easy, and the first occupation of the cave probably dates back to this time. Deposits appear to have continued accumulating until the cave mouth was almost blocked. Subsequent erosion once again rendered the cave inaccessible save by a precarious climb. The deposits along the drip-line by the cave mouth have become cemented into a hard breccia, but inside the cave toward the rear they remain unconsolidated. Residual deposits adhering to the rock wall between Cave 2 and Shelter 1A, as indicated in the composite section (fig. 3.1), suggest that it was layer 27 which first reached the height of the cave floor, during the MSA II stage. However, the artifacts scattered profusely on the surface of the truncated deposits inside Cave 2 were of Howieson's Poort type.

The position of the square meter test cutting inside Cave 2 is shown on the general plan (fig. 2.1). The sections of this cutting (fig. 3.13) showed the identical black carbonaceous soil layers with laminated ash hearths of the Howieson's Poort levels beneath Shelter 1A and produced the same industry, as shown in table 6.10.

Comparison of this assemblage with that from the Howieson's Poort levels beneath Shelter 1A (layers 10 to 21) enables it to be correlated with the lower part of that sequence, mainly on the presence of trapezes. However, there is no identical proportion of tool classes or rock types, and it is impossible to be certain exactly to which layer or layers this material from Cave 2 should be equated. The two most significant features apart from the trapezes are the low counts of fine silcrete artifacts throughout and the large amount of quartz in layer 2. There was a considerable decrease in the use of fine silcrete in layers 18 and 19 of Shelter 1A relative to the layers above and below them, and layer 18 was also rich in quartz. On these grounds it is likely that layers 1 to 5 of Cave 2 are contemporary with layers 18 to 19 of Shelter 1A.

7 Summary of and Conclusions on the MSA and Howieson's Poort Industries at KRM

Divisions have been made on the evidence of the stratigraphy, placing the long sequence of industries into eight phases: four stages of the MSA, one of Howieson's Poort, and three of the LSA. Their chronological order is clear, and details have been given of artifact classes within the various layers which constitute each phase. The purpose of this chapter is to consider the industrial changes throughout the MSA and Howieson's Poort sequences and what they may reflect of the economy and society of the people at KRM. The LSA is considered in chapter 9.

Dating is discussed separately in chapter 14, but it is obvious from the vast buildup of occupational deposits that a very long period is involved. Some 22 m of deposits are concerned, a thickness comparable to the tels of early urban civilization in the Near East and produced by a similar cause: a restricted area of occupation. In one case there was restriction by the town boundaries or defenses, in the other a limited area of adequate shelter. But there are numerous coastal caves in South Africa and elsewhere that were used by prehistoric hunters, yet with only a fraction of this thickness of occupational deposits. The greatest thickness recorded is the LSA midden (c. 10 m) at Matjes River (Louw 1960). At Mossel Bay (Goodwin and Malan 1935) there is c. 1 m of LSA and MSA deposits. Inland, the MSA layers of the Cave of Hearths in the Transvaal are only about 4 m thick (Mason 1962). So few MSA coastal sites have been excavated in South Africa that it is not possible to give even a rough estimate of the average thickness of the deposits, but nothing has been recorded to suggest anything greater than a quarter of the KRM accumulation. Other sites of comparable size may exist, especially along the Tzitzikama Coast, but at present KRM is unique. The reasons must be many, a combination of favorable factors some of which can be deduced from the results of the excavations, some of which can only be inferred or guessed. It is reasonable to assume that during the Upper Pleistocene period there would have been an equally variable environment to attract a rich faunal biomass. The Tzitzikama forests would have been more extensive, and there were numerous vleis in the open veld between the mountains and the sea, in addition to the rivers and the rocky coastline. It is stressed that KRM occupies a central position in this highly varied environment, unequaled elsewhere in the Eastern Cape Province. Whatever the causes of the large depositional sequence, the successful interaction between the populations and the environment had a positive influence on the stone industries.

To comprehend the sequence of stone industries it is necessary to know not only their relative order, which the stratigraphy has given, but also whether the occupation was continuous or intermittent. There are no sterile layers from the bottom of MSA I to the top of MSA III, but would desertion of the site for a long period, say 500 years, leave detectable evidence? Erosion, as now, may have been greater than any natural accumulation, so there would be no sterile deposit. Longer periods of desertion would almost certainly produce detectable truncation of earlier deposits, weathered sterile soils, or accumulations of scree or hill-wash. None of these things was seen. Sandier horizons, as immediately below the Howieson's Poort layers or throughout much of MSA III, may indicate less activity on the site. None is sterile, but a few centimeters of sand could well form in a century or so when the site was deserted and have many of the artifacts of the next occupation impressed into it. No amount of "microexcavation" is likely to detect this.

Although it seems most unlikely that the site was ever uninhabited for long periods, the laminated aspect of most of the MSA deposits accords better with some degree of oscillations of occupational intensity. Seasonal or periodical movement may be inferred by the multitude of thin ash, soil, and sand lenses found, particularly in the MSA I layers of Cave 1 and the MSA II layers of Shelter 1A. Conversely, the uniform soil of 1-15 suggests a long, unbroken occupation on the same spot. Similarly, the thick, black carbonaceous soils of the Howieson's Poort layers point to considerable activity in one place with ash layers indicating minor changes in hearth positions throughout. Broadly, the sequence can be regarded as a continuous one, from top to bottom, and it remains as a monument to the adaptive resourcefulness of Upper Pleistocene people, who appear to have come to terms with their environment in a manner far more successful than is usually imagined.

Perhaps the most significant fact is that, in 17 of the extant deposits, there was found a Middle Stone Age industry both at the very bottom and at the top, but the differences between these industries are far outweighed by the similarities. The proportions of artifact types throughout MSA I and II show no radical changes as can be seen in figure 7.1. However, the same diagram does emphasize some of the differences between these MSA stages and the more recent MSA IV. The other major discovery was the appearance of a morphologically distinct industry, identified as Howieson's Poort, wedged into the upper part of the sequence. It is critical for an understanding of South African prehistory to know whether this Howieson's Poort Industry represents the intrusion of people from outside the region with different cultural and possibly physical heri-

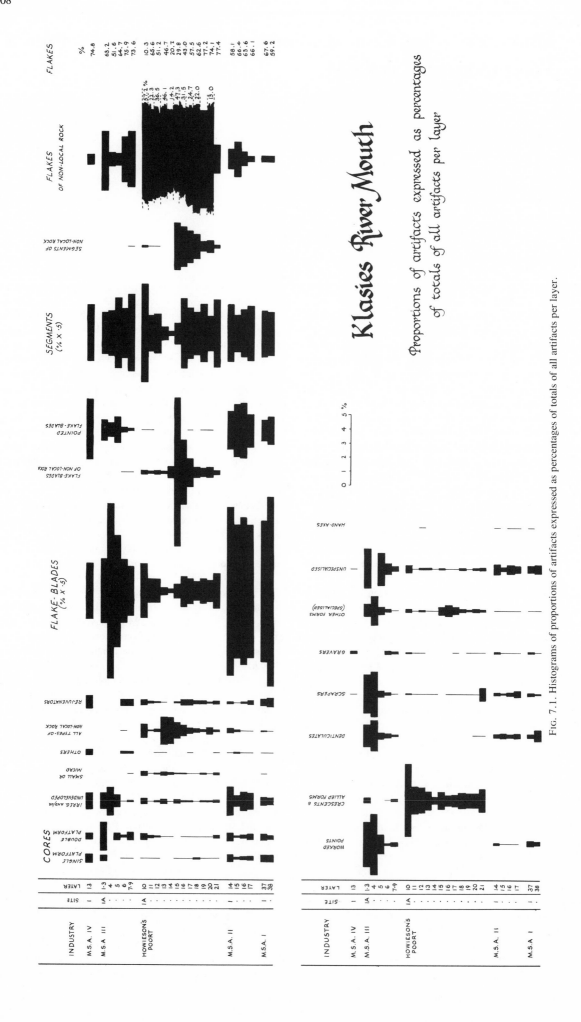

FIG. 7.1. Histograms of proportions of artifacts expressed as percentages of totals of all artifacts per layer.

tage, or the reaction of the indigenous population to a change of circumstances. The KRM evidence is strongly in favor of the former.

Tables 7.1 and 7.2 and figure 7.1 have been compiled to show in concise form much of the numerical data contained in detailed descriptions of the industries, while figure 7.2 illustrates the proportions of flake-blade segments found and nonlocal rocks used, expressed as percentages of total artifacts per layer in Cave 1. They are likewise subject to many of the vagaries and errors of subjective classification, apart from misleading figures produced by the inevitable variation of the total numbers of artifacts found in various layers (table 7.2). For example, the percentages calculated for most of the layers of the MSA III stage are mainly based on very small numbers and are correspondingly less reliable than those from all the layers below. Variation of activity at certain parts of the site at particular points in time will also have distorted the proportions of artifact types. Nevertheless, the tables express clearly all the observations made during study of the artifacts and it is reasonable to suppose that a few other things they show may also have some validity. Lengths of flake-blades are also diagrammatically compared in figure 7.3. The variations in the lengths of flake-blades through the different layers mainly reflect changing industrial traditions, but availability of raw material and the type of occupational deposit will also have affected them. For example, the small size of the flake-blades in the MSA IV industry may be accounted for by a lack of large quartzite cobbles, for at this time the sea had receded and dune sand covered the old beaches. Layer 14 of Cave 1 is a rubble deposit, whether it is a storm beach, a tumble layer, or both, whereas layer 15 beneath it is a slow buildup of fine occupational soil. This may explain the differences between these two layers of flake-blades within the 1–2 in. category.

The contrast of the Howieson's Poort Industry with the MSA industries above and below it is clearly shown in figure 7.11: some classes of artifacts (flake-blades and segments of nonlocal rock, crescents, and allied forms) are virtually restricted to the Howieson's Poort, and others are much varied in their proportions (cores of nonlocal rock, flake-blades, flakes of nonlocal rock, unspecialized worked flakes). Some classes are virtually absent from the Howieson's Poort (pointed flake-blades, worked points, denticulates). It is this overall contrast that forces the conclusion that this is an intrusive industry. If it were not so, more of the artifact classes would be expected to remain fairly constant through the MSA II and into the Howieson's Poort. The reversion to a similar Middle Stone Age stage, MSA III, does not show on the table so strikingly, but this is attributed to the fair quantity of Howieson's Poort material which was bound to become mixed up with the lower occupational layers of MSA III. All the tool forms peculiar to the Howieson's Poort disappear, with a few rare exceptions which can be explained as above. The change is so marked that, again, an intrusion is indicated.

If the MSA stages are considered alone, the table shows no significant differences in any of the artifact classes throughout the four phases recognized, with the exception of a marked increase in the proportion of worked points and other worked flakes in the upper part of MSA III. There is also an increase in the number of worked points and denticulates in MSA I and several other less marked differences throughout. These are more conveniently considered by taking the industries separately, and this is done below, with account also taken of differences other than numerical ones.

MSA I

This earliest stage of the MSA at KRM is characterized by large numbers of finely struck flake-blades of the local quartzite.

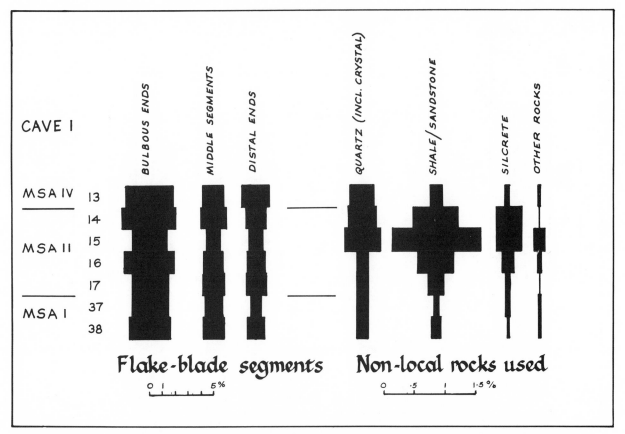

FIG. 7.2. Flake-blade segments and nonlocal rocks used in Cave 1, expressed as percentages of total numbers of artifacts per layer.

Table 7.1. Totals of Stone Artifacts Found at KRM Main Site (Caves 1 and 2, Shelters 1A and 1B)

	MSA IV	MSA III			HOWIESON'S POORT INDUSTRY					MSA II				MSA I		
	CAVE 1	SHELTER 1A			SHELTER 1A			CAVE 2	TOTAL	CAVE 1	SHELTER 1A		TOTAL	CAVE 1	SHELTER 1B	TOTAL
	Layer 13	1968	Initial Cutting	Total	1968	Layers 15–16, CAVE 1 only	Initial Cutting				1968	Initial Cutting				
Cores	56 ⊕	68	22	90 ⊕	887	24	187	99	1197 ⊕	1508	295	150	1953	358	50	408
Core prep. and rejuv.	19 ⊕	29	8	37 ⊕	230	9	15	82	336 ⊕	110	246	90	446	140	19	159
Flakes	1572	4030	789	4819	53979	1166	9654	8249	73048	39875	12853	12708	65346	18121	2313	20434
Flake-blades	170	186	391	577	3195	105	515	1179	4994	13410	2090	1057	16557	6372	909	7281
Segments	170	464	164	628	5880	127	593	972	7572	4549	1164	703	6416	1823	431	2254
Pointed flake-blades	91	15	13	28	21		11	2	34	1968	75	358	2401	479	58	537
Worked points		18	16	34	6				6 ⊕	55	42	31	128	112	30	142
Worked flakes	8 ⊕	84	26	110 ⊕	463	9	43	23	538 ⊕	802	121	68	991	390	63	453
Crescents and allied forms		8		8 ⊕	1245	13	82	34	1374 ⊕		6	6	12			
Handaxes										1			1	2		2
? Handaxes					1				1	3	1		4	1		1
Hammerstones										2			2			
Nonlocal rock: Flakes	15 *	206	40	246 *	25075	896	965	779	27715	843	191	127	1161 **	115	26	141 **
Flake-blades				96	1246	96		58	1400							
Segments				50	1049	50		22	1121							
TOTALS	2101			6577					119336				95418			31812

SUMMARY:

MSA IV Industry	2,101
MSA III Industry	6,577
Howieson's Poort Industry	119,336
MSA II Industry	95,418
MSA I Industry	31,812
GRAND TOTAL..........	255,244

⊕ including those made of nonlocal rock
* including flake-blades and segments
** including flake-blades

Table 7.2. Artifact Totals for Shelter 1A, Initial Cutting, Including Side Cutting A

(These totals are also included in the tables for artifacts of the MSA II stage)

| Layer as excavated --- | 1 | 2 | 3 | 4 | 5 | 6 | 7 | 8 | 9 | 10 | 11 | 12 | 13 | 14 | 15 | 16 | 17 | 18 | 19 | 20 |
as published, if different ---	---						7-9	10-12	13-16	17-21	22	23-24	25	26	27	28-29	30	31	32-33	34
Cores																				
Single platform								1	1			6	3	5	4	21	1		5	4
Double platform			2				13	1	1			4	3	6	7	8			7	9
Small or micro					2	4		22	16	18	5	5	3	1						
Others						1				4		8	3	3	9	11			2	11
Core prep. and rejuv.						2	6	13		15	4	3	3	1	10	14			42	13
Flakes	7	1	16	20	2	291	452	778	657	8219	625	3088	1257	458	1420	2425	70	74	1603	1754
Flake-blades	1		8	14	19	60	94	85	58	372	109	361	48	25	57	155	6	2	95	294
Pointed flake-blades			1		4	8	3	7	4		7	13	34	29	66	79	2	1	82	45
Flake-blade segments																				
Bulbous ends				2	3	32	36	27	16	218	53	128	12	5	11	24	3	2	42	77
Middle segments						12	28	16	11	197	40	116	8	4	3	31	1		11	28
Nonbulbous ends					3	12	36	13	9	86	18	52	6			5			6	17
Worked flakes																				
Points			3	2		5	7	7				26		1		1				3
Denticulates			1	2		1	1				1	8			1				3	
Scrapers			2	1	1	2			1	1	3	3		2	2					
Gravers																			2?	
Borers												1								
Unspecialized			2		3	9	1	7	8	15	3	13		4					9	10
Crescents										31	5	1								
Trapezes										12										
Quartz																				
Cores	3	2						12	32	7	11				1					
Flakes						2	9	50	245	140	43	5		1	1	5				4
Crescents, etc.								1	1		1									
Worked flakes										1										
Other nonlocal rock																				
Cores								11	20	27	1				1					1
Flakes			1		2	8	13	25	93	412	16	11		1		3	2		27	5
Crescents, etc.								1	3	16	2									
Worked flakes									4	15										
Red ocher							1													
TOTALS	11	3	36	41	39	449	699	1086	1180	9806	292	3854	1380	546	1593	2783	85	79	1936	2276

GRAND TOTAL.......... 28,074

Pointed flake-blades of similarly fine quality were also struck in fair quantity, and several were further fashioned into worked points of various forms. In addition, worked points were made on flake-blades or just flakes. Shallow flaking was used on some, and two were partly bifacial.

Many of the flake-blades and pointed flake-blades were thin and symmetrical, and a special technique was used for rounding and reducing the thickness of the striking platform. Before being struck from the core, the edge of the striking platform was delicately worked back until a critical flaking angle was reached and the stone bruised instead of chipped. The flake-blade was then struck from the core, probably with the use of an intermediate punch, close to its edge, so that only a little platform was left, with its edges battered by the preparatory process. Some further thinning of the platform may have been done after the flake-blade had been struck. Flake-blades with such battered striking platforms were found only rarely in later stages, more in MSA III than II, but only in MSA I was this technique commonly practiced. The flake-blades of the MSA industry found in Cave 5 were of similar good quality with battered striking platforms, and mainly on the basis of this criterion, they are thought to be of the same stage.

Cores from this stage reflect the systematic work, and well-developed single and double platform cores outnumber those which are irregular and/or undeveloped. Single platform cores predominated, and rejuvenation flakes were numerous (fig. 7.1).

Although about half the worked flakes were of unspecialized forms, denticulates and scrapers were often neat and symmetrical. Denticulates predominated markedly, and some were more regularly made than any seen in later stages. A few well-formed gravers were found and nonlocal rock was occasionally used for flakes.

MSA II

This stage extends over the longest period of occupation at KRM, possibly to be measured in tens of thousands of years. It is found within Cave 1 and beneath Shelter 1A, making a total depth of over 12 m. Beneath 1A the layers rest conformably on those of MSA I, but in Cave 1 there was some time interval between the two stages.

The main differences between this and the previous stage are the decline in the quality of the flake-blades, the rise in the number of pointed flake-blades, and a corresponding decrease in the number of worked points.

It was hoped that the sizes of flake-blades might give an indication of industrial trends. To some extent they do, but not in a very marked, convincing manner. However, there was a general, if slight and unsteady, decrease in flake-blade size between the beginning of MSA I and the end of MSA II (fig. 7.3). The numbers of flake-blades remained fairly constant throughout the whole of MSA II.

Worked flakes, generally of poor quality, were found in small numbers, with unspecialized forms predominating. Denticulates and scrapers were the commonest specialized forms, and occasional specimens were surprisingly neat and symmetrical. Gravers also occurred in small numbers. There was a slight increase in the use of nonlocal rock at the end of MSA II.

Corresponding to the decline in the quality of the flake-blades, there was a distinct rise during this stage in the number of irregular and/or undeveloped cores. There was no rise in single platform cores, in spite of the increased number of pointed flake-blades from such cores, and it may be that many of these single platform cores were whittled down to irregular ones.

Apart from the stratigraphical indications, the similarity of the industry in Cave 1 to that beneath the Howieson's Poort levels beneath Shelter 1A is so marked that it is concluded that they are the same. However, one cannot be sure which levels correspond exactly to each other, but a comparison of the flake-blade sizes (fig. 7.3) from the MSA II levels at both parts of the site suggests a correlation. It was concluded that 1-14 was a rubble layer produced by the fall of material from outside down the steep living slope beneath Shelter 1A and that for reasons of safety, if nothing else, occupation was confined to Shelter 1A. There are two main rubble layers at Shelter 1A itself, a major one immediately beneath the Howieson's Poort layers (layer 22), and a minor one 1.5 m below (layer 26). The histograms (fig. 7.3) for the flake-blade sizes of 1A-23 to 26 correspond well with that for 1-14. Those for 1A-22 demonstrate a marked increase in flake-blades of the smallest category, almost certainly due to intrusion of material from the layer above. It this is so, layers 27 to 32 probably extend over the same period as layers 15 to 17 in Cave 1.

Howieson's Poort Industry

The main differences between this industry and the underlying MSA I and II stages have been outlined. They are so radically different that it is more pertinent to consider the changes within the industry itself, as represented by the sequence through layers 10 to 21 beneath Shelter 1A.

Of course, there are features common to all stages of the industry; for example, there is a drastic reduction in both size and number of flake-blades of the local quartzite. Even when added to the totals of flake-blades of nonlocal rock, the proportions are less than half those in the earlier stages of the MSA. Flakes and segments of nonlocal rock show a corresponding marked increase. All this must reflect a change in the needs of the community, and a likely explanation is the adaptation of new hunting techniques.

The worked points and some of the pointed flake-blades from the MSA stages have been interpreted as spearheads. These weapons are missing from the Howieson's Poort Industry at KRM, and so it seems that the stone-tipped heavy spear had been discarded. The numerous semimicrolithic crescents, trapezes, and related forms present are considered to be their replacement, set into small slots along a wooden spearshaft to act as barbs or points. In the same manner, small flake-blades or micro–flake-blades, segments, or just flakes of nonlocal rock may have been selected from a stockpile and set as barbs into spearshafts or arrowheads, although there is no direct evidence that they used bows. Thin pieces of the local quartzite are extremely brittle whereas the nonlocal rocks such as silcrete, shale, and quartz are strong and sharper, and this must be the reason for their laborious search for these rocks. The concern with microlithic pieces most likely indicates the use of small spears. These could be thrown further and, if the barbs were tipped with poison, would increase their hunting success considerably. Arrows, also, would require very small tips and barbs, and it is difficult to believe that some of the very small pieces could have served any other use.

The crescents, trapezes, triangles, obliquely blunted points, and allied forms constitute such definite types that they presumably served different functions. Small notches, edge-chipping, or smoothing indicate use, possibly by hafting in some cases. An analysis of these types by layers has been

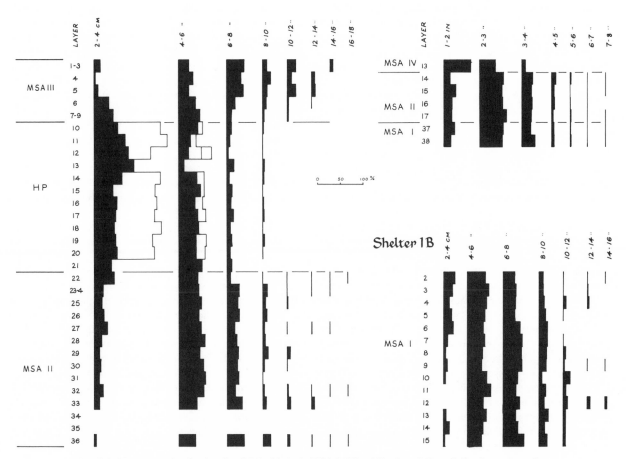

FIG. 7.3. Histograms showing lengths of flake-blades in MSA I–IV and Howieson's Poort Industries, expressed as percentages of totals of flake-blades per layer. Layers 34 and 35 beneath Shelter 1A have not been included, as the saturated nature of these layers prevented complete or satisfactory control over their excavation. It can be seen that throughout the period of the MSA I and II industries there was a slight trend toward diminution of flake-blade size. The very marked reduction of size within the Howieson's Poort Industry shows plainly and is in great contrast to the MSA II and III industries which enclose it. This is regarded as corroboration for the interpretation of the Howieson's Poort Industry as a separate industrial complex that was intrusive and did not evolve from the local MSA industries. The large number of small flake-blades in the lower levels of MSA III is almost certainly the effect of mixing of material derived from Howieson's Poort levels. A distinction has been made between the local quartzite and other nonlocal rocks used for flake-blades in the Howieson's Poort Industry, as it was such an important and essential part of it. The number of flake-blades of nonlocal rocks in the MSA industries is so small that they have been included with the quartzite. The measurements of flake-blades found in Cave 1 are in inches, as they were made prior to a decision to change to metric units in 1969 (see footnote to table 5.3).

made, and it shows that trapezes were restricted to layer 15 and below, with one exception from layer 10. Significantly, there are several changes in the proportions of various artifact classes at this point in the vertical sequence: flake-blades of local quartzite decrease, there is a sudden increase in flake-blades of nonlocal rock which rapidly dies out, and the snapping of flake-blades of nonlocal rock into segments virtually stops. There is also a marked decrease in notched flakes and outils écaillés above layer 15, and crescents become more common. These changes may be connected with the supply of fine silcrete, one of the most suitable fine-grained rocks for this type of industry and one of the most available types in the district, with the exception of quartz, which had limited uses. From layer 15 to the top of the Howieson's Poort sequence there is a marked drop in the use of silcrete and a corresponding rise in the use of quartz. Flake-blades and segments of local quartzite also increase. If there had been any stratigraphical evidence, it would have justified dividing the industry into two phases, above and below layer 15, but there is no sign of any break.

The worked flakes form an interesting aspect of this industry, suggesting various specialized activities. Gravers and scrapers were neatly made, generally on thin flake-blades of local quartzite, whereas notched forms and outils écaillés were invariably of silcrete or indurated shale. The diagram (fig. 7.1) is misleading in that very few worked flakes appear to exist in the industry, but this is because the large number of flakes of local and nonlocal rock has swamped the proportions. Scrapers were predominantly rounded end-scrapers. Denticulates were absent save for some in the lowermost layers, which could have been derived from earlier MSA layers.

Flake-blades were probably punched off cores: the striking platforms were reduced to a minimum, and the bulb was negligible. Cores were correspondingly systematic. Small cores or microcores of local quartzite appear to have been worked in the same manner, on a smaller scale, as those of fine-grained rock, and they were slightly more numerous in the upper part of the industry, possibly as a result of the same silcrete deficiency mentioned above. In figure 7.1 only small cores or microcores of local quartzite are shown in a separate column, whereas nearly all cores of nonlocal rock are in this size category. The increase in cores of nonlocal rock above layer 15 was due mainly to the working of quartz.

Segments of broken flake-blades occur throughout all layers of the MSA stages and also in the Howieson's Poort Industry. Invariably there are similar proportions between the various segments, with bulbous ones predominating and slightly more middle segments than nonbulbous ones. It is not possible to conclude whether these flake-blades had broken into segments as a result of accident or design, and our opinion is that most are the result of accident but some may have been deliberately broken, either to remove a clumsy bulb of percussion or a brittle, thin nonbulbous end, or to obtain a neat rectangular middle segment. Small middle segments of fine-grained non-local rock would certainly have made a spear more lethal if several were set in slots along one or opposite edges. Other composite tools could also have been made with them.

Flake-blades are just as likely to snap into two pieces, so the proportions between the three types of segments may not signify much. However, in layer 17 within the Howieson's Poort levels, where there were numerous segments of local quartzite, there were slightly more middle segments than bulbous ends (637:630). In the same layer there were more segments of fine silcrete than there were flake-blades of the same rock (455:336) although the proportions of the types of segments were not unusual (255 bulbous to 149 middle to 51 nonbulbous). It does appear, in this instance at least, that small flake-blades were being snapped with intention. There were similar high proportions of segments to flake-blades of nonlocal rock in the layers below, but those of local quartzite were not unusual.

The Howieson's Poort Industry found in the test section in Cave 2 is best related to the sequence beneath Shelter 1A by its contained crescents and allied forms and by the types of nonlocal rock used. Trapezes were present, but very little silcrete was used. Quartz was the predominant nonlocal rock used. The layers in the Shelter 1A sequence which best fit these proportions are layers 18 and 19.

MSA III

Sandier levels immediately above the Howieson's Poort Industry probably indicate less activity on the site; but none was sterile, and lines of soil or hearths prove some occupation during their formation. This MSA stage was very similar to MSA II. It contained all the same artifact classes with the addition of a few small, unifacial points that appear distinctive. The proportions in which the artifact classes occur cannot be used for comparison with the earlier stages with much confidence, for they are based on much smaller numbers. There are also included several features which recall the Howieson's Poort Industry: a few crescents and many more flakes of nonlocal rock than found in the earlier MSA stages. The crescents and a few other pieces considered distinctive of the Howieson's Poort occur, with one exception, in the lower layers and are thought to be most likely derived. However, the use of nonlocal rock may be part of the actual industry.

There appear to be more flake-blades in the larger size categories in the upper layers, whereas the greater number of smaller ones in the lower layers could also be caused by an admixture of earlier material.

Some of the worked flakes are more specialized than those from the earlier MSA stages, especially flake-blades that are steeply backed or worked all along one edge, which make efficient cutting knives. These occurred in all layers, and during the excavation of the Initial Cutting, one fine example was found in layer 9 lying on top of the uppermost Howieson's Poort level and beside a large, well-made worked point. Denticulates and scrapers are common but undistinctive, except for an unusual "thumbnail scraper" in Cave 1, layer 3. Apart from this piece, there was nothing else that might suggest intrusion of LSA material.

It does look as though there were signs of development and change in this stage, and it is unfortunate that 6 m of higher levels eroded away before there was any chance of examining them.

MSA IV

The reasons for placing this stage between MSA III and the LSA middens have been explained, the main one being that if so much sand had been blowing about earlier it would have left an obvious trace in the stratigraphy beneath Shelter 1A. It was suggested (chap. 3) that the sand containing this stage accumulated during a period when mobile sand was prevalent as a result of a low sea level. If this was the case, the KRM site may then have been several kilometers inland, overgrown, and subject to blowing sand, making it an unfavorable living site. This would explain the lack of hearths and occupational soils. The small quantities of stone artifacts, bone fragments, and shells accord with casual visits to the cave for shelter by people who lived elsewhere.

This stage is clearly related to the other MSA stages although there are slight differences. It did not contain anything significantly characteristic of the Howieson's Poort. Flake-blades were less common than in the earlier MSA stages, but there was an increase in the number of pointed flake-blades. However, the size proportions of both these categories were different, as figures 7.1 and 7.3 show. There were no flake-blades over 4 in. (10 cm) long, and most of the pointed flake-blades were unusually small. The size range is more typical of the Howieson's Poort flake-blades. There were few flake-blades of nonlocal rock, and worked flakes were rare, which might be expected if the site was not being used for habitation. Single platform cores slightly predominated over double platform ones, although irregular and/or undeveloped cores were commonest.

If industrial development reflects cultural evolution, it must be concluded that the first part, possibly half, of the long sequence represents a static society, even if a successful one. The arrival of the Howieson's Poort Industry suggests a new people with different traditions and a manner of life alien to the earlier occupants of the site, who disappear until the site was vacated by the intruders. The later MSA stages show minor differences which may be the result of some connection with the Howieson's Poort. It is interesting to speculate that the Howieson's Poort "intruders," despite their significantly different industry, successfully inhabited the same ecological niche for a period of intense occupation. Regrettably, no human remains were recovered from these layers. This sequence is considered in relation to other known Middle Stone Age and Howieson's Poort sites in South Africa in chapter 15.

8   Other Finds in the MSA and Howieson's Poort Industries

Evidence for the Use of Bone

The great majority of the bones from all levels were broken, and it would be surprising if some had not been broken with the intent of using one or more of the parts produced as tools. The identification of such intent is beset with difficulties because of all the other reasons bone can get smashed, and signs of use may easily be confused with natural decay, fracture, or the gnawing of carnivores and rodents (Singer 1959). Certain bones are obviously more useful than others for performing such functions as cutting, scraping, rasping, hammering, and pounding. An analysis of bones found on the site, and a search for types of fracture and possible signs of use do not reveal a pattern reflecting intentional or purposeful fracture. It would be difficult to recognize the occasional intentional fracture for marrow removal or use of splinters or fragments. The purpose here is to describe finds which may show that bone may have been regarded as a useful material from which tools could be made. We are concerned with identifying those bones which have been modified and shaped into specific tool forms, not fractured pieces which may have then been utilized, as at Kalkbank (Mason, Dart, and Kitching 1958).

All the many thousands of bones from the MSA levels were examined, and it can only be concluded that bone was not used as a raw material for tools in those industries. The nearest approach to the shaping of bones was two pieces of broken ribs with serrations cut down their edges (fig. 8.1, nos. 1, 2) and a small fragment with four thin lines scored across it parallel to each other (fig. 8.1, no. 3). These specimens are described below:

a) A small rib fragment with serrations cut along the edge. Both surfaces are striated with thin cut lines. It was found in Cave 1, West Cutting H, in layer 15+, i.e., the upper part of layer 15 apparently disturbed by the accumulation of the rubble layer 14. (Catalog no. 27069.)

b) Part of a rib, unfortunately broken in the course of excavation and incomplete, with similar serration of the edges as on no. 27069. One part, as shown, also has similar striations. The position of the two pieces in relation to each other as shown in the figure is not definite. It came from the saturated layer 36 beneath Shelter 1A and is partly mineralized. (Catalog nos. 31819, 31820.) This artifact resembles similar objects with edge notches found in the Upper Paleolithic industries of Europe, some of which bear face marks interpreted by Marshack (1972) as numerical notation. Unfortunately, there is nothing to substantiate such an interpretation of this specimen.

c) A small fragment of a bone shaft with four thin parallel

lines scratched across it. The fracture at the narrow end is very straight and parallel to the other lines and may be the result of a deeper cut. The bone is smoothed and is dark, possibly as a result of burning. It was found in layer 20 beneath Shelter 1A. (Catalog no. 26733.)

Another bone was found in layer 15 within Cave 1 which was first thought to be a tool. It was a flat, sickle-shaped piece 10 cm long and little more than 0.5 cm thick. Six comblike prongs at one end and two at the opposite one gave it the appearance of a carefully made comb which would have been ideal for teasing furs. Certainly, it may have been put to this use, but Dr. John Grindley, formerly director of Port Elizabeth Museum, kindly identified it as part of the shoulder girdle, possibly the cleithrum, of a large fish. The apparent prongs are sutures.

Bone in the Howieson's Poort levels was much more poorly preserved than in most of the MSA levels. This is thought to be due mainly to the greater intensity of occupation at this stage, as shown by the thick, black carbonaceous soils and innumerable ash hearths. Fire had affected a large number of the bones, and small amorphous pieces about thumb-nail size occurred with very much greater frequency than anything larger or of recognizable shape. However, all were examined, and it was not until the last stage of excavation was reached that anything was seen that could indicate a bone industry. In 1A-19, in a Howieson's Poort level associated with trapezes and much use of fine red silcrete, an elegant, delicate ground bone point was found (fig. 8.1, no. 4). Nothing else was later found, and it remains a unique find but for which it would have been concluded that there was no bone industry in the Howieson's Poort at KRM. The presence of one unusual artifact is always suspicious and must prompt queries as to whether it was intrusive or had even been "planted." All that can be said is that it came from compressed, laminated levels that showed not the slightest sign of disturbance and all the usual precautions had been taken to remove the surface layer on the scree slope where layer 19 outcropped. It should be noted that layer 19 overlay in part some large rocks which had fallen onto layer 22 and that the edges of irregular rocks are notorious for attracting roots and small burrowing animals; but this bone point was found in Transect B2, well away from where layer 19 overlay these rocks. The bone is stained and in identical condition to other bones in the same layer, being quite unlike the yellow, greasy bones typical of the LSA middens. Nor can the bone have been "planted," as the integrity of the excavation staff was beyond reproach and casual laborers would have neither the knowledge

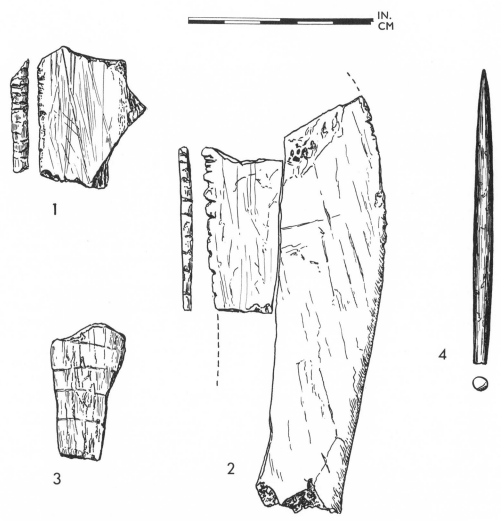

FIG. 8.1. Bone industry: nos. 1–4. MSA II and Howieson's Poort Industry. 1, 2: ribs with serrated edges, MSA II. 3: bone with thin parallel grooves, MSA II. 4: bone point, Howieson's Poort Industry.

nor the incentive to do such a thing. The artifact can be accepted as evidence for a Howieson's Poort bone industry on the existing facts.

The bone point (Catalog no. 42160) is 7.7 cm long and of near-circular section, 0.5 cm at its greatest diameter. Slight striations from the original shaping can still be seen but are mainly obscured by the polishing which completed its manufacture or may have been imparted by utilization. It tapers gradually to a point, and this is completely unbroken save for an extremely minute chip visible under a magnifying glass which may be an ancient break or wear, for it is similarly stained to the rest of the bone. The butt end is cut straight across or, more accurately, broken across, for two slight ridges can be seen on the underside which would result from snapping, and the artifact could be considered complete. It could have served as a pin or awl, but identical thin bone points in other contexts are generally considered as arrowheads.

The evidence for the lack of any bone industry in the MSA at KRM reflects that from other MSA sites in South Africa. The ground bone point appears to be the only evidence known and published for bone artifacts with a Howieson's Poort Industry, and in view of its refined workmanship, this is surprising. Nothing was found at Montagu Cave. Ground bone "daggers" made of split wart-hog tusks have come from the post–Howieson's Poort levels at the Border Cave (Beaumont 1979) and ground bone points in the Early LSA at the same site. Bone points have also been found in a pre-Robberg undifferentiated

blade industry at Boomplaas Cave (J. Deacon, personal communication).

Shell

Broken shell can be used for so many purposes that it would be unusual if no advantage had been taken of it. A few pieces with unusually straight edges, as though snapped with care and intention, were retained, but it was later found impossible to decide whether they were accidental fractures. Nor could anything be detected along their edges that definitely denoted some form of use. Only in one instance were three pieces of limpet shell found that appeared to have been snapped and chipped into a similar form to the stone crescents (fig. 6.5, nos. 28–30), already referred to in chapter 7. They were found within the same square meter in layer 11 beneath Shelter 1A, and this in itself strongly supports the idea that they had been made purposefully. Similar crescents made of shell were found in the Glentyre and Oakhurst rock shelters (Fagan 1960) in layers attributed to an LSA Wilton Industry. J. D. Clark (personal communication) suggested that pieces of shell may become worn to such a shape if used for scraping. These are the first shell crescents to be reported from a Howieson's Poort Industry.

The tops of a few of the limpet shells had small irregular holes which looked as though they may have been punched out with a narrow, pointed implement. However, similar recently perforated shells were found along the modern beach, so it seems that a natural cause was just as likely to have been responsible.

Ostrich Eggshell

The presence of small fragments of ostrich eggshell in some layers proves that ostrich eggs were collected, presumably as food, but there was nothing to show that they may have served a secondary purpose as water containers or bowls. No signs could be found on any of the fragments of perforations being made with a sharp tool, such as a quartzite flake, nor were there any scratches on the surface of the eggshell or anything else remotely connected with engraving or decoration. Several fragments were blackened by burning.

The distribution of the fragments is more interesting, for, although only small numbers were found in any of the layers, there were relatively many more fragments in the Howieson's Poort layers and none in the MSA I. Seven pieces came from the MSA II layers, all in Cave 1, and three from MSA III. In contrast, there were 95 pieces of ostrich eggshell in the Howieson's Poort levels, none being below layer 17. There distribution was:

Layer	Pieces of Ostrich Eggshell
10	7
11	1
12	16
13	1
14	26
15	19
16	21
17	4

Ocher (Plate 51)

Throughout all the industries a few small pieces of softish, oxidized rocks were found which would have been suitable for the production of pigments. Most of them showed marks of smoothing or scratching, occasionally so well developed that they could be described as crayons. Invariably, this raw material for pigment was red, varying in hardness from a highly oxidized sandstone similar to that occurring in cracks within the local quartzite to a soft, greasy hematite that must have been imported. A few pieces of relatively soft, yellow sandstone were found, and these, too, may have been used for producing a yellow pigment. Small fragments of pink, red, and yellow shale may also have been collected for the same purpose, but none had or retained the characteristic scratching and smoothing found on some of the softer red pieces.

The cross-hatching of thin lines found on some of the pieces is reminiscent of the marks seen on the surfaces of slate palettes of the Later Stone Age (cf. pl. 50). They are consistent with the dragging of a sharp flake across their surfaces. Such an action produces a fine powder of the rock which, when mixed with animal fat and possibly other ingredients such as egg white, makes a good paint. One of our assistants, D. A. Parish, conducted an experiment with such a piece of red ocher and, mixing a powder of it with some fat, produced an opaque paint of a pleasing red hue which he applied to the surface of some local beach pebbles. The color remained fast in spite of some exposure to rain and sun.

Nothing was found which could have been used to produce a white paint although numerous pieces of a soft, white rock were associated with the Howieson's Poort Industry at the type site. The pieces of red ocher which justify the name of crayons were not numerous, and the largest and most distinctively shaped was found at the top of the MSA II Industry, in 1-14 (pl. 51, center; Catalog no. 27578).

Red ocher appears to have been used more extensively in the Howieson's Poort Industry, as shown by the following table of the number of pieces found:

MSA IV	3 pieces
MSA III	25 pieces
Howieson's Poort	144 pieces of which 42 are doubtful[1]
MSA II	20 pieces in Cave 1
	16 pieces beneath Shelter 1A
MSA I	11 pieces in Cave 1
	3 pieces beneath Shelter 1B

An unusual broken crayon of red ocher was found in 1A-21, the lowest Howieson's Poort layer. About 3 cm remained of what had originally been a cylindrical piece of soft ocher, now broken at each end. On one side were three shallow depressions which were perfectly circular, and so presumably drilled out, two of 0.7 cm diameter and a lower one of 0.4 cm diameter and about the same depths. Nothing else like this was found in any of the other layers, nor anything else on bone or stone to suggest that a technique of drilling was employed. The bottoms of the semiperforations are smooth concavities, suggesting the use of a bone or wooden drill.

There is no evidence whatsoever to indicate for what purpose the red paint was used. As has been seen, the negative evidence from Cave 1C suggests it was not parietal art. The inference is that it was for artifactual or personal adornment. The use of pigments as far back in time as MSA I renders the attribution of actual mining for pigment by MSA people at the Lion Cavern, Ngwenya, Swaziland (Beaumont 1973b) a little less surprising. It certainly suggests that coloring materials were considered of great value and were possibly regarded as imparting magical rather than just decorative qualities.

Human Bones

If human burial was practiced by the occupants of the site throughout the whole sequence from MSA I to MSA IV, including the Howieson's Poort Industry, it cannot have been at the living site. Not a trace of any intentional interment was found, nor any pits which might have been intended for such. The several human fragments which were found during the course of the excavation lay isolated in the soil in the same manner as the other faunal remains. It can hardly be coincidental that nearly all the human bones found were mandible or skull fragments, and that, apart from a near-complete clavicle and the very small part of a radius, postcranial bones were absent. The lack of femora, in view of their strength and durability, is particularly remarkable. Some selection is indicated, although the small numbers of remains do not accord with any activity or tradition. Human remains with Middle Stone Age associations are uncommon in South Africa (Wells 1957; Tobias 1971; DeVilliers 1973), and in some of the cases the associations are doubtful as most have been chance finds. It is not the concern of this section to discuss the morphology of the fragments but to list the finds made and add comments on the circumstances of their discovery where necessary (see chap. 11). This we do in table 8.1.

1. These are pieces which may be no more than highly weathered, oxidized local quartzite.

Table 8.1. Distribution of Human Skeletal Remains according to Layers in Caves or Shelters

	Shelter or Cave	Layer	Catalog No.
WITH MSA IV		Nil	
WITH MSA III			
2 parietal skull fragments, both blackened by apparent burning	1A	6	40243, 40244
WITH HOWIESON'S POORT		Nil	
WITH MSA II			
Mandible fragment with right PM2, M1, and M2	1	14 West Cutting F	13400
Molar tooth with fragment of mandible attached	1	14 West Cutting F	14691
Premolar and 2 molar teeth	1	14 West Cutting F	14692, 14693, 14694
Mandible fragment with symphysis-no teeth	1	14 West Cutting F	14695
Molar tooth	1	14 West Cutting F	14696
Malar bone	1	14 West Cutting F	16651
Innominate bone fragment	1	14 West Cutting F	16720
Clavicle, near complete	1	14 West Cutting H	26076
Parietal fragment and 3 indeterminate skull fragments	1	14 West Cutting K-L	27574, 27575, 27576, 27577
Mandible fragment with right M1, M2, and M3	1	14+ West Cutting F	16424

This rubble deposit is a mixture of layers 14 and 16, so the contents may relate to either layer.

	Shelter or Cave	Layer	Catalog No.
Parietal fragment	1	15+ West Cutting H	27038

This is the top of layer 15 where it has become a little mixed with the rubble of layer 14, hence this fragment probably relates to the latter.

	Shelter or Cave	Layer	Catalog No.
Proximal end of radius fragment — slightly blackened by burning	1	15 Main Cutting A	27889
Frontal bone fragment with part of supraorbital ridge and nasal bone	1	16 Main Cutting A	16425
Mandible fragment, found in three places without teeth — blackened by burning	1	17 Main Cutting A	21776
2 skull? fragments[1]	1	17 Main Cutting A	24006, 24007
Skull? fragment[1]	1A	25 Initial Cutting	21696

Table 8.1. Continued

	Shelter or Cave	Layer	Catalog No.
Large piece of right parietal	1A	36 East Cutting T	41658

This bone was found in an extension of this cutting between the north side and the rock wall. It was immediately beneath a thin slab of cemented occupational deposit which had apparently fallen from Cave 2 above on the eroded slope of layer 36. There was .7 m of wet, rubbly scree between this slab and the present surface. Adhering to the bottom of the fallen slab was part of an antelope mandible, but although in contact with the slab, the human parietal bone was not attached to it. It probably belongs to layer 36, and its position beneath the slab is fortuitous, but the possibility exists that it was purposely placed there and thus belongs to a period subsequent to the total accumulation of occupational deposits beneath Shelter 1A.

Right parietal fragment with 2 associated skull? fragments	1A	34 Initial Cutting	26730, 26731, 26732

These fragments came from the clay at the top of the saturated deposits.

WITH MSA I

Parietal? fragment with some associated skull? fragments	1	37 Main Cutting A	26909, 26910
Nondescript fragment of cranium[2]	1	37 West Cutting H	27070
27 skull fragments some of which are ? human[1]	1	38 Main Cutting A	24374 to 24400 (serially)
Mandible with right PM2 and M1 and left M1 and M2	1B	10	41815

The most complete mandible found at Klasies River Mouth. Found beside but not under a large lump of soft calcrete lying on the surface of this layer. It rested with the ramus upright.

Fragment of condyle of mandible	1B	10	41820

1. Missing from South African Museum collection and not described. It is possible that they were identified as being nonhominid and moved.

2. Not described in chapter 11.

9   The LSA Occupations and Industries

The Middens in Cave 1 (Plates 7, 40–42)

Excavation has revealed inside Cave 1 a considerable accumulation of shells and bones, which formed a mound on the higher east side of the cave overlying the eolian sand of KRM-1 to 13 (fig. 9.1). Contained stone and bone artifacts clearly differentiate this period of occupation from that of the preceding MSA and relate it to LSA Strandlopers, whose sites and remains abound along much of the Tzitzikama Coast and elsewhere. These middens in Cave 1 together with their contents are described below, but a brief consideration of the manner in which middens form is first provided so that the validity of the evidence from them can be assessed.

Middens are piles of domestic rubbish that have accumulated close to but not usually beneath the habitation spots of those who created them. They may be located either on open beaches or dunes, or at the mouths of caves or within them, or in rock shelters. Coastal middens, apart from soil and sand, are inevitably composed mainly of discarded shells and fish bones, as marine food was presumably the staple diet of people living beside the sea. However, animal (including human) bones are often found in middens. Some degree of hygiene and comfort demanded that the living spaces within a cave were relatively free of such litter, so it was thrown or carried and tipped on a convenient area such as toward the rear of a cave. Gradually the rubbish produces a mount which will tend to advance toward the point of origin of the rubbish until it virtually overwhelms the living space. Ultimately, all the living space will be rendered uninhabitable unless a decision is made to dump rubbish elsewhere.

If rubbish is tipped on a midden in small quantities daily, a near-homogeneous pile will accumulate. If larger quantities are dumped at longer intervals, say, weeks or months, or even years, then evidence of the tip-lines or piles may be discerned by excavation. Long intervals of nonoccupation or nontipping may allow soils to develop on the surface, or rockfalls, blown sand, or silt may become concentrated at a particular level. Trampling on the midden by the occupants may produce layers of crushed shell which reflect temporary surfaces. The exigencies of space sometimes caused hearths to exist on a midden, but generally only on its periphery or in its initial stages when it presented no great obstacle, especially if there was a considerable time interval between the builders of the hearth and the previous disposers of the rubbish. There is thus little if any correspondence between time and thickness in a midden: a thick, homogeneous mass of shell and bone may have formed in a few years or even months, whereas three superimposed

tip-lines each only a few centimeters thick may span centuries. Because the signs of tip-lines, crushed layers, and incipient soils may be very faint, the difficulties of actual excavation are in proportion to the difficulties of interpretation. Their limitations for producing detailed evidence of the actual living conditions of the occupants are rather greater than the more usual situation of rubbish and soil accumulating slowly underfoot around them, as, for example, beneath a rock shelter. Most of the rubbish dumped at any one time on a midden is likely to be contemporary with the occupation, but occasional cleaning of the site or the digging of pits for various purposes might well scrape up material of earlier periods. Even so, the difference in time is not likely to be very great, unless the cleanup was particularly thorough. For these reasons it was felt that there was little to be achieved by the meticulous examination of every change discernible within the middens. However, where development of soils or other continuous features within the midden indicated definite breaks in its construction, the separate examination of the layers above and below was felt to be justified, with perhaps special attention to the break itself, which may represent a surface removed in time from either of them. Similarly, horizontal positions of the various objects in the midden have little meaning, as most, if not all, of them have been haphazardly tipped or thrown onto it.

In practice, major breaks in the sequence of the midden buildup may not be obvious until after excavation has disclosed more than is at first visible. KRM 1-1 to 12 (fig. 9.1) are layers discerned during excavation which were considered likely to qualify as major breaks, but KRM 1-7 was the only layer which was found to be continuous, associated with a well-developed soil, compacted, and containing crushed shell. This was also the only horizon at which lime cementation had occurred on the surface, suggesting a considerable time interval before the deposition of the next layer. The cementation was slight but best developed in Main Cutting C. The surface of KRM 1-7 is thus interpreted as the top of an earlier midden, abandoned but subjected to the trampling of people or animals. There is almost 1.5 m of midden above this without any such break. The tops of the other layers certainly constitute breaks of some sort, but they are not thought to be of particular significance. The lack of sharp or continuous breaks and well-developed soils, and the homogeneous nature of KRM 1-1 to 6 all suggest a rapid buildup of the midden, to be dated more likely in centuries than millennia. This interpretation is substantiated by two radiocarbon dates obtained from various parts of the midden, those in layer 1-1 and on the surface of 1-7 both being in the first

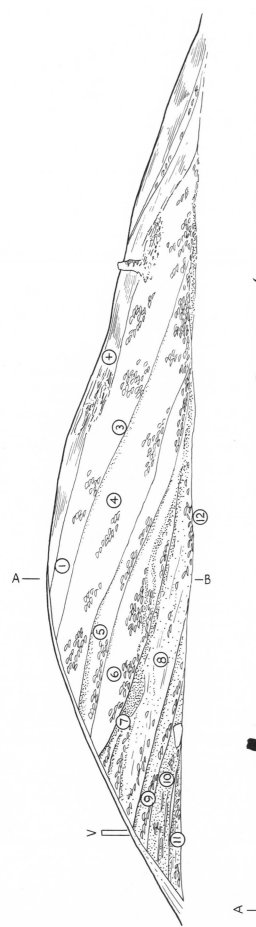

Klasies River Mouth Cave 1

Sections along and across L.S.A. midden deposits

INITIAL CUTTING

FIG. 9.1. Sections along and across the LSA deposits of the Initial Cutting in Cave 1.

millennium B.C. Two others in KRM 1-7 and 10 were both in the third millennium B.C. Layers 1-1 to 6 thus represent an Upper Midden, or KRM Later Stone Age II (LSA II), and layers 1-7 to 12 a Lower Midden, or KRM Later Stone Age I (LSA I).

The divisions between the various layers in the Lower Midden are a little clearer than in the Upper, but insufficient to justify classification as major breaks. Toward the rear of the cave they became increasingly difficult to separate. All of the Lower Midden was far more compact than the Upper, and toward the cave mouth it merged into true occupational soils with hearths (KRM 1-9 to 11). A longer time span is indicated for its development. The condition of the shells in the vertical sequence also substantiates this twofold division of the midden, for that above KRM 1-7 was generally much fresher than that below. The bone was also fresher, appearing yellow and greasy.

The horizontal distributions of the Upper and Lower Middens are shown on the plans, figures 9.2 and 9.3. They covered a similar area, but the Lower was slightly more extensive. They were best preserved in the central part of the Main Cutting, but in the Rear Chamber they were much disturbed and mixed with underlying layers. Burrowing animals or human activity may have been responsible for this disturbance.

The Upper Midden (KRM 1-1 to Top of 1-7): LSA II

This was mainly confined to the higher, east side of the cave, where a few meters of space still remained between the surface of earlier deposits and the roof. The drawn section along the Initial Cutting (fig. 9. 1.) is along its major axis. That along the Main Cutting (fig. 3.2) is a little oblique to it and thus slightly different. Very little of this Upper Midden was revealed on the west side of the central balk: it was found that earlier deposits had already almost filled in the low area beneath the overhang. The small amount of shell and other midden debris which had run down the mound toward the west side was partially cemented and also disturbed by animal burrows (fig. 3.4, 3.5). A small patch of shell and bone had been dumped in Grid G near the Rear Alcove. A description of the layers follows (see fig. 9.1).

Layer +. Fine, laminated, dark sandy soil, patchily cemented by calcite. Toward the rear, a thin lens of sand and shells appeared within this soil.

Layer 1-1. Shell midden mixed with dark sand near the east wall of the cave.

Layer 1-2. Thin lens of shells restricted to the area near the east wall of the cave.

Layer 1-3. Shell midden mixed with dark sand near the east wall of the cave.

Layer 1-4. Thick shell midden.

Layer 1-5. Thin soil, black and well developed near the top of the mound, which merged into loose shell midden. The shells were compressed near the top of the mound.

Layer 1-6. Thick shell midden with discontinuous soil layers, particularly near the rear of the mound.

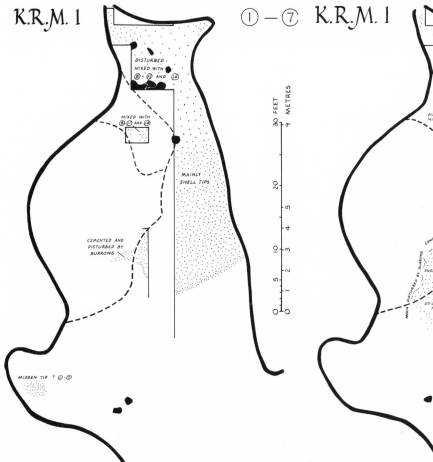

FIG. 9.2. Cave 1 plan of LSA Upper Midden (layers 1 to 7).

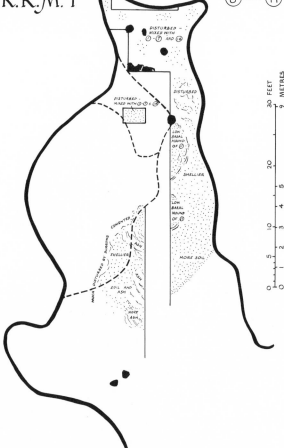

FIG. 9.3. Cave 1 plan of LSA Lower Midden (layers 8 to 11).

Top of Layer 1-7. Surface of dark soil, black in places. It was compressed and contained crushed shells.

During this time the occupants of the cave must have been living in the wide mouth, for the remainder of the cave was too blocked with earlier material to offer any other position, save perhaps behind the mound of the Lower Midden, toward the rear, but this would have been dark, dank, and undesirable. However, it made an obvious place to throw or tip rubbish.

The original curve of the tip-lines at the front of this midden are truncated by the slope produced by natural erosion. Only a small amount appears to have suffered, probably less than a meter. Fresh shells that were found in the fine scree in front of the cave may have been derived from here.

There are no signs of calcite formation during the growth of the midden, but the capping of up to 30 cm of fine, laminated soil is locally cemented by calcite. This has penetrated a little into layers 1-1 to 3 and even into parts of layer 1-4. At one point, toward the rear, a small stalagmite about 30 cm high has developed on layer 1-1 and may still be in process of formation. This soil capping appeared to be partly subaerial and was completely sterile on the east side of the cave in the Main Cutting. On the other side, in the West Cutting G and H, this top soil was loose and much more organic. It appeared to have been disturbed, for it produced a fine oval perforated pendant made of slate (fig. 9.6, no. 5), various flake-blades, flakes and cores, a smoothed rib bone, several bones including a felid skull in fragments, shell, and a broken glass bottle. A thick, backed scraper-knife (fig. 9.4, no. 11) came from the adjacent grid J.

The Lower Midden (KRM 1-7 to Top of 1-12): LSA I

This midden was smaller than the one above, and its highest part was closer to the cave mouth. The occupants at this time were probably living a little way back from the entrance, on the west side, a very favorable spot at present for protection from wind or rain. Their hearths are superimposed on each other, contained within layers which become shellier toward the rear. As with the Upper Midden, in the Rear Chamber the midden is much disturbed and mixed with earlier and, in this case, more recent deposits. A description of the layers follows (see fig. 9.1)

Layer 1-7. A dark, compact soil at the top of and merging into the underlying shelly layer. Material on its surface has been related to the Upper Midden.

Layer 1-8. Shell midden with discontinuous lenses of loose soil.

Layer 1-9. Shell midden with a near-continuous, slightly developed soil at its top.

Layer 1-10. Brown sandy soil with ash hearths toward the front of the midden and shellier at the rear.

Layer 1-11. Loose dark brown to black soil and shell which formed irregular low heaps on the surface of the underlying layer. It was flecked with charcoal, and there were traces of ash hearths in the very front near the cave mouth.

Layer 1-12. Brown sand and lenses of silt. This was dug as a separate layer but proved to be the weathered surface of the yellow eolian sand with its lenses of silt. Much of it was cemented by lime, either as a crust or penetrating deep into the underlying sand to form hard masses.

The Lower Midden has suffered considerable erosion since it was formed, to judge from the truncation of its lower layers toward the front of the cave (see comments by Butzer, chap. 4). Originally it must have extended on the east side at least as far as the drip-line at the entrance. The initial occupation of this period was on the surface of the windblown sand (layer 1-13), a surface which was already partially cemented by calcite. A soil (layer 1-12) had formed in the upper part, and this was also partly cemented. Two low heaps of soil and food refuse (layer 1-11) were later covered by further wider spreads of soil and rubbish (layer 1-10). As the accumulations developed into a mound and thus became unsuitable for sitting or lying on, so the layers almost totally comprised food debris in the form of shells and bones (layers 1-7 to 9).

No evidence was found for any calcite formation during this period of the midden's growth. A large sandstone slab and a rectangular slate palette were found lying flat on the surface of layer 1-12.

Toward the Rear Chamber a gley soil had developed at the level which was equivalent to the surface of layer 1-12. Patches of powdery, red iron oxide lay on and within cracks of dark clay a few centimeters thick. Also in this area were found two unusual ribbed and pointed stalagmites, 20 and 28 cm long. They had been broken from their place of formation and lay flat on the surface of this gley soil. Some human activity was indicated, but if this was of a ritual nature there was nothing else to substantiate it. Two other similar ribbed stalagmites, 25 and 30 cm long, were found in the bottom levels of the Lower Midden nearby in Main Cutting B. Layers 1-7 to 11 converge here and constitute a thickness of only 30 cm. They are somewhat jumbled, and it is not possible to isolate one layer from another at this point. Ribbed stalagmites of this nature were only found in Cave 1C, which had been blocked since the time of the MSA II stage, so if this was their source, the LSA occupants probably found them in the MSA deposits which they appear to have disturbed in the Rear Chamber of the cave.

As with the Upper Midden, bones and artifacts were scattered throughout all the layers. Some artifacts were a little more numerous on the west side of the cave (West Cutting H and K). Toward the rear of the cave on the west side there is a spread of the typical food refuse and other rubbish of the Lower Midden, but most of it has been disturbed by animal burrows (possibly porcupine) or human activity. Some of the midden here is cemented by calcite, and burrowing animals have taken advantage of this and let it form the roof of their burrows. However, in places the weight of the cemented midden has been too much and large lumps have collapsed into the burrow, with a corresponding disturbance of the unconsolidated layers above. Much of the material from here could not be related with certainty to particular levels and was thus discarded. Figure 3.5 shows a section across this part of the cave.

Table 9.1 summarizes the stone and bone artifacts and other finds from the Upper and Lower Middens. Material from the surface of layer 1-12 is recorded separately, as it seems certain that LSA and MSA material is mixed together at this level.

Summary and Conclusions concerning LSA I and LSA II

As with most coastal middens of the LSA in Southern Africa, there is little evidence of a vigorous stone industry in either the Upper or the Lower Midden at KRM. The numbers of the various tool classes found are shown in table 9.1, and it can be seen that specialized forms are rare. There are a few systematic cores, but flakes have mainly been struck haphazardly from convenient, available beach pebbles and are accordingly ir-

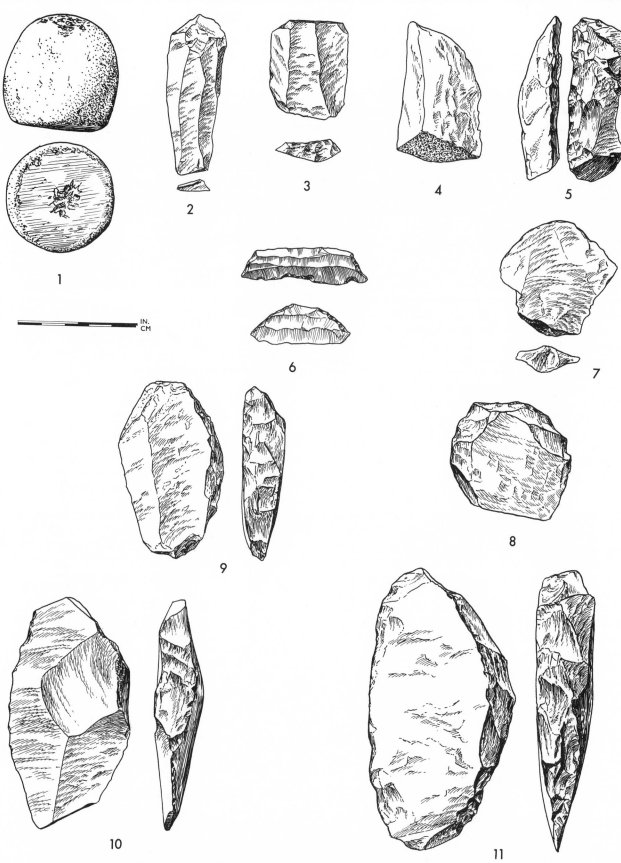

Fɪɢ. 9.4. Artifacts from LSA Middens I and II—Cave 1. 1: rubbing stone with central pecked hollow. Also used as a hammerstone. 2: flake-blade. Snapped, probably in striking, just below bulb. 3: bulbous end of broken flade-blade. Trace of ? notch remaining on one side of snap. 4: crude flake. 5: small pick or chisel of fine, gray yellow silcrete. 6: crescent, partially blunted, of fine, red silcrete. 7: crude flake; cortex on reverse. 8: crude thick scraper. Cortex on major part of reverse. Striking platform worked away. Bulbous end shown uppermost. 9–11: thick, backed scraper knives ("giant crescents"). Nos. 10 and 11 made on large side-struck flakes. No. 9 shown with bulb uppermost. All have signs of use along the thin edge, heavy use on 11. The flake-blades, such as 2, 3, and the occasional trapeze or crescent, are considered to be derived from earlier MSA or Howieson's Poort levels. They occur on the surface of the scree slope beneath Shelter 1A, and their occurrence in the middens suggests they were collected for reuse.

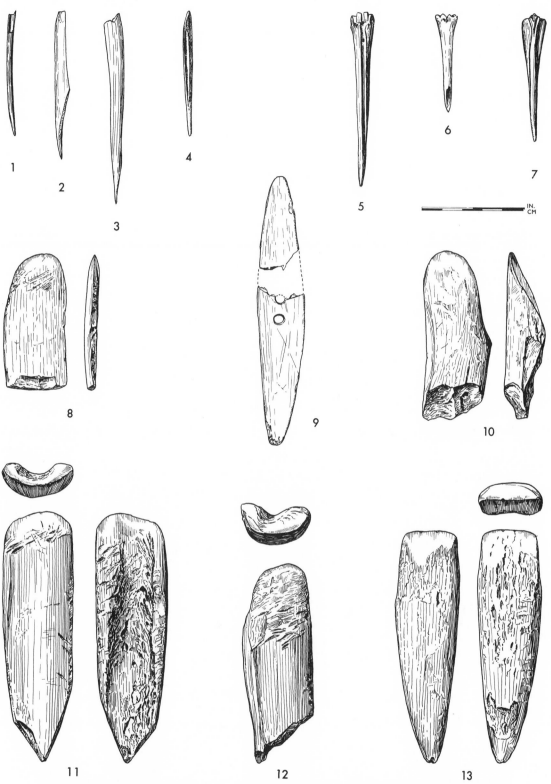

FIG. 9.5. Bone industry: nos. 1–13. LSA I and II. 1: awl or pin made on a delicate bird bone. Tip polished and portion of bone interior exposed. 2, 3: splinters of thin bone, probably bird, with tips polished to acute points. 4: awl or pin made on splinter of a small long bone. Extreme tip snapped off. 5–7: awls with polished tips. Nos. 5, 6 are made from small antelope metapodials and 7 from a bird bone. 8: thin chisel cut from fragment of a large rib. 9: flat pieces of rib bone, tapered at both ends and with two perforations in the center. Probably a pendant or even a "wirra-wirra." 10: chisel, ground onto a thick piece of bone, initially shaped by "flaking." 11, 12: gouges on pieces of hollow long bones. 13: chisel.

Table 9.1. Distribution of Materials Recovered from the Upper and Lower Middens

	Upper Midden LSA II	Lower Midden LSA I	Layer 1-12
A. STONE ARTIFACTS (Fig. 9.4)			
Cores			
Single platform	5	1	2
Double platform	2	7	1
Micro		2	2
Irregular and/or undeveloped	12	24	6
Rejuvenators		2	2
Choppers	2	3	
Flakes	233	698	618
Flake-blades	33	213	59
Pointed flake-blades	3	23	35
Flake-blade segments			
Bulbous ends	2	30	26
Middle segments		21	37
Nonbulbous ends	1	12	15
Worked flakes			
Denticulates		2	
Scrapers		4	
Thick, backed scraper-knives	17	1	
Hollow scrapers		1	2
Gravers		1	1 ?
Points	1	1	
Borers	1		2
Unspecialized	8	11	3
Crude picks	3		
Unifacial point		1	
Crescents of fine silcrete	1	1	
Trapezes of black, siliceous indurated shale		1	
Nonlocal rock			
Fine silcrete flakes		3	1
Indurated shale flakes	2	5	3
Quartz cores	1		
Quartz flakes		5	
Other rock flakes		1	
	327	1074	815

TOTAL = 2,216

B. BONE ARTIFACTS (Fig. 9.5)			
Chisel	2	5	
Gouge	1	1	
Awl	3	5	1
Spatula		1	
Perforated oval disc	1		
Burnisher	1	1	
Worked fragment		2	1
	8	15	2

Table 9.1. Continued

	Upper Midden LSA II	Lower Midden LSA I	Layer 1-12
C. QUERNS and POUNDERS (Figs. 9.4, 9.6)			
Quern	3	2	
Hammerstone	5	1	
Rubbing stone		3	
Upper grinder with pecked hollows	2		
Bored stone, broken		1	
	10	7	
D. MISCELLANEOUS (Fig. 9.6)			
Grooved stone, broken		1	
Slate palette		1	
Fragments of slate	1		
? Line sinkers	1	2	
Red ocher		1	1
Ostrich eggshell			1
Perforated cowrie		1	
	2	6	2

regular and crude. Length rarely exceeds breadth, and cortex is common on either the dorsal side of the flakes or their striking platforms. A few corelike pieces have battered edges and warrant classification as choppers.

The artifacts from KRM 1-12, as mentioned above, are likely to be a mixture of the MSA IV stage of 1-13 and the artifacts used by the first LSA occupants, and, not surprisingly, the majority of them do reflect the earlier industry, i.e., a high proportion of flake-blades less than 8 cm long and small pointed flake-blades. Well-struck flake-blades identical to those found in the MSA stages do occur throughout the middens, but decrease in numbers with the buildup of the occupational refuse. In view of the coarse nature of their general stonework, it seems highly unlikely that the occupants of the midden made these flake-blades, which demand high knapping skills. In some cases it can be seen clearly that they were old MSA flake-blades that had been reutilized, for signs of slight secondary working or heavy use have cut through a faint staining or weathering of their surfaces. Such flake-blades would have been lying abundantly on the scree slopes outside the cave mouth, and in our opinion, this was the source of all these artifacts, including the segments of broken flake-blades. A similar reuse of MSA materials was noted at Matjes River (Louw 1960). Similarly, the isolated examples of a unifacial point, two crescents, and a trapeze are considered to originate from earlier industries.

The only specialized tools that can definitely be ascribed to the LSA here are the large flake-tools described as thick, backed scraper-knives. In other contexts they have been referred to as giant crescents, but this is misleading, as they bear no affinity to the crescents of the Howieson's Poort Industry: they are not made on flake-blades, micro or otherwise, and obviously had a completely different use. However, it does describe their shape. They are wedge-shaped, and the crescentic backing affords an excellent handgrip if the opposing sharp edge is to be used as a knife. Sometimes this edge also has been blunted by secondary working, possibly to make the tool serviceable for some other function such as scraping. It must be significant that of the 18 tools found of this type, 17 came from the Upper Midden. The odd one from the Lower Midden was toward the rear of the mound in Main Cutting B, where layers 1-9 to 11 could not be separated with certainty and were thus dug as one unit. It was below layer 1-8, however, and nothing was noted to indicate that it might be intrusive. Similar thick, backed scraper-knives were found in the tail of the midden in Cave 5 (see below). Figure 9.4 includes drawings (nos. 9–11) of these tools from Cave 1. There was nothing else to indicate any significant difference between the LSA I and LSA II stone industries except that the only smoothed grindstone rubbers with pecked hollows came from the Upper Midden.

The bone industries of LSA I and II. Well-made bone tools were found in both the Upper and the Lower Middens (table 9.1). Several are illustrated in figure 9.5. The chisels and gouges are made on fragments of large long bones with the cutting edges ground on them at one end from both sides. Although described as chisels and gouges, there is nothing on their blunt ends to indicate that they were ever used in conjunction with a wooden or stone mallet: in fact their jagged or pointed ends would have made it difficult to do so. Some use in the hand is indicated, unless they were originally inserted into wooden sleeves.

Some of the awls are very delicate, and most are made on splinters of bird bones ground to a needlelike point at one end. One of the so-called burnishers is made on a nearly complete bird tibia. The small gougelike end is highly polished, as is much of the surface of the rest of the tool. The other burnisher is made on a long bone fragment, polished at one end. The spatula is made of a rib.

The only bone artifact which may be an ornament or be nonfunctional is figure 9.5, number 9. It was unfortunately broken in the course of excavation, but it was broken in such a way that we were able to reconstruct it. It is made on a flat

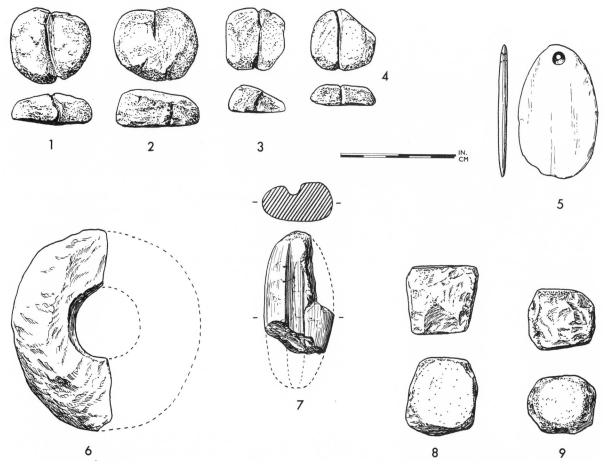

FIG. 9.6. Miscellaneous: nos. 1–9. LSA industries. 1–4: small pieces of shale with grooves. (Nos 1, 3, 4 are from Cave 1; no. 2 from Cave 4.) The flat underside in each case has no groove. Possibly line sinkers. 5: perforated slate pendant. 6: broken bored stone of fine-ground rock. 7: broken grooved "stone" made of soft limestone. 8,9: cubes made from flat quartzite pebbles, the cortex left untouched on upper and lower faces. Flaked and battered into shape. No sign of any smoothing, but some of the battering may indicate their use as hammerstones.

bone, probably part of a rib, tapering to a rounded point at both ends and having two small perforations in the middle. It could have been a child's toy (*wirra-wirra*) or a pendant.

Miscellaneous (figure 9.6). As can be seen from table 9.1, very few other objects were found in the middens. Querns and rubbing stones suggest the collection and use of edible seeds and roots. The one broken bored stone (fig. 9.6, no. 6) found came from the Lower Midden but in a very confused part of it near the Rear Chamber, exposed in the South Trench of that area. It is made of a dark, fairly fine grained quartzite foreign to the district.

The broken grooved stone (no. 7) was found in the tail of the Lower Midden in Main Cutting C. It was made of a soft, dark material resembling fired clay, which was identified chemically as limestone by M. Kastner, Department of Geophysical Sciences, University of Chicago.

All three grooved pieces of shale are shown (nos. 1, 3, 4), and these may be evidence for line fishing, as they would make ideal sinkers. Two came from the Lower Midden, layer 1-8 and the top of layer 1-9. The other was in the Upper Midden but at the bottom of layer 1-6, so it may also relate to the Lower Midden.

Evidence for painting was very slight, with only few pieces of ocher occurring in the middens, and yet the major part of a fine slate palette, rectangular with beveled edges, was found lying on layer 1-12 in West Cutting M, at the very bottom of the Lower Midden (pl. 52). It bore clear traces of red ocher, indicating that pigments were certainly being mixed.

The lack of ostrich eggshell beads is surprising, with only one example in layer 1-12. Such small items could have been missed, but routine 1/8 inch sievings failed to reveal any.

Food supply. In both middens fish and bird bones greatly outnumber mammalian bones. Details of the bones and shells found are given in chapters 12 and 13, respectively, but it can be summarized here for convenience that the staple diet of the occupants of Cave 1 at this time was fish, bird, and shellfish. However, the hunting of game was not rare. The people of the Lower Midden appear to have been the greater hunters and caught at least six species of antelope. Buffalo and hippopotamus are confined to the Lower Midden. Seal was also hunted in fair numbers, although there are no longer any seal colonies on this part of the Tzitzikama Coast. Stranded whales and dolphins supplemented their varied food supply. The quern stones and rubbers suggest the collection of local seeds, nuts, fruits, roots, and other edible vegetation.

Mussels and limpets were the favorite or most readily obtainable shellfish. Winkles and turbo shells were collected in large numbers as well as the land snail, *Achatina zebra*. It is interesting that many of the limpets were obtained from rock surfaces only exposed at low tides.

The effect of the diet on human dentition is noted in chapter 11 (specimen 614).

Klasies River Mouth Shelter 1D

A small cutting, 1×2 m, was made beneath the overhang of the small rock shelter at the campsite, on the east side and 47 m from the sea (see map, fig. 1.2, for general position and pl. 43). The surface at the highest point of the cutting, inside the drip-line, was 17 ft. (5.2 m) above sea level, dipping away from the shelter to a more gentle slope toward the sea from 13 to 7 ft. (4 to 2.1 m) above it. It was on this platform that their camp was situated, and the object of the cutting was to locate the bedrock bench and discover what traces of human occupation, if any, were to be found upon it. No archeological material was to be seen on the present surface beneath the shelter but it seemed a likely place for occupation, and it was not surprising that excavation showed that LSA Strandlopers had taken advantage of it.

The sections (fig. 9.7) show five main occupational layers banked up against the dark, humified sand of layer 6[1] which rested on bedrock at 10 ft. (3 m) above sea level. Details of layers and a description of their contents follow.

Layer +. Twenty-five to fifty centimeters of fine dark, sandy humus thickening to nearly 1 m toward the rock face. This proved to be sterile of shells, bones, stone artifacts, or modern rubbish and is regarded as a natural colluvial deposit.

Layer 1. Similar to the above deposit but containing numerous shells and some bird bones, as well as a crudely flaked pebble, two flakes, and a slab of soft, pink shale, 10×12 cm.

Layer 2. Sandier humus than above with few shells or bones. No stone artifacts were found.

Layer 3. Fine sandy humus with very few shells but numerous bone fragments, mainly of bird but also including antelope. Scattered through this layer were parts of a disarticulated human skeleton. Only part of the body was present, represented by a mandible fragment, leg bones, and arm bones together with a scapula fragment and other postcranial bones. The skull was not found but may well remain in the unexcavated part of the same layer beyond the cutting. Stone artifacts comprised one crude core and 10 flakes, one with unspecialized secondary working. There were also 15 sherds of fine dark ware with a burnished surface and containing some small subangular sand frit. Two sherds are parts of perforated lugs.

Layer 4. Fine sandy humus with large rock fragments in the upper part. The layer was over 1 m thick under the actual shelter but contained very few bone fragments or shells. In the upper part was a large rim and body sherd of a necked pot with a thin, overturned, rounded rim (fig. 9.8). It was of thin ware with a black core and brown exterior and a medium admixture of angular sand grains. The surface was slightly smoothed and burnished and undecorated save for a little trimming of the step to the rim. There was no sign of any lugs or bosses. This is one of the most common forms of Strandloper pottery (cf. Hangklip [Rudner 3] type C2; Rudner 1968). There were no stone artifacts.

Layer 5. Similar fine sandy humus but with numerous shells in good condition. There was also a little bone, mainly of bird, and also the left half of a human mandible. Two sherds of

1. In this section all layer numbers refer to those excavated in Shelter 1D.

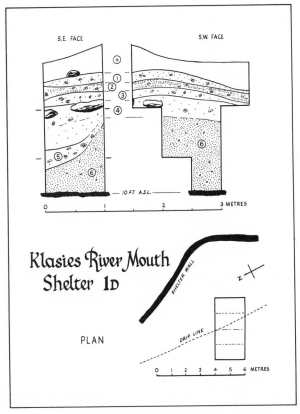

Fig. 9.7. Plan for Shelter 1D.

poorly fired buff gray ware with large frit were found and one flake.

Layer 6. Dark, uniform, humified sand with a few rare shells and small angular rock fragments apparently derived from the rock wall or overhang. It was found to be sterile of bone fragments, stone artifacts, or other cultural material. It rested directly on bedrock and is thus considered to have formed prior to the first occupation of shelter.

The bedrock platform at about 3 m probably relates to a high sea level of about this height, thus making the third wave-cut platform for which there is good evidence at KRM. The other two, higher ones are represented by the floors of the caves. It has been shown that the first MSA occupation of the site was contemporary with the 6–8 m beach. This lower rock platform was presumably cut after the sea had receded from the 6–8 m

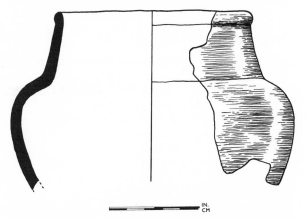

Fig. 9.8. Klasies River Mouth, Shelter 1D. Sherd of necked pot from layer 4.

Table 9.2. TIME SPAN OF CAPE LSA SITES

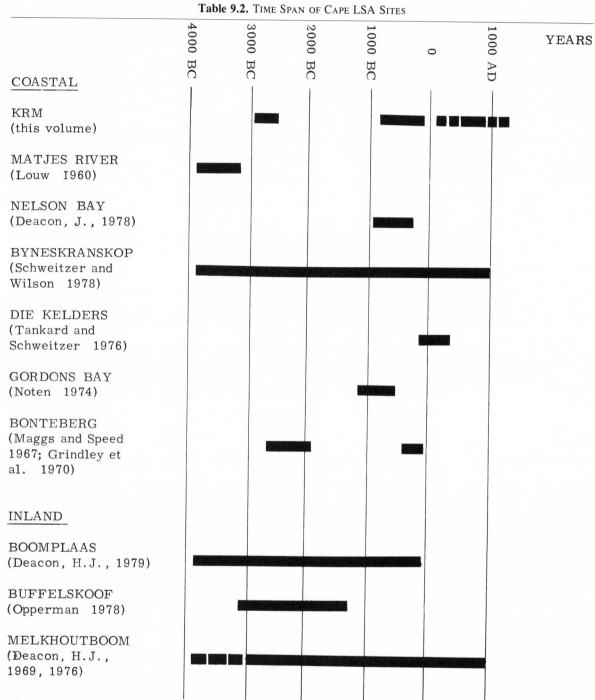

level, and, to judge from the archeological evidence, the shelter at the back of it was not used until pottery-using Strandlopers took advantage of it. There is nothing to indicate that the LSA people responsible for either the Upper or the Lower Middens in Cave 1 used the shelter: their litter *may* be under another part of the shelter, but the finding of sherds in the lowest occupational level makes it seem doubtful.

The dark, fine sandy humus of layer 6 immediately above the bedrock is considered to be the result of soil washing down from the steep slopes around the shelter, a process which appears to have continued throughout the occupation and is still going on; hence the thick layer + sealing it.

The KRM LSA in Relation to Some Other LSA Sites in the Cape Province

The so-called Strandloper or midden sites which abound along the southern Cape Coast are a notable feature of South African archeology. They testify to a rigorous exploitation of marine resources, and in many cases there is some evidence (J. Deacon 1976a) that a mobile population was involved which practiced a form of transhumance. Comparisons of artifacts found at the coastal sites with those thought to be contemporary inland are confounded by the adaptations imperative to the marked change of habitat. As with most LSA middens, the stone artifacts from the three phases of the LSA represented at KRM are mainly crude, sparse, and lacking a formal typology. The three phases, separated on the basis of stratigraphy, radiocarbon dating, and the presence or absence of pottery, are:

LSA Phase 1
    Cave 1   2745 B.C. ± 180 (GX-0973)
                2805 B.C. ± 95 (GX-0970)
    Cave 5   2160 B.C. ± 60 (GX-1378)
LSA Phase 2
    Cave 1   575 B.C. ± 85 (GX-0969)
                845 B.C. ± 85 (GX-0971)
    Cave 5   335 B.C. ± 105 (GX-1397)
LSA Phase 3
    Shelter 1D   Ceramic

In contrast to the stonework, the bone industry of phases 1 and 2 is quite sophisticated (fig. 9.5).

The evidence from KRM does little to resolve the problem of the origins or affinities of the people who produced the middens. Sampson (1974) classifies them as Coastal "Strandlopers" within his Phase 6 of the LSA, ceramic or preceramic. There is certainly nothing in the KRM LSA assemblages such as small scrapers or microlithic elements to show any links with Wilton Industries, as at the Nelson Bay Cave, Robberg (Deacon 1978) Byneskranskop (Schweitzer and Wilson 1978), all coastal cave sites west of KRM. However, such observations have limited value, and as Deacon (1974) comments, terms are needed which "would express the integration of technological, subsistence and demographic factors." In this case the vital factor is the exploitation of the marine resources and the areas favored at particular periods. Table 9.2 indicates the periods of occupation at some LSA sites in the Cape where controlled excavation and radiocarbon dating has enabled this to be assessed.

The ever-increasing number of radiocarbon dates available for LSA sites in the whole of South Africa has focused attention on the question of the contemporaneity or otherwise of the Smithfield and Wilton complexes (see discussion in H. J. Deacon, 1972 and J. Deacon, 1974). The absence of Smithfield dates in the range of 9500–4600 B.P. prompts the conclusion

that the Smithfield and Wilton Industries were not contemporary throughout the Holocene. Those industries occurring immediately prior to the Wilton that had been labeled Smithfield were given other names to avoid linking them with the Smithfield B of the historic period. Sampson (1974) defines "Smithfield" as only that group of industries that postdate the Wilton complex of the South African interior. Such "pre-Wilton" industries have been given several names, but they highlight one of the most remarkable realizations in South African archeology within the last decade, namely, that many stone assemblages that can be referred to as LSA extend well back into the Late Pleistocene period. This was first evident from the radiocarbon dating of the "Early LSA" at the Border Cave (Vogel 1970) and at Rose Cottage and the Heuningsneskrans Shelter near Ohrigstad. LSA–type industries were "pushed back" to more than 30,000 years. The dates for the "Smithfield A" of Matjes River, hitherto regarded as early, now seemed late! Similarly, very early dates for LSA–type industries were soon forthcoming from Nelson Bay Cave (Klein 1972a), Byneskranskop (Schweitzer and Wilson 1978), Buffelskloof (Opperman 1978), and Boomplaas (Deacon 1979). Sampson (1974) had suggested "Oakhurst Complex" to cover this post–MSA, pre-Wilton series of assemblages, but the terms "Albany Industry" and "Robberg Industry" have become accepted for two of the identifiable industries, with type sites at Nelson Bay Cave for the Robberg Industry (Klein 1974) and at Wilton for the Albany Industry (Klein 1974; J. Deacon 1972).

The Robberg and Albany Industries span the time ranges of approximately (as currently known) 20,000–12,000 B. P. and 12,000–8000 B. P., respectively. In the Cape they have been found at Boomplaas, Buffelskloof (Albany Industry only), Nelson Bay Cave, and Melkhoutboom. However, at KRM there is nothing to suggest any occupation of the caves and shelters by people with these industrial traditions. At KRM, this is the time of apparent nonoccupation. As has been seen, there is a hiatus between MSA IV and the earliest LSA midden (LSA Phase 1) which must be at least 30,000 years, more likely 50,000 years. This hiatus may be explained by such factors as (i) recession of the coastline during the Late Pleistocene; (ii) higher precipitation, rendering the cases and shelters damp and uncomfortable; and (iii) blocking of the cave mouths and partial burying of the shelters by dune sand.

There is evidence for all three of these factors at KRM Main Site, but they may not all have applied to KRM Caves 3 and 4, and future investigation may reveal something to fill part of this hiatus. Similarly, although there was nothing found in the tail of the huge midden at KRM Cave 5 between the Phase 1 LSA and an MSA I industry, a very different sequence could exist in the front of the midden which remains unexplored.

Particularly relevant to this hiatus period at KRM is the evidence from Die Kelders (Tankard and Schweitzer 1976). Overlying the MSA succession in that cave (also on the coast of the Indian Ocean, 160 km from Cape Town) are yellow iron-stained sands. These sands are eolian and totally sterile of stone artifacts, large mammal bones, or shell fragments. They are related by the excavators to a time when the shoreline was distant (hence no shell fragments) and indicate a time of nonoccupation between about 35,000–40,000 years and the first LSA occupation about 2000 B. P. This is a somewhat similar order of time and sequence to KRM.

The most recent phase of the LSA at KRM (Phase 3 under Shelter ID) contains sherds. It may be relevant that pottery has come from middens at Bonteberg radiocarbon dated to c. 100 B.C.

10 KRM Cave 5

The long, tunnel-like cave just over 2 km east of the main complex of caves and rock shelters at KRM referred to as Cave 5 (see map [fig. 1.2] and pls. 44, 45) has its entrance almost completely blocked by a very large midden. The top of this midden is at 94 ft. (28 m) above sea level, and the width of the cave at this point is only about 5 m. The original entrance was probably very much wider, at the level of the rock floor, but the midden accumulation entirely conceals it. The original level of the floor at the entrance can be estimated from the profile of the present surface inside the cave (fig. 10.1) and an extrapolation of the downward slope of the bedrock exposed in the cutting. This would be 60 ft. (18 m) and corresponds to the bedrock floor of Cave 2 and probably Cave 3 and Cave 4. If this is so, it means that 34 ft. (10 m) of archeological deposits have accumulated in the entrance, and the section exposed suggests that almost all of this is from the LSA.

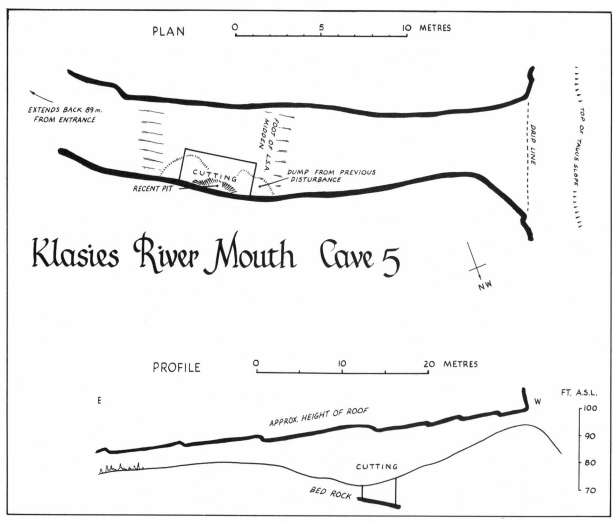

FIG. 10.1. Cave 5— plan and profile.

A small cutting, 4 × 2 m, was made inside the cave at the foot of the LSA midden (plan [fig. 10.1] and pls. 46, 47), where a shallow depression against the north wall and surrounding thrown-up soil marked some recent disturbance. A slight rise toward the rear of the cave at this point coupled with the presence of MSA stone artifacts on the surface indicated the possibility of earlier occupational soils outcropping from beneath the midden. The cutting was designed to test this relationship and also to discover whether conditions were suitable for the preservation of faunal remains in any earlier deposits.

Two sections are illustrated (fig. 10.2) at right angles to each other, and the following layers and features are identified:

Layer +. Recent disturbance, mainly thrown-up and spread soil connected with the shallow depression close to the cave wall.

Layer 1+. Recent disturbance, as above, but slightly more compact. There was no sharp division between these soils, but some of the lower ones may represent disturbance prior to the digging of the shallow pit.

Pit A. Cut into the uppermost disturbed layers and sectioned on the south side of the cutting. In plan it was oval-shaped and extended about .5 m toward the west wall and probably the same distance on the unexcavated side. It was just over 1 m deep, and the bottom was cut through into layer 3.

Layer 1. Fine gray ash and sand which was confined to the west end of the cutting and did not extend as far as the cave wall. The maximum thickness was 10 cm and cut through by Pit A.

Layer 2. Loose shell with pebbles and rock fragments with a few lenses of fine ash and sand.

Layer 2a. The lower part of layer 2 on the west side of the cutting.

Layer 2b. A continuation of layers 2 and 2a on the east side of the cutting, where they merged into a much more compacted shelly cave soil. Much of the shell was crushed, and there were signs of a shallow pit cut through it on the south face, in turn cut through by the digging of Pit A.

Layer 3. Mainly loose shell sealed by a nearly continuous layer of fine ash and sand up to 5 cm thick. This layer rested on the clean sand of layer 4a and was sharply divided from it, except toward the cave wall on the east side, where it rested directly on layer 5 and was a little mixed with it.

Layer 4a. Loose, clean yellow sand sloping down in a wedge from the west side of the cutting, i.e., toward the entrance, where it was nearly 1 m thick. It thinned to nothing and was not present on the east side of the cutting. Traces of a hearth with charcoal fragments were found at the base.

Layer 4b. Loose, paler sand than the layer above, up to 30 cm thick on the west side but thinning to nothing eastward. The upper part, at the junction with layer 4a, was cemented by lime, and several bone fragments, artifacts, and shells adhered to the bottom of this cemented part.

Layer 5. A brown, compact sandy occupational soil with ash and hearth layers that extended over the entire west side of the cutting, but was not excavated on the east side. It was probably the weathered part of the underlying layer, which varied only in color.

Layer 6. Light brown sandy soil with some ash and hearth layers.

Layer 7. Clean, sandy, angular shingle and gravel resting on the irregular surface of the quartzite bedrock.

Archeology of Layers

All these layers produced archeological material, and this is described below, divided into four sections on the basis of the stratigraphy outlined above: (i) recent disturbance (layers + and 1+); (ii) LSA (layers 1 to 3 and Pit A); (iii) intervening eolian sand (layers 4a and b); and (iv) MSA (layers 5 to 7).

Recent Disturbance

Work commenced by removing and examining all the loose soil and shell which surrounded or was partly in the pit that had been dug against the cave wall (fig. 10.1). This pit was very shallow, no more than .5 m deep, and of irregular shape, and had all the aspects of being a comparatively recent uncontrolled excavation. The volume of the disturbed soil (+) was found to be 3–4 times the volume of this pit, and from this it could be concluded that a low mound originally existed against the wall. It was such a mound, perhaps, that attracted the previous diggers, and its size (? 3 m long and .75 m high) accords well with a low mound over an interment. Almost certainly a burial had been dug out carelessly from this part, for in 1957 John Abel of Port Elizabeth found a human right parietal bone close to the pit, and our examination of the thrown-up soil produced several human bones including an occipital and left parietal fragments,

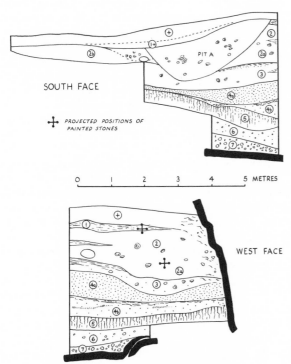

Klasies River Mouth Cave 5

SOUTH FACE

✛ PROJECTED POSITIONS OF PAINTED STONES

0   1   2   3   4   5 METRES

WEST FACE

FIG. 10.2. Cave 5—South and West Faces.

a right temporal bone, a right humerus, a right scapula fragment, and some ribs (see chap. 11).

The several artifacts found in the disturbance comprised a few stone artifacts of unspecialized form presumably derived from earlier layers, some pot sherds, and a few modern objects that give some indication of the date of the disturbance or, more likely, repeated disturbances. They comprise a wooden pipe-bowl, a piece of rusty sheet iron apparently part of a child's spade, a small fragment of decayed leather, and a used PF1 flashbulb.

Three sherds were found, and it is significant that no other sherds were found in any of the undisturbed layers below. Pottery was entirely absent from the Main Site at KRM (Caves 1 and 2 and Shelters 1A and 2A) either on the surface or in any of the deposits. A few sherds were found within the occupational layers in Shelter 1D and on the midden spreads along the beach between the Main Site and Cave 3 (see map [fig. 1.2]). Jalmar Rudner of Cape Town, South Africa, submits the following note entitled "Pottery Fragments from KRM Cave 5":

Catalog no. 29331, KRM 5

A fragment of a shoulder with a very short neck and a slight body-neck junction ridge (sign of slight subcarination). The rim is overturned and beveled outward with a trimming groove. The material is black and well fired with fine, or no, admixture. There are remains of a red burnish on the neck. The vessel was built in rings. There are two bored holes above each other on the side of the sherd, probably for repairing a crack. Their sides are almost parallel, outer diameter 5 mm, inner 4 mm. The thickness of the rim is 6 mm and of the wall 9 mm. Estimated outer rim diameter $R = \pm 10.0$ cm and maximum body diameter $D = \pm 14.0$ cm. Ratio $D/R = 1.40$.

This is probably part of a bag-shaped pot of a similar type (B2) as a pot found in a game pit at Nekkies near Knysna (Rudner, in preparation, Fig. VII:3) or Strandloper ware from Jeffreys Bay, Kromme Bay, Gamtoos River, and Mossel Bay (Rudner 1968, figs. XXV:4, XXVI:2, XXXII:88, and XXXII:77).

All the features of this fragment are common among Strandloper pottery. Bag-shaped pots of Type B2 occur on the Southwestern Cape coast but also between Fish Bay and Port Elizabeth. Overturned and tapered, including beveled, rims are mostly found between Hangklip and Port Alfred. Black material and fine or no admixture reach their maximum occurrence in the Port Elizabeth area. Bored holes are only found on the South West Africa (Namibia) and northern Namaqualand coast and again east of Fish Bay. Wall thicknesses of more than 8 mm occur mostly in the Port Alfred and East London areas. The slight carination is more common inland, e.g., in the Prince Albert District.

Catalog no. 29333, KRM 5

A typical horizontally pierced, internally reinforced Hottentot and Strandloper lug, probably conical in shape and with a maximum thickness of about 30 mm and aperture diameter of about 17 mm. The material is brown to black with a fine sand admixture, and it is burnished. This type of lug is found all along the coast of the Cape and is the type of lug expected with a pot like no 29331.

Catalog no. 29326, KRM 5

A potsherd found on the surface of the thrown-up soil. It is light red brown, is well fired, and has a medium quartz admixture. The surface has a light brown burnish. The wall thickness is 6–7 mm.

Light-colored material is more rare east of Cape Agulhas, but it does occur. The same is the case with the medium quartz admixture. The wall thickness is average for Strandloper pottery.

Conclusions

The three fragments represent typical Strandloper ware from the area in question. The same type of ware is also found in shelters, some of them containing paintings, in the mountain ranges along the coast, suggesting that the same people used the shelters and created the middens probably at different seasons. On the Cape south coast, where there are shelters, there was perhaps no need for seasonal movements. In early historical times the coast between Mossel Bay and Kromme River was the area of the Houteniqua Hottentots.

The only other object of note from the disturbance was a fragment of an elegant slate palette with ground, rounded edges.

Upon removal of the obvious loose disturbance it was not found possible to discern any features save a general disturbance along the cave wall. However, the soil below was slightly more compact, and this was removed as a separate layer (1+) for a depth of about 10 cm until the plan of the underlying deposits could be seen clearly. For the most part, this layer probably represented the cave surface prior to the digging of the pit. It contained no human bones or modern objects but one sherd of black ware that might be associated with the sherds from the layer above, a bone chisel made on a short but thick fragment of a large shaft bone, two stone flakes, one unspecialized worked flake, and a pebble grindstone rubber which was well smoothed with traces of yellow ocher and battered at both ends. Bone and shell were plentiful, including a large trumpet shell (*Charonia*). The only other trumpet shell recorded from KRM was also from 5-2a.

As might be expected with such unconsolidated deposits, there were signs of disturbance along the cave wall, and material from this area was recorded separately so that it should not be confused with material found in the undisturbed midden deposits. Burrowing animals may have been responsible for much of this disturbance. Apart from a few stone artifacts a wooden pounder was found, broken in two.

Later Stone Age

The loose filling of Pit A produced no bone tools, but a few crude stone artifacts and a remarkable number of smoothed, pecked, or battered pebbles, many bearing traces of red or black pigment. Three pebbles had well-worn facets at one end, one having a slight central depression pecked out. There were nine pebbles with various degrees of pecked facets, three bearing traces of pigment and one slightly smoothed as well. Seven other pebbles had distinct pigment adhering to them, and at least 12 other rock fragments bore traces of black or brown ocher. Several other pebbles about the size of tennis balls were in the filling and were presumably the result of selection. These, too, may have served some use which has not left obvious signs.

Only 16 stone artifacts were found, comprising three irregular cores, four crude choppers, a thick, backed crescentic scraper-knife (fig. 10.3, no. 1), an unspecialized worked flake, a flake-blade with a prepared striking platform, and six flakes. One of the larger flakes had a smear of red ocher on the dorsal cortex. There was also a small piece of shale.

Pit A gave the impression of having been dug and filled in immediately. Its size was certainly suitable for a human burial, but it had not been used for this, nor was there any other evidence to show its purpose. The dark cave soil which is mixed with overlying disturbed layers was quite absent from the filling of the pit and precludes its having been dug since this soil formed.

The fine gray sand and ash of layer 1 which was cut through by Pit A, and confined to only a small part of the west side of the cutting, produced five stone artifacts: a crude core or chopper, a crude core on a thick flake, a worked flake thickly backed on both edges, and two flakes. It also produced a flattish beach boulder 27 × 15 cm which, when washed, was seen to bear a faded but quite recognizable painting in black of a man and four fish or dolphins (pl. 48). This important discovery is described at the end of this chapter, together with another painted pebble found in the layer below.

Layer 2, including 2a and 2b, represented the tail of the LSA midden and was presumably more humified and compacted by trampling on the east side of the cutting because it was here not protected by later accumulations. Stone artifacts comprised two cores, three crude pebble choppers, 37 flakes, one flake-blade, three thick, backed scraper-knives (fig 10.3, nos. 3, 4, 8), one denticulated scraper (no. 5), two un-

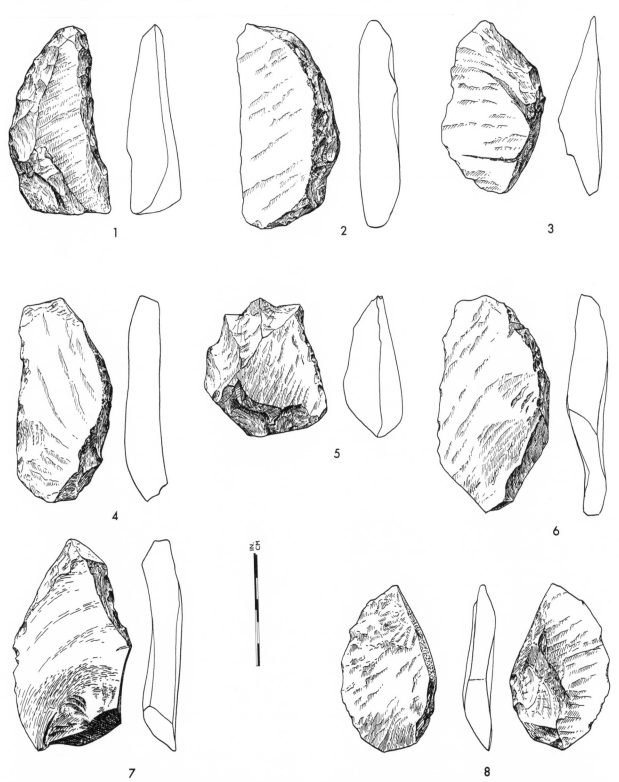

FIG. 10.3. KRM Cave 5. Thick, backed scraper-knives: nos. 1–8. LSA Industry. These appear to have been steeply flaked in a crescentic form to afford a comfortable grip while applying heavy pressure on the opposite sharp edge. This latter edge often shows signs of edge damage presumably caused by such use, e.g., no. 4, which bears bruised chipping along both faces of its thin edge, and no. 7 has a few jagged notches. However, there is no obvious damage to the knife-like edge of the elegant example, no. 2, and no. 1 is worked on both edges. No. 5 is atypical, and no. 8 presumably has the same form, but its suitable primary shape allowed its use without further flaking. Although a distinctive tool type, it probably served a variety of functions. Similar tools come from the LSA Lower Midden in Cave 1.

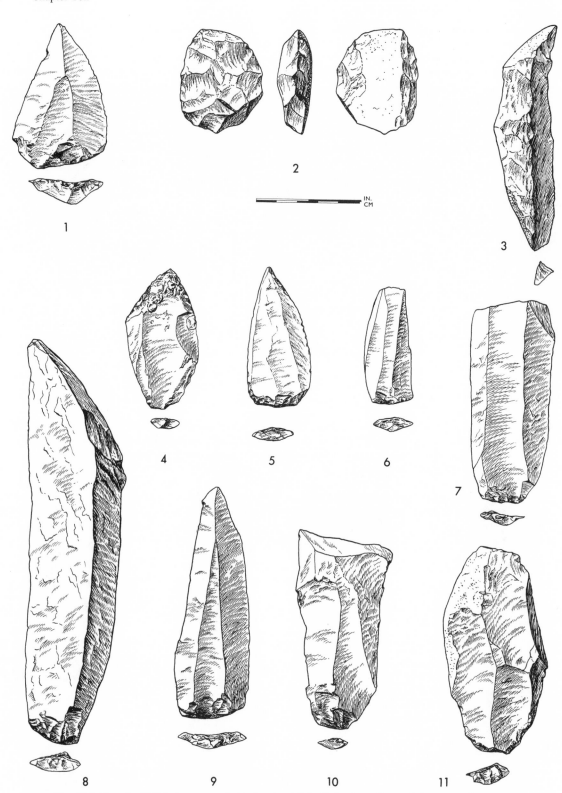

FIG. 10.4. Cave 5—MSA industry: nos. 1–11. 1: pointed flake-blade. 2: small two-platform core. 3: core rejuvenation flake. 4, 5: worked points. 6–11: flake-blades. This industry is similar to the MSA I in Cave 1 and Shelter 1B. Several of the striking platforms of the flake-blades have the same "bruised" appearance, characteristic of this stage (especially nos. 5–9). The worked point (no. 4) has limey encrustation on its tip. All derive from layer 5.

specialized worked flakes, and eight pebbles with either worn or pecked facets, some with traces of ocher on them. One pebble with a well-smoothed facet and a central pecked depression came from layer 2b, as did the only ostrich eggshell bead. There was a bored piece of calcite and three pieces of yellow and gray soft shale, but the most significant finds were a complete slate palette (pl. 50) and a flat pebble with a red grid pattern painted on both sides (pl. 49). The painted pebble is described at the end of this chapter. The palette was found in two pieces, separately, but they can be rejoined. It is waisted at one end to form a handle, similar to a modern artist's palette. The edges were chipped to shape and the roughness removed by grinding. Both surfaces have the characteristic crosshatching of grooves found on LSA slate palettes almost certainly resulting from the pulverizing of pigment with stone flakes. The fracture surfaces of the two pieces of this palette are unscratched, so it must have been thrown aside when it broke. The presence of this palette, grinding stones with traces of ocher, and the painted pebble itself all in the same layer conclusively indicates that there was artistic activity within the cave.

This layer also produced a large trumpet shell, similar to the one in the disturbed layer (1+) above.

The lowermost LSA layer (3) was little different in composition from the one above: the same loose shell with a little more silt. It produced many more stone artifacts, mainly of MSA types (fig. 10.4), and it became evident as excavation proceeded that these were coming from the area of the cutting where this layer directly overlay the weathered soil of layer 5 and had presumably been derived from it. There were 96 flake-blades (28 of which had reduced, battered striking platforms), 23 segments of flake-blades, four pointed flake-blades, one worked point, four other worked flakes, two single platform cores, and one double platform core, all of which are characteristic of the local MSA industry. It is impossible to know to which Stone Age industry the 268 flakes and eight irregular cores may belong. However, one smoothed grindstone rubber with a central pecked depression is of LSA type, as are probably the two unusual, small cuboid cores made from flat pebbles (fig. 9.6, nos. 8, 9). Similar cores come from the Wilton layers and above at Matjes River (C. G. Sampson, personal communication).

Also in this lowermost LSA level were four flakes or shatter-pieces of quartz, a piece of slate (possibly used as a palette), a piece of red ocher, and a bird's broken shaft bone bearing two circumferential thin cut marks.

The small number of artifacts and the unspecialized nature of many of them do not offer much chance of reliable correlations with other LSA sites in the district, but the presence of the crescentic, thick, backed scraper-knives does suggest a connection with the LSA II industry of Cave 1. There is a radiocarbon date for shells from layer 1 of 315 B.C. ± 105 (Geochron GX-1397), and this agrees with similar dates from Cave 1 in the Upper Midden. Much evidence for earlier phases of the Later Stone Age probably exists in this large midden that now blocks the entrance of Cave 5.

Intervening Eolian Sand

The sands, designated as layers 4a and 4b, intervene between the MSA occupational soils of layer 5 and below, and the LSA middens above. They contain no distinctive LSA cultural objects, but several stone artifacts of MSA type:

Layer 4a
    1 double platform core
  29 flakes
  14 flake-blades (3 with battered striking platforms)
    5 segments
    1 pointed flake-blade
    1 scraper with shallow secondary working
    1 piece of red ocher
Layer 4b
    1 core rejuvenator
  10 flake-blades (5 with battered striking platforms)
    5 segments
    3 pointed flake-blades
    1 denticulate
  38 flakes

These artifacts indicate an MSA date for the sands, but there is contradictory evidence from a radiocarbon date obtained from a small hearth at the base of layer 4a (2140 B.C. ± 160 [Geochron GX-1378]). It is significant that this hearth is on the cemented junction between layers 4a and 4b, and the interpretation offered is that layer 4b represents the eolian sand *in situ* which, if not of MSA date, predates any LSA occupation, a surface which was partially cemented by lime-rich water dripping from the cave roof. The initial LSA occupation, represented by the small hearth, may have disturbed this sand at a higher level nearer the cave mouth and it spread downward to form layer 4a. Excavation of a larger area might well produce LSA material in this upper sand, mixed with the derived earlier artifacts.

Middle Stone Age (Figure 10.4)

The contained artifacts which do not include any LSA types and the partially cemented capping of eolian sand indicate that layers 5 and 6 are true MSA occupational soils. The lower one rests on sandy shingle and gravel and is correspondingly sandier and cleaner than the upper. There is no sharp break between them, and so the stone artifacts found are tabulated together in Table 10.1. Mixed with the clean, sandy angular shingle and gravel (layer 7) resting on bedrock were three flake-blades, one worked flake, and five flakes.

The flake-blades in all these MSA layers are mainly of good quality, and the distinctive thinning and battering of the striking platforms suggest a correlation with the MSA I stage of Cave 1 and Shelter 1B. The worked points agree with this, one being particularly elegant with slight trimming of its base and tip. It likewise rests on bedrock and probably represents the first MSA occupation of this part of the Tzitzikama Coast.

Bone and shell were both found to be well preserved in all the MSA layers, especially in layer 5. The bone was hard and partly mineralized. It was mainly very broken and fragmentary, but bird, tortoise, and mammalian species could be identified and the latter are listed in chapter 12 and the shells in chapter 13. There were no human remains.

Painted Stones from Cave 5 (Plates 48 and 49)

The vertical positions of the two painted stones that were found in Cave 5 have been projected onto the section of the west face of the cutting that was made (fig. 10.2). There is a meter of shell accumulation between them, but this is unlikely to indicate much difference in time, for, as has been seen, layers 1 to 3 appear to represent one stage in the build-up of the midden at its foot. Shells from layer 1, directly associated with the black painting of a man and four fish or dolphins on the larger stone, have been radiocarbon dated to 315 B.C. ± 105 (Geochron GX-1397; 2285 ± 105 B.P.). The smaller stone with its red grid pattern on both faces came from layer 2, where it was found in association with a complete slate palette and evidence for the crushing of ocher to make pigments. This fortunate discovery places art objects from this region into their archeological context for the first time (Singer and Wymer 1969).

Both stones are beach pebbles of the local quartzite, selected because of their flatness. The larger (Catalog no. 29350) is 27 cm along its major axis, and the painting is executed in solid black pigment with some thin white lines (pl. 48). It depicts a man and four fish or dolphins, probably the latter because of their size and shape.[1] Their bellies are neatly

1. P. B. Best, Marine Biology unit, South African Museum, kindly advised us that the distinctive shape of the dolphin head (no beak) is suggestive of either Heaviside's dolphin (*Cephalorhyncus heavisidei*) or the dusky dolphin (*Lagenorhyncus obscurus*). The shape of the dorsal fin (almost triangular and quite small) favors the former, although for both species it is inaccurately placed relative to the tail. The

Table 10.1. VARIETIES OF MSA ARTIFACTS FROM CAVE 5

Cores
     Small double platform 1
     Small irregular 1
     Rejuvenators or core preparation flakes. . .6

Flake-blades 102

1	at	18-20 cm	(		with battered striking platforms			)
1	"	12-14 cm						
5	"	10-12 cm	(	4	"	"	"	"	)
18	"	8-10 cm	(	12	"	"	"	"	)
32	"	6- 8 cm	(	15	"	"	"	"	)
36	"	4- 6 cm	(	12	"	"	"	"	)
9	"	2- 4 cm						

Segments 55

    33 bulbous segments (15 with battered striking platforms)
    11 middle segments
    11 nonbulbous segments

Pointed flake-blades 10

Worked points. 3

Worked flakes. 2

    1 rounded end-scraper on flake-blade; 1 worked from both sides
    along one thick edge.

Flakes. 396

Nonlocal rock flakes 5

    3 of quartz
    1 of indurated shale
    1 of grey shale

Red ocher crayon 1

outlined in white. They form a regular pattern of two pairs, all in a formal, rather lifeless side view. The man has his legs bent, and, although infrared photography has done much to exaggerate the contrast between the pigment and other marks on the stone, the position of his arms remains indistinct. It is possible that the stone is meant to be viewed upright and the man is seated and holding a stick which could be a fishing rod, in which case he would be gazing at a swollen portrayal of his successful catch. Evidence for line fishing in the South African LSA coastal middens is very tenuous, but the small pieces of grooved shale found in Cave 1 (another was on the surface of the midden at Cave 4) qualify well for line sinkers. Hooks would not be expected to survive if made of thorns. However, the "rod" is very faint and may be no more than misleading stains on the stone. An alternative interpretation of the painting, favored by us, places the stone horizontally with the man in the top left corner: he is then swimming in company of four dolphins. Whatever the interpretation, it is a tastefully composed and cleanly executed example of prehistoric art.

The smaller stone from layer 2a (pl 49) has a red grid pattern on both faces, being brighter and better preserved on one side (Catalog no. 29477). The pattern is the same on both sides and is the first pattern of this type discovered in South Africa (J.

Rudner, personal communication). However, Phillipson (1969) reports schematic rock paintings of grid type on a wall panel at Nakapapula rock shelter, Zambia, in which a grid similar to that on the KRM stone is noted. A date earlier than the eighth century A.D. is suggested for the Napakapula paintings on the basis of radiocarbon dating.

Many other stones were washed and examined for possible paintings. Several bore faint traces of black or red staining, and some were considered to be possible faded paintings. Infrared photography of the more likely ones failed to substantiate this.

The Tzitzikama Coast is famous for its painted gravestones, now in the South African and Port Elizabeth Museums, found by FitzSimons during his investigations of many of the caves in the 1920s (FitzSimons 1923; Rudner 1971). The records are insufficient to show the exact associations of the earlier finds, and there is nothing but the art itself to connect them with these discoveries from KRM.

Since the discovery of these painted stones in KRM Cave 5, four other painted stones have been found in the inland cave of Boomplaas (Deacon, Deacon, and Brooker 1976); associated with a Wilton LSA Industry, these have been radiocarbon dated at 4450 B.C. ± 75 (UW-306) and 5 B.C. ± 75 (UW-336). A similar date has been obtained for a grave covered by a painted stone in a cave at Plettenberg Bay: A.D. 25 ± 33 (Pta-014) (Rudner and Rudner 1973), whereas painted stones at Apollo 11 Cave in South West Africa has been radiocarbon dated to c. 24,000 B.C.

---

present distribution of these species is poorly known, but indications are that *L. obscurus* does not range as far east as KRM while *C. heavisidei* has only been recorded from the Cape Peninsula and west coast of South Africa.

11 Human Skeletal Remains

The scanty human (compared with the rich faunal) fragmentary remains were scattered in isolated fashion throughout the sequences (fig. 11.1). Their locations and circumstances of discovery are noted in chapter 8. For the sake of quick reference, they will be summarized here according to sequences and described. Their analysis relative to remains found elsewhere in Africa must of necessity be limited because of their incomplete nature. Certain basic conclusions may be ventured, but because of the wide variations in sapient populations and the fragmentary nature of specimens recovered elsewhere, the use of techniques such as multivariate analysis and D^2 values is premature.

Sequence	Specimen Numbers
MSA IV	Nil
MSA III	40243, 40244
MSA II	13400, 14692, 14691, 14693, 14694, 14696, 14695, 16424, 16425, 27038, 21776, 41658, 16651, 26076, 27574-7, 26730-2, 27889, 16720
MSA I	26909, 27070, 41815, 41820
LSA	614, 43110 (see below)

Two additonal series were recovered: (1) fragments of cranial and postcranial parts in recently disturbed layers either on or just below the surface of Cave 5 (see chap. 10); (2) fragments in Shelter 1D (see chap. 9). Because of the rather "fresh" appearance and fragmentary nature of the LSA specimens in these latter series and because of the lack of comparative described postcranial material, these specimens will be listed only and not described or compared in this monograph. However, because of its location at such depth, specimen 43110 from 1D-5 is described later in the chapter.

1. KRM 5 (Plates 52, 53, 54)

   a) Surface and +:

41038	Fragment of basioccipital region, belonging to 41040
41039	Fragment of temporal
41040	Right temporal
41041	Right humerus (juvenile)
41042	Fragment of right scapula
41043/4	Ribs
43113	Fragment of left parietal

We are grateful to Dr. Patricia Smith, University of Tel Aviv, for assistance with the analysis of the dentitions, and to Dr. Philip Rightmire, SUNY at Binghamton, for information based on his examination of some cranial fragments at the South African Museum.

   b) Layer 2a:

41254	Fragment of petrous part of temporal

2. KRM 1D (Plate 55)

All specimens are from layer 3 unless stated otherwise

43068a,b,c	Left fibula (adult)
43069	Left ulna, upper three-fourths
43070	Left radius, shaft
43071a–d	Left humerus (adult female)
43072a,b	Left scapula, glenoid and olecranon process
43072c	Scapula fragment, axillary border (fits 43077)
43073	Proximal phalanx, big toe
43074	Proximal part of second metacarpal
43075	Femur, fragment of distal condyle
43076	Fibula, midshaft
43077	Fragment of scapula, axillary border (fits between 43072a and 43072c)
43078	Fragment of right first rib
43079	Rib fragment
43080	Rib fragment
43081	Bone fragment
43082	Distal part of left first metacarpal
43085	Bone fragment
43086	Cuneiform
43087	Cuboid
43088	Capitate
43110	Layer 5: part of the left ramus and body of a mandible with 3 worn small molars in sockets showing chronic periodontitis. This specimen is described below

Numerous fragments of ribs (unnumbered).

It is likely that the remains found in 1D-3 belong to one individual. This suggests a considerable cultural shift from the MSA remains, which comprise anatomically isolated skeletal fragments.

MSA III
40243, 40244: KRM 1A-6

Two small fragments of the parietal bone of the skull were found in 1A-6. Both appear charred, 40244 more than 40243. The thicknesses of the fragments are

40243 _____ 6.5 mm max., 4.5 mm min.
40244 _____ 6.0 mm max., 4.0 mm min.

The inner aspects show faint vascular grooves.

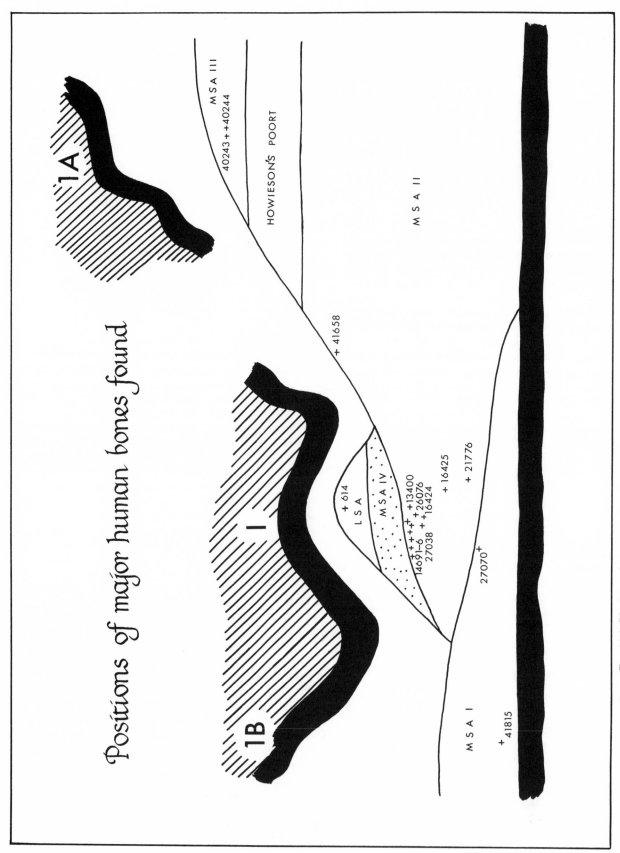

Fig. 11.1. Diagrammatic representation of the locations of the major human bones recovered. The numbers are the catalog numbers of the individual fragments found.

MSA II
13400: KRM 1-4, (Plates 56 and 64)

This is a portion of the corpus of a mandible, extending from the socket of the right third molar to the socket of the left second premolar. It is robust with a thickened lower border or basal bar, and a torus mandibularis lingual to the second premolar and first molar. The chin is weakly developed, with the labial aspect of basal and alveolar bone forming a continuous straight line when viewed from the side. A weak pogonion (mental protuberance) is about one-third up from the lower border of symphysis, and below that point the chin slopes backward with a slight convexity (fig. 11.2, pl. 56) to gnathion. On the labial side of RP$_3$ about 6 mm of the alveolar margin is broken away but the edge is suggestive of some alveolar eversion, or possibly bony reaction to gingival irritation.

The height of the body at the symphysis is 32.5 mm while at M$_1$ it is about 31 mm, suggesting that the upper and lower borders of the mandible are parallel such that there is no significant increase in the vertical dimension in the symphysial region. A section through this region (fig. 11.2) shows a teardrop appearance which is produced mainly by the bulge of the genial tubercles. This chin region is almost vertical. The sockets of the anterior teeth have had the buccal bone broken away. The genial tubercles form a prominent mass whose diameter measures 10.5 mm vertically and 7.5 mm horizontally. Laterally and below it, along the inner edge of the lower border, there is a marked oval depression on each side for the attachment of the anterior belly of the digastric muscle. Two mental foramina of approximately equal size are present on the right side, one below M$_1$ and one below Pm$_2$. The formina are bounded below by a thickened, continuous bar of bone which continues downward and forward almost to the inferior border of the corpus opposite the digastric impression. Seen from the superior aspect, the lingual surface of the symphysis faces superiorly and posteriorly. Measured labiolingually, the basal bone in the symphysial region is thicker than the alveolar bone. At the genial tubercles, the symphysis measures 14.8 mm. The inferior border at the symphysis measures 12 mm. Opposite M$_1$ (at the torus mandibularis) the thickness is 17.5 mm while below it the flattened inferior border is 10.7 mm thick. Thus the robusticity index at M$_1$ is about 56 percent, while at M$_2$ it is about 55 percent.

Teeth: Only the second premolar and first and second right molars were found securely *in situ,* but four other loose teeth (see below) were found adjacent: 14691, 14692, 14693, and 14694 (pl. 57). The teeth present have a 5Y cuspal pattern, and are narrow buccolingually. They decrease in size from M$_1$ to M$_3$. There is some wear due to attrition with exposure of dentine but no evidence of alveolar recession, and the sockets of the missing teeth are discrete, indicating postmortem loss. There are no accessory tubercles present, and the teeth are not taurodont. However, there is some hypercementosis of the root apices.

The condition of the bone and state of wear of the teeth would indicate an age at death of 20–25 years. Because of advanced wear of teeth, the diameters of the teeth are less than those of less worn or unworn teeth with which they may be compared.

14692   This is a lower left first premolar, fitting into the appropriate socket in 13400. It is single rooted, with hypercementosis apically. There are two lingual cusps, and there is exposure of dentine in the occlusal surface.

14691   A lower left first molar, with hypercementosis of the distal root. Cuspal pattern is 5Y; dentine is exposed on the occlusal surface. It is set in a fragment of mandible and fits the appropriate socket in 13400.

14693   A lower left second molar, cuspal pattern 5Y, with dentine exposed on the distolingual cusp. There is a distinct seventh cusp on the lingual aspect. The tooth fits the socket distal to 14691. The close proximity of the mesial root to the distal root is similar to the pattern of the above teeth and those found in 13400.

14694   A lower left third molar, 5-cusped, with faceting of the occlusal surface.

14696   This is a *left* lower first or second molar, characterized by the buccolingual breadth of crown and roots which give the tooth a quadrangular appearance. The cuspal pattern is partially obliterated by wear, but five cusps can be distinguished. The wide separation of the mesial and distal roots and their shortness distinguish it from the above teeth. The roots are short, and there is marked separation of buccal and lingual root canals in both roots. The anterior root is bifurcated at its tip. It is also less worn that the teeth of the right side in 13400. It was found further away from 13400 than 14691-4 and adjacent to another mandibular symphysial fragment, 14695. Radiographs of 13400 show that the roots are long and bulky.

The measurements of the teeth are given in table 11.1.

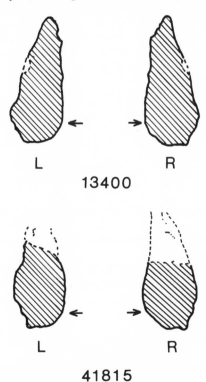

13400

41815

Fig. 11.2. Contours of casts of 13400 and 41815 sectioned through symphysis menti. Arrow points to mental protuberance (pogonion).

14695: KRM 1-14 (Plate 59)

Fragment of mandibular body including the symphysis, sockets for all four lower incisor teeth, and both canine sockets broken away along the distal margins. There is some erosion of bone

Table 11.1. MEASUREMENTS (MM) OF TEETH IN SPECIMEN 13400 AND ASSOCIATED LOOSE
TEETH

Specimen	Mesiodistal	Buccolingual (max.)
14692 (P_1)	c. 7.7	8.7
14691 (M_1)	12.8	11.3
14693 (M_2)	12.5	10.5
14696 (M_2)	12.1	11.1
14694 (M_3)	11.4	9.8
13400 (P_2)	8.0	9.0
(M_1)	12.8	11.1
(M_2)	11.9	10.5
(P_2 - M_2)	32.7	
(P_2 - M_3)	c. 44.1	
(M_1 - M_3)	c. 36.4	

along the inferior surface and anteriorly at the symphysis, but the mental eminence is not markedly developed even when this surface loss is accounted for. As there is some fracturing of the alveolar margin, a measurement of corpus height cannot be accurate. The bone is thick, and the genial tubercles are well developed. Measurements:

Symphysial thickness   15.0 mm
Symphysial height   > 25 mm

16424: KRM 1-14+ (Plate 58)

This constitutes part of the right corpus of a mandible, carrying the three molars. The bone is very slender and gracile. The teeth are small, with a 5+ pattern on the M_2 and M_3. M_1 is weathered, and the enamel is chipped so that the cuspal pattern cannot be distinguished. The teeth are taurodont, but all apices are fully formed and closed, suggesting an age at death of 20–22 years. The roots are perfectly proportioned to crowns—not pathological (e.g., hypopituitary dwarf). The root socket for P_2 is small. The uniquely small teeth are set in relatively large jaws, but the proportion is perfect. It is adult, but if M_3 was not *in situ,* one may have mistaken it for a child's jaw! There are no signs of fire shrinkage. The low ramal height, five-cusped but small molars, and mesotaurodontism are all Bushman features. The small size and gracility of the bone suggest that this fragment belonged to an unusually small female. There are many resemblances to the later (LSA), but more robust, specimen 43110 (see below).

The broken edges of the ramus and corpus are "smoothed," the appearance suggesting water action or weathering or both. The buccal aspect of the anterior end of the corpus is broken away, leaving the socket of P_2 intact. The inferior border is narrow and rounded, the outermost layer of the bone appearing to be split off. The front part of the corpus is discolored (including M_1), possibly charred. The inferior border of the ramus is much thinner than that of the adjacent corpus. The oblique line, for the attachment of the buccinator, is reasonably well formed, leaving a shelf lateral to M_3 equaling about one-third of the width of the bone there. The bone is broken away over the mandibular foramen, displaying a relatively large, rounded space for the inferior dental nerve and vessels. The rounded smooth edge above the foramen indicates that this is close to the upper end of the foramen. It is thus possible to estimate the approximate breadth of the ramus here (see below). The groove for the mylohyoid nerve and vessels is clearly demarcated, and the mylohyoid ridge is prominent. The height of the corpus at P_2/M_1 is slightly more than 20 mm. The maximum thickness at this point is 13.2 mm. The thickness of the inferior border of the corpus here is approximately 8 mm, while the thickness of the inferior border of the ramus (in the region of the facial vessels' groove) is almost 6 mm. The latter groove is poorly demarcated.

The distance from the mandibular foramen to the anterior border of the ramus is approximately 20 mm, suggesting that the total width of ramus here is about 35 mm. (See also tables 11.2 and 11.3.)

Measurements of teeth (M-D = mesiodistal, B-L = buccolingual):

	M-D	B-L
M_1	c. 9.5	c. 8.5
M_2	9.3	8.8
M_3	8.3	8.0
M_1–M_3	c. 27.2	

Radiographs of 16424 show that the roots are gracile and tapering. Taurodontism in M_2 and M_3 is obvious. The apices of the M_3 root are quite closed, which confirms the age estimate of 20–23 years.

The teeth and jaws from MSA II reveal that the remains of at least four individuals are represented, and the jaw fragments indicate the presence of at least two different types: three massive jawed and one gracile.

16425: KRM 1-16 (Plate 59)

Fragment of frontal bone in glabellar region, with frontonasal suture intact and portion of right supraorbital ridge. The frontonasal suture is almost obliterated, while the internasal suture

Table 11.2. DIMENSIONS AND ROBUSTICITY INDEX OF THE BODY OF THE MANDIBLE AT M_1 IN KRM SPECIMENS AND SELECTED SPECIMENS FROM ELSEWHERE

Specimen	Height at M_1	Thickness at M_1	Robusticity Index	Source of Data
1) KRM:				
#13400	c 31	17.5	c 56	Present study
#16424	c 20	13.2	c 66	"
#21776	c 35	c 18	c 51	"
#41815	c 33.5	16.4	c 49	"
2) African Upper Pleistocene and Post-Pleistocene:				
Border Cave (Third White Ash layer)	29.5	13.6	46.1	De Villiers 1976
Border Cave 2	26.0	11.4	43.8	"
Tuinplaas (Springbok Flats)	35.0	18.0	51.4	"
Fish Hoek (Skildergat) P4	32.1 [R] 31.6 [L]	15.7 [R] 15.6 [L]	48.9 [R] 49.4 [L]	Tobias 1971
Cave of Hearths (adolescent)	25.8	15.9	61.6	"
Wadi Halfa	27.0 [R] 26.0 [L]	12.0 [R] 12.0 [L]	44.4 [R] 46.2 [L]	"
Diré-Dawa	34.0	16.0	47.0	"
Boskop	24.3	14.9	61.3	"
Cape Flats	32.4 [R] 33.9 [L]	14.4 [R] 15.0 [L]	44.4 [R] 44.2 [L]	"
3) African Middle Pleistocene:				
Ternifine I	36	19	53	Tobias 1971
Ternifine II	35	17	48.5	"
Kanam	c 40	16.5	c 41.3	"
Olduvai Hominid 22	29.0	20.3	70.0	"
Olduvai Hominid 23	c 30.5	20.4	c 66.9	"
4) Modern:				
S. African Negro (male, n=50) mean	28.83	13.57	47.25	De Villiers 1976
S. African Negro (female, n=50) mean	27.70	13.12	47.71	"
San Bushman (male, n=14) mean	24.49	12.91	53.34	"
San Bushman (female, n=8) mean	24.58	13.10	53.54	"

Table 11.3. Mesiodistal and Buccolingual Diameters of Mandibular Premolars and Molars in KRM and Selected Specimens

Specimens	Pm$_1$ MD	Pm$_1$ BL	Pm$_2$ MD	Pm$_2$ BL	M$_1$ MD	M$_1$ BL	M$_2$ MD	M$_2$ BL	M$_3$ MD	M$_3$ BL	Data From
KRM #13400	7.7	9.0	8.0	9.0	12.8	11.1	11.9	10.5	-	-	Present Study
KRM #14691-3/4	c 7.7	8.7	-	-	12.8	11.3	12.5	10.5	11.6	9.9	Present Study
KRM #14696	-	-	-	-	12.1	11.1	-	-	-	-	Present Study
KRM #16424	-	-	-	-	(9.5)	8.5	9.3	8.8	8.3	8.0	Present Study
KRM #43110	-	-	-	-	-	-	10.2	9.1	9.8	8.8	Present Study
Kalomo	-	-	-	-	10.5	10.5	11.1	10.5	12.0	11.0	Schepers 1935
Cave of Hearths	7.7	8.6	-	-	12.1	11.1	12.0	10.3	-	-	Tobias 1971
Haua Fteah 1	-	-	-	-	-	-	11.9	11.5	10.9	10.8	Tobias 1967
Haua Fteah 2	-	-	-	-	-	-	-	-	11.4	10.6	Tobias 1967
Near East Mousterian	7.7	8.6	7.5	8.9	11.7	11.3	11.3	10.8	11.5	10.6	Smith, unpub.
I. Ihraud	-	-	-	-	14.5	12.5	-	-	-	-	Smith, unpub.
W. Halfa (male)	7.6	9.3	7.5	8.4	12.5	12.7	12.3	12.0	12.1	11.7	Green et al. 1967
W. Halfa (mixed)	7.6	9.3	7.4	10.0	12.1	11.5	11.8	11.5	11.8	11.5	Green et al. 1967
I. Hahaba	7.8	9.5	7.7	9.8	12.3	11.2	12.8	10.9	-	-	Green et al. 1967
Negro S. Africa	7.6	9.0	8.0	9.3	12.0	11.3	12.0	11.3	11.9	11.2	Abel 1933
Bantu S. Africa	7.1	8.2	7.2	8.1	11.0	10.5	11.0	10.3	11.1	10.4	Shaw 1931
Hottentot	-	-	-	-	10.8	10.4	10.5	10.4	11.6	11.1	Singer, unpub.
	-	-	-	-	9.9	10.6	10.0	9.9	9.5	9.5	Singer, unpub.
Bushmen	6.9	7.5	7.2	7.6	11.3	10.2	11.0	10.0	10.0	9.3	Drennan 1929
Fish Hoek (P4)	6.6	7.3	6.8	7.8	11.1	10.1	10.8	10.4	10.4	9.9	Singer, unpub.
European	6.4	7.3	6.6	7.8	10.7	10.3	10.0	9.7	10.0	9.5	Brabant et al. 1964
Pygmy	7.2	8.1	7.3	8.7	11.6	10.9	10.9	10.2	10.6	9.8	Brabant et al. 1964
Cape Colored	-	8.1	-	8.4	10.0	10.5	-	10.7	-	10.9	Singer, unpub.
Diré-Dawa	-	(7.0)	-	(6.5)	(9.5)	(9.0)	(10.5)	(10.0)	(10.0)	(9.0)	Vallois 1951
Springbok Flats (Tuinplaas)	-	-	-	(7.6)	(9.1)	(10.7)	(9.2)	(10.6)	(10.0)	10.0	Schepers 1941
Boskop	-	-	-	-	-	-	(10.5)	(9.5)	9.5	11.0	Schepers 1935
Kabua 1	-	8.0	-	9.0	-	-	12.0	12.2	11.7	11.5	Whitworth 1966

Note. Values in brackets are for severely abraded teeth. KRM specimen #41815 is not included because the teeth are worn down to the crown-root junction.

is relatively nonserrated. The broken nasal bones are about two-thirds of their original length, as the internasal crest forming part of the root of the nose and articulating with the perpendicular plate of ethmoid is clearly visible inferiorly. The upper edge of the frontal process of the maxilla is broken away. The right superior orbital margin is slightly rounded and fairly horizontal in position, and medially there is a prominent supraorbital bulge which meets its fellow in a rather bulging glabellar region (but not as prominent as in the Florisbad skull) with a slight dimple in the metopic suture region. The nasal bones are set at a definite angle to the frontal bone, and the internal area is angulated, indicating that this area is not as flat as one expects in some typically orthognathous Bushmen and Hottentots. There is a marked supraorbital notch. The inner surface of the fragment displays an average-sized frontal sinus. The thickness of the frontal at the glabella is more than 18 mm, but not much more. The smallness of the fragment does not permit reasonable assessment of the exact degree of slope of the frontal bone, but some sloping is present; i.e., the frontal is unlikely to have been truly vertical. There is not anything about this fragment that could not be assigned to *Homo sapiens*. The bulging

glabella and angulated nasal bones are suggestive of non-Bushman features, but the horizontal position of the superior orbital margin is not. On the basis of the remains of the nasal bridge and medial wall of right orbit, the interorbital width is estimated as about 30 mm.

27038: KRM 1-15+ (Possibly 14) (Plates 61 and 62)

This parietal fragment shows a portion of the sagittal suture—with open serrations and no evidence of fusion with the opposite side. Parallel to this edge, on the inner aspect, is the groove for the sagittal sinus, suggesting that this fragment belongs to the right side. Anteriorly are erosions of the arachnoid granulations, and ending at the sinus are two clearly marked and large grooves for the middle meningeal vessels. The maximum thickness near the suture is 9 mm, and inferiorly 8 mm.

21776: KRM 1-17 (Plate 60)

Part of the left corpus of the mandible, found in three pieces and blackened, possibly charred. The black staining is mostly on the lingual aspect. The cracked appearance suggests firing, but the inferior border is slightly crushed too. At the symphysis the small piece of the right body contains one and a half sockets for incisors, while the left corpus extends back to include part of the M_2 socket. The latter area is split but not very distorted. The sockets are large. The mental foramen, opposite P/M_1, is large. A chin is present, and the alveolar area suggests mild prognathism. The chin appears to be more obvious because it is less "receding" (rounded) inferiorly than specimen 13400 and also because of the alveolar prognathous appearance.

At the symphysis, the thickness is 17.0 mm and the height is c. 36.0 mm. Opposite M_1, the thickness is c. 18.0 mm and the height is > 31.0 mm (probably about 35.0 mm). The thickness of the alveolus between RI and LI is 7.0 mm. The robusticity index at the symphysis is about 47 percent. The robusticity index at M_1 is about 51 percent.

The inferior border is thick and rounded, but is difficult to measure, as it slopes rapidly to the maximum thickness at the level of the genial tubercles. Just laterally to the tubercles the thickness is 15 mm. It seems unlikely that a torus mandibularis was present. The compression of the bone in the region of M_2 gives the corpus an artificial appearance of being very robust here, and the mylohyoid line is also artificially accentuated for the same reason. The lingual aspect of the symphysis does not have the same concave shelving behind the incisors, downward and backward, as in specimen 13400. Lateral to the symphysis, the inferior border has a slight hollowed concavity. It seems that the alveolar and inferior borders have the same parallel tendency as in no. 13400.

41658: KRM 1A-36 (Plate 66)

This parietal bone was found in an extension of East Cutting T between the north side and the rock wall (see chap. 8). It was found with numerous flakes: blades, pointed flake-blades, bifacial shallow-flaked, worked flakes, and one Stillbay flake blade. Specimen 41658 comprises mainly part of the right parietal bone, a small protion of the adjacent left parietal bone, and a piece of the right frontal bone adjacent to the coronal suture.

On the endocranial aspect the faint straightish groove (pockmarked with minute vascular foramina) for the frontoparietal suture almost bisects the fragment. Just posterior to it is the upper portion of the "stem" of the anterior division of the middle meningeal vessels where it bifurcates into its branches which proceed toward the sagittal suture (pl. 66). The main branch nearest and parallel to the coronal suture usually demarcates the general position of the precentral sulcus. Near the posterior edge of the fragment are the grooves for the "middle" branches (which are usually the anterior branches of the posterior division). The shortness of the "stems" indicates that the lower border of the fragment is in the region of the temporal ridge, a portion of which can be seen faintly in the posterior half of the fragment's external surface. The bregmatic portion of the sagittal suture is fused and thickened, and on each side of it (especially on the right parietal bone) there are a number of granular pits (to lodge the arachnoid granulations). The position of the coronal suture is confirmed by X-ray on which it is noted that there is a sinuous density just anterior to bregma: this may possibly represent a fused metopic suture (normally rare in living African populations).

The bone posteriorly is thick, the measurements being as follows (mm):

Antero-inferior	9.0
Postero-inferior	7.0

Mid-anterior border	8.2
Mid-posterior border	9.7
Maximum thickness at sagittal suture	7.0
Para-sagittal	4.5

The external surface has a mottled roughness on the upper half which could be the result of weathering erosion (pl. 66). At the antero-inferior angle are three grooves running upward and backward produced by the supraorbital vessels. Near the middle of the posterior border, externally, is a dimple—either an erosion or a healed injury.

The fragment gives the impression of being relatively low-vaulted and narrow, with a frontal that does not slope backward as much as in the Saldanha skull. It belongs to an old individual (on basis of suture fusion).

16651: KRM 1-14 (Plate 65)

Left zygomatic (malar) bone, almost complete but damaged along its maxillary border. There is also slight erosion of bone along the inferior margin. The remaining fragment is rather flat in facial aspect, and there is little suggestion of incurving toward the zygomaticomaxillary suture. The bone is large but within the range of size variation in modern African population. There is a large zygomaticofacial foramen, and the ascending orbital margin is broken near the frontozygomatic suture.

Measurement is difficult because of the problem of landmarks, especially anteriorly at the point where the zygomaticomaxillary suture should cross the inferior orbital margin. Maximum malar length is about 42 mm, but this is an underestimate of the actual length. Malar subtense cannot be taken.

26076: 1-14 (Plate 65)

Left clavicle, broken away at the sternal end and damaged at the acromial end (inferiorly). It is small, lightly built, and the ligamentous attachments for the coracoclavicular ligaments and the deltoid muscle are discernable. Measurements (mm):

Antero-posterior diameter (midpoint)	10
Supero-inferior diameter (midpoint)	8
Antero-posterior diameter (acromial end)	16.5
Supero-inferior diameter (acromial end)	11

27574, 27575, 27576, and 27577: KRM 1-14
(Plates 61 and 63)

Fragments of cranial vault. Specimen 27574 is the largest, measuring c. 55 by 65 mm; meningeal markings are apparent, but much of the ectocranial surface bone has been worn away. It is possible that it belongs to a juvenile. Specimen 27575 seems to belong to a parietal bone, but identification cannot be precise. Numbers 27576 and 27577 are small fragments, not diagnostic. Specimens 27575 and 27576 can be joined to each other. It is possible that all the fragments belong to a single individual.

26730, 26731, and 26732: 1A-34 (Plate 63)

Fragments of cranial vault. Specimen 26730 is the largest (c. 70 by 50 mm) of the three, and probably a fragment of right parietal bone with meningeal markings present endocranially. Posteriorly about 35 mm of the lamboid suture are preserved. Specimens 26731 and 26732 are smaller fragments, blackened (probably by fire) and not diagnostic.

27889: KRM 1-15

A fragment of a radius. Much of the head is eroded away, and only a small part of the articular surface remains. The shaft is broken off c. 20 mm beyond the tuberosity; the latter is not robustly developed. The fragment is suggestive of a small, lightly built individual. The specimen appears to have been blackened by burning.

16720: KRM 1-14

A fragment of innominate bone, possibly right, that could belong to the pubic portion of the acetabular rim.

MSA I
26909: KRM 1-37 (Plate 61)

Another parietal fragment of a skull, measuring c. 45 by 50 mm, rather badly eroded over portions of its ectocranial surface. Faint meningeal markings can be elicited endocranially (26910, a companion piece, is missing from the South African Museum collection).

27070: KRM 1-37 (Plate 61)

This thin fragment of skull measures c. 40 by 60 mm, the one edge being part of a suture. The external surface is rather smooth, while the internal has a chip of bone cemented to it near one corner, and a small pit is found in the opposite corner. The thinness of the fragment, varying from 3.5 to 7 mm, contrasts markedly with specimen 41658 and less so with specimen 20738.

41815: KRM 1B-10 (Plates 67 and 68)

This well-mineralized, relatively intact mandible was found beside, but not under, a large lump of soft calcrete lying on the surface of this layer. It rested with the ramus upright (pl. 67). Most of the corpus is intact, except that a small triangular portion of the alveolus between LI_2 and RI_2 is broken out. Only right P_2, M_1 and left M_1, M_2 are present. The other alveolar sockets are present and appear normal. However, RM_3 is lost, but the entire socket is absent on the left, the appearance suggesting congenital absence. X-ray indicates that LM_3 is not embedded (i.e., unerupted) in the bone. The socket for RM_3 is shallow and single. M_1 (R and L) and LM_2 are worn down to their roots, while both M_1 have exposure of root canals. There are signs of abscesses at the root apices of both M_1. The LP_4 root socket is present, while the socket of LP_3 shows signs of abscess cavity; in addition, the left canine socket shows chronic abscess formation.

There is no taurodontism evident, and judging from the root/crown size, the M_1 and M_2 seem to have been large—they compare fairly with the root sizes of 14691 and 13400.

The teeth are heavily worn down to the roots (stage 6 of Brothwell 1963, p. 69) with dentine erosion in the right P_2, M_1 and left M_1. The LM_2 is ground down with very little enamel remaining as a ridge around the tooth. From the appearance of the sockets, it appears that quite a bit of the alveolar margin is resorbed, so that the height of the mandible in the living healthy individual would have been 2–3 mm greater.

The right mental foramen is double—the larger is above, the smaller below (opposite P_1–P_2). The left mental foramen is single, though a small foramen is present 8.7 mm behind and

slightly below it. The corpus is robust with bulging triangular mental protuberance (fig. 11.2). Lingually, there is a slight shelflike ridge in the region of the genioglossus attachment. There is a thick ridge extending down from the lower end of the coronoid process to the chin, passing between the two mental foramina on the right and below the mental foramen on the left (between it and the smaller foramen posteriorly).

On the left, the inferior border is broken from the angle for about 7 cm anteriorly. On the right side, the inferior border has a marked concavity in the region of the facial artery groove. The lower border of the ramus is broken just posterior to this. The mylohyoid line is markedly ridged and bulges in the region of M_2–M_3 on the left and right. From this bulge a marked ridge (in the region of the attachment of the superior constrictor) projects upward to a triradiate bulge anterior to the inferior alveolar foramen.

The left ramus is rather badly broken, only part of the coronoid process remaining. On the right, it is a little better preserved with most of the coronoid process intact. The coronoid process is rather massive, rounded, and low with a marked supero-anterior ridge for attachment of temporalis muscle.

Measurements (mm). Taken at crown-root junction (or on root):

Tooth	Mesiodistal	Buccolingual
Right P_2	5.5	7.0
Right M_1	9.8	9.5
Left M_1	9.7	9.4
Left M_2	10.9	10.0

M_1–M_2 (left): 20.8
M_1–M_3 (right): c. 32.5

Thickness of body. Measured on right side:

Opposite gonion	14.2
Opposite I_2	14.8
Opposite P_2	15.0
Opposite M_1	16.4
Opposite M_2	18.4
Opposite M_3	18.1

Height of body:

Opposite right I_2–C	31.2
At right C–P_1	33.6
At right M_1	33.5 (measured on buccal aspect)

Height of right coronoid process from tip to a point just behind the facial artery concavity: >62 mm (a piece fragmented off inner and inferior part). Distance from lingula to anterior border of ramus (parallel to inferior border): 23 mm. Length from anterior edge of alveolar foramen to anterior border: c. 21 mm. Therefore approximate estimated breadth of ramus: ±33 mm (i.e. very broad). On X-ray, the left M_2 shows two mesial roots (usually considered to be a mongoloid characteristic). Distance between the two mesial points of incisor sockets: 21.5 mm (measured from most mesial point). Length between anterior points of coronoid process: c. 102.0 mm. Minimum length between right and left M_3: 55.0 mm. Maximum length across right and left M_3 (outermost surface of body of mandible): 90.0 mm. Gnathion-gonion (angle of mandible estimated): 100 mm. Gnathion-most distal point on right side: 84 mm. Bigonial breadth (estimated): 110 mm. Bigonial breadth (actual across broken rami): 100 mm. Breadth across mental foramina (main): 50 mm. Robusticity index: 48.93 percent. The dental arch of 41815 is wide and "open" posteriorly, and the teeth are in a short curve. The ramus angle appears to have had a large flange.

41820: KRM 1B-10

A fragment of a mandibular condyle found immediately next to 41815 and probably belonging to its right ramus. It is very broad, and the neck is especially massive. Side-to-side breadth of condyle: 24.3 mm. Maximum thickness (A–P): 10 mm. Breadth of neck: c. 15.0 mm. These figures suggest that the ramus was massive.

Notes on the Wear on the Teeth (MSA II and I)

13400. Occlusal wear plane is flat and occlusobuccal angle is rounded, suggesting that attrition took place as a result of chewing activities that involve wide lateral excursion of the mandible. No enamel chipping or sharp edges noted, which thus indicates a lack of foreign abrasive particles, i.e., suggests meaty or fibrous diet but not grit or sand. This is inferred despite the extensive shellfish diet.

16424. Less worn than 13400 but the same applies.

14691, 14692, and 14693. Slightly less worn than 13400, but this could be within the range of variation expected in terms of bilateral asymmetry. However, the wear patterns are similar.

14694. M_3: similar to 13400 wear.

14696. M_1 (?M_2) with markedly more attrition on buccal than on lingual cusps. The occlusobuccal angle is smooth and rounded (as above). This probably reflects a difference in jaw relationship rather than a different diet or abrasive action.

13400 and 16424. Suggests a tête-à-tête arrangement anteriorly with the maxilla, which resembles the arrangement one gets in short, wide arches (similar to Fish Hoek mandibles). This is also the kind of pattern found in Neandertal jaws.

41815. Very severely worn. The occlusal plane is flat. From the viewpoint of diet, it is similar to 13400.

LSA
614: KRM 1, Lower Part of Upper Midden
(Layer 6/7) (Plate 70)

Fragment of left side of corpus containing alveolar region from M_2–M_1 and broken at the level of the mental foramen. From the alveolar height in this region, M_1 height was probably 32–35 mm. The I_1, C, and M_2 were lost postmortem, and I_1 is broken off at root level. The crown of the LI_2 is completely worn away and the occlusal surface rounded over. P_3, P_4, and M_1 are similarly worn to root level, but the occlusal plane dips lingually, leaving a sharp, thin enamel wall on the buccal aspect of the teeth. There is a large abscess cavity lingually to the roots of M_1.

43110: KRM 1D-5 (Plate 71)

The fragment comprises part of the left corpus and ramus of an adult male mandible. The coronoid process is missing, and anteriorly the fragment terminates in an oblique fracture, revealing the lingual margins of the tooth sockets of P_3 and P_4, and bucally the distal margin of the mental foramen between the apices of the tooth sockets of P_4–M_1. All three permanent molars are present and moderately worn (for measurements,

see table 11.3). The occlusal surfaces of the teeth are flattened, with dentine extensively exposed on M_1 and M_2, and slightly exposed on M_3. Calculus is present around the roots of the teeth in the area of root bifurcation, suggesting that the alveolus had resorbed considerably. The bifurcation of the roots is fairly low down, as found in mesotaurodontism.

Notes on the Wear on the Teeth (LSA)

614. There is severe wear anteriorly, where there is "rounding" type of wear as seen in Fish Hoek jaws (e.g., skeleton P2), but there is a reversed slope to the occlusal surface in the premolar and molar region. This means that the mandible was deviated to the left side, so that when he was chewing, the mandible was lateral to the maxillary teeth. The thin wedge of enamel sticking up on the buccal side suggests either that he may have not had much grinding force (? due to arthritic changes in the temporomandibular joint) or that the abrasion was due to gritty food or sandy substances rather than to the chewing mechanism. The apical abscess is probably secondary to severe wear. The appearance also suggests the possibility of a change of diet, e.g., to shellfish food, as compared with 13400.

43110. The occlusal plane is flat. He had a "sticky" diet, and possibly a more cereal type of diet—based on increased calculus lingually at the base of the crown and general resorption of bone.

Discussion

In comparison with the faunal fragments, the hominid remains are scanty. Furthermore, the MSA deposits yielded mostly cranial and dental fragments. The data suggest that the MSA humans did not bury their dead in the caves and that these remains really should be considered in the same light as the faunal remains (see below).

The discussion will deal mainly with the dental and mandibular specimens, the frontonasal fragment (16425 from MSA II), and the parietal fragment (41658 from MSA II).

Despite the relatively small size of specimen 41658, one can state that the vault is rounded and the frontal unlikely to have the "flattened" (i.e., low) appearance that one finds in the Broken Hill and Saldanha skulls. The apparently low and narrow vault would tend to differentiate it from the Florisbad skull and place it more in line with the Skūhl specimens. It is not possible, or even desirable, to make extensive comparisons of this fragment with other African material, and especially with specimens supposedly associated with MSA cultural material. However, the specimen is thicker and represents a larger skull than many of the Fish Hoek skulls, and it does not have the same shape (in the same region) as the Plettenberg Bay skull, the Boskop skull, or the Tuinplaas skull. In modern terms, it seems to have the low vault of the Bushman and the narrower skull of the Hottentots and Negroes.

In 16425, the superciliary and glabellar region is rather unlike that of the Border Cave 1 cranium, but bears a resemblance to the modern Bushman (A 1175) figured by De Villiers (1973, pl. 11, fig. 4) and certainly to the Matjes River 1 specimen.

It also resembles the frontonasal region of the Fish Hoek (Skildergat) P4 skull, but it differs markedly from the other skulls of that cave, all of which are broad and flat-nosed (bridge) with no glabellar, supraorbital, or superciliary bulging. Thus one could continue comparing a number of specimens, but in the current hazy state of phylogenetic relationships of prehistoric (versus protohistoric and historic) populations, this line of investigation will not be very conclusive. One *can* state that this specimen is unlike the Saldanha, Broken Hill, and Florisbad skulls, that it bears some resemblance to a few of the MSA–related skulls (which have been described in Bushman-Hottentot-Negro terms of varying degrees), and that similar examples may be found in collections of modern southern African indigenous populations. It is precisely this confusion of the amalgam of morphological characteristics (i.e., the amount of Bushman, Hottentot, or Negro characters) present in fossilized material that leads us to believe that such amalgams, found in the appropriate time periods, reflect the negroid ancestors of the modern populations, the latter deriving by microevolutionary mechanisms (Singer and Weiner 1963).

This view is borne out further by the evidence of the fragmentary jaws and teeth recovered at the site. For example, the larger teeth from KRM fall within the size range of modern Bantu (P. Smith, personal communication).

Specimen 13400 bears some features in common with the generalized Neandertals and approaches them in robusticity (see Tobias 1971, table 1, which gives a robusticity index range of 41.2 to 57.7; cf. our table 11.2). The teeth are also comparable in size, although perhaps narrower buccolingually as compared with the mesiodistal diameter. The weak chin and multiple mental foramina are common to many of the Neandertals, but the distinguishing feature of 13400 is the absence of any increase in vertical dimension at the mandibular symphysis. This, together with the large tooth size, sets this specimen apart from other South African fossils, but it is found in the Rabat specimen (although these teeth have a buccal cingulum) and indicated in the Diré-Dawa and Haua Fteah fossils. In later specimens, it may be recognized in Kenya (Njoro River and the Bromhead Site), as well as Zuurberg (near the KRM site). The toothless specimen 21776 is also rather massive but with a slightly more prominent chin.

Specimen 16424, much smaller than 13400, cannot be matched by other known fossil specimens. The small teeth fall outside the range given by Brabant (1965) for Pygmies and Drennan (1929) for Bushmen, but it does fall within the range of recent European teeth (table 11.3).

The simultaneous presence of gracile and rugged forms at one site is, of course, found at a number of sites, e.g., the australopithecine sites, Elmenteita in Kenya, the Zuurberg in South Africa, etc. This wide range of variation may be explained in a number of ways, including more than one population variety in the region of the site. More important, this apparently anomalous presence of two very different forms (especially at KRM with its rather "unified" culture), indicating the extremes of the range of variation, suggests the potential of subsequent generations and the microevolutionary possibilities through gene drift and/or selection. Apart from its size and ruggedness, specimen 13400 has all of the characteristics associated with Bushman mandibles (for example, see Salmons 1925). It is interesting that the closest resemblances are found with much later material and with specimens from North Africa. The squarish ramus and relatively large teeth are features in which it approaches modern Bushmen much more closely than the so-called Boskopoids or pre-Bushmen.

If one does a cluster analysis of the mesiodistal and buccolingual diameters of the mandibular premolars and molars of the KRM specimens and selective comparative material (see table 11.3), one obtains an inconclusive result which adds little to that which can be deduced from the table of measurements, namely, that the specimens can be divided into two groups:

1. The more primitive looking specimens (13400, 14691, 14693, 14694, and 14696) resemble the Cave of Hearths specimen, but differ from modern South African Negroes and Near Eastern Mousterians mainly in the relative narrowness of the teeth buccolingually. They do relate to modern Bushmen and MSA/LSA Fish Hoek specimens from the point of view of shape, but not very closely. But there can be no reason to believe that these specimens and the Cave of Hearths specimen would be massive enough to fit skulls like the Saldanha and Broken Hill skulls, as Tobias (1971) seems to believe of the Cave of Hearths mandible.

2. The second group seems more recent, but 16424 is small, even by Bushman standards, and clusters separately, although it probably should be grouped with them.

Even more puzzling is the discovery of 41815 in the temporally early MSA I deposits of Shelter 1B. Other than the large teeth, it is a very non-Neandertal-like mandible with a well-formed chin and a medium-height, squarish ramus more nearly resembling Hottentot and Negro mandibles than those of Bushmen. The robusticity index is not very helpful by itself—e.g., it relates this specimen to Rabat, Kanam, Fish Hoek, Diré-Dawa, Baringo, Sangiran B, etc., differing markedly from the Cave of Hearths. It lies somewhere between 13400 and 16424. It does resemble the Cave of Hearths mandible in its rare congenital absence of the LM_3.

The specimen is only slightly larger than some of the Fish Hoek specimens (which are certainly much later in time), and the teeth (if one guestimates the sizes of the crowns from the crown-root junctions' size) would possibly fall into the size range of modern Hottentots, Negroes, and the Cave of Hearths.

Specimen 41815 has a mandibular curve identical to Tabun I, but the chin in the former is more pronounced, the corpus is sturdier and has no internal shelf sloping up to the incisors, and the ramus is taller and broader. It has a more rounded arch than the Tuinplaas (Springbok Flats) mandible, and although the rami are smaller in shape and size, the corpus is much shorter A–P and suggests a smaller, wider face (which is what one would expect in a Bushman-like face). Although similar in size (A–P) to some Fish Hoek mandibles, e.g., P2, the corpus is more robust, the arch wider, and the bicoronal (and therefore bicondylar) breadth greater, again suggesting a broader face than these specimens have.

Again, it is possible to continue such comparisons with many other specimens, but the major conclusion that one can reach with absolute certainty is that in MSA I times a very sapient individual was present at KRM, with a broad and possibly orthognathous face, with a mandibular ramus somewhat in between that of a Bushman and a Negro (in modern terms), and with teeth possibly in a like size category. In MSA II times we have remains of jaws that fall into at least two groups—gracile and robust— the latter being more "primitive" and somewhat Neandertal-like and the former more akin to modern African populations. None can be linked morphologically with the Saldanha, Broken Hill, and Florisbad specimens. The features in the isolated KRM specimens, and especially 16424, would raise the possibility of a mosaic or pattern of generalized negroid features (in the genetic sense referred to in Singer and Weiner 1963) that would indicate ancestral forms of modern Negro, Bushman, and Hottentot peoples.

The most important conclusion is that 41815 represents the earliest *Homo sapiens sapiens* directly associated with an MSA culture in southern Africa or elsewhere. It must yet be compared with specimens like those from Omo, about which data are not available.

These data confirm not only that *Homo sapiens sapiens* occupied this southern region of Africa ''by the advent of the 'final MSA,' that is, before 50,000 BC at the latest'' (Vogel and Beaumont 1972) but that they indeed manufactured the early stages of the MSA more than 100,000 years ago.

Furthermore, the KRM material, when considered with the Border Cave adult mandible found in the intact Third White Ash stratum (dated to about 90,000 B.P.) (De Villiers 1976), would indicate that a reconsideration must be given to the popular misconception that ancestral Negroes (see Singer and Weiner 1963) were not present in South Africa prior to fairly recent times. It is not considered appropriate to discuss here the rather complicated and incomplete evidence relating to the origins of modern indigenous Negro, Bushman, and Hottentot populations. Attempts have been made to do this recently—for example, by Rightmire (1976, 1978)— but the approaches have been inadequate in scope. The KRM material, albeit very scanty, as well as remains from other sites (Border Cave, Skildergat, etc.), tends to bear out the extrapolative inferences from the biological data on modern indigenes (Singer and Weiner 1963) by evidencing a mosaic of characters linking the three modern indigenous populations in their ancestral forms. Consequently, it should not be surprising when investigators (for example, Rightmire 1979) analyze human fossils from South Africa (by whatever means) and categorize them as having similarities with at least two of the modern populations but with a bias toward one or the other. More extensive fossil population samples will be needed to unscramble the biological omelette in a more precise and meaningful way and before phylogenetic implications become objectively obvious.

12 The Nonhominid Fauna

The nonhominid mammalian fauna recoverd at KRM during the excavations has been studied by Richard G. Klein, Department of Anthropology, University of Chicago, who has published a detailed analysis (Klein 1976a) and a number of articles including and relating to these data (Klein 1974, 1975a) to which the reader is referred. In order to avoid unnecessary duplication, only some tables and conclusions that have direct relevance to other chapters in this volume will be included here, while other observations will be added by the authors.

It has not been possible to obtain a report on the relatively abundant bird skeletal remains (submitted to G. Avery, South African Museum, for study), but it appears that most of these were marine birds, particularly black back gulls (*Larus dominicanus*), contrary to the statement by Volman (1978). In modern times these are very common coastal birds, especially near human settlements, where there is refuse to be scavenged. It would be interesting to relate the ratio of bird bones to other skeletal remains for each cultural sequence. Klein (1976a) hints that there may have been a reduction in the number of marine birds (and seals) during the Howieson's Poort and MSA II and MSA IV times, reflecting the onset of coastline retreat. On the basis of eggshells recovered (see chap. 8), it may be surmised that there was a relative absence of ostrich in the MSA and a relative abundance in the Howieson's Poort times. However, the ostrich populations need not have changed but the hunter-gatherer habits or needs may have differed during these cultural periods (see below).

The fossil reptiles, represented by sea turtles, tortoises, and snakes, comprise a very small sample and remain unstudied.

The scanty fish remains were studied by C. Poggenpoel, South African Museum, who counted the specimens in the LSA layers (table 12.1) mainly on the basis of identifiable dentaries. None of the latter was present in the sample of fish bones from the MSA deposits.

These marine species could have been harvested by fishing or trapping, or washed up carcasses may have been scavenged on the beaches. The aim of one of Klein's analyses was to estimate the minimum numbers of individuals by which each species was represented in each level of the site (tables 12.2, 12.3, 12.4, and 12.5). To this end, anatomical and taxonomical determination of the bones of the nonbovid species was feasible, but this was not possible for the bovid remains. The minimum counts for the various bovid species in these tables were calculated strictly on the basis of cranial remains, especially teeth. The bovid postcranial remains were divided into four arbitrary size classes (table 12.6), roughly equivalent to those used by Brain (1969, 1974). These size classes are (1) *small,* including Blue Duiker, Grysbok, Oribi; (2) *small medium,* including Vaalribbok, Mountain Reedbuck, Springbok, Bushbuck; (3) *large medium,* including Southern Reedbuck, Blue Antelope, Bastard Hartebeest, Wildebeest, Kudu; and, (4) *large,* including Eland, Cape Buffalo, Giant Buffalo.

Only the MSA levels in Cave 1 provided a sample of bovid postcranial material large enough for detailed interpretation

Table 12.1. Minimum Numbers of Individuals by Which Various Fish Species Are Represented in the KRM 1, LSA Levels

Fish species and popular name	LSA I		LSA II			
	1	6	7	8	9	11
Cymatoceps nasutus, Biskop	–	1	–	9	7	1
Sparadon durbanensis, Musselcracker	–	–	–	2	1	–
Rhabdosargus globiceps, White Stumpnose	–	–	–	1	1	1
Coracinus capensis, Galjoen	–	–	1	4	1	1
Diplodus sargus, Dassie	–	1	1	3	1	–
Lithognathus lithognathus, Steenbras	–	1	1	–	–	–
? Myliobatis aquila, Eagle Ray	–	–	1	1	–	–

Table 12.2. Minimum Numbers of Individuals by Which Each Mammalian Species Is Represented in the Various Horizons of KRM 1

	LSA II	LSA I	MSA IV	MSA II					MSA I	
	1-6	7-12	13	14	15	16	17a	17b	37	38/39
Papio ursinus, Chacma Baboon	2		1	3	1	1			1	
Canis mesomelas, Black-backed Jackal		1					1			
Mellivora capensis, Honey Badger				1		1				
Aonyx capensis, Clawless Otter	2			2	1	2	1	1	1	
Genetta sp., Genet	?1									
Herpestes ichneumon, Egyptian Mongoose				1	1	1				
H. pulverulentus, Cape Grey Mongoose				2		1	1	1		
Atilax paludinosus, Water Mongoose				1						1
Hyaena brunnea, Brown Hyena				1	1	1				
Felis libyca, Wildcat						1				
Felis cf. caracal, Caracal				1	1		1			
Panthera pardus, Leopard	1			4	1	1	1	2	1	
Arctocephalus pusillus, Cape Fur Seal	7	8	3	20	5	17	4	4	7	4
Mirounga leonina, Elephant Seal				1						
Loxodonta africana, Elephant					1	1	1			
Procavia capensis, Rock Hyrax		2	3	15	5	15	3	6	2	2
Diceros bicornis, Black Rhinoceros				2		1	1		1	
Equus cf. quagga, Quagga				1		1			1	1
Potamochoerus porcus, Bushpig	?1			1	1				2	2
Phacochoerus aethiopicus, Warthog					1					2
Hippopotamus amphibius, Hippopotamus	1	2		4	1	2	1	2	5	1
Cephalophus monticola, Blue Duiker	2	3								
Raphicerus melanotis, Cape Grysbok	1	7		21	14	5	6	3	4	
Ourebia ourebi, Oribi					1	1				
Pelea capreolus, Vaalribbok	2	2	2	1		3	1			
Redunca cf. arundinum, Southern Reedbuck		1		1	1		1		2	2
R. fulvorufula, Mountain Reedbuck	1	1				1	2		3	1
Hippotragus leucophaeus, Blue Antelope			4	8	4	6	7	7	11	5
Alcelaphus buselaphus, Hartebeest	5	3	2						1	2
Damaliscus sp., Bastard Hartebeest				1		1				
Connochaetes sp., Wildebeest				1	1	2	2	2		5
Antidorcas sp., Springbok				1		2	1			
Tragelaphus scriptus, Bushbuck			1	6	8	2	3	1	1	2
T. strepsiceros, Kudu				2		5	1	2	3	
Taurotragus oryx, Eland		1	3	27	10	23	12	8	10	11
Syncerus caffer, Cape Buffalo	7	7	4	5	3	9	4	8	7	4
Pelorovis antiquus, Giant Buffalo*			2	13	1	9	4	5	11	7
Hystrix africae-australis, Porcupine	3	1	1	10	4	3	1		2	1
Georychus capensis, Mole Rat				2	3	1	1			
Lepus capensis, Hare				1						
Delphinidae, Dolphins		2	1	2	2	1	1	1	2	1
Other Cetacea, Whales				1					1	?1

*Other authors have referred to the extinct Giant Buffalo as "Homoioceras" sp. or "Homoioceras bainii."

Table 12.3. Minimum Numbers of Individuals by Which Each Mammalian Species Is Represented in the Various Horizons of KRM 1A

	MSA III					Howieson's Poort			MSA II									
	1-3	4	5	6	7-9	10-11	13-16	17-21	22	23-24	25	26	27	28-29	30	31	32-33	34
Papio ursinus, Chacma Baboon			2			2		1										
Herpestes pulverulentus, Cape Grey Mongoose								2										
Atilax paludinosus, Water Mongoose			1															
Panthera pardus, Leopard			1															
Felis libyca, Wildcat						1		1	1									
Felis cf. caracal, Caracal				1		1												
Arctocephalus pusillus, Cape Fur Seal		1	3	3	2	5		6	1	3	2		2	4	2	2	5	2
Loxodonta africana, Elephant								1										
Procavia capensis, Rock Hyrax	4	1	2	3	3	4	4	4		1	1	1	1	1			2	1
Equus cf. quagga, Quagga				2	3	3		6										
Hippopotamus amphibius, Hippopotamus			1				1	2										
Raphicerus melanotis, Cape Grysbok	2		1	1		6		2				1	1		1	1	1	1
Pelea capreolus, Vaalribbok			1			2											1	1
Redunca arundinum, Southern Reedbuck				1	1	1		3		1	1		1					
Hippotragus leucophaeus, Blue Antelope	2		1		1	5		3	1	2		1	1	2		1	2	1
Damaliscus sp., Bastard Hartebeest			1		3													
Connochaetes sp., Wildebeest				1	3			1										
Tragelaphus scriptus, Bushbuck								1										
T. strepsiceros, Kudu								1			2		1					
Taurotragus oryx, Eland	1	3	1	3	3	1		7		2	1	2	6		1		3	3
Syncerus caffer, Cape Buffalo *	2	1	4	1	6	2		4		3		1	1					
Pelorovis antiquus, Giant Buffalo			1	1	5			2	1	1				2				1
Hystrix africae-australis, Porcupine						1		1						1			1	
Delphinidae, Dolphins						?1												

*See table 12.2.

Table 12.4. MINIMUM NUMBERS OF INDIVIDUALS BY WHICH EACH MAMMALIAN SPECIES IS REPRESENTED IN THE VARIOUS HORIZONS OF KRM 1B AND 1C

| | KRM 1B -- MSA I | | | | | | | | | | | | | KRM 1C-MSA I | |
	1-3	4	5	6	7	8	9	10	11	12	13	14	15	36	37
Papio ursinus, Chacma Baboon	1														
Canis mesomelas, Black-backed Jackal	1														
Atilax paludinosus, Water Mongoose							1								
Arctocephalus pusillus, Cape Fur Seal	3	2	1	2	3	2	1	3	2		1		1	2	4
Procavia capensis, Rock Hyrax	3		3	3	1			1	2		1				
Potamochoerus porcus, Bushpig											1				
Hippopotamus amphibius, Hippopotamus				?1							1				
Raphicerus melanotis, Cape Grysbok	4		1		2									1	1
Pelea capreolus, Vaalribbok			1												
Hippotragus leucophaeus, Blue Antelope				2				1							
Alcelaphus buselaphus, Hartebeest						1	1								1
Connochaetes sp., Wildebeest						1		1							
Tragelaphus scriptus, Bushbuck				1											1
Taurotragus oryx, Eland	4	1		1			2	1						1	1
Syncerus caffer, Cape Buffalo	1														1
Pelorovis antiquus, Giant Buffalo *					1										
Hystrix africae-australis, Porcupine				1											
Lepus capensis, Hare												1			
Delphinidae														1	

*See table 12.2.

Table 12.5. MINIMUM NUMBERS OF INDIVIDUALS BY WHICH EACH MAMMALIAN SPECIES IS REPRESENTED IN THE VARIOUS HORIZONS OF KRM 1D AND 5

| | KRM 1D-LSA III | | | | | KRM 5-LSA II(?) | | | 5-Mixed | | 5 - MSA I(?) | | |
	1	2	3	4	5	Pit A	1	2	3	4	5	6	7
Papio ursinus, Chacma Baboon							1	2					
Genetta genetta, Smallspotted Genet							1						
Felis cf. caracal, Caracal									1				
Arctocephalus pusillus, Cape Fur Seal			2	1	1	2	2	5	3	?1			
Mirounga leonina, Elephant Seal			1										
Potamochoerus porcus, Bushpig								2					
Hippopotamus amphibius, Hippopotamus								1					
Cephalophus monticola, Blue Duiker								2					
Raphicerus melanotis, Cape Grysbok								1				1	2
Ourebia ourebi, Oribi													1
Pelea capreolus, Vaalribbok								2					
Connochaetes sp., Wildebeest									1				
Tragelaphus scriptus, Bushbuck								2				2	
Taurotragus oryx, Eland													1
Syncerus caffer, Cape Buffalo							1	2					
Pelorovis antiquus, Giant Buffalo *									1				
Hystrix africae-australis, Porcupine								1					
Delphinidae, Dolphins							1	1					

*See table 12.2.

Table 12.6. MINIMUM NUMBERS OF DIFFERENT-SIZED BOVIDS REPRESENTED BY CRANIAL AND POSTCRANIAL REMAINS IN THE MSA DEPOSITS OF KRM 1

	Small Bovids	Small Medium Bovids	Large Medium Bovids	Large Bovids
Minimum numbers represented by:				
Cranial remains	55	42	92	200
Postcranial remains	54	42	56	95

Note. For definitions of the size categories see the text.

(Klein 1976a). The data in table 12.6 give no reason to suppose that species frequencies based solely on cranial material would be seriously altered if the postcranial remains were to be specifically identified.

Figure 12.1 illustrates the relative frequencies of different bovid taxa in the various culture-stratigraphic units at KRM and Nelson Bay Cave. The identified species of terrestrial mammals at KRM reveal that hunting concentrated on the artiodactyls. Klein's dental data (table 12.7) suggest that the eland remains are mostly those of adults, while those of the other

large bovids, the buffalo, include an approximately equal number of young individuals. This higher proportion of immature individuals may reflect a difficulty the hunters may have had in killing the formidable and treacherous buffalo.

The data indicate quite clearly that the KRM fauna is composed mostly of extant taxonomic forms and only a small number of extinct forms. The presence of marine animals throughout the MSA sequence suggests that the sea was never very far away. This is the earliest known evidence for the systematic exploitation of marine resources.

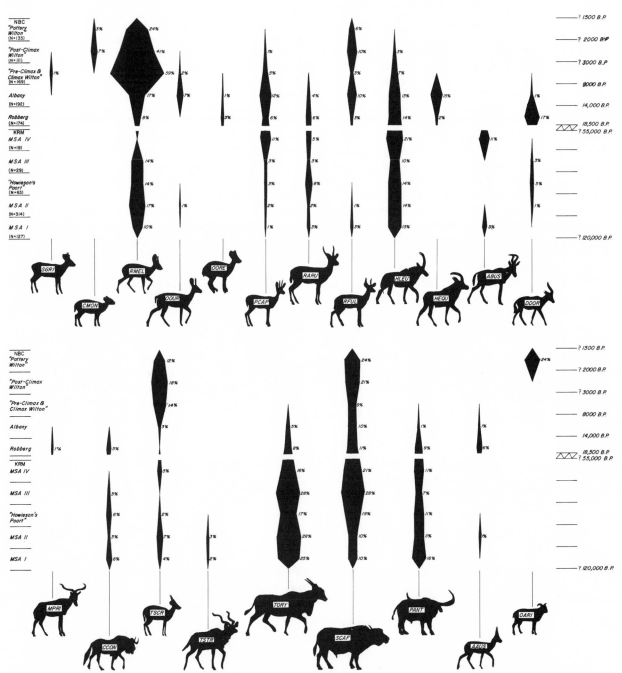

FIG. 12.1. The relative frequencies of different bovid taxa in the various culture-stratigraphic units of Klasies River Mouth and Nelson Bay Cave. Note that the samples from the different units vary considerably in size so that not all the fluctuations in the figure are statistically significant. Note also the major time break between the top of the Klasies (MSA) sequence and the bottom of the Nelson Bay (LSA) one. SGRI = *Sylvicapra grimmia*, CMON = *Cephalophus monticola*, RMEL = *Raphicerus melanotis*, OOUR = *Ourebia ourebi*, OORE = *Oreotragus oreotragus*, PCAP = *Pelea capreolus*, RARU = *Redunca* cf. *arundinum*, RFUL = *Redunca fulvorufula*, HLEU = *Hippotragus leucophaeus*, HEQU = *Hippotragus equinus*, ABUS = *Alcephalus buselaphus*, DDOR = *Damaliscus* sp., MPRI = *Megalotragus priscus*, CCON = *Connochaetes (Connochaetes)* sp., TSCR = *Tragelaphus scriptus*, TSTR = *Tragelaphus strepsiceros*, TORY = *Taurotragus oryx*, SCAF = *Syncerus caffer*, PANT = *Pelorovis antiquus*, AAUS = *Antidorcas australis*, OARI = *Ovis aries*. (Klein 1976.)

Table 12.7. NUMBERS OF LARGE BOVIDS IN DIFFERENT DENTAL AGE STATES IN THE MSA DEPOSITS OF KRM

| | Dental Age States | | | | | | |
	I	II	III	IV	V	VI	VII
<u>Taurotragus</u> <u>oryx</u>, Eland	10	10	13	20	23	62	14
<u>Syncerus</u> <u>caffer</u>, Cape Buffalo	21	13	4	7	5	16	5
<u>Pelorovis</u> <u>antiquus</u>, Giant Buffalo (=<u>Homoioceras</u> sp.)	28	2	2	4	4	21	6

Note. The dental age states are defined to include animals in which (I) dP4 was unworn; (II) M1 was erupting to erupted, but essentially unworn; (III) M2 was erupting to erupted, but essentially unworn; (IV) M3 was erupting to erupted, but essentially unworn; (V) P4 was erupting to erupted, but essentially unworn; (VI) P4 was in early to mid-wear; and (VII) P4 was in late wear.

The KRM MSA I–III sequence indicates that the coast was close by, though a relative reduction in marine remains in the most recent MSA levels may reflect the initiation of coastline retreat (? at the beginning of the Last Glacial). Klein (1976*a*) states that fluctuations in the frequencies of different kinds of antelopes and of equids in the MSA sequence *suggest* changes in vegetation from more open (? at the very end of the Penultimate Glacial or beginning of the Last Interglacial) to more closed (? in the full Last Interglacial) back to more open (? in the earlier Last Glacial). Although some authors (Klein 1974, 1975*a*, 1976*a*; Hendey and Deacon 1977) continue to draw positive conclusions concerning the environmental cover and related climatic changes from the presence or absence of certain terrestrial fauna in occupation sites, it is suggested that such conclusions can only be of a doubtful nature (though possibly suggestive in some cases) unless confirmed by adequate pollen samples. Hunting habits, economic pressure (such as drought or severe cold that may affect the animal populations and hence the distances that hunters may have to walk for successful hunting), population density, and other factors are variables that can often not be evaluated from the excavation (see also Singer and Heltne 1966) or by studies of present-day environments (Moffett and Deacon 1977). The *presence* of certain animal forms does indicate environmental features within hunting distance of the site, but *absence* of various forms need not indicate extinction or lack of certain environmental features. Thus most experienced prehistorians view with caution the extrapolations that may be possible from the recovery of faunal remains from a site. Certainly, assertive inferences of major biotic and climatic changes may only be made when a number of sites in a particular region demonstrate similar trends in hunting preferences associated with similar pollen diagrams. The KRM deposits were considered unsuitable for pollen analysis.

The KRM MSA levels have provided the earliest known evidence for the systematic exploitation of marine resources, while at the same time suggesting that MSA peoples exploited both marine and terrestrial resources differently and perhaps less effectively than LSA peoples in the same habitat.

Plates

PLATE 1. General view of the cave and rock shelter complex from the east. Beyond is the Coastal Platform at +170–200 m and the Tzitzikama Mountains on the skyline. The highest point is Mount Formosa.

PLATE 2. View from Cave 2. In the middle foreground is a wave-cut platform at 6–8 m above present sea level.

PLATE 3. General view from east prior to excavation to show positions of Caves 1 and 2, and Shelters 1A and 1B.

PLATE 4. General view of Caves 1 and 2 and Shelter 1A from south, prior to excavation.

PLATE 5. Relative positions of Caves 1 and 2. The occupational soils in the upper Cave 2 are partially cemented, and the harder parts show as laminae, truncated by later erosion. Irregular masses of calcite hang inside and around the mouths of both caves.

PLATE 6. View of the rock face between Shelter 1A and Cave 2. Residual masses of laminated occupational strata are cemented to the rock, partially covered by irregular calcite formations, and high above the surface of the present occupational soils beneath Shelter 1A.

PLATE 7. The surface at the mouth of Cave 1 before excavation. Eolian sand (layer 13) is exposed to the left of the ranging pole, and some LSA Midden deposits are exposed at the top.

PLATE 8. Cave 1—Main Cutting, West Face.

PLATE 9. Cave 1—West Cutting, East Face.

PLATE 10. Cave 1—Main Cutting from mouth of cave before removal of layers below layer 15 beyond grid a.

PLATE 11. Cave 1—West Cutting G–F, North Face.

PLATE 12. Cave 1—West Cutting H–J, North Face.

PLATE 13. Cave 1—Main Cutting. Detail of layers 13, 14, and 15 before removal of layers below.

PLATE 14. Cave 1—West Cutting H. Skull of leopard skeleton in layer 15+.

PLATE 15. Cave 1—East Cutting Q, North Face. Shingle and bedrock exposed below layers 38 and 39. The pole stands on clean sand considered to be part of the 6–8 m beach. Occupational material was found between this level and the shingle and is accepted as evidence for the initial occupation thus being contemporary with the 6–8 m sea.

PLATE 16. Shelter 1A—top of scree slope before excavation.

PLATE 17. Shelter 1A—Initial Cutting.

PLATE 18. Shelter 1A—Side Cutting A. Cemented deposits adhere to the rock wall above the present surface and indicate their former extent. They grade into the existing layers. The name board rests on the sandstone bedrock.

PLATE 19. Shelter 1A—Top, Middle, and Bottom Cutting completed.

PLATE 20. Shelter 1A—Top Cutting, Northeast Face.

PLATE 21. Shelter 1A—Top Cutting. A large block of fallen calcite is contained within the lower levels.

PLATE 22. Shelter 1A—Initial Cutting. Close-up of carbonaceous layers containing Howieson's Poort Industry (East Face, layers 13 to 21).

PLATE 23. Shelter 1A—Bottom Cutting. The clean sand exposed on the step is the top of layer 30.

PLATE 24. Cave 2—North and East Faces of Cutting.

PLATE 25. Shelter 1B—before excavation.

PLATE 26. Shelter 1B—section of West Face.

PLATE 27. Top of mouth of Cave 1C exposed by removal of layer 36. The saturated deposits above link with those of the Initial Cutting and Side Cutting A of Shelter 1A.

PLATE 28. The interior of Cave 1C looking toward the rear. Several fallen stalagmites, especially those above the name board, were possibly smashed by human activity prior to MSA II.

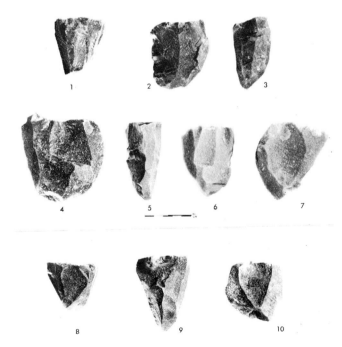

PLATE 29.-Single platform cores: nos. 1–10. MSA II. Flakes or flake-blades have been struck from one striking platform, shown uppermost in each case. After preliminary dressing the core could be used in two ways: (i) A series of roughly parallel flake-blades might be struck around the circumference of the striking platform, generally around only part of it (e.g., nos. 2, 4, 6). If the knapping was continued around most or all of the platform, a conical form resulted (e.g., nos. 1, 3, 5). (ii) Two or more large flakes might be struck from one side so that a central ridge was formed. The upper part of this ridge was removed by a small flake struck immediately behind it, and after a final preparation of the striking platform, a final, larger flake was removed from behind this one. If struck successfully, a pointed flake-blade was produced. No. 10 clearly shows the facet from the striking of such a pointed flake-blade. This type of single platform core is a specialized form of tortoise core.

At all stages, in both forms of cores, constant dressing (preparation) of the striking platform was necessary to maintain correct striking angles. Similarly, rejuvenation flakes along the edge of the striking platform were removed when necessary.

PLATE 30. Double platform cores: nos. 1–6. MSA II. These were intended for the production of parallel-sided flake-blades. The majority had striking platforms opposing each other on the same face of the core, but sometimes the platforms were opposed on different sides. The more regular examples had their shape maintained by dressing from the sides, at right angles to the direction of flake-blade removed. This dressing could develop into another striking platform and hence result in a multiplatform core. As with single platform cores, constant dressing of the striking platform was necessary to assist accurate knapping, and rejuvenation flakes were removed when necessary to maintain a clean edge to the platform. All the cores illustrated are from 1-17b.

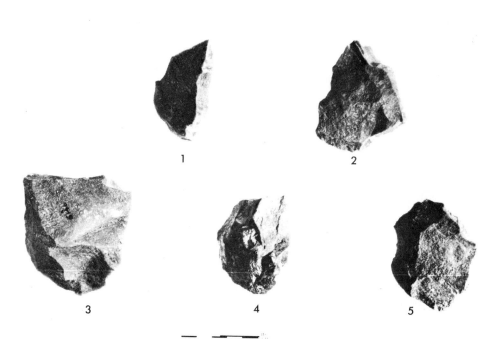

PLATE 31. Irregular and undeveloped cores: nos. 1–5. MSA II. These constitute a large proportion of the cores found in all the MSA industries. Many are probably whittled-down cores of single or double platform type, others must reflect knapping failures in the initial preparation of regular core types or are just trial pieces during the selection of suitable knapping stone.

PLATE 32. Other cores: nos. 1–4. MSA II. 1–3: discoidal cores, possibly used as missiles. 4: tortoise core.

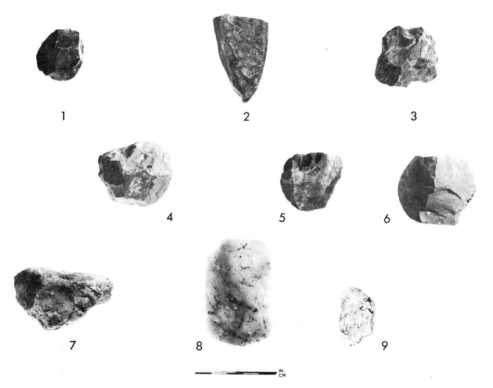

PLATE 33. Cores of nonlocal rocks: nos. 1–9. MSA II. Small pebbles and pieces of nonlocal rocks were sometimes used in the MSA industries, particularly indurated shale, silcretes, and quartz, all considerably finer-grained than the quartzite in general use. Beach and river pebbles were probably collected in the course of other activities. It was worked in a similar manner to the local rock, but the small size of the pebbles or pieces rarely allowed the production of any flakes or flake-blades of comparable size. The small flakes of fine-grained rock were probably prized for special purposes because of their keener edges and for being less brittle. 1, 2, 3, 6: indurated shale; 4, 5: fine silcrete; 7, 8: quartz; 9: quartz crystal.

PLATE 34. Cores: nos. 1–9. MSA IV. 1, 2, 3: single platform; 5: double platform; 8: pebble chopper-core; 4, 6, 7, 9: irregular and/or undeveloped.

PLATE 35. Cores: 1, 4, 5, 7, 8; MSA III. Cores of nonlocal rock: 2, 3, 6, 9; MSA II. 1, 4, 5, 7, 8: double platform; 2: chalcedony; 3, 6, 9: indurated shale.

PLATE 36. Cores: nos. 1–9. MSA II. 1–4, 6: single platform; 5, 9: double platform; 8: core; 7: irregular and/or undeveloped. See plates 29, 30, 31, 32, 33, 35 for illustrations of other cores from this stage.

PLATE 37. Cores: nos. 1–9. MSA I. 6–9: single platform; 1, 2: double platform; 3–5: irregular and/or undeveloped.

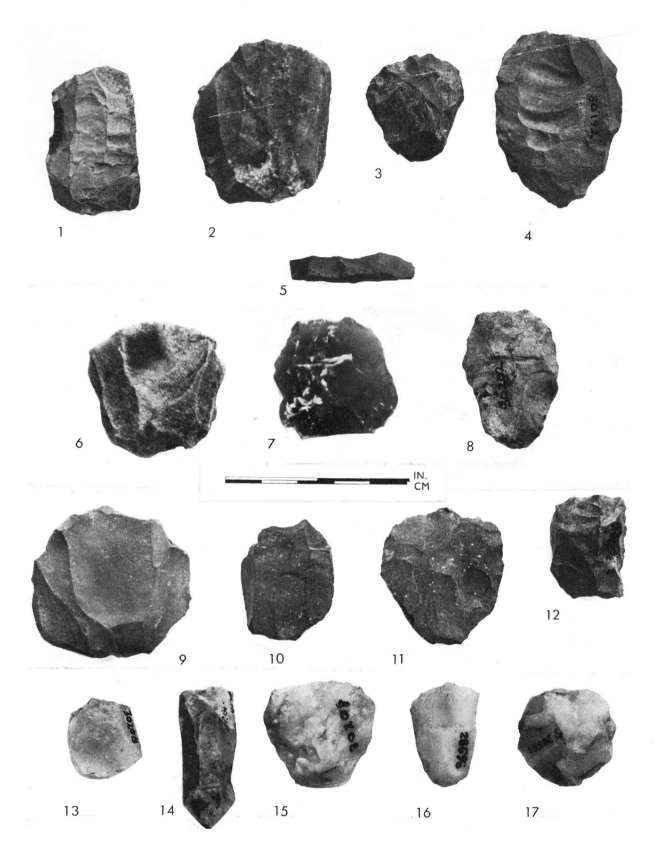

PLATE 38. Cores of nonlocal rock: nos. 1–17. Howieson's Industry. The demand for microblades in this industry led to the use of any fine-grained rocks which were available, fine silcrete being the most desirable. Small cores and microcores were of various types, including elegant double platformed types (e.g., no. 1) and occasional tortoise cores (e.g., no. 4). Rejuvenation flakes (no. 5) attest to the delicate preparation of striking platforms before the removal of microblades. 1, 2, 3, 4, 5: fine silcrete; 6, 8: coarse silcrete; 7: chalcedony; 9, 10, 11, 12: indurated shale; 15, 16, 17: quartz; 13, 14: quartz crystal.

PLATE 39. Quartzite cores: nos. 1–10. Howieson's Poort Industry. These vary considerably from those in the MSA stages above and below the Howieson's Poort levels, mainly in the greater proportion of small cores and microcores, the occurrence of flat rectangular ones with side trimming (e.g., nos. 2, 8) for microblades, and the absence of the type of single platform core for producing one or more pointed flake-blades. No. 10 is a core-rejuvenating flake.

PLATE 40. Cave 1—Main Cutting. Section through LSA Upper and Lower Middens.

PLATE 41. Cave 1—Main Cutting. Tail of LSA Middens.

PLATE 42. Cave 1—Main Cutting. Developed soil at base of layer 6
dividing LSA Upper and Lower Middens.

PLATE 43. Shelter 1D—position of cutting.

PLATE 44. Cave 5—general view from west. The cave mouth is
obscured by shadow and vegetation. It is one-quarter up the rock face
above the highest sand in the middle foreground.

PLATE 45. Cave 5—entrance, almost entirely blocked by mound of LSA Midden.

PLATE 46. Cave 5—position of cutting at base of tail of LSA Midden.

PLATE 47. Cave 5—West Face of Cutting. The second label down is pinned into layer 1, in which a painted stone was found.

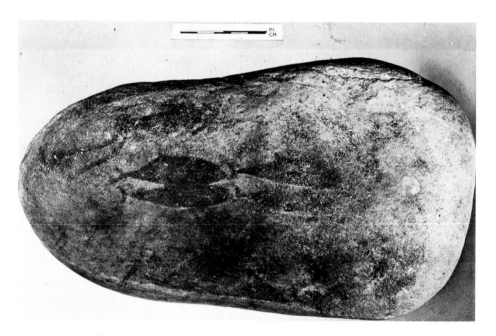

PLATE 48. Cave 5—stone with black painting of a human and four fishes or dolphins.

PLATE 49. Cave 5—stone with red painting of grid pattern on both sides.

PLATE 50. Slate palette from the tail of the LSA Midden inside Cave 5. It was in the same part of the Midden (layer 2) as several rubbing stones and a flat pebble with a red grid pattern painted on each side (pl. 49).

PLATE 51. Pieces of red ocher from KRM. *Upper left*, 1943; *center*, 27578; *upper right*, 21057; *lower left*, 19146; *lower right*, 27379.

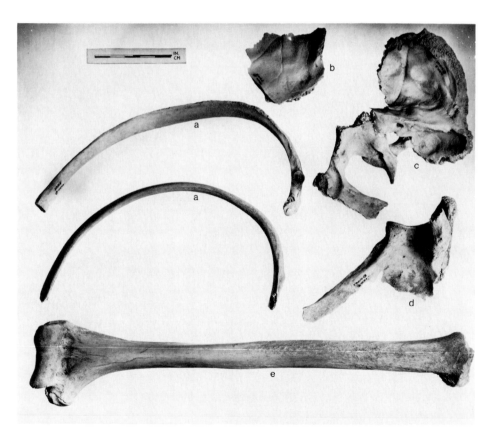

PLATE 52. Human remains from Cave 5. LSA. (a) 41043/4: ribs, inferomedial aspect. (b) 41039: skull fragment, endocranial aspect. (c) 41038: temporal and occipital fragments, endocranial aspect. (d) 41042: scapula fragment, anterior surface. (e) 41041: shaft and distal end of humerus, anterior surface.

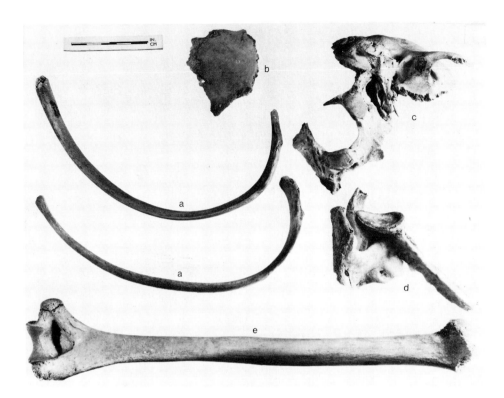

PLATE 53. Human remains from Cave 5. LSA. Reverse side of specimens shown in pl. 52.

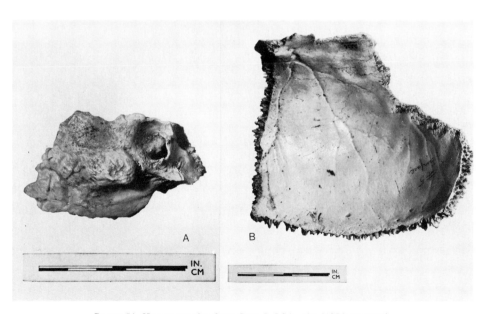

PLATE 54. Human remains from Cave 5. LSA. (A) 41254: temporal bone fragment, exocranial aspect. (B) 43113: parietal bone fragment, endocranial aspect.

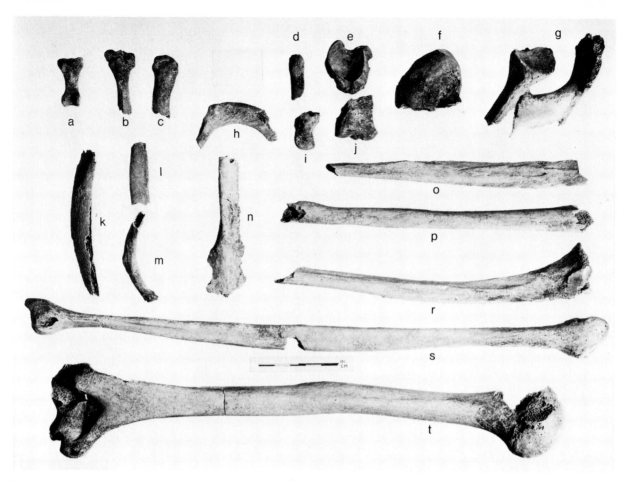

PLATE 55. Human remains from Shelter 1D. (a) 43073: proximal phalanx, hallux. (b) 43074: proximal part of second metacarpal. (c) 43082: distal part of left first metacarpal. (d) 43085: bone fragment. (e) 43086: cuneiform. (f) 43075: femur fragment (condyle). (g) 43072a, b: left scapula fragments. (h) 43078: right first rib fragment. (i) 43088: capitate. (j) 43087: cuboid. (k) 43080: rib fragment. (l) 43079: rib fragment. (m) 43085: bone fragment. (n) 43072c: scapula fragment. (o) 43076: fibula, mid-shaft. (p) 43070: left radius, shaft. (r) 43069: left ulnar, proximal fragment. (s) 43068a, b, c: left fibula. (t) 43071a–d: left humerus.

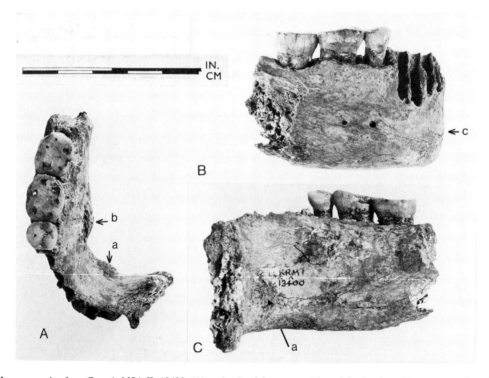

PLATE 56. Human remains from Cave 1. MSA II. 13400: (A) occlusal view. (B) right buccal (lateral) view. (C) lingual (medial) aspect of right corpus. (a) genial tubercles; (b) torus mandibularis; (c) mental foramina.

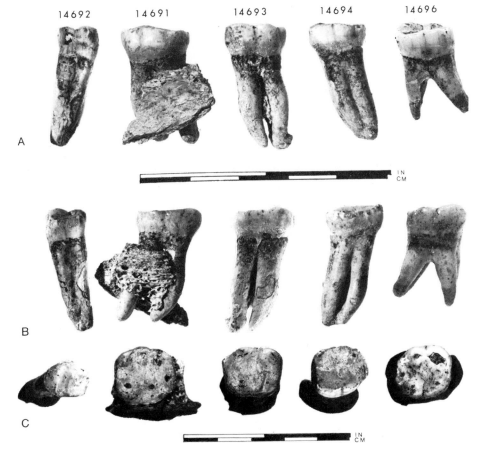

PLATE 57. Human remains from Cave 1. MSA II. Loose teeth: upper
row (A) is buccal aspect (14692 mesial aspect); middle row (B) is
lingual (14692 distal aspect); lower row (C) is occlusal view.

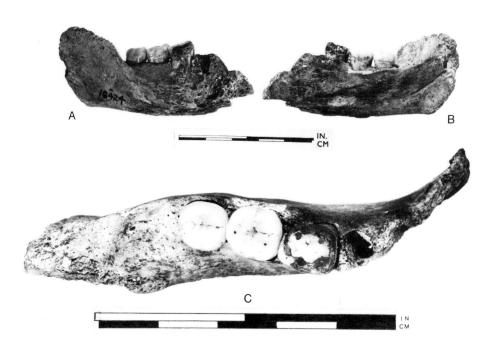

PLATE 58. Human remains from Cave 1. MSA II. 16424: (A) buccal
view; (B) lingual view; (C) occlusal view (a different scale).

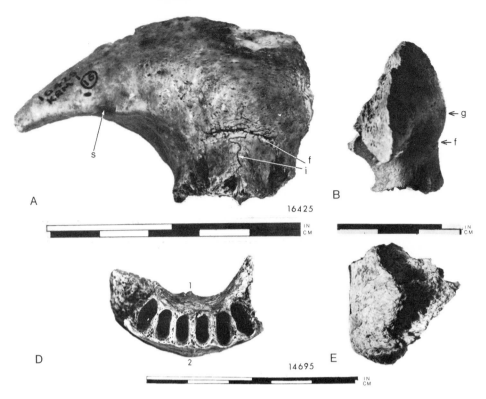

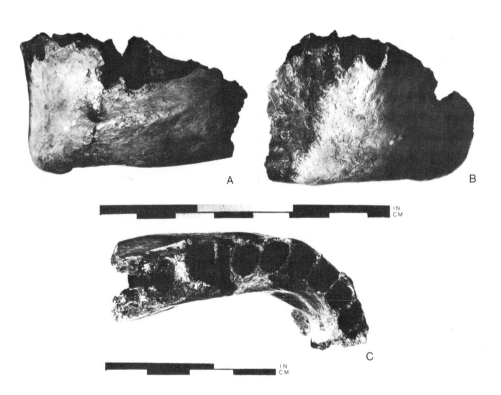

PLATE 59. Human remains from Cave 1. MSA II. 16425: Frontonasal region. (A) frontal view. (B) right lateral view. (g) glabella; (f) frontonasal suture; (i) internasal suture; (s) supraorbital notch. 14695: (D) occlusal view, showing sockets, genial tubercles (1) and mental protuberance (2). (E) left buccal aspect with symphysis on left.

PLATE 60. Human remains from Cave 1. MSA II. 21776: (A) left buccal aspect. (B) anterior aspect. (C) occlusal view, showing sockets for the teeth.

PLATE 61. Human remains from Cave 1: parietal bones, endocranial aspect. (A) 27038 (MSA II). (B) 27070 (MSA I). (C) 27574 (MSA II). (D) 26909 (MSA I).

PLATE 62. Human remains from Cave 1: parietal bones, exocranial aspect. Specimens in same order as pl. 61.

PLATE 63. Human remains from Cave 1 (27576, 27577) and Shelter 1A
(26730–26732). MSA II. Cranial bones, endocranial aspect. (A)
27577; (B) 27575–6 joined; (C) 26732; (D) 26731; (E) 26730.

PLATE 64. Human remains from Cave 1 and Shelter 1A. Cranial bones,
exocranial aspect. Specimens in same order as in pl. 63.

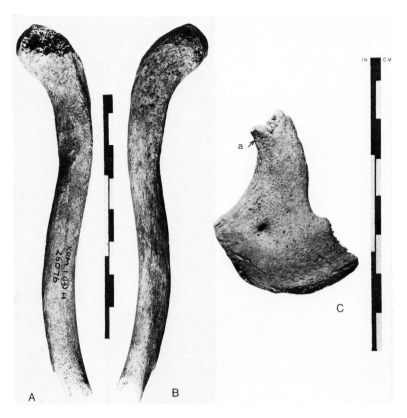

PLATE 65. Human remains from Cave 1. MSA II. 26076: left clavicle, lateral two-thirds. (A) inferior aspect. (B) superior aspect. 16651: left zygomatic bone, lateral aspect (C). Note the large zygomaticofacial foramen. (a) region of frontozygomatic suture.

PLATE 66. Human remains from Shelter 1A. MSA II. 41658: parietal fragment. (A) endocranial aspect: (a) fused coronal suture. (b) groove for stem of anterior division of middle meningeal vessels. (c) groove for "middle" branches of middle meningeal vessels. (d) fused sagittal suture. (B) exocranial aspect.

PLATE 67. Position of discovery of human mandible (41815) in 1B-10.

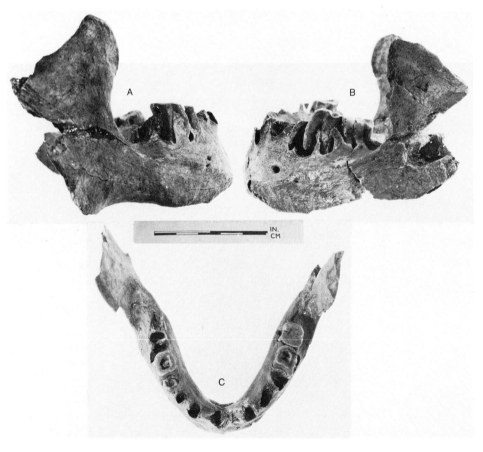

PLATE 68. Human mandible 41815. MSA I. (A) right buccal aspect. (B) left buccal aspect. (C) occlusal aspect.

PLATE 69. Cave 1, West Cutting F, northwest corner. Site of discovery of human mandible 13400 within layer 14. Above the coarse pebbles of this layer are the laminated sands of layer 13 and layer + and the extreme western apse of the cave.

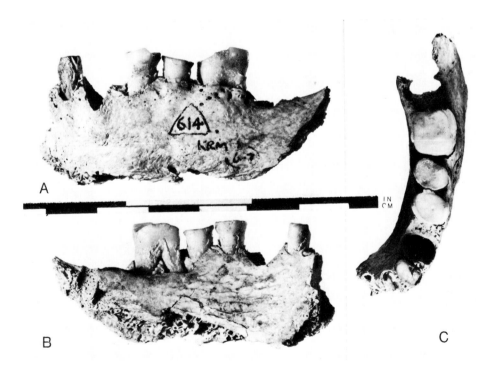

PLATE 70. Human remains from Cave 1, lower part of LSA Upper Midden. 614: fragment of left corpus of mandible. (A) buccal aspect. On the left is left I₂ with crown totally worn down to the root. (B) lingual aspect. (C) occlusal aspect.

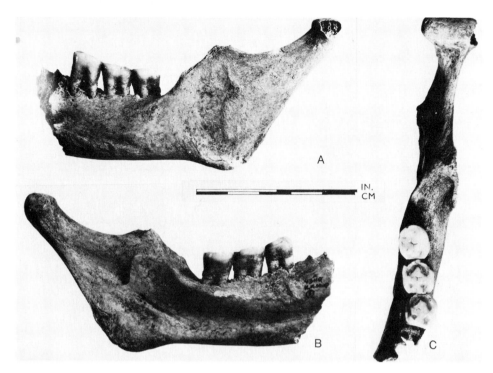

PLATE 71. Human remains from Shelter 1D. LSA. 43110: part of left corpus and ramus of mandible. (A) buccal aspect. (B) lingual aspect. (C) occlusal aspect.

PLATE 72. A specimen of *Turbo sarmaticus* from the KRM deposits showing drill holes at c. 2 mm intervals from which samples have been removed for isotopic analysis.

13 The Molluscan Fauna
*Elizabeth A. Voigt**

Introduction

During the excavation of the long sequence of archeological deposits at the KRM caves, samples of shells were obtained from many levels. Very little detailed information was then available on the molluscan content of prehistoric deposits. The author undertook a detailed analysis of this aspect in 1967 (Maggs and Speed 1967), from which it became obvious that, within certain limitations (Speed 1969), the molluscan fauna, which is often neglected by archeologists during excavations, was capable of yielding valuable dietary and environmental information.

Klasies River Mouth has presented a unique opportunity to collect information on man's utilization of marine resources over an exceptionally long period. Although adequate samples are not available from every level, sufficient material was retained to give us information relating to all six cultural periods represented in the caves. The aim of the analysis was to define the molluscan species present and to analyze these in terms of environmental conditions, and dietary and collecting habits.

The Collection and Analysis of the Samples

The sampling methods at KRM varied. In many cases, particularly in Cave 1, only species samples were collected; i.e., one specimen of each species present was collected from the sieves while a particular layer was being excavated. However, other samples were much more useful in that a defined quantity, such as two full sieves (measuring 3 ft. × 2 ft. of ¼ in.

* Elizabeth A. Voigt is with the Department of Archaeozoology, Transvaal Museum, Pretoria, South Africa.

Two preliminary reports have been published by the author: "Klasies River Mouth Cave: An Exercise in Shell Analysis," *Bulletin of the Transvaal Museum,* no. 14 (Sept. 1973), pp. 14–15, and "Stone Age Molluscan Utilization at Klasies River Mouth Caves," *South African Journal of Science* 69 (1973): 306–9.

The author is deeply grateful to Professor R. Singer for his permission to study the collection from KRM and also to Mr. J. Wymer and their team for collecting the somewhat weighty material during the excavations. Mr. B. Kensley, formerly malacologist at the South African Museum, Cape Town, was of considerable assistance in checking species identifications. Special thanks are due to the late Miss Helen Tiedt of the Transvaal Museum for her faultless and patient typing of the manuscript and tables, and to Mrs. E. du Plooy for typing the revised version. Mr. F. Thackeray assisted with the tables and checked the manuscript, and Dr. R. Klein made useful comments. Thanks also go to the South African Museum for the loan of the material and to the Transvaal Museum for the facilities and assistance offered during the analysis.

mesh) or all the identifiable fragments, was retained. It is these larger samples which have been used in the comparative work.

The state of preservation of the shells was variable; in many cases intact shells, some of which still retained their coloring, were collected from MSA levels. However, in other levels of similar age, the shell was so fragmented that it was only possible to record a species as being "present." In such cases the species are recorded in the tables with a cross (X) which is not included in the totals for levels.

The samples were analyzed according to the methods described in Maggs and Speed, (1967, pp. 90–91). In some samples, *Patella* spp. had lost their apices, so that minimum numbers were calculated by inspecting the remaining bodies and counting these. Where *Turbo* sp. columellae were less common than opercula, opercula were used in the count. Bivalves were divided into left and right valves, the maximum number of one side representing the minimum number of individuals. Those which could not be divided into left or right were divided equally between the two classes. Initially chiton plates were counted and divided by eight; in the large samples the plates were divided into terminal and medial plates; terminal plate numbers were divided by two, medial by six. The highest number was taken as representing the minimum number of individuals. The number of *Burnupena* spp. present was calculated on the basis of either apices or columellae, depending on which were more numerous.

This system of analysis provided all the data for the species identification and percentage tables. Since the total quantity of shell was not retained from any part of the excavation, it was not possible to analyze the degree of fragmentation of the shells.

The species identifications have been done with as much accuracy as possible with assistance from a malacologist and comparative material. The oysters represented are probably *Crassostrea margaraticea.* All the rock mussels appear to belong to the warm water species *Perna perna.* Those valves that were too fragmentary for species identification have been grouped as Mytilid fragments, but their texture and size suggest that they are also *P. perna.* Where specific identification was difficult, certain *Patella* species have been grouped together. This group may contain fragments of *Cellana* sp., which were not identified but could be present.

All chiton plates have been grouped as *Dinoplax gigas,* although another species may be present. Some specimens attained a considerable size.

The discussion of the molluscan fauna will be strictly temporal, with the youngest (Shelter 1D) material discussed first.

155

Table 13.1. KRM 1D—Percentages of Molluscan Species on Basis of Minimum Numbers of Individuals

LEVEL		Patella argenvillei	Patella barbara	Patella longicosta	Patella miniata	Patella oculus	Total Patellidae	Burnupena cincta	Burnupena lagenaria	Haliotis spadicea	Oxystele sinensis	Oxystele tigrina	Perna perna	Turbo sarmaticus	Total Non-Patellidae	Total Marine Mollusca	Terrestrial Mol. Achatina zebra	Total collection
1	No.	3	–	16	–	3	22	1	–	–	20	12	3	16	52	74	1	75
	%	4.0	–	21.3	–	4.0	29.3	1.3	–	–	26.7	16.0	4.0	21.3	69.3	98.7	1.3	99.99
	% Patellidae	13.6	–	72.7	–	13.6												
2	No.	–	–	–	–	–	–	–	–	–	–	–	–	1	1	1	–	1
3	No.	–	–	–	–	–	–	–	–	–	1	–	2	1	4	4	–	4
4a	No.	–	–	6	–	1	7	–	–	–	5	6	9	4	24	31	–	31
	% Patellidae			85.7		14.3	22.6											
5	No.	1	1	11	1	8	22	1	1	1	74	24	27	33	161	183	1	184
	%	0.5	0.5	6.0	0.5	4.4	12.0	0.5	0.5	0.5	40.2	13.0	14.7	17.9	87.5	99.5	0.5	100.00
	% Patellidae	4.6	4.6	50.0	4.6	36.4												
TOTAL NO.		4	1	33	1	12	51	2	1	1	100	42	41	55	242	293	2	295
	% of Total	1.4	0.3	11.2	0.3	4.1	17.3	0.7	0.3	0.3	33.9	14.2	13.9	18.6	82.0	99.3	0.7	100.00

The Molluscan Fauna

One of the primary aims of the study was to identify the molluscan species represented in each cave or shelter.

Shelter 1D (LSA [Ceramic])[1]

This is the youngest deposit in the sequence. The shells are included in a fine black soil and are fresh enough for the *Turbo sarmaticus* specimens to have retained their outer colored layer. A fair sample was collected from each of the five layers. This "shell occupation" is probably quite recent and, in view of the lack of detailed information about modern species present at KRM, can best be grouped together to form one unit which can be regarded as a "modern" sample.

The minimum number of individuals of each molluscan species and the percentage of the sample represented by each species are given in table 13.1. The list of species, although more limited, compares well with the modern list compiled by Stephenson (1944). In particular, *Patella granatina* and *Patella compressa* are absent in both samples. The high number of *Oxystele* sp. and *T. sarmaticus* specimens and *P. perna* confirms the visual impression gained at the KRM site, where it was noticed that these three genera were accessible and occurred in large numbers in some places along the coast. There are no sandy beach species present in the sample, nor are there any examples of *D. gigas*.

Cave 5 (LSA II)

In this analysis the two shell fragments labeled "Pit A II" were omitted, as was layer +, which only contained one beach-worn specimen of *Charonia pustulata*. The material from the hearth in layer 4 was combined with the rest of layer 4, the only

additional species in the hearth being represented by a single specimen of *Oxystele sinensis*.

Several *T. sarmaticus* specimens in layers 2 and 4 still retained their outer colored layer. In layer 4b there was a complete specimen of *P. perna* with the two halves still joined and only slightly open along their outer edge. This was one specimen which apparently did not get eaten, as cooked specimens tend to open flat. The minimum number of individuals and the percentage of the sample represented by each species are shown in table 13.2.

Several of the samples collected can be used for comparative purposes, although they tend to be rather small. Totals of the units from a single layer resulted in reasonable sized samples for layers 1, 2, and 4. The samples from layers 3, 5, and 7 are small, but layer 6 yielded a good sample.

In layers 1 and 2, *Patella* and *Oxystele* species are prominent, whereas in layers 5 and 6, *P. perna* and *T. sarmaticus* outnumber the Patellidae. In layer 4, *Patella longicosta* and *T. sarmaticus* are almost equal, but both are outnumbered by *P. perna*. Once again *P. granatina* and *P. compressa* are absent, but *Donax serra,* a sandy beach specimen, begins to make an appearance in this cave, as does *D. gigas*.

KRM 1-1 to 12: LSA I and II

The samples from these LSA layers are disappointingly small; only two of them—layers 4 and 5 to 6—can be used for comparative purposes, and even then they are very different in size. In layer 4, the *Patella* and *Oxystele* species, *P. perna*, and *T. sarmaticus* are all very well represented, with the same number of *Patella* species as are present in Cave 5.

In layers 5 to 6, the Patellidae are the most common, with a fair sample of *P. perna*.

D. serra is absent again, as is *P. compressa. P. granatina* was recorded only in 1-38.

Seventeen of the modern species recorded by Stephenson occur in this layer, as compared with ID-12 and 5-21. This list

---

1. This refers to the LSA level with pottery, as described in chapter 9 and referred to as LSA III in Klein's tables in chapter 12.

Table 13.2. KRM 5—Percentages of Molluscan Species on Basis of Minimum Numbers of Individuals

S P E C I E S

LEVELS		Patella argenvillei	Patella barbara	Patella cochlear	Patella granularis	Patella longicosta	Patella miniata	Patella oculus	Patella tabularis	TOTAL PATELLIDAE	Burnupena cincta	Burnupena lagenaria	Phalium labiata	Donax serra	Gryphaea margaritacea	Haliotis midae	Haliotis spadicea	Oxystele sinensis	Oxystele tigrina	Oxystele sp.	Perna perna	Turbo sarmaticus	Charonia pustulata	Argobuccinum gemmifera	Dinoplax gigas	TOTAL NON-PATELLIDAE	TOTAL MARINE MOLLUSCA	Terrestrial mollusca	TOTAL SAMPLE
1	No.	1	4	2	-	14	-	5	2	28	-	-	-	-	-	2	1	3	11	-	2	7	-	-	1	27	55	2	57
1	%	1.8	7.0	3.5	-	24.6	-	8.8	3.5	49.1	-	-	-	-	-	3.5	1.8	5.3	19.3	-	3.5	12.3	-	-	1.8	47.4	96.5	3.5	-
1+	No.	1	-	-	-	1	-	-	1	3	-	-	-	-	-	1	-	1	2	-	1	1	1	-	-	7	10	1	11
TOTAL	No.	2	4	2	-	15	-	5	3	31	-	-	-	-	-	3	1	4	13	-	3	8	1	-	1	34	65	3	68
LEVEL	%	2.9	5.9	2.9	-	22.1	-	7.4	4.4	45.6	-	-	-	-	-	4.4	1.5	5.9	19.1	-	4.4	11.8	1.5	-	1.5	50.0	95.6	4.4	-
	% Patellidae	6.5	12.9	6.5	-	48.4	-	16.1	9.7	-	-	-	-	-	-	-	-	-	-	-	-	-	-	-	-	-	-	-	-
2	No.	7	-	3	-	6	1	1	2	20	6	-	1	1	1	2	2	4	3	-	2	2	-	-	-	24	44	3	47
2a	No.	1	-	-	-	2	-	-	2	5	-	-	-	-	-	2	1	2	4	-	3	2	-	-	-	14	19	2	21
2b	No.	-	-	-	-	-	-	1	1	2	-	-	-	-	-	-	-	-	-	-	-	-	-	-	-	-	2	-	2
TOTAL	No.	8	-	3	-	8	1	2	5	27	6	-	1	1	1	4	3	6	7	-	5	4	-	1	-	38	65	5	70
LEVEL	%	11.4	-	4.3	-	11.4	1.4	2.9	7.2	38.6	8.6	-	1.4	1.4	1.4	5.7	4.3	8.6	10.0	-	7.2	5.7	-	1.4	-	54.3	92.9	7.2	-
	% Patellidae	29.6	-	11.1	-	29.6	3.7	7.4	18.5	-	-	-	-	-	-	-	-	-	-	-	-	-	-	-	-	-	-	-	-
3	No.	-	1	-	-	1	-	1	1	4	-	-	-	1	-	-	1	1	1	-	2	1	-	-	-	7	11	2	13
4	No.	2	-	-	1	11	-	2	4	18	-	2	-	1	-	-	2	1	-	1	15	4	-	-	-	22	40	1	41
4b	No.	2	-	-	-	2	-	-	5	23	-	3	-	-	-	-	3	-	-	-	21	16	-	-	-	47	70	2	72
TOTAL	No.	2	1	-	-	14	-	2	4	23	-	3	-	2	-	-	3	1	1	-	21	16	-	-	-	47	70	2	72
LEVEL	%	2.8	1.4	-	-	19.4	-	2.8	5.6	31.9	-	4.2	-	2.8	-	-	4.2	1.4	1.4	-	29.2	22.2	-	-	-	65.3	97.2	2.8	-
	% Patellidae	8.7	4.4	-	-	60.9	-	8.7	17.4	-	-	-	-	-	-	-	-	-	-	-	-	-	-	-	-	-	-	-	-
5	No.	1	-	-	-	7	-	3	2	3	-	11	-	-	-	-	-	3	3	1	14	6	-	-	-	27	38	-	38
	%	2.6	-	-	-	18.4	-	7.9	-	29.0	-	-	-	-	-	-	-	7.9	7.9	2.6	36.9	15.8	-	-	-	71.1	100.0	-	-
6	No.	-	1	-	2	5	-	3	1	12	-	-	-	-	-	1	1	5	4	-	41	13	-	-	1	67	79	-	79
	%	-	1.3	-	2.5	6.3	-	3.8	1.3	15.2	-	-	-	-	-	1.3	1.3	6.3	5.1	-	51.9	16.5	-	-	1.3	84.8	100.0	-	-
	% Patellidae	-	8.3	-	16.7	41.7	-	25.0	8.3	-	-	-	-	-	-	-	-	-	-	-	-	-	-	-	-	-	-	-	-
7	No.	-	-	-	-	1	-	1	-	2	-	-	-	-	-	-	-	-	1	-	9	2	-	-	-	12	14	-	14
TOTAL	No.	13	6	5	2	51	1	17	15	110	8	3	1	3	1	8	12	17	29	1	95	50	1	1	2	232	342	12	354
	%	3.7	1.7	1.4	0.6	14.4	0.3	4.8	4.2	31.1	2.3	0.9	0.3	0.9	0.3	2.3	3.4	4.8	8.2	0.3	26.8	14.1	0.3	0.3	0.6	65.5	96.6	3.4	-

of species is shown in table 13.4; the full list of species is given in table 13.3.

KRM 1-13: MSA IV

All 12 of the species in this sample have been recorded in the vicinity in modern times. Patellidae predominate in numbers but constitute only 5 percent of the assemblage. *P. granatina, P. compressa,* and the sandy beach species are again absent. *P. perna* is very poorly represented.

The full list of species is given in table 13.4. The sample can be compared with 1-5 to 6 and 15: even though the samples are small, they are roughly comparable in size.

KRM 1A-1 to 9: MSA III

All the samples from this MSA stage are small; between them they include 13 of the modern species recorded in the area. *P. granatina* is present in small quantities in these layers.

Patellidae are the most common group, with *P. perna* very rare and few examples of *Turbo* spp. Other species are very sparsely represented; the entire list is shown in table 13.5. For comparative purposes the total number of specimens from these layers are utilized, but even this gave a small total sample.

KRM 1A-10 to 21: Howieson's Poort

The shell from these layers was heavily fragmented. By combining the material from layers 15 and 16, four reasonable samples became available for comparative purposes—layers 15/16, 19, 20, and 21.

A decrease in the frequency of Patellidae with increasing depth is associated with a marked increase in *P. perna* and *T. sarmaticus. P. granatina* is well represented, and one juvenile *P. compressa* appears in layer 20. Seventeen of the modern recorded species are present. Two of these are sand-dwelling bivalves, i.e., *D. serra* and *Tellina alfredensis. D. gigas* is

Table 13.3. Minimum Numbers of Individuals per Molluscan Species

MOLLUSCAN SPECIES	+ Scree	+ 4	5	5-6	5-7	7-12	7-12 ⊕	Later Stone Age Total	13	14	15	16	17a	17b	TOTAL	37	38	38 E Cutting Q	TOTAL	Middle Stone Age Total	TOTAL
		LATER STONE AGE							MSA IV		MIDDLE STONE AGE II						MIDDLE STONE AGE I				
Patella argenvillei	-	3	15	-	5	x	x	x	23	3	-	1	x	1	-	2	2	46	7	55	60	83
P. barbara: tabularis	-	-	-	-	4	-	-	-	4	-	-	-	-	-	-	-	-	-	-	-	-	4
P. barbara	-	2	9	x	-	x	x	x	11	2	-	-	x	-	-	x	-	-	-	-	2	13
P. cochlear	-	1	28	-	6	x	x	-	35	2	-	-	-	1	-	1	-	-	-	-	3	38
P. granatina/ oculus	-	1	-	-	-	-	-	-	1	16	-	2	x	-	-	2	-	4	-	4	22	23
P. granatina	x	-	-	-	-	-	-	-	-	-	-	-	-	-	-	-	-	1	-	1	1	1
P. granularis	-	-	2	-	-	-	x	-	2	2	-	-	-	-	-	-	-	1	-	1	3	5
P. longicosta	-	6	142	x	26	x	x	x	174	4	x	8	x	1	-	9	8	47	4	59	72	246
P. oculus	-	-	13	-	3	x	-	-	16	12	-	2	-	3	2	7	-	1	11	12	31	47
P. tabularis	-	-	4	-	-	-	x	-	4	-	x	1	x	-	2	3	1	1	-	2	5	9
Patella species	-	-	2	-	-	-	-	-	2	1	x	2	-	-	-	2	-	3	2	5	8	10
Bullia rhodostoma	-	-	-	-	-	-	-	-	-	-	-	-	-	-	-	-	-	1	-	1	1	1
Burnupena cincta	x	1	6	-	-	-	x	-	7	-	-	-	-	1	-	1	3	16	-	19	20 -	27
Burnupena lagenaria	-	1	3	-	2	-	x	-	6	1	-	-	x	-	-	x	-	9	-	9	10	16
Burnupena species	-	-	-	-	-	-	-	-	-	-	-	-	-	-	1	1	-	-	-	-	1	1
Juvenile Patellidae	-	-	1	-	-	-	-	-	1	-	-	-	-	-	-	-	-	1	3	4	4	5
Donax serra	-	-	-	-	-	x	-	-	-	x	-	-	-	-	-	-	-	8	19	27	27	27
Gryphaea margariticea	-	-	-	-	-	-	-	-	-	-	-	-	x	-	-	x	-	-	-	-	-	-
Haliotis midea	-	-	-	-	-	x	x	-	-	x	-	-	x	-	-	x	-	1	1	2	2	2
Haliotis spadicea	-	3	-	x	1	x	x	-	4	1	-	-	-	-	-	-	-	-	2	2	3	7
Oxystele sinensis	-	1	34	x	4	-	x	-	39	3	-	-	-	1	-	1	-	2	3	5	9	48
Oxystele tigrina	-	-	49	-	5	x	x	-	54	2	-	-	-	-	-	-	-	5	3	8	10	64
Oxystele species	-	-	-	-	1	-	-	-	1	-	-	-	-	-	-	-	-	-	1	1	1	2
Perna perna	-	1	63	-	12	x	x	x	76	4	-	3	x	1	-	4	-	2	86	88	96	172
Phalium labiata	-	-	-	-	-	-	-	-	-	-	-	1	-	-	-	1	-	-	2	2	3	3
Mytilid fragments	-	-	8	x	-	-	-	-	8	2	-	-	-	-	-	-	-	-	34	34	36	44
Turbo cidaris	-	-	-	-	-	-	-	-	-	-	-	(1)	-	-	-	1	-	-	-	-	(1)	(1)
Turbo sarmaticus	-	-	34	x	9	x	x	-	43	3	-	22	x	30	9	61	7	13	13	33	97	140
Turbo species	-	1	-	-	2	-	-	-	3	1	-	-	-	-	-	-	-	-	-	-	1	4
Balanus maxilaris	-	-	-	-	-	-	-	-	-	-	-	-	x	-	-	*	-	-	-	-	-	-
Dinoplax gigas	-	1	1	-	-	-	-	-	2	-	-	-	-	-	-	-	-	-	1	1	1	3
Total No. of marine mollusca	x	12	414	x	80	x	x	x	516	59	x	43	x	39	14	96	22	162	191	375	530	1046
Terrestrial Mollusca																						
Achatina zebra	-	1	3	x	2	x	x	x	6	-	-	-	x	1	-	1	-	-	1	1	2	8
Cyclostoma ligatum	-	-	-	-	-	-	-	-	-	-	-	1	-	-	-	1	-	-	-	-	1	1
Total No. of terrestrial mollusca	-	1	3	x	2	x	x	x	6	-	-	1	x	1	-	2	-	-	1	1	3	9
Total No. of specimens	x	23	417	x	82	x	x	x	522	59	x	44	x	40	14	98	22	162	192	376	533	1055

⊕ Porcupine lair filling   x = Present, not countable.   Figures in brackets = identification uncertain.

Table 13.4. Percentages of Well-represented Molluscan Species on Basis of Minimum Numbers of Individuals (x denotes species present, not countable)

		Patella argenvillei	*Patella barbara*	*Patella barbara/ tabularis*	*Patella cochlear*	*Patella granatina/ oculus*	*Patella granatina*	*Patella granularis*	*Patella longicosta*	*Patella oculus*	*Patella tabularis*	*Patella* spp.	TOTAL PATELLIDAE	*Burnupena cincta*	*Burnupena lagenaria*	*Donax serra*	*Oxystele sinensis*	*Oxystele tigrina*	*Perna perna*	*Turbo sarmaticus*	Others	TOTAL NON-PATELLIDAE	TOTAL MARINE MOLLUSCA	TERRESTRIAL MOLLUSCA	TOTAL
LATER STONE AGE:																									
Level 4	No.	15	9	-	28	-	-	2	142	13	4	2	215	6	3	-	34	49	63	34	10	199	414	3	417
	%	3.6	2.2	-	6.7	-	-	0.5	34.1	3.1	1.0	0.5	51.6	1.4	0.7	-	8.2	11.8	15.1	8.2	2.4	47.7	99.3	0.7	
	% Patellidae	7.0	4.2	-	13.0	-	-	0.9	66.1	6.1	1.9	0.9													
Levels 5/6	No.	5	-	4	6	-	-	-	26	3	-	-	44	-	2	-	4	5	12	9	4	36	80	2	82
	%	6.1	-	4.9	7.3	-	-	-	31.7	3.7	-	-	53.7	-	2.4	-	4.9	6.1	14.6	11.0	4.9	43.9	97.7	2.4	
	% Patellidae	11.4	-	9.1	13.6	-	-	-	59.1	6.8	-	-													
Levels 4 + 5/6	No.	20	9	4	34	-	-	2	168	16	4	2	259	6	5	-	38	54	75	43	14	235	494	5	499
	%	4.0	1.8	0.8	6.8	-	-	0.4	33.7	3.2	0.8	0.4	51.9	1.2	1.0	-	7.6	10.8	15.0	8.6	2.8	47.1	99.0	1.00	
	% Patellidae	7.7	3.5	1.6	13.1	-	-	0.8	64.9	6.2	1.5	0.8													
MIDDLE STONE AGE. PHASE IV																									
Level 13	No.	3	2	-	2	16	-	2	4	12	-	1	42	-	1	-	3	2	4	3	4	17	59	-	59
	%	5.1	3.4	-	3.4	27.1	-	3.4	6.8	20.3	-	1.7	71.2	-	1.7	-	5.1	3.4	6.8	5.1	6.8	28.8	100.0	-	
	% Patellidae	7.1	4.8	-	4.8	38.1	-	4.8	9.5	28.6	-	2.4													
MIDDLE STONE AGE. PHASE II																									
Levels 14-17b	No.	2	x	-	1	2	-	-	9	7	3	2	26	1	x	-	1	-	4	61	3	70	96	2	98
	%	2.0	-	-	1.0	2.0	-	-	9.2	7.1	3.1	2.0	27.5	1.0	-	-	1.0	-	4.1	62.2	3.1	71.4	97.9	2.0	
	% Patellidae	7.7	-	-	3.9	7.7	-	-	34.6	26.9	11.6	7.7													
MIDDLE STONE AGE. PHASE I																									
Level 38	No.	46	-	-	-	4	1	1	47	1	1	3	104	16	9	8	2	5	2	13	3	58	162	-	162
	%	28.4	-	-	-	2.5	0.6	0.6	29.0	0.6	0.6	1.9	64.2	9.9	5.6	4.9	1.2	3.1	1.2	8.0	1.9	35.8	100.0	-	
	% Patellidae	44.2	-	-	-	3.9	1.0	1.0	45.2	1.0	1.0	2.9													
Level 38, E. cutt. Q	No.	7	-	-	-	-	-	-	4	11	-	2	24	-	-	19	3	3	86	13	44	168	192	-	192
	%	3.7	-	-	-	-	-	-	2.1	5.7	-	1.0	12.5	-	-	9.9	1.6	1.6	44.8	6.8	22.9	87.5	100.0	-	
	% Patellidae	29.2	-	-	-	-	-	-	16.7	45.8	-	8.3													
Total level 38	No.	53	-	-	-	4	1	1	51	12	1	5	128	16	9	27	5	8	88	26	47	226	354	-	354
	%	5.0	-	-	-	1.1	0.2	0.2	14.4	3.4	0.2	1.4	36.2	4.5	2.5	7.6	1.4	2.3	24.9	7.3	13.3	63.8	100.0	-	
	% Patellidae	41.4	-	-	-	3.1	0.8	0.8	39.8	9.4	0.8	3.9													
TOTAL	No.	78	11	4	37	22	1	5	232	47	8	10	455	23	15	27	47	64	171	133	68	548	1003	7	1010
	%	7.7	1.1	0.4	3.7	2.2	0.1	0.5	23	4.7	0.8	1.0	45.1	2.3	1.5	2.7	4.7	6.3	16.9	13.2	6.7	54.3	99.3	0.7	

Table 13.5. KRM 1A—Percentages of Molluscan Species in Layers 5 to 21 (MSA III, Howieson's Poort) on Basis of Minimum Numbers of Individuals (figures in parentheses denote number of juveniles in sample; x denotes species present, not countable)

		Patella argenvillei	Patella barbara/ tabularis	Patella barbara	Patella compressa	Patella granatina/ oculus	Patella granatina	Patella granularis	Patella longicosta	Patella oculus	Patella species	TOTAL PATELLIDAE	Bullia rhodostoma	Burnupena lagenaria	Burnupena species	Donax serra
MIDDLE STONE AGE PHASE III																
5+	No.	-	-	-	-	-	-	-	-	7	(1)	8	-	-	-	-
6	No.	1	2	-	-	1	4	-	-	2	2	12	-	-	-	x
7	No.	-	-	-	-	1	-	-	-	-	-	1	-	-	-	3
8	No.	-	-	1	-	11	6	-	-	-	-	18	-	-	-	-
9	No.	-	-	-	-	12	2	-	-	1	-	15	-	-	-	1
TOTAL	No.	1	2	1	-	25	12	-	-	10	3	54	-	-	-	5
	%	1.0	2.0	1.0	-	24.5	11.8	-	-	9.8	2.9	52.9	-	-	-	4.9
	% Patellidae	1.9	3.7	1.9	-	46.3	22.2	-	-	18.5	5.6	-	-	-	-	-
HOWIESON'S POORT																
10	No.	3	-	-	-	8	-	-	-	-	2	13	-	-	1	1
11	No.	3	-	-	-	2	-	-	-	1	1	7	-	-	-	1
12	No.	1	-	-	-	-	-	-	-	-	2	3	-	-	-	-
13	No.	1	-	-	-	1	-	-	-	-	-	2	-	-	-	1
14	No.	2	-	-	-	1	1	-	-	-	1	5	-	-	-	-
15/16	No.	-	-	-	-	54	5	-	1	6	1	67	-	-	-	1
	%	-	-	-	-	71.1	6.6	-	1.3	7.9	1.3	88.2	-	-	-	1.3
	% Patellidae	-	-	-	-	80.6	7.5	-	1.5	9.0	1.5	-	-	-	-	-
17	No.	-	-	2	-	4	1	-	-	1	3	11	-	-	-	-
18	No.	-	-	-	-	1	-	-	-	-	2	3	-	-	-	-
19	No.	2	-	-	-	1	4	2(1)	-	8	-	17	-	-	-	-
	%	2.4	-	-	-	1.2	4.9	2.4	-	9.8	-	20.7	-	-	-	-
	% Patellidae	11.8	-	-	-	5.9	23.5	11.8	-	47.1	-	-	-	-	-	-
20	No.	5	-	1	(1)	-	19	8(5)	-	21	18	73	(1)	1	1	6
	%	0.8	-	0.2	0.2	-	2.8	1.2	-	3.1	2.7	10.9	0.2	0.2	0.2	0.9
	% Patellidae	6.9	-	1.4	1.4	-	26.0	11.0	-	28.8	24.7	-	-	-	-	-
21	No.	-	-	-	-	-	-	4(1)	2	-	2	8	-	-	-	3(1)
	%	-	-	-	-	-	-	4.4	2.2	-	2.2	8.9	-	-	-	3.3
	% Patellidae	-	-	-	-	-	-	50.0	25.0	-	25.0	-	-	-	-	-
TOTAL	No.	17	-	3	1	72	30	14	3	37	32	209	1	1	2	13
	%	1.6	-	0.3	0.1	6.9	2.9	1.3	0.3	3.5	3.1	20.0	0.1	0.1	0.2	1.2

exceptionally well represented in two layers. The full list of species is given in table 13.5.

The Cave 2 deposit also dates from this cultural stage, but no shells were available.

KRM 1-14 to 17b: MSA II

This phase is not well represented in the sample; the MSA II material from Shelter 1A is better for comparative purposes.

Patellidae and *T. sarmaticus* are the dominant species present. *P. granatina* and *D. gigas* are absent again, and there are no sandy shore species.

The species list appears in table 13.4.

KRM 1A-22 to 33: MSA II

These levels have yielded what are probably the finest extant samples of shells of this age. Once again, the three groups Patellidae, *P. perna,* and *T. sarmaticus* are best represented.

Layers 24 and 25 included large quantities of *D. serra.* The *P. granatina* and *P. granatina/oculus* groups are the dominant *Patella* species. *D. gigas* is one of the most common species in layers 30 and 31, while *P. compressa* is also present.

The sample from "layer 28 to 29" was omitted from the final tables since it was a small sample in which all the species were already represented much better in layers 28 and 29. The only exception was a single specimen of *Fissurella mutabilis.*

Of the 27 species present, 22 appear in the modern record, the highest degree of similarity within the sequence.

The full list appears in table 13.6.

KRM 1-37 to 38: MSA I

The sample from layer 38 (38 and 38 East Cutting Q) is a good size for comparative work. Layer 37 is poorly represented and includes only two species other than *Patella* spp.

The two samples from layer 38 differ in some respects. The sample from layer 38 consists mainly of *Patella* spp., with a fair representation of others. However, East Cutting Q yielded far fewer specimens of *Patella* spp., but a large number of *P. perna* specimens. *D. serra* is well represented in both samples.

There is only one specimen each of *P. granatina* and *D. gigas.*

Individual numbers per species appear in table 13.4.

KRM 1B-1 to 13: MSA I

The material from this shelter was again very fragmented; only one sample large enough for comparative purposes (layer 12) was obtained.

Patellidae and *P. perna* are fairly constantly distributed throughout, but no specimens of *T. sarmaticus* occur below layer 12. *D. gigas* occurs in only three layers, and the sand dwellers are totally absent. One interesting feature is the sud-

cf *Gryphaea*	*Haliotis midae*	*Haliotis spadicea*	*Oxystele tigrina*	*Oxystele* species	*Perna perna*	*Tellina alfredensis*	*Turbo cidaris*	*Turbo sarmaticus*	*Turbo* species	cf *Amblychilepas scutella*	*Dinoplax gigas*	TOTAL NON-PATELLIDAE	TOTAL MARINE MOLLUSCA	*Achatina zebra*	*Trepidophora ligata*	TOTAL TERRESTRIAL MOLLUSCA	TOTAL SAMPLE
-	-	-	-	-	-	-	1	2	1	-	-	4	12	-	-	-	12
1	-	-	-	-	-	-	-	5	-	1	1	8	21	3	-	3	24
-	-	-	-	-	1	-	1	-	-	-	-	5	6	-	-	-	6
-	-	1	-	-	1	-	-	5	-	-	-	7	25	2	-	2	27
-	1	-	1	-	1	-	12	1	-	-	1	18	33	1	-	1	34
1	1	1	1	-	3	-	14	13	1	1	2	42	97	6	-	6	103
1.0	1.0	1.0	1.0	-	2.9	-	13.7	12.8	1.0	1.0	2.0	41.2	96.1	5.9	-	5.9	-
-	-	-	-	-	-	-	-	-	-	-	-	-	-	-	-	-	-
-	-	-	-	-	7	3	-	8	-	-	-	20	33	-	-	-	33
-	-	-	-	-	5	4	-	5	-	-	1	16	23	-	-	-	23
-	-	-	-	-	2	-	-	-	-	-	-	2	5	-	-	-	5
-	-	-	-	-	3	-	-	-	-	-	-	4	6	-	-	-	6
-	-	-	-	-	5	1	1	15	-	-	-	22	27	-	-	-	27
-	-	-	-	-	-	-	-	8	-	-	-	9	76	-	-	-	76
-	-	-	-	-	-	-	-	10.5	-	-	-	11.8	-	-	-	-	-
-	-	-	-	-	-	-	-	-	-	-	-	-	-	-	-	-	-
-	-	-	-	-	-	-	-	9	-	-	2	11	22	-	-	-	22
-	1	-	-	-	4	-	-	6	-	-	-	11	14	-	-	-	14
-	1	-	1	-	18	cf1	1	22	-	-	21	65	82	-	-	-	22
-	1.2	-	1.2	-	22.0	1.2	1.2	26.8	-	-	25.6	79.3	-	-	-	-	-
-	-	-	-	-	-	-	-	-	-	-	-	-	-	-	-	-	-
1	7	-	-	-	157	-	1	397	1	-	15	588	661	7	1	8	669
0.2	1.1	-	-	-	23.5	-	0.2	59.3	0.2	-	2.2	87.9	98.8	1.1	0.2	1.2	-
-	-	-	-	-	-	-	-	-	-	-	-	-	-	-	-	-	-
-	2	1	-	1	32	-	-	39	-	-	4	82	90	-	-	-	90
-	2.2	1.1	-	1.1	35.6	-	-	43.3	-	-	4.4	91.1	-	-	-	-	-
-	-	-	-	-	-	-	-	-	-	-	-	-	-	-	-	-	-
1	11	1	1	1	233	9	3	509	1	-	43	830	1039	7	1	8	1047
0.1	1.1	0.1	0.1	0.1	22.3	0.9	0.3	48.6	0.1	-	4.1	79.3	99.2	0.7	0.1	0.8	-

den increase in the *Burnupena* species in layer 12; they are a very minor factor in the other layers.

P. granatina occurs in layers 7 and 12 only.

These layers share only 11 species with the modern list; a full list appears as table 13.7. Percentages are given only for layers 12 and 13. The material from layers 13, 13a, and 13b has been combined in order to derive a larger sample—one which comes from the oldest part of the sequence.

The KRM Mollusca and the Present-Day Fauna

Stephenson prepared a survey of the South African intertidal fauna; the section relevant to KRM appeared in print in 1944. Two of his stations, at Storms River and Jeffreys Bay, straddle the KRM area. Thus it was possible to draw up a list of extant species (the "Recent" column in table 13.8) by using this publication, the work of Day (1969), and some information gathered by the author during a visit to KRM.

Several interesting points emerge. The eastern limit of the distribution of *P. granatina* is given as Cape Agulhas and that of *P. compressa* as Danger Point (near Gansbaai), both being west of longitude 20°. The identification by the author of the latter species may be open to question in spite of the care taken; nevertheless, it suggests that further work should include a special alertness for this species, which is indicative of the presence of the giant kelp, *Ecklonia maxima,* and may therefore be linked with temperature changes.

However, there is no doubt concerning the identification of *P. granatina*. Complete specimens and specimens retaining their coloring were common. This species is unknown along this coast in modern times. Koch (1949, p. 502) lists it as an essentially cold water species. The species reaches its peak in MSA II (1A-29). It is rare in MSA I, but increases at a comparatively steady rate up to MSA III. It is entirely absent from MSA IV and the succeeding LSA I and II, and it was not recorded in the MSA II layers of Cave 1.

The presence of this species suggests a general lowering of the sea temperature during MSA I–III. Unfortunately, it is not possible to equate this lowering of sea temperature unequivocally with the onset of the Last Glaciation, but it is probable that it does in fact tie in with this climatic change. The absence of *P. granatina* from 1-13 (MSA IV) could be related to the presumed drop in sea level, although other shellfish species are present.

Stephenson notes that *Patella argenvillei* is not as abundant or as large on this part of the coast as on the west coast. It is present at KRM, but never forms a very large part of the total collection, suggesting that it may not have been very abundant locally or could not be collected easily on the steep shore. The littoral distribution of the species is more limited on the south coast at the present time, being scattered through the Lower Balanoid to Cochlear zone. On the west coast it extends further down into the Lower Cochlear/Argenvillei zone.

Oxystele variegata is listed by Stephenson as being the most common *Oxystele* species in 1944; in 1968 large quantities of

Table 13.6. KRM 1A (CONTINUED)—PERCENTAGES OF MOLLUSCAN SPECIES IN LAYERS 22 TO 33 (MSA II) ON BASIS OF MINIMUM NUMBERS OF INDIVIDUALS (FIGURES IN PARENTHESES DENOTE NUMBER OF JUVENILES IN SAMPLE; X DENOTES SPECIES PRESENT, NOT COUNTABLE)

Layer		*Patella argenvillei*	*Patella barbara/tabularis*	*Patella barbara*	*Patella cochlear*	*Patella compressa*	*Patella granatina/oculus*	*Patella granatina*	*Patella granularis*	*Patella longicosta*	*Patella oculus*	*Patella tabularis*	*Patella* spp.	TOTAL PATELLIDAE	*Bullia rhodostoma*	*Burnupena cincta*	*Burnupena lagenaria*	*Burnupena* spp.
22	No.	3(2)	-	-	-	(1)	-	-	-	5(2)	7	-	4	20	-	-	-	2
	%	4.6	-	-	-	1.5	-	-	-	7.6	10.6	-	6.1	30.3	-	-	-	3.0
	% Patellidae	15.0	-	-	-	5.0	-	-	-	25.0	35.0	-	20.0	-	-	-	-	-
23	No.	10	-	4	1	-	15	1	2	19(2)	107	3	10	172	4	1	3	-
and	%	2.2	-	0.9	0.2	-	3.3	0.2	0.4	4.1	23.3	0.7	2.2	37.5	0.9	0.2	0.7	-
24	% Patellidae	5.8	-	2.3	0.6	-	8.7	0.6	1.2	11.1	62.2	1.7	5.8	-	-	-	-	-
25	No.	4	6(1)	-	2	-	35	2	-	13	71	-	-	133	-	-	10	-
	%	1.6	2.3	-	0.8	-	13.6	0.8	-	5.1	27.6	-	-	51.8	-	-	3.9	-
	% Patellidae	3.0	4.5	-	1.5	-	26.3	1.5	-	9.8	55.4	-	-	-	-	-	-	-
26	No.	3	2	-	-	-	5	-	-	-	27	-	-	37	-	-	8	-
	%	3.7	2.4	-	-	-	6.1	-	-	-	32.9	-	-	45.1	-	-	9.8	-
	% Patellidae	8.1	5.4	-	-	-	13.5	-	-	-	73.0	-	-	-	-	-	-	-
27	No.	14	-	4	2	-	5	18	-	-	78	6	1	128	-	7	3	-
	%	5.2	-	1.5	0.7	-	1.9	6.7	-	-	29.0	2.2	0.4	47.6	-	2.6	1.1	-
	% Patellidae	10.9	-	3.1	1.6	-	3.9	14.1	-	-	60.9	4.7	0.8	-	-	-	-	-
28	No.	-	-	-	1	-	91	35	4	4	23	2	1	161	-	11	12	2
	%	-	-	-	0.3	-	27.7	10.7	1.2	1.2	7.0	0.6	0.3	49.1	-	3.4	3.7	0.6
	% Patellidae	-	-	-	0.6	-	56.5	21.7	2.5	2.5	14.3	1.2	0.6	-	-	-	-	-
29	No.	5	-	2	-	-	421	239	-	4	47	-	1	719	-	-	-	-
	%	0.7	-	0.3	-	-	56.5	32.1	-	0.5	6.3	-	0.1	96.5	-	-	-	-
	% Patellidae	0.7	-	0.3	-	-	58.6	33.2	-	0.6	6.6	-	0.1	-	-	-	-	-
30	No.	9	-	-	1	-	60	42	-	8(2)	26	-	18	164	-	2	2	-
	%	2.5	-	-	0.3	-	16.4	11.5	-	2.2	7.1	-	4.9	44.8	-	0.5	0.5	-
	% Patellidae	5.5	-	-	0.6	-	36.6	25.6	-	4.9	15.6	-	11.0	-	-	-	-	-
31	No.	9	-	-	1	-	138	8	-	3	105	-	8	272	-	2	-	1
	%	1.7	-	-	0.2	-	26.0	1.5	-	0.6	19.8	-	1.5	51.2	-	0.4	-	0.2
	% Patellidae	3.3	-	-	0.4	-	50.7	2.9	-	1.1	38.6	-	2.9	-	-	-	-	-
32	No.	4	-	2	1	-	1	-	-	14	6	2	-	30	-	1	-	-
and	%	5.6	-	2.8	1.4	-	1.4	-	-	19.7	8.5	2.8	-	42.3	-	1.4	-	-
33	% Patellidae	13.3	-	6.7	3.3	-	3.3	-	-	46.7	20.0	6.7	-	-	-	-	-	-
TOTAL	No.	61	8	12	9	1	771	345	6	70	497	13	43	1836	4	24	38	5
	%	1.9	0.3	0.4	0.3	0.03	24.3	10.9	0.2	2.2	15.7	0.4	1.4	57.9	0.1	0.8	1.2	0.2

Oxystele tigrina and *O. sinensis* were recorded, both of which common in the archeological deposits.

No specimens of *Choromytilus meridionalis* were found in the deposits; as at present, *P. perna* was the common mussel, indicating that sea temperatures remained within the range of tolerance of this species throughout the sequence.

Fragments of *Achatina zebra* were found in most of the layers (table 13.8). Connolly (1939, p. 298) states that this species occurs along the south coast from George to East London, and Wymer (personal communication) reports having seen specimens on the slopes around KRM. It is thus reasonable to include this species in the list of recent species in table 13.8.

Shoreline Ecology at KRM

The overall picture as represented by the mollusca remains the same throughout the sequence, with the exception of the presence of certain species. Intertidal pool and rock-dwelling mol-lusca are dominant throughout. Sandy shore species such as *D. serra, Bullia rhodostoma,* and *T. alfredensis* occur intermittently, indicating that a sandy shore existed not far from the caves.

P. perna colonies were present throughout the LSA stages, but the species is poorly represented during MSA III and IV and all of the Howieson's Poort stage until 1A-19 to 21. The numbers of available molluscs increased again in MSA II and decreased in MSA I. This fluctuation may reflect changes in sea temperature.

However, it is possible that the collecting pattern may reflect a change in the shoreline ecology. Figure 13.11 summarizes the data on collecting zones for the six cultural stages and compares them with the pattern of collecting reflected in the assemblage from a modern midden at Nthlonyane in the Transkei. The modern sample reflects a collecting pattern extending down the shore to the sublittoral fringe. The collecting area was greatly increased by the exposure of a very extensive rocky shelf at low tides.

Crepidula porcellana	Donax serra	Haliotis midae	Oxystele sinensis	Oxystele tigrina	Oxystele spp.	Perna perna	Mytilid fragments	Siphonaria sp.	cf. Thais sp.	Turbo cidaris	Turbo sarmaticus	Turbo spp.	Dinoplax gigas	TOTAL NON-PATELLIDAE	TOTAL MARINE MOLLUSCA	Achatina zebra	Tropidophora ligata	TOTAL TERRESTRIAL MOLLUSCA	TOTAL SAMPLE
-	1	2	-	-	-	9	-	-	-	-	27	2	1	44	64	1	1	2	66
-	1.5	3.0	-	-	-	13.6	-	-	-	-	40.9	3.0	1.5	66.7	97.0	1.5	1.5	3.0	-
-	-	-	-	-	-	-	-	-	-	-	-	-	-	-	-	-	-	-	-
-	82	2	-	4	-	109	-	-	-	2	71	-	6	284	456	2	1	3	459
-	17.9	0.4	-	0.9	-	23.8	-	-	-	0.4	15.5	-	1.3	61.9	99.4	0.4	0.2	0.7	-
-	-	-	-	-	-	-	-	-	-	-	-	-	-	-	-	-	-	-	-
-	34	2	7(1)	5	-	21	-	-	-	5	35	(3)	1	123	256	1	-	1	257
-	13.2	0.8	2.7	2.0	-	8.2	-	-	-	2.0	13.6	1.2	0.4	47.9	99.6	0.4	-	0.4	-
-	-	-	-	-	-	-	-	-	-	-	-	-	-	-	-	-	-	-	-
1	-	1	4	3	-	7	-	1	-	-	17	-	1	43	80	1	1	2	82
1.2	-	1.2	4.9	3.7	-	8.5	-	1.2	-	-	20.7	-	1.2	52.4	97.6	1.2	1.2	2.4	-
-	-	-	-	-	-	-	-	-	-	-	-	-	-	-	-	-	-	-	-
-	(1)	5	2	6	-	33	-	1	1	4	68	(2)	6	139	267	2	-	2	269
-	0.4	1.9	0.7	2.2	-	12.3	-	0.4	0.4	1.5	25.3	0.7	2.2	51.7	99.3	0.7	-	0.7	-
-	-	-	-	-	-	-	-	-	-	-	-	-	-	-	-	-	-	-	-
-	-	2	-	7	-	47	-	-	-	-	86	-	-	167	328	-	-	-	328
-	-	0.6	-	2.1	-	14.3	-	-	-	-	26.2	-	-	50.9	100.0	-	-	-	-
-	-	-	-	-	-	-	-	-	-	-	-	-	-	-	-	-	-	-	-
-	-	4	1	-	-	1	-	-	-	1	12	2	2	23	742	3	-	3	745
-	-	0.5	0.1	-	-	0.1	-	-	-	0.1	1.6	0.3	0.3	3.1	99.6	0.4	-	0.4	-
-	-	-	-	-	-	-	-	-	-	-	-	-	-	-	-	-	-	-	-
-	2	2	-	-	-	12	-	-	-	-	150	-	32	202	366	-	-	-	366
-	0.5	0.5	-	-	-	3.3	-	-	-	-	41.0	-	8.7	55.2	100.0	-	-	-	—
-	-	-	-	-	-	-	-	-	-	-	-	-	-	-	-	-	-	-	-
-	-	3	-	-	2	23	24	-	-	2	148	6	47	258	530	1	-	1	531
-	-	0.6	-	-	0.4	4.3	4.5	-	-	0.4	27.9	1.1	8.9	48.6	99.8	0.2	-	0.2	-
-	-	-	-	-	-	-	-	-	-	-	-	-	-	-	-	-	-	-	-
-	-	2	1	-	-	14	-	-	-	-	22	-	1	41	71	-	-	-	71
-	-	2.8	1.4	-	-	19.7	-	-	-	-	31.0	-	1.4	57.8	100.0	-	-	-	-
-	-	-	-	-	-	-	-	-	-	-	-	-	-	-	-	-	-	-	-
1	120	25	15	25	2	276	24	2	1	14	636	15	97	1324	3160	11	3	14	3174
0.03	3.8	0.8	0.5	0.8	0.1	8.7	0.8	0.1	0.03	0.4	20.0	0.5	3.1	41.7	99.6	0.4	0.1	0.4	

The Nthlonyane bar graph is visually most similar to that of MSA IV and MSA !. This suggests that possibly during these stages a more extended rocky littoral was available to the occupants of the KRM caves. Such an extension of the littoral would occur with a lowering of the sea level, a factor discussed in greater detail below. The evidence for such an extension of the shoreline is perhaps scanty; the possibility exists, however, that the examination of other molluscan assemblages in terms of zonation (such as at Nelson Bay Cave) might produce further evidence for such a change in shorelines.

The Interpretation of the KRM Molluscan Fauna
The Molluscan Fauna and the Chronological Sequence

The occurrence of marine mollusca throughout the sequence indicates that the sea was accessible to the occupants of the caves at all times. The earliest levels of the sequence are thought to date to around 125,000 years ago (see chap. 14); a major hiatus occurs in the sequence between MSA IV and the LSA deposit. It is very possible that during this period the shoreline advanced to such an extent that it was not available to the occupants of the cave as a source of food. This hiatus in the sequence is at least partially covered by shell midden deposits in the Nelson Bay Cave.

Rice (in Klein 1972a, pp. 185–192) found a shift in the shell species from *Choromytilus meridionalis* to *P. perna* with decreasing age in the Nelson Bay Cave middens. This shift indicates an increase in temperature from cold water conditions, to which *C. meridionalis* is suited, to warm water conditions similar to the present-day temperatures which support *P. perna*. The shift presumably took place after the MSA IV stage at KRM and possibly represents the close of the Last Glacial.

The KRM sequence does not show a similar shift in mussel species. However, as mentioned earlier, the cold water species *P. granatina* appears at the expense of *P. perna* in three of the MSA stages. At the same time, we have at KRM some slender evidence of shoreline regression in MSA I and IV; in MSA I

Table 13.7. KRM 1B, MSA I—Percentages of Molluscan Species on Basis of Minimum Numbers of Individuals (figures in parentheses denote number of juveniles in sample)

LEVEL		*Patella argenvillei*	*Patella cochlear*	*Patella granatina/ oculus*	*Patella granatina*	*Patella longicosta*	*Patella oculus*	*Patella species*	TOTAL PATELLIDAE	*Burnupena cincta*	*Burnupena lagenaria*	*Burnupena species*	*Haliotis midae*	*Oxystele sinensis*	*Perna perna*	*Turbo sarmaticus*	*Dinoplax gigas*	TOTAL NON-PATELLIDAE	TOTAL MARINE MOLLUSCA	*Achatina zebra*	*Tropidophora ligata*	TOTAL TERRESTRIAL MOLLUSCA	TOTAL SAMPLE
7	No.	-	-	-	1	-	-	-	1	-	-	-	-	-	-	1	-	1	2	-	-	-	2
9	No.	1	-	1	-	1	-	-	3	-	-	-	-	-	4	6	-	10	13	1	-	1	14
10	No.	-	-	-	-	2 (1)	-	2	4	-	1	-	1	cf3	8	3	1	17	21	-	-	-	21
11	No.	1	-	-	-	3	1	-	5	4	2	2	-	-	7	2	-	17	22	-	-	-	22
12	No.	5	(2)	-	3	14 (2)	-	8	32	25	18	-	1	-	7	26	2	79	111	-	1	1	112
	%	4.5	1.8	-	2.7	12.5	-	7.1	28.6	22.3	16.1	-	0.9	-	6.3	23.2	1.8	70.5	99.1	-	0.9	0.9	-
	% Patellidae	15.6	6.3	-	9.4	43.8	-	25.0	-	-	-	-	-	-	-	-	-	-	-	-	-	-	-
13	No.	-	-	-	-	4	1	3	8	6	2	1	-	1	16	-	1	27	35	-	-	-	35
	%	-	-	-	-	11.4	2.9	8.6	22.9	17.1	5.7	2.9	-	2.9	45.7	-	2.9	77.1	100.0	-	-	-	-
	% Patellidae	-	-	-	-	50.0	12.5	37.5	-	-	-	-	-	-	-	-	-	-	-	-	-	-	-
TOTAL	No.	7	(2)	1	4	24	2	13	53	35	23	3	2	4	42	38	4	151	204	1	1	2	206
	%	3.4	1.0	0.5	2.0	11.7	1.0	6.3	25.7	17.0	11.2	1.5	1.0	2.0	20.4	18.5	2.0	73.3	99.0	0.5	0.5	1.0	-

SPECIES

the highest proportion of *D. serra* also occurs (7.6 percent). This may reflect an increased area of sandy shoreline available for utilization.

The increase in frequency of *P. granatina* (combined with *Patella oculus*) indicates a lowering of sea temperature. Thus warm and cold phases appear to be represented in the sequence, as shown in the summary of the evidence given below.

Cultural Phase	Mollusc Proportions (%)	Shoreline	Climatic Assumption
LSA	No *Patella granatina*, up to 24.2 of *Perna perna*	. . .	Present-day (i.e., warm)
MSA IV	47.5 *P. granatina* 6.8 *P. perna*	? Regression	Cold
MSA III	46.1 *P. granatina* 2.9 *P. perna*	. . .	Cold
Howieson's Poort	10 *P. granatina* 22.6 *P. perna*	. . .	Warm
MSA II	53 *P. granatina* 8.7 *P. perna*	. . .	Cold
MSA I	4.8 *P. granatina* 24.9 *P. perna*	? Regression	Cooling

The above evidence could be interpreted as reflecting the onset of the Last Glacial (MSA I), cold phases of the Last Glacial (MSA II, III, and IV), and a warm phase of the Last Glacial (Howieson's Poort). The presence of shells throughout the sequence indicates that, although temperatures were lower at certain stages of the sequence, at no time had world temperatures dropped to such an extent that they were associated with a major regression, thus placing the shoreline beyond the reach of the occupants. The possibility of a regression in MSA I is not easy to fit into this sequence, especially with the high proportion of *P. perna*. This phase appears to represent a gradual lowering of temperatures at the end of the Last Interglacial. An alternative interpretation would be to see MSA I as being extremely old and representing the very last stages of the previous cool period (Riss Glaciation); this interpretation is unlikely in view of the absence of evidence for a long hiatus.

The Cultural Use of the Shell

The KRM caves yielded the oldest evidence for the utilization of marine mollusca by man.

Such a collection can be expected to yield information on the cultural use of shells as well as on man's dietary and collecting habits.

There is a small amount of evidence for the cultural importance of shells in the KRM sequence. In 5-2, a slightly beachworn specimen of *Argobuccinum gemmifera* was found. This is a deep water species; the condition of the shell suggests that it was collected dead on the beach. Therefore it must have been carried back to the shelter for aesthetic reasons. Layer 2 also contained a specimen of *Phalium labiata*, which was probably brought back to the cave for the same reason. Layer 2a of the same cave yielded a more exciting piece of cultural evidence. One of the largest specimens of *Patella tabularis* was stained with red ocher in the area within the muscle scar. The upper layers of this cave yielded two painted stones (Singer and Wymer 1969 and chap. 10), one of which was painted red. The pigment the shell contained either could have been used for painting on stone or could have been used for body painting. Whatever its eventual use, the shell formed a perfect "paint-pot."

Perforated shells are not uncommon in archeological sites. In 1A-13 (MSA IV), a specimen of *P. oculus* had a rough-edged conical hole broken through from the ventral surface on the broader end of the shell and slightly off-center. The specimen was presumably intended as an ornament.

During the sorting of material from 1A-18 and 21 (Howieson's Poort), two *T. sarmaticus* opercula were found with unusual edge damage. In both cases the thick edge of the opercula was flattened and the protuberances on the outer face broken off. When the edge was examined under a high-powered microscope, it showed a smooth, polished surface without striations. The wear was highly suggestive of abrasion by a human agency, although some natural agent might have been involved.

These specimens suggest that a close watch should be kept for similar phenomena in other deposits, as an operculum would make quite an efficient skin scraper. In layer 19a (Howieson's Poort) one specimen of *P. longicosta* also exhibited what appears to be a ground edge. In layer 16 of the same cave, some prehistoric workman had begun a perforation in the body whorl of a *Burnupena cincta* but had not completed his task.

KRM 1-15 (MSA II) and 38 (MSA I), included three specimens of *Phalium labiata*, all of which were probably brought back to the cave as curiosities in the same way as the specimens in 5-2.

Thus there is a small amount of evidence[2] for the cultural importance of shells at KRM, but the shells supply most information on a very essential aspect of prehistoric man's life—his diet.

Dietary Preferences and Food Gathering Habits at KRM

It is possible to define prehistoric dietary preferences on the basis of percentages of species in a sample, but the limitations laid down by the author in 1969 (Speed 1969, pp 193–195) must always be borne in mind. In any such analysis it is necessary to assume that the sample is a random sample representative of the individual midden and reflecting the availability of species in the area. Given these limitations, it is possible to say a good deal about differences and similarities in dietary preferences and collecting habits throughout the 125,000 years covered by the KRM sequence.

In the percentage tables for Cave 1 (table 13.4), the portion of the sample labeled "Others" includes *Bullia rhodostoma, P. labiata*, juvenile Patellidae, *Haliotis midae* and *H. spadicea, Oxystele* sp., Mytilid fragments, *Turbo* sp., and *Dinoplax gigas* (only three specimens of which occur in the whole sample from Cave 1). In Shelter 1A, the same category includes *Crepidula porcellana, Fissurella mutabilis* (both of which are nonfood species), *H. spadicea, Oxystele* sp., cf. *Amblychilepas*

2. See also discussion of shell crescents in chapter 8.

scutellum (nonfood), cf. *Thais* sp., and the oysters. The "Total Terrestrial Mollusca" category in this table includes *Achatina zebra* and *Tropidophora ligata*.

The Later Stone Age. Samples compared: 1D-1 and 5 (table 13.1); 5-1, 2, 4, and 6 (table 13.2); 1-4 and 5 to 6 (table 13.4).

In Shelter 1D, the Patellidae constitute less than one-third of the sample from layer 1 (29.3 percent) and only 12.0 percent from layer 5. *T. sarmaticus* is a constant factor in both layers (21.3 percent and 17.9 percent, respectively). Both *Oxystele sinensis* and *P. perna* are less important in layer 1 than in layer 5: in layer 5, *O. sinensis* is the dominant species in the sample (40.2 percent); *P. perna* is slightly more common in layer 5 than the Patellidae. *O. sinensis* contributes almost an equal amount to the sample from layer 1 as the Patellidae. When analyzed statistically by means of the G-test, it was confirmed that the two layers did not differ significantly ($P > 0.1$) when the *O. sinensis* and *P. perna* samples were omitted, but that they differed significantly ($P < 0.01$) when they were included in the test. It is thus reasonable to state that the overall collecting pattern for the two layers did not differ significantly except in the incidence of *O. sinensis* and *P. perna*. Therefore, Patellidae are marginally the major contributors in layer 1, followed by *O. sinensis,* whereas in layer 5, *O. sinensis* is the most important contributor (40.2 percent).

Within the Patellidae, *P. longicosta* is the most common species.

This pattern, with Patellidae constituting less than 50 percent and *Oxystele* being the second major species, is similar to that from the Bonteberg Shelter pottery levels (layer 2b, Maggs and Speed 1967, p. 88). At Bonteberg, however, *Burnupena* spp. constituted a large part of the sample. The major *Patella* species at Bonteberg were the *P. granatina/oculus* group.

Terrestrial mollusca form a very small part of the diet in both layers.

In Cave 5, Patellidae constitue a major proportion of the sample in layers 1, 2, and 4, with a maximum of 45.6 percent in layer 1.

In 5-1, the second most important species are *O. sinensis* and *Oxystele tigrina* (25.0 percent total), followed by *T. sarmaticus. P. perna* makes a very small contribution (4.4 percent). In layer 2, the Patellidae are the dominant species, with *Oxystele* spp. being the second largest contributor. The proportion of *T. sarmaticus* drops to less than half the proportion found in layer 1, while the proportion of *P. perna* increases to almost double that of layer 1.

In layer 4, the *Oxystele* species are of minor importance; *P. perna* (29.2 percent) and *T. sarmaticus* (22.2 percent) contribute similar high proportions to the sample. The full swing around in preference comes in layer 6, in which the *Oxystele* species and *T. sarmaticus* contribute a fair quantity, but *P. perna* contributes more than half of the sample while the Patellidae are of equal importance (15.2 percent) with *T. sarmaticus*.

In layers 1, 4, and 6, *P. longicosta* is the most common of the *Patella* species; in layer 2 *P. longicosta* and *P. argenvillei* are of equal importance.

The relative percentages of the species are shown in table 13.2.

Thus the Cave 5 sample shows an increasing dependence upon Patellidae in the diet as one moves from the older to the younger levels. The oldest level, layer 7, is dominated by *P. perna* (64.3 percent). Layer 4 includes few *D. serra* speci-

mens. *Burnupena cincta* and *D. gigas* are of little dietary importance. *Haliotis* spp. form a small percentage throughout.

The Cave 5 samples contrast sharply with the Bonteberg Shelter prepottery LSA level; at Bonteberg, *Patella* spp. constituted 50 percent of the sample, with *P. granatina/oculus* the dominant species. *Oxystele* and *Burnupena* species were also the second most important species in the diet.

When samples from layers 1, 2, 4, and 6 were tested by means of the G-test for significant differences, it was found that there was a significant difference between the four layers. This difference can probably be accounted for by the shift in emphasis from *Patella* spp. to *P. perna* as discussed above.

In Cave 1, *Patella* species constituted just over half of the sample. In layer 4, the order of preference is then *O. sinensis* and *O. tigrina* (19.9 percent total), *P. perna,* and *T. sarmaticus.* In layers 5/6, *P. perna* is more common than either the *Oxystele* or *Turbo* group, each of which constitutes about 10 percent of the total; however, it is a small sample. *Burnupena* spp. constitute a very small part of the collection, and *D. serra* is entirely absent. The total percentages are shown in table 13.4.

Within the *Patella* species, *P. longicosta* is the most common species in both samples, constituting over 60 percent of the sample. The second most common is *P. cochlear.*

When the two levels were tested statistically against each other using the G-test, it was found that $P > 0.2$, so that the samples showed no significant difference.

The LSA sequence shows a definite change in dietary preferences. In the most recent (Shelter 1D) deposits, *Patella* spp. are of minor importance and *Oxystele* spp. constitute the major part of the diet. In Cave 5, *P. perna* is a major contributor in those levels in which the frequency of Patellidae and of *Oxystele* spp. decreases. However, in Cave 1, the cycle is reversed, with the Patellidae becoming the dominant group.

P. longicosta is the most favored *Patella* throughout, constituting 60 percent or more of the samples in 5-4 and 1-4. *P. argenvillei, P. oculus,* and *P. cochlear* are the next most common species.

These preferences are represented graphically in figure 13.1.

When the LSA samples from 1D-5, 1-4 and 5/6, and Cave 5 were tested using the G-test, it was found that there was a highly significant difference between the samples with respect to the quantities of Patellidae, *Oxystele* spp., *P. perna,* and *Turbo* spp. It is thus justifiable to state that significant differences in collecting patterns do occur within the LSA sequence.

Middle Stone Age IV and III. Samples compared: MSA IV: 1-13; MSA III: 1A-5 to 9.

In the only layer belonging to MSA IV, the Patellidae form the major portion of the sample. *Oxystele* species, *P. perna,* and *T. sarmaticus* make up a decreasing percentage of the sample. The *P. granatina/oculus* group is the most common *Patella* species; together with *P. oculus* it contributes 66.6 percent of the sample (table 13.4).

In MSA III in the Shelter 1A sequence, the individual layers yielded very small samples. Therefore all five levels were combined for comparative work.

Patellidae again contributed the major portion of the sample (52.9 percent), the next biggest contributor to the diet being *T. sarmaticus* and *T. cidaris* (26.5 percent). The *Oxystele* spp. were represented by only one specimen, and *P. perna* and *D. gigas* were also poorly represented. *D. serra* was more com-

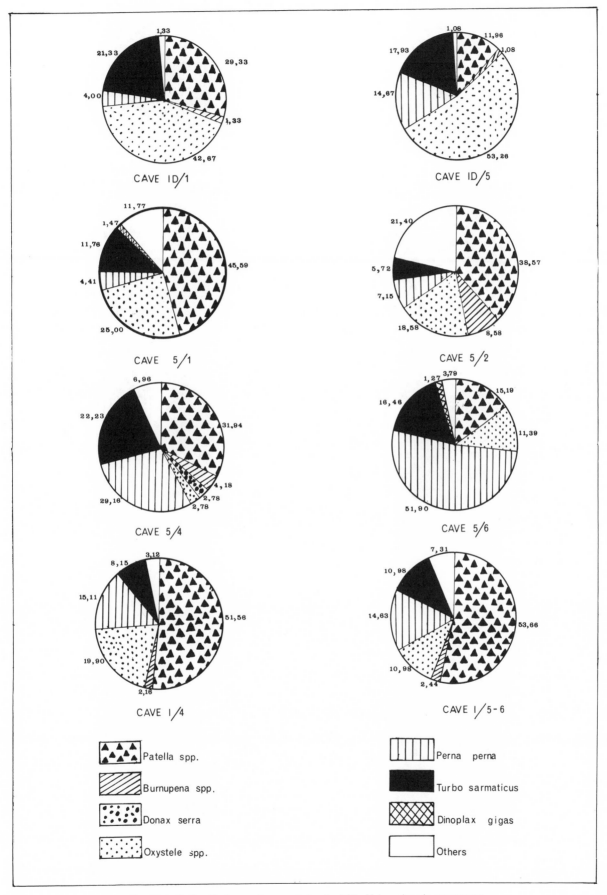

FIG. 13.1. Shell-collecting preferences during the LSA. Values given in percentages.

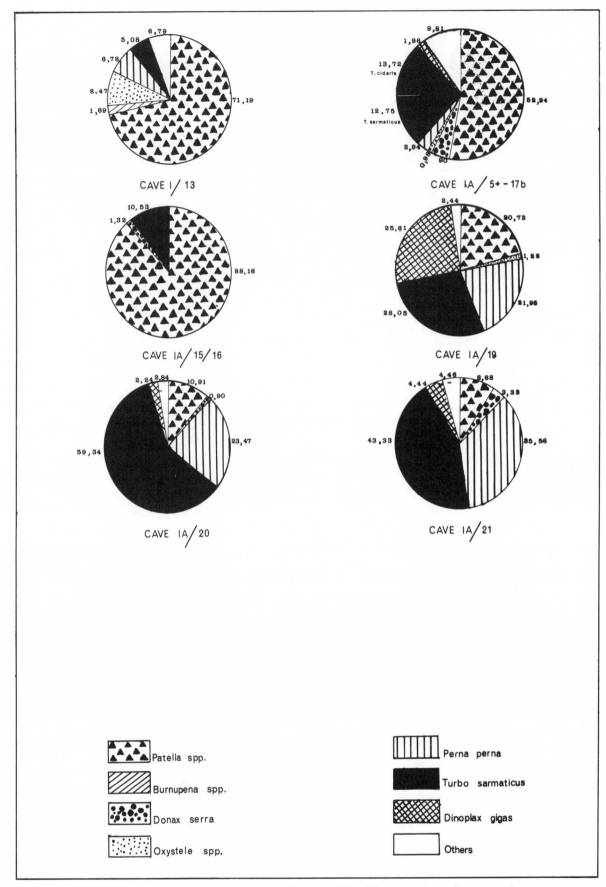

F̶ɪɢ. 13.2. Shell-collecting preferences during MSA IV and III and Howieson's Poort. Values given in percentages.

mon than any one of these last four species. The total percentages are shown in table 13.5.

Within the Patellidae, the group of *P. granatina* and *P. oculus* constituted the major part of the sample (87.0 percent).

In both these MSA stages, the Patellidae are dominant (71.2 percent and 52.9 percent), with *P. granatina/oculus* very much the dominant *Patella* species. MSA IV has a wider range of less important species, whereas MSA III has a high proportion of *T. sarmaticus* and a few other less important species. Unlike the samples from the LSA layers, *Oxystele* and *Perna* species do not show up as preferences in these MSA phases.

When the two samples were tested against each other using the G-test, it was found that there was a highly significant difference between them ($P < 0.001$). This was undoubtedly due to the large number of *Turbo* spp. present in Shelter 1A.

The dietary preferences are represented diagrammatically in figure 13.2.

Howieson's Poort. Samples compared: 1A-15/16, 19, 20, and 21 (table 13.5).

This cultural stage is represented only in Shelter 1A. In layers 10 to 14, Patellidae form less than 50 percent of the sample except in the small sample from layer 12. In layers 15/16 they constitute 88.2 percent of the sample, the rest of which is made up of a small percentage of *D. serra* and 10.5 percent *T. sarmaticus*.

In layer 19, the Patellidae constitute only 20.7 percent of the sample, with *T. sarmaticus* (26.8 percent), *D. gigas* (25.6 percent), and *P. perna* (22.0 percent) making up the rest of the sample. The percentage of Patellidae drops still further in layers 20 and 21, with the percentages of *P. perna* and *T. sarmaticus* also changing. *T. sarmaticus* constitutes 59.3 percent and 43.4 percent of the respective samples, and is thus the most common species in both samples.

Layer 20 included two nonfood species: one specimen of *Littorina* sp. and one small *Drillia* sp.

Within the *Patella* species, the *P. granatina/oculus* group constitutes up to 97.0 percent of the *Patella* specimens. The other *Patella* samples are much smaller.

In this cultural stage there was a marked shift in preferences away from Patellidae to a heavy dependence, first, on *T. sarmaticus* and, second, on *P. perna*. The group *P. granatina/oculus* remains the commonest *Patella* spp. in the big samples.

Layers 15/16 of Shelter 1A show some similarity in preferences to the MSA III and IV layers, in that all three samples show a marked dependence on Patellidae. There is also a very limited utilization of species in this layer.

The samples from layers 15/16, 19, and 21 were too small to be worth testing statistically; layer 20 yielded one of the largest individual samples in the assemblage. Although Patellidae and *P. perna* are important in both the Howieson's Poort and the LSA levels, the Howieson's Poort levels are characterized by continuous utilization of *T. sarmaticus*.

The dietary preferences for MSA III and IV and for Howieson's Poort are represented graphically in figure 13.2.

Middle Stone Age II. Samples compared: 1-14 to 17b (table 13.4); 1A-23/24, 28, 29, and 31 (table 13.6).

In Cave 1, the MSA II levels showed a marked preference for *T. sarmaticus* (62.2 percent). Patellidae constituted only 27.5 percent of the sample, and *P. perna* a very small percentage. There were no *D. serra* specimens in the sample. *P. longicosta* was the most favored *Patella* species, followed closely by the *P. granatina/oculus* group (34.6 percent).

In Shelter 1A, the *Patella* percentages decreased gradually with time during the MSA II layers, dropping from a peak of 96.5 percent in layer 29 to 30.3 percent in the youngest levels.

In layers 23/24, Patellidae are the most common species but constitute only 37.5 percent of the sample. *P. perna* are the next most common species (23.8 percent) followed by *D. serra* and *T. sarmaticus*. *D. serra* is an important food item in both these layers and in layer 25.

Patellidae constitute 49.1 percent of the sample in layer 28, with *T. sarmaticus* the second most common species, followed by *P. perna*. *D. serra* drops completely out of the picture as a dietary item, but the *Burnupena* species constitute 7 percent of the sample.

In layer 29, Patellidae make up the major part of the sample, whereas in layer 31 they contribute just over 50 percent, with *T. sarmaticus* once again being the second major dietary item (27.9 percent). In layer 32, the Patellidae drop below 50 percent and *P. perna* and *T. sarmaticus* contribute equally to the sample, whereas in layer 30, *T. sarmaticus* contributes a major 41.0 percent. Layers 32 and 33, although yielding a very small sample, return to the pattern set by layer 31. *D. gigas* contributes almost 9 percent to the samples from layers 30 and 31.

Within the *Patella* spp., the major contributors to the diet throughout are the *P. granatina/oculus* group in varying combinations: 71.5 percent (layers 23/24); 92.6 percent (layer 28); 98.3 percent (layer 29); and 92.3 percent (layer 21).

Therefore throughout the MSA II sequence the Patellidae were a favorite, and in at least one case an almost exclusive food item, with a steady decrease in their importance in the upper levels of the stage in Shelter 1A. *T. sarmaticus* replaces *P. perna* as a second major contributor, and in one layer (23/24), *D. serra* assumes considerable importance. *D. gigas* is also a good contributor in two layers (30 and 31). *Patella* collecting concentrated on the two species *P. granatina* and *P. oculus*, although *P. longicosta* was equally important in Cave 1. These variations were shown to differ significantly when analyzed by means of the G-test.

These preferences are represented graphically in figure 13.3.

Middle Stone Age I. Samples compared: 1-38 (table 13.4); 1B-12 (table 13.7).

Shellfish collecting takes on a different pattern again in this stage. In Cave 1, the contribution of the Patellidae again drops below 50 percent, and *P. perna* emerges as a major item in the diet. *D. serra* and the *Burnupena* species each contribute just over 7 percent to the diet, as does *T. sarmaticus*. *D. gigas* is no longer a useful contribution, but a fair percentage is made up by *Oxystele* and *Haliotis* species. Among the Patellidae, the large species *P. argenvillei* figures for the first time as a major contributor, followed by *P. longicosta*.

In Shelter 1B, the *Patella* are replaced as major dietary contributors by the *Burnupena* spp. (layer 12: 38.4 percent). *T. sarmaticus* contributes almost the same number of specimens as the Patellidae, but future favorites such as *P. perna* and *Oxystele* species are as yet making little contribution to prehistoric diets at KRM. *P. longicosta* appears in layer 12 as the first favorite limpet food at this early stage of an exceptionally long sequence (table 13.7).

In fact, with the early establishment of the collecting of *P. longicosta*, *P. perna*, and *T. sarmaticus*, MSA I lays down the foundation of thousands of years of marine mollusc exploitation. It is unusual, perhaps, that the *Burnupena* species should figure so prominently at this stage; this may be due to the ease

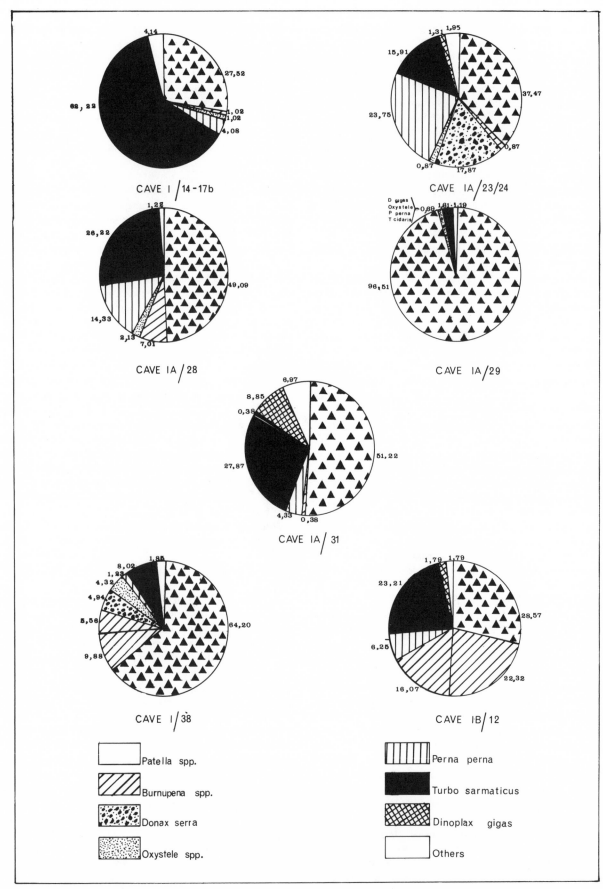

Fig. 13.3. Shell-collecting preferences during MSA II and I. Values given in percentages.

with which they can be collected, and one suspects that their place is later taken by the *Oxystele* species. Rice (Klein 1972*a*, p. 189) found a similar increase in the number of *Burnupena* specimens at the base of the Nelson Bay Cave sequence, a fact which he suggests may have paleoenvironmental implications. *Burnupena* spp. were also major contributors in the Bonteberg Shelter sample.

The dietary preferences for MSA I are represented in figure 13.3.

The KRM assemblage shows a variation in species representation throughout the sequence. The largest samples from each cultural unit were examined for significant variation by means of the G-test; the result showed a highly significant difference among them. These variations in species can be intepreted as reflecting either availability or selective collecting relating to dietary preferences. Since the spectrum of species present in any one section of the sequence indicates that the full range of species was present, it is assumed that the variations reflect selective collecting. This was borne out by fieldwork in the Transkei, where it was found that only certain species were collected even though other edible species were present.

Thus it can be seen that preferences resulted in swings between Patellidae and other species such as *T. sarmaticus*, *P. perna*, and *Oxystele* species. It is surprising to find that small species such as *Oxystele*, *Burnupena*, and *Dinoplax* could each in their own time make a reasonable contribution to the prehistoric diet at KRM.

In summary, it can be seen that the sequence began with a fairly even distribution of species in MSA I. Definite preferences begin to be detectable in MSA II.

During the earliest Howieson's Poort stage these performances swung completely away from the *Patella* spp. toward *Turbo*, *Perna*, and even *Dinoplax* species, which made a surprisingly large contribution to the prehistoric diet. The younger Howieson's Poort and the MSA III and IV stages exhibit a steady increase in the number of Patellidae, a pattern which persisted into the LSA period. However, in the younger LSA levels, the *Patella* species again lost favor in the face of concentrated collecting of *P. perna* and *T. sarmaticus*.

These vertical fluctuations are shown diagrammatically in figure 13.4, which can be compared with the figure published in the preliminary report on the Nelson Bay Cave (Klein 1972*a*, p. 185–87).

The Nelson Bay Cave shell samples display similar fluctuations within their single cultural period, as is shown in the KRM sequence. *P. granatina* is not identified in the sample, and *P. perna* occurs only in the upper part of the sequence, having superseded *C. meridionalis*. The *Burnupena* species are more constantly present at KRM than in the Nelson Bay Cave, but *D. serra* is far more common, with two good peaks, at Nelson Bay than at KRM, as is *P. perna*. *Oxystele* spp., *T. sarmaticus*, and *Dinoplax* are more common in individual layers at KRM than at Nelson Bay Cave.

Robertshaw (1977, p. 68) found marked variations in the frequency of *C. meridionalis* in relation to *Patella* spp. in a shallow shell midden excavated at Paternoster in the southwestern Cape Province. The midden yielded two reliable dates of 870 ± 50 B.P. and 855 ± 45 B.P. In layer 1 of the midden, Patellidae and *C. meridionalis* contributed almost equal quantities (48.6 percent and 44.9 percent, respectively). In layers 2 to 5, Patellidae contributed 91.9–94.3 percent and *C. meridionalis* 2.0–6.4 percent; in the lowest layer the proportion of Patellidae dropped a little, but this group was still dominant. The frequencies of the two most common species show a

reversal at the same point; thus *P. granularis* and *P. granatina* contributed 35.3 percent and 58.7 percent, respectively, in layer 1, whereas in layers 2 to 6 the percentages are 35.9–36.8 percent and 46.8–50.9 percent, respectively. *D. serra* is present only in the upper two layers, and *Oxystele* spp. are present throughout but are not common. Therefore it would appear that the people responsible for this midden showed a very strong preference for the two groups Patellidae and *C. meridionalis*, and a swing from the one to the other can be identified in layer 2. Similar variations in other middens along the coast have been noted, but quantitative data are not available in the literature.

Collecting Habits at KRM

The shells from KRM can yield information on actual shellfish (and therefore food) collecting habits as well as dietary preferences. Most shell species occur within limited zones on the shore (Stephenson 1944) so that it should be possible to define the precise location along the shore where most of the collecting took place. The zones used here are as defined by Stephenson, and the zonation of collecting is depicted graphically in figures 13.5 to 13.10. It should be noted that several species, such as *T. cidaris* and *Oxystele* spp., occur in pools in the Lower Littorina as well as in the Upper Balanoid zones.

The Later Stone Age (Table 13.9)

In Shelter 1D, 70.3 percent of the specimens collected were gathered in the Upper Balanoid zone. A further 22 percent were collected from the Lower Balanoid and Lower Balanoid/Cochlear zone interface. In Cave 5, 45.3 percent of the collecting was done in the Upper Balanoid zone, with 24.2 percent from the Lower Balanoid zone and 14.6 percent from the Lower Balanoid/Cochlear zone interface. From the Cochlear zone and below, 15.2 percent was collected; i.e., a greater proportion of the Cave 5 specimens came from the lower zones, which are frequently splashed even at Low Water Spring tides.

In Cave 1, the zones in which most collecting was done were the Lower Balanoid to Cochlear zones (59.5 percent). Only 29.7 percent of the collecting was done in the Upper Balanoid zone.

From the above evidence, it appears that more molluscs were collected in the upper zones, which are exposed at Low Water Spring tide, during the occupation of Shelter 1D than in the earlier LSA Stages (fig. 13.5).

Middle Stone Age IV and III (Table 13.10)

In MSA IV, 47.4 percent of the collecting was confined to the Upper Balanoid zone and the interface between this and the Lower Balanoid zone, i.e., to areas which are completely exposed or only splashed at Low Water Spring tide. The lower intertidal zones were exploited much less intensely, with yields of 3.4–8.5 percent. The zonation of collecting in MSA III follows the same pattern (figs. 13.6 and 13.7).

Howieson's Poort (Table 13.10)

During this period 57.2 percent of the collecting occurred in the Upper Balanoid zones or above; 1.1 percent was collected in sandy areas, and 22.6 percent of the diet came from the Lower Balanoid zone.

Table 13.8. SPECIES LIST FOR KRM CAVES AND SHELTERS AND MODERN FAUNA

	RECENT	L. S. A.			M.S.A. IV	M.S.A. III	HOWIESONS POORT	M. S. A. II		M. S. A. I	
		KRM 1D	KRM 1: 1-12	KRM 5	KRM 1: 13	KRM 1A: 1-9	KRM 1A: 10-21	KRM 1: 14-17b	KRM 1A: 22-33	KRM 1: 37-38	KRM 1B 7-13
Patella argenvillei	x	x	x	x	x	x	x	x	x	x	x
P. barbara	x	x	x	x	x	x	x	x	x	-	-
P. cochlear	x	-	x	x	x	-	-	x	x	-	x
P. compressa	-	-	-	-	-	-	x	-	x	-	-
P. granatina	-	-	x	-	-	x	x	-	x	x	x
P. granularis	x	-	x	x	x	-	x	-	x	x	-
P. longicosta	x	x	x	x	x	-	x	x	x	x	x
P. miniata	x	x	-	x	-	-	-	-	-	-	-
P. oculus	x	x	x	x	x	x	x	x	x	x	x
P. tabularis	x	-	x	x	-	-	-	x	x	x	-
cf *Amblychilepas scutella*	x	-	-	-	-	x	-	-	-	-	-
Argobuccinum gemmifera	x	-	-	x	-	-	-	-	-	-	-
Bullia rhodostoma	x	-	-	-	-	-	x	-	x	x	-
Bunupena cincta	x	x	x	x	-	-	-	x	x	x	x
B. lagenaria	x	x	x	x	x	-	x	x	x	x	x
Charonia pustulata	x	-	-	x	-	-	-	-	-	-	-
Crassostrea sp.	x	-	-	x	-	x	x	x	-	-	-
Crepidula porcellana	x	-	-	-	-	-	-	-	x	-	-
Donax serra	x	-	x	x	-	x	x	-	x	x	-
Fissurella mutabilis	x	-	-	-	-	-	-	-	x	-	-
Haliotis midae	x	-	x	x	-	x	x	x	x	x	x
H. spadicea	x	x	x	x	x	x	x	-	-	x	-
Oxystele sinensis	x	x	x	x	x	-	-	x	x	x	x
O. tigrina	x	x	x	x	x	x	x	-	x	x	-
Perna perna	x	x	x	x	x	x	x	x	x	x	x
Phalium labiata	-	-	-	x	-	-	-	x	-	-	-
Siphonaria sp.	x	-	-	-	-	-	-	-	x	-	-
Tellina alfredensis	x	-	-	-	-	-	x	-	-	-	-
cf *Thais* sp.	x	-	-	-	-	-	-	-	x	-	-
Turbo cidaris	x	-	-	-	-	x	x	x	x	-	-
T. sarmaticus	x	x	x	x	x	x	x	x	x	x	x
Dinoplax gigas	x	-	x	x	-	x	x	-	x	x	x
TERRESTRIAL MOLLUSCA											
Achatina zebra	x[+]	x	x	x	-	x	x	x	x	-	x
Cyclostoma ligatum	-	-	-	-	-	-	-	x	-	-	-
Tropidophora ligata	-	-	-	-	-	-	x	-	x	-	x
No. of species	29	13	20	23	12	16	21	16	27	18	14

+See page 162.

Table 13.9. LSA ZONATION OF COLLECTING

Zone	Cave 1D	Total	Cave 5	Total	Cave 1	Total
Sandy shore	-	-	*D. serra*	0.7	-	-
U. Balanoid	*Oxystele* spp. 50.2 *Turbo sarmaticus* 18.9 *Burnupena* spp. 0.8 *H. spadicea* 0.4	70.3	*Oxystele* spp. 14.2 *T. sarmaticus* 14.2 *Burnupena* spp. 3.5 *H. spadicea* 2.8 *P. granularis* 0.7	45.3	*Oxystele* spp. 18.4 *T. sarmaticus* 8.6 *Burnupena* spp. 2.2 *P. granularis* 0.4	29.7
U/L Balanoid	*P. oculus*	4.2	*P. oculus*	4.2	*P. oculus*	3.2
Lower Balanoid	*Perna perna*	11.6	*P. perna*	24.2	*P. perna*	15.0
L. Balanoid/ Cochlear	*P. longicosta*	10.4	*P. longicosta*	14.5	*P. longicosta*	33.7
Cochlear	*P. argenvillei*	1.5	*P. argenvillei* 4.2 *H. midae* 2.8 *P. cochlear* 1.7	8.6	*P. cochlear* 6.8 *P. argenvillei* 4.0	10.8
Cochlear/ sublittoral fringe	*P. barbara*	0.4	*P. tabularis* 4.5 *P. barbara* 2.6	6.6	*P. tabularis*	0.8

173

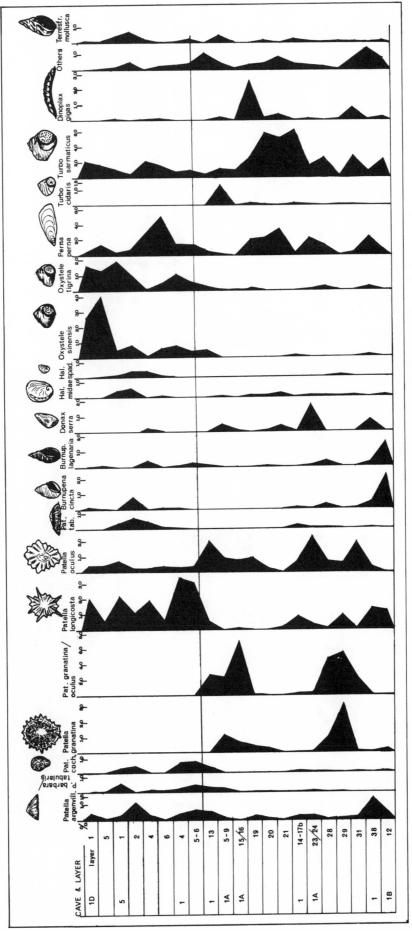

FIG. 13.4. Variations in species distributions during KRM sequence.

174

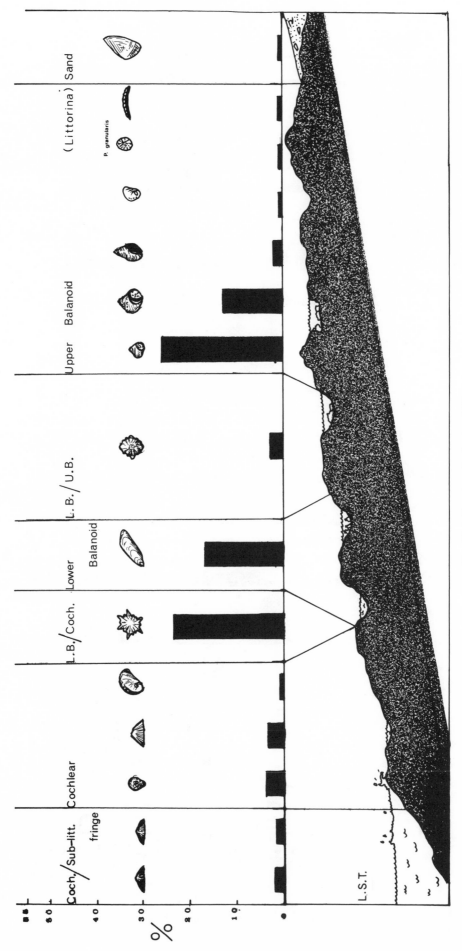

Fig. 13.5. Zonation of collecting: LSA.

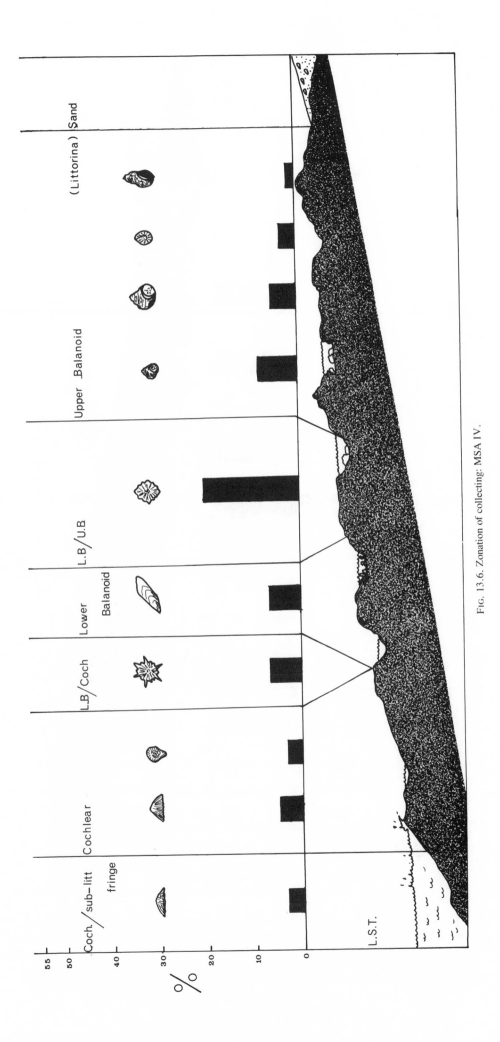

FIG. 13.6. Zonation of collecting: MSA IV.

176

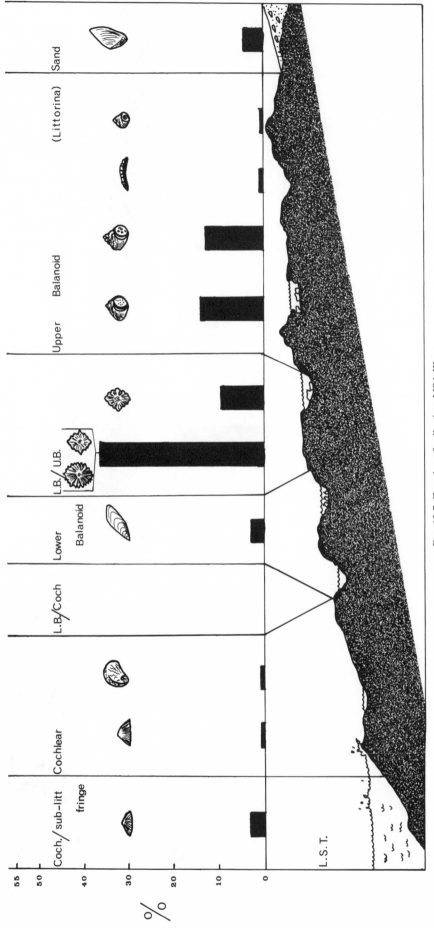

Fig. 13.7. Zonation of collecting: MSA III.

Therefore it can be seen that during these later MSA and Howieson's Poort stages, just above or below half of the collecting was concentrated in zones which were completely exposed during Low Water Spring tides (fig. 13.8).

Middle Stone Age II and I (Table 13.11)

In MSA II in Shelter 1A, 73.5 percent of the collecting was once again in the Upper Balanoid or the Upper/Lower Balanoid zones. Only a small proportion comes from lower down on the shore. Of the sample, 4.0 percent was collected on a sandy shore. In Cave 1, collecting during the same period is also largely in the Upper Balanoid zone, with smaller proportions coming from each of the other zones.

During MSA I in Cave 1, a large part of the diet came from the Lower Balanoid zone and lower on the shore (54.5 percent). The Upper Balanoid zone still supplied a small proportion of the diet. The contribution made by the sandy shore environment is the largest in the sequence. However, this is in direct contrast to Shelter 1B: the majority of the shells in this

sample came from the Upper Balanoid zone (figs. 13.9 and 13.10).

The evidence thus indicates that the majority of the collecting was done in the Upper Balanoid zone and on the interface between the Upper and Lower Balanoid zones. The exception to this situation is the assemblage from MSA I in Cave 1; the increase in species from sandy shores and from lower zones in the intertidal area may both support the suggestion made earlier that this was a period marked by some degree of shoreline regression, with a greater area of sand and of intertidal pools available to the occupants of the cave.

Most of the shells in the assemblage came from rocky shore environments. The shell collectors must have virtually immersed themselves in the water in order to obtain species such as *Patella argenvillei*, *P. cochlear*, and *Haliotis midae*. Observations by the author on the Transkei coast indicate that women collecting shellfish will go waist-deep into the water to collect some species. However, the majority of the species—*P. oculus*, *P. granatina*, *P. longicosta*, *Oxystele* spp., *T. sarmaticus*, etc.—could have been collected quite easily and with

Table 13.10. MSA III, MSA IV, AND HOWIESON'S POORT ZONATION OF COLLECTING

Zone	Cave 1, Layer 13 (MSA IV)	Total	MSA III	Total	Howieson's Poort	Total
Sandy shore	–	–	*D. serra* 4.9	4.9	*D. serra*	1.1
U. Balanoid	*Oxystele* spp. 8.5		*T. cidaris* 13.7		*T. sarmaticus* 50.8	
	T. sarmaticus 5.1		*T. sarmaticus* 12.8		*D. gigas* 4.4	
	P. granularis 3.4		*D. gigas* 2.0		*P. granularis* 1.5	
	Burnupena spp. 1.7	18.6	*Oxystele* spp. 1.0	29.4	*Oxystele* spp. 0.1	
					Burnupena spp. 0.1	57.2
U/L Balanoid	*P. oculus* 20.3		*P. oculus* 9.8		*P. oculus* 3.8	
	P. gran/oculus 27.1	47.4	*P. gran/oculus* 36.3	46.1	*P. gran/oculus* 6.3	10.1
L. Balanoid	*P. perna*	6.8	*P. perna*	2.9	*P. perna*	22.6
L. Balanoid/Cochlear	*P. longicosta*	6.8	–	–	*P. longicosta*	0.3
Cochlear	*P. argenvillei* 5.1		*P. argenvillei* 1.0		*P. argenvillei* 0.8	
	P. cochlear 3.4	8.5	*H. midae* 1.0	2.0	*H. midae* 1.1	1.9
Cochlear/sublittoral fringe	*P. barbara*	3.4	*P. barbara/ tabularis*	2.9	*P. barbara*	0.1

Table 13.11. MSA I AND II ZONATION OF COLLECTING

Zone	MSA II: 1A	Total	Cave 1	Total	MSA I: Cave 1	Total	1B
Sandy shore	*D serra* 4.0	4.0	–	–	*D. serra* 7.6	7.6	–
U. Balanoid	*T. sarmaticus* 15.4		*T. sarmaticus* 62.2		*T. sarmaticus* 7.3		*Burnupena* spp. 38.4
	D. gigas 2.7		*Burnupena* spp. 1.0		*Burnupena* spp. 7.1		*T. sarmaticus* 23.2
	Burnupena spp. 1.4		*Oxystele* spp. 1.0	64.3	*Oxystele* spp. 3.7		*D. gigas* 1.8
	Oxystele spp 0.6				*P. granularis* 0.2	18.3	
	P. granularis 0.3						
	T. cidaris 0.2	20.5					
U/L Balanoid	*P. oculus* 13.7		*P. oculus* 7.1		*P. oculus* 3.4		
	P. gran/oculus 39.3	53.0	*P. gran/oculus* 2.0	9.2	*P. gran/oculus* 1.4	4.8	*P. gran/oculus*
Lower Balanoid	*P. perna*	8.7	*P. perna*	4.1	*P. perna*	24.9	*P. perna*
L. Balanoid/ Cochlear	*P. longicosta*	1.5	*P. longicosta*	9.2	*P. longicosta*	14.4	*P. longicosta*
Cochlear	*P. argenvillei* 1.2		*P. argenvillei* 2.0		*P. argenvillei* 14.4		*P. argenvillei* 4.5
	P. cochlear 0.1	1.3	*P. cochlear* 1.0	3.1			*P. cochlear* 1.8
							H. midae 0.9
Cochlear/sublittoral fringe	*P. barbara/ tabularis*	0.5	*P. tabularis*	3.1	*P. tabularis*	0.2	–

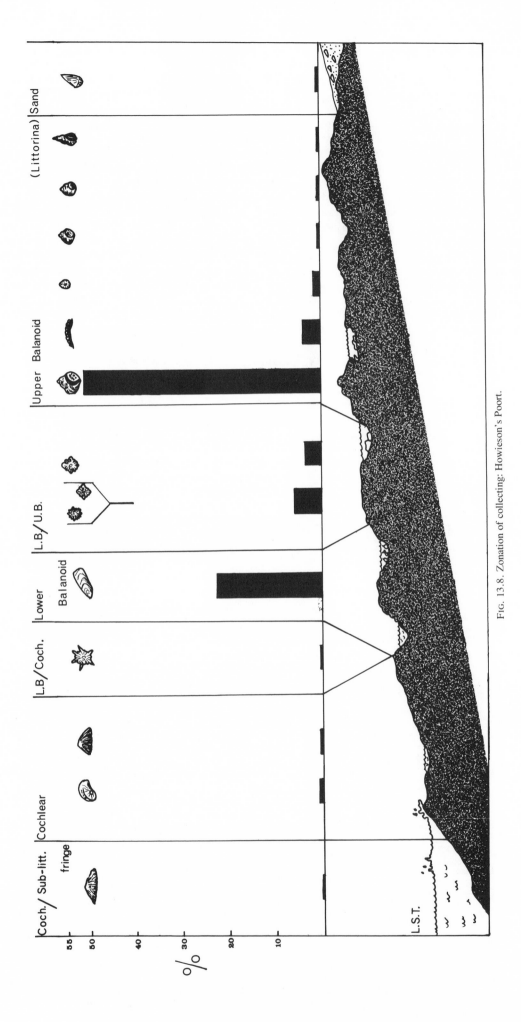

FIG. 13.8. Zonation of collecting: Howieson's Poort.

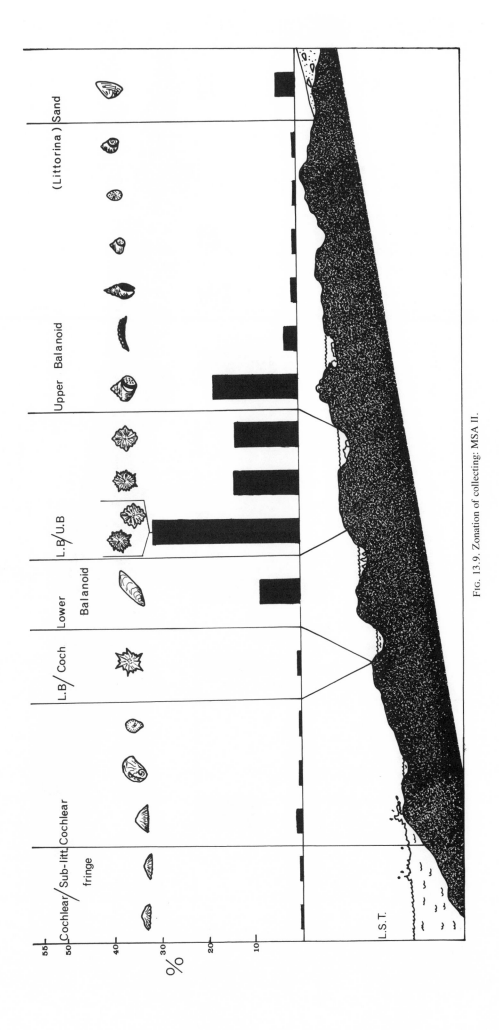

Fig. 13.9. Zonation of collecting: MSA II.

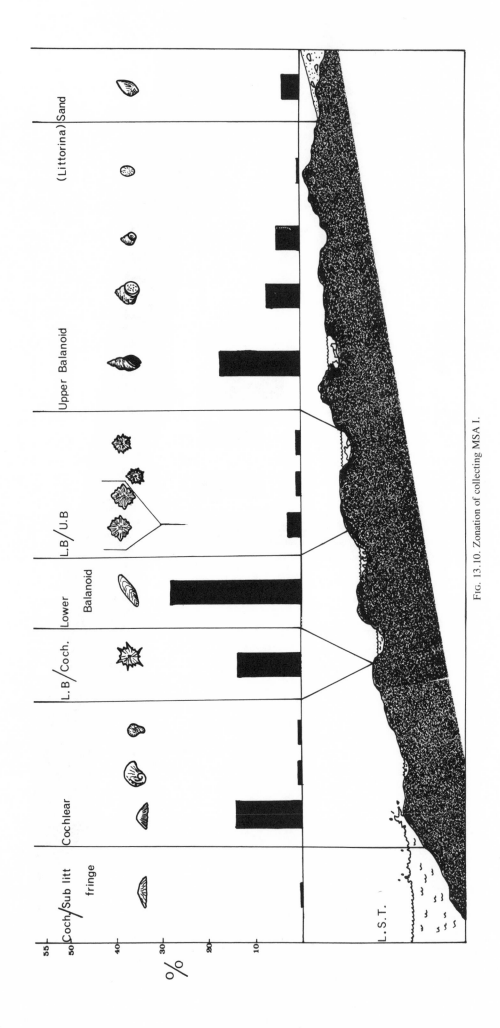

Fig. 13.10. Zonation of collecting MSA I.

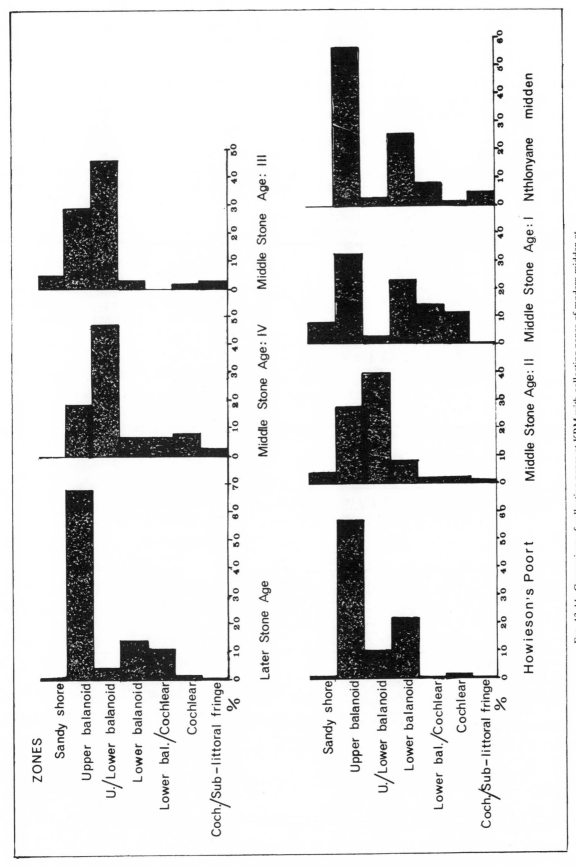

Fig. 13.11. Comparison of collecting zones at KRM with collecting zones of modern midden at Nthlonyane, Transkei. Originally published in *Archaeozoological Studies* (Voigt 1975, p. 92), this figure is reproduced with the kind permission of the Elsevier/North-Holland Biomedical Press, Amsterdam.

the minimum of contact with the sea from rock pools and ledges. The sandy shore species such as *D. serra* and *T. alfredensis* could have come from the small beach area at the mouth of the Klasies River and from the large sandy area about two miles east of the caves.

The Paternoster midden excavated by Robertshaw (1977) shows a similar concentration on the upper intertidal zones with respect to collecting. The presence of middens containing almost entirely *H. midae* has also been noted in the area, suggesting almost exclusive utilization of the lower intertidal zones. However, there is an added problem in the interpretation of the presence of *H. midae* in that there is some evidence in folklore that this species used to occur higher on the shoreline and that its present low level is due to overexploitation. Nevertheless, it is probably still reasonable to regard *H. midae* as representing utilization of lower levels of the intertidal zone.

Unfortunately, it is impossible to define with any accuracy the range of prehistoric shell collectors; on ethnographic evidence a minimum collecting range of 2 km would be reasonable. Present-day Bantu-speaking peoples will walk up to 8 km in order to obtain seashells to supplement their protein-deficient diet (Bigalke and Voigt 1973, p. 259). Ethnological evidence also indicates that shellfish are carried back to the homesites intact and are not removed from their shells as implied by Parkington (1976, p. 132). The only concession made to weight by the Transkei shell collectors is to remove the larger pieces of seaweed, etc., from the shells and to sluice the worst of the sand from the shells. It was quite usual to see a line of women gracefully swaying their way up the footpaths leading over the hills and homeward, each with a 4 gallon can balanced on her head, the cans being full of *P. perna* and *Cellana capensis* (Bigalke 1973).

Mollusc Size Ranges at KRM

During the analysis of the shell assemblage, measurements of maximum length, breadth, and height were made of all possible specimens of the Patellidae, *Turbo* spp., *Oxystele* spp., and *Burnupena* spp. Since the analysis and original preparation of this report, metric data on Patellidae have appeared in a number of publications (Parkington 1976; Robertshaw 1977; Buchanan et al. 1978). When the present report was revised in 1978, it was decided to include some of these metric data.

Patellidae

Although a large number of Patellidae were measured, only about 50 percent of the sample was sufficiently intact to provide maximum lengths. Since this is the measurement utilized in the literature, only the intact maximum dimensions of specimens have been utilized below.

Table 13.12. KRM LSA—Maximum Dimensions of Limpets

SPECIES	SITE	MEAN mm	SD mm	RANGE mm	NO. OF MEASUREMENTS
Patella argenvillei	KRM 1/4-6	49.7	5.5	42-58	6
	KRM 5	62.4	6.3	52-73	12
Patella oculus	KRM 1D/1-5	64.8	9.4	52-80	6
	KRM 1/4-6	49.0	6.2	41-58	5
	KRM 5	60.0	6.1	53-69	8
Patella longicosta	KRM 1D/1-5	65.0	7.9	52-88	25
	KRM 1/4-6	55.0	5.9	40-72	110
	KRM 5	60.0	7.9	43-76	35
Patella granularis	KRM 1/4-6			22.0	1
	KRM 5			26.0	1
Patella cochlear	KRM 1/4-6	47.0	4.0	40-55	17
	KRM 5	50.0	9.0	42-60	3
Patella tabularis	KRM 5	105.0	19.9	79-133	12
Patella barbara	KRM 1/4-6	53.0	4.0	50-57	3
	KRM 5	65.0	8.0	56-75	5
Patella granatina	KRM 1/4-6			50.0	1

Table 13.12 provides the means, standard deviation, and range of eight *Patella* species from the LSA levels. In all cases, the mean for Cave 5 specimens is higher than that for Cave 1; the few specimens from Shelter 1D have a higher mean than those from Cave 5. Therefore the evidence indicates a slight reduction in size between the three caves. This reduction cannot be satisfactorily linked with the carbon dating of these deposits, as larger shells were being collected by the later inhabitants.

The few *Patella granatina* and *P. granularis* specimens from KRM fall far below the means quoted by Parkington (1976, p. 137), Robertshaw (1977, p. 68), and Buchanan et al. (1978, p. 93).

The means and standard deviation of the small quantity of measurable limpets from the MSA levels are given in table 13.13. Many of the MSA specimens yielded maximum breadth measurements; if comparative data were available, these could be utilized.

The sample is too small to be able to make reliable statements on limpet sizes in relation to time. However, the few specimens of *P. granatina* fall within the size range of those described by Parkington, Robertshaw, and Buchanan et al.

In table 13.14 the same data are given for the Howieson's Poort levels. In the case of *P. oculus* and *P. longicosta* the highest mean comes from the lowest levels; with *P. granatina,* however, the highest value is for the uppermost levels. The sizes of *P. granularis* are well below those published for the west coast sites; the *P. granatina* means fall within the upper range and above the means from these sites.

The smaller size of *P. granularis* relative to the west coast specimens is in accordance with the statement by Stephenson (quoted in Branch 1974, p. 170) that this species decreases in size eastward.

Therefore there is no evidence within the KRM data for the suggestion that larger shells were collected in earlier levels, i.e., that prolonged exploitation led to a reduction in overall shell size. The exception to this is *P. oculus;* the mean for Howieson's Poort specimens is in all cases higher than that of the LSA specimens. Nevertheless, it cannot be said that human predation resulted in a decrease in size within the sequence.

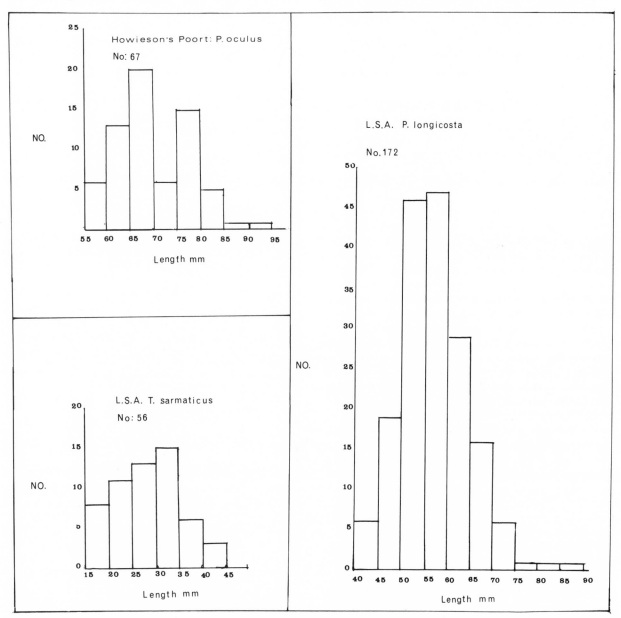

FIG. 13.12. Maximum dimensions of *P. oculus* from Howieson's Poort layers.
FIG. 13.13. Maximum dimensions of *P. longicosta* from LSA layers.
FIG. 13.14. Maximum dimensions of *T. sarmaticus* opercula from LSA layers.

Table 13.13. KRM MSA—Maximum Dimensions of Limpets

SITE AND SPECIES	MEAN mm	SD mm	RANGE mm	NO. OF MEASUREMENTS
MSA III (Cave 1A/5-9)				
Patella oculus	76.1	1.4	74-78	9
Patella barbara			56.0	1
Patella granatina	63.7	5.1	59-70	4
MSA II (Cave 1/14-17b)				
Patella oculus	74.8	11.6	62-90	4
Patella longicosta	65.2	16.8	49-88	4
Patella cochlear			54	1
Patella tabularis			135, 137	2
MSA I (Cave 1B)				
Patella argenvillei			36, 69	2
Patella longicosta	66.6	11.4	53-81	8
Patella granatina			64, 67	2

MSA IV -

NO MEASUREMENTS AVAILABLE

Figures 13.12 and 13.13 show the size distribution of *P. oculus* in the Howieson's Poort layers (1A-10 to 19) and of *P. longicosta* in the LSA layers (1-4 to 6, Cave 5, Shelter 1D). Unfortunately, the *P. oculus* sample is small; however, both samples show a clear utilization preference for shells above the size of 55 mm (*P. oculus*) and 40 mm (*P. longicosta*). In both cases the upper size limit is higher than that given by Branch (1974). On the basis of the age calculations made by Branch, if it is assumed that east coast growth rates are similar to those of the west coast, the age of the shells when collected can be postulated. On this basis, all the specimens of *P. oculus* collected at KRM would have been older than one year. Branch states that the maximum length achieved on the west coast is c. 79 mm (1974, p. 173), but that life expectancy is short (c. two years). This would suggest either that east coast specimens are generally much larger in size or that their life span is longer, thus enabling them to reach a greater size. In the case of *P. longicosta,* it can be postulated that the peak of collecting concentrated on specimens of between five and seven years old. It would be interesting to compare east and west coast growth rates and sizes in order to see whether the apparent larger size in the KRM sample is an artifact of environment or of time, i.e. that the species reached a larger size during the Late Pleistocene and Holocene.

Turbo Sarmaticus

The operculum of *T. sarmaticus* was well represented in the KRM molluscan sample. Those specimens that were well enough preserved were measured for maximum length and minimum breadth. Table 13.15 lists the means, standard deviation, and range of the maximum dimension of those opercula which were adequately preserved to allow this measurement to be made.

There is little difference between the means of the MSA and Howieson's Poort stages. However, the means for the LSA are

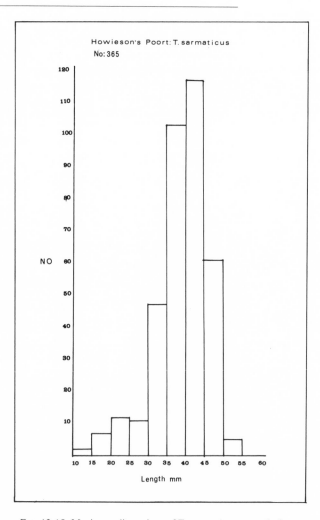

FIG. 13.15. Maximum dimensions of *T. sarmaticus* opercula from Howieson's Poort layers.

Table 13.14. KRM HOWIESON'S POORT—MAXIMUM DIMENSIONS OF LIMPETS

SPECIES AND LEVEL		MEAN mm	SD mm	RANGE mm	NO. OF MEASUREMENTS
CAVE 1A:					
Patella argenvillei:	10-14	58.7	19.5	29-69	4
	15,16			72, 72	2
Patella oculus:	10-14	70.3	7.6	58-83	36
	15,16	70.8	7.6	57-81	20
	17-19	79.9	8.8	70-91	6
Patella longicosta:	10-14	55.7	23.4	20-83	16
	15,16	44.3	24.8	19-72	4
	17-19	69.9	5.6	64-77	7
Patella granularis:	10-14	25.1	3.2	20-28	7
	15,16			21,20	2
Patella cochlear:	10-14			27,32	2
	15,16			31,32	2
	17-19			36	1
Patella tabularis:	10-14			112,5	1
	15,16	103.7	7.3	96-111	3
	17-19			105	1
Patella barbara:	10-14			65,9	1
	15,16			93,45	2
	17-19			64	1
Patella granatina:	10-14	74.4	7.5	64-82	5
	15,16	65.1	12.1	17-81	27
	17-19	68.0	2.7	63-70	5

Table 13.15. MAXIMUM DIMENSIONS OF OPERCULA OF *T. SARMATICUS*

PHASE		MEAN mm	SD mm	RANGE mm	NO. OF MEASUREMENTS
Later Stone Age:	Cave 1D/1-5	36.5	4.5	27-41	13
	Cave 1/4	24.8	5.8	15-33	26
	Cave 5	27.9	5.7	16-37	17
MSA PHASE III:	Cave 1A/5-9	40.2	8.2	20-48	9
MSA PHASE II:	Cave 1/14-17	39.3	2.8	32-43	25
MSA PHASE I:	Cave 1B	38.5	5.8	33-48	6
HOWIESON'S POORT:	Cave 1A/10-14	39.8	7.2	13-55	214
	Cave 1A/15/16	39.6	4.2	26-50	84
	Cave 1A/17-19	38.9	8.4	13-47	67

much lower than for the earlier stages. As in the limpet sample, Cave 5 has a higher mean than Cave 1 and Shelter 1D has the highest mean. Since the operculum size is directly proportional to body size (G. Robinson, personal communication), these figures are a direct reflection of the size of the animal being collected.

Figures 13.14 and 13.15 show graphically the size distribution of the total LSA and Howieson's Poort samples. It is interesting to note that Cave 1 yielded a large number of specimens falling below 22 mm; in Shelter 1A very few specimens fell below this level. The LSA sample is small; nevertheless, the size distribution suggests a preference for the 20–35 mm size class. In this case, the paucity of large specimens (over 40 mm) suggests that these larger animals may not have been available.

The Howieson's Poort people collected *T. sarmaticus* extensively; the size distribution shows a very definite preference for a relatively narrow size range of 35–45 mm. Thus the people responsible for this portion of the vast accumulation of deposits were preferentially collecting specimens which were considerably larger than those collected by the LSA people. At this time, too, specimens of up to 55 mm were available for collecting.

The above results suggest strongly that similar work on other mollusc assemblages could produce additional useful information.

Conclusions

The analysis of the shellfish remains from KRM has provided data on temperature changes, dietary preferences, economic (collecting) activities, and the biology of the shellfish. The series of caves yielded the oldest and most extensive record of man's exploitation of marine resources. The presence of a cold water species is useful in indicating climatic changes within the sequence. A similar situation has been recognized in Nelson Bay Cave. In New Zealand, a cold water patellid, *Cellana denticulata,* has been identified in shell middens, thus permitting similar paleoenvironmental postulations in that country (Rowland 1976).

The significance of the analysis lies in the incredibly long period of mollusc utilization. It has shown that selectivity in collecting was practiced, and it has thrown some light on marine resource utilization by the occupants of the great caves overlooking the rugged Tzitzikama Coast.

14   Dating

Former Sea Levels

It was seen that outside the mouth of Cave 1 the earliest MSA industry found at the site rested on the sand of the 6–8 m raised beach. Hearths, stone artifacts, and bone fragments were mixed with and partly buried by clean marine sand, and this was taken as evidence for the earliest occupation being contemporary with a sea level of this height. Occupation was apparently in close proximity to the water, with this part of the living floor subject to occasional inundations. The sand suggests a sheltered spot similar to the small inlet or cove beside our campsite, well protected from the incessant pounding of the waves on the nearby rocks. A few rolled flakes and one rolled handax in the beach shingle of the 6–8 m sea may indicate even earlier occupation nearby, when the lower caves were still being cut. The conclusion that the MSA I stage was contemporary with the 6–8 m sea is significant, for it offers the best chance for dating the initial occupation. Absolute dates for Upper Pleistocene sea levels in other parts of the world have been estimated by radioactive methods, and it remains to consider whether a correlation with any of them is justified.

Along the entire coast, from Cape Province to Natal, there is good evidence for former sea levels at about 18–20 m and 6–8 m, in the form of raised beaches, wave-cut platforms, and caves or niches in the cliffs at these levels (Davies 1951, 1967, 1969, 1971). Their consistent height argues against any later tectonic movement. Krige (1927) referred to the two levels, respectively, as the Major and Minor Emergences. Davies refers to them as Beaches IV and V in his sequence (Davies 1951 and elsewhere), and they are often more loosely referred to as the 60 ft and 20 ft beaches. At KRM it can hardly be coincidental that Caves 2, 3, 4, and 5 have their floors at about the higher level and Cave 1 at the lower. There is also a well-preserved remnant of the 6–8 m wave-cut platform or raised beach immediately east of the Main Site (fig. 1.2, pl. 2). Along the coast nearby are more subtle traces of these former levels in the topography of the cliffs. Butzer and Helgren (1972) summarize the evidence for 5–12 m beaches in this area and equate them with the Last Interglacial or Eem (see also chap. 4).

A key site for the archeological dating of the higher Beach IV in the Cape Province is Cape Hangklip, on the east side of False Bay, where a prolific Acheulian Industry overlies Beach IV (Gatehouse 1955; Mabbutt 1955; Sampson 1962). As Acheulian industries are not found on Beach V, it can be concluded that this beach is more recent than the final Acheulian industries of South Africa. At the opposite end of the time scale, material on the Beach can, of course, date from any time

between the exposure of the Beach as a dry surface to the present day. The unique significance of the evidence from KRM is the very strong inference that the earliest occupation is actually contemporary with the 6–8 m sea.

It is necessary to jump to North Africa to find beaches at this level which have been firmly dated by radioactive methods. If correlations are to be made, this involves the assumption that sea levels are worldwide phenomena and there has been no tectonic movement at either place. These premises are generally accepted, although other complications may need to be taken into account, such as the sea reverting to a former level after one transgression or regression or more. Faunal evidence, especially molluscan, may sometimes corroborate correlations by altitude. In Morocco the beach at about 7.5 m is termed Ouljian. Dates from deep sea cores by the ^{230}Th/^{231}Pa method place this beach between 97,000 and 69,000 years. Dates by the ^{230}Th/^{234}U method from molluscs give 90,000 to 70,000 years, so there is good agreement (Biberson 1966). This puts the Ouljian Beach in the Last Interglacial or Eemian period of European glacial chronology. Zeuner (1959) had independently concluded that the 7.5 m world sea level (his Late Monastirian) was Last Interglacial and, on the basis of Milankovitch's astronomical time scale, had given a date of 180,000 to 120,000 years.

If Beach V in South Africa is to be equated with the Ouljian of North Africa, which Davies (1967) accepts, this places the earliest occupation at KRM between 90,000 and 70,000 years. The more recent end of this period is likely, as time must be allowed for the cutting of the lower cave, so a date of c. 75,000 years is suggested (see also chap. 4).

Radiocarbon Dates

Thirty-three samples were submitted to the Geochron Laboratory, Cambridge, Massachusetts, from various layers at KRM, mainly in the form of charcoal fragments. Samples were obtained from all the industrial stages recognized at the site except MSA IV, for no suitable charcoal was found in the layer (1-13) containing it. Preference was given to samples from the long sequence of deposits extending from Cave 1 to Shelter 1A, containing industries MSA I, MSA II, Howieson's Poort, and MSA III, in the hope that the chronology and the duration would be clarified. A continuous increase in age with depth would do much to confirm the reliability of the results of the radiocarbon measurements themselves, and it is unfortunate to

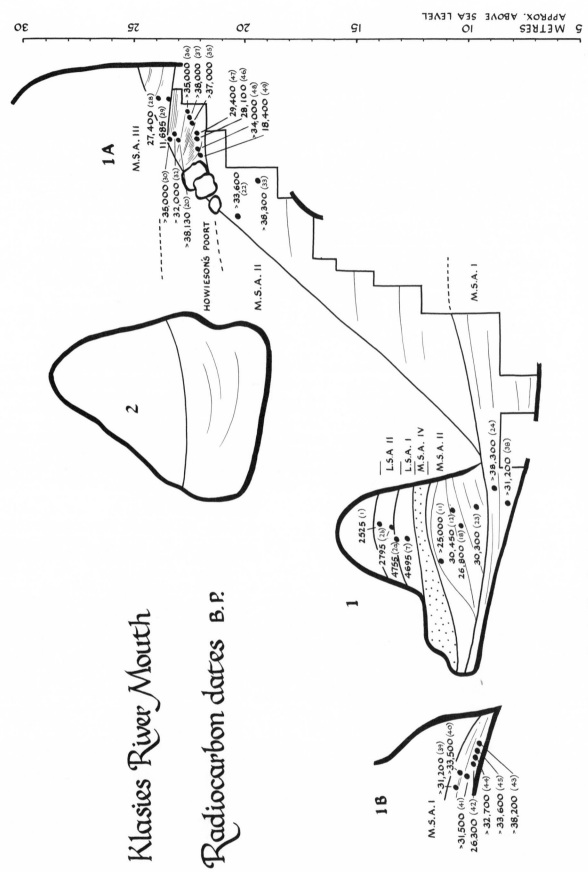

FIG. 14.1. The radiocarbon dates are all expressed in radiocarbon years (i.e., they are uncalibrated).

report that the reverse is true: the results which are tabulated and figured diagrammatically in this chapter show at once the anomalous figures that come from measurements of the samples for radiocarbon. Most significant are the early dates for the Howieson's Poort Industry, all but one of which are as early or earlier than those obtained from the underlying MSA II and MSA I stages (figs. 14.1 and 14.2). Many of the dates are expressed as minimum ones, and thus may not differentiate between long periods or time intervals preceding them, perhaps going beyond the limits of radiocarbon measurability. Yet other dates expressed as probabilities are equally anomalous.

There are only six dates for LSA deposits, four from the Cave 1 middens and two from Cave 5. These, at least, make a logical sequence and are probably reliable. From observations

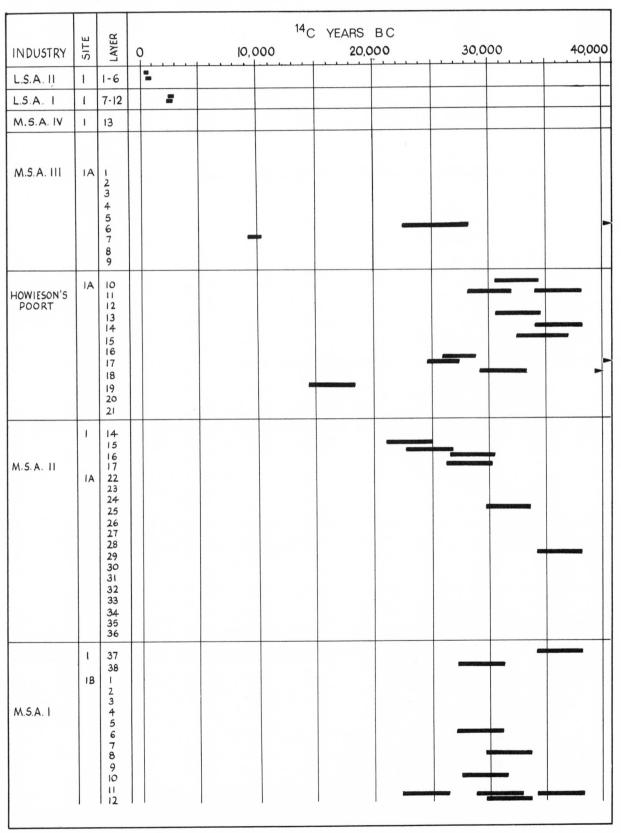

FIG. 14.2. Radiocarbon dates (expressed in radiocarbon years) from Klasies River Mouth plotted against vertical sequence of stone industries. ► indicates dates obtained by J. C. Vogel (see text).

Table 14.1. Positive Radiocarbon Measurements from KRM Made by Geochron Laboratories

Sample No.	Date	Date B.C. (= B.P. minus 1950)	S.D. (±)	Industry and Layer	Geochron Lab No.
1	2525	575	85	LSA II	GX0969
2b	2795	845	85	LSA II	GX0971
2a	4755	2805	95	LSA I	GX0970
7	4695	2745	180	LSA I	GX0973
28	27,400	25,450	3300/2300	MSA III (1A-6)	GX-1373
29	11,685	9735	450	MSA III (1A-7)	GX-1374
				Howieson's Poort	
30	>35,000	>33,050	95% certainty	(1A-10)	GX-1375
32	>32,000	>30,050	95% certainty	(1A-11)	GX-1376
20	>38,130	>36,180	95% certainty	(1A-10-12)	GX0983
36	>35,000	>33,050	95% certainty	(1A-13)	GX-1380
37	>38,000	>36,050	95% certainty	(1A-14)	GX-1381
35	>37,000	>35,050	95% certainty	(1A-15)	GX-1379
47	29,400	27,450	1600	(1A-17)	GX-1391
46	28,100	26,150	1500	(1A-17)	GX-1390
48	>34,000	>32,050	95% certainty	(1A-18)	GX-1392
49	18,400	16,450	650	(1A-19)	GX-1393
22	>33,600	>31,650	95% certainty	MSA II (1A-25)	GX0985
33	>38,300	>36,350	95% certainty	MSA II (1A-29)	GX-1377
11	>25,000	>23,050	95% certainty	MSA II (1 -15)	GX0974
12	30,450	28,500	950	MSA II (1 -16)	GX0975
18	26,800	24,850	1400	MSA II (1 -16)	GX0979
23	30,300	28,350	1400/1600	MSA II (1 -17)	GX-1395
24	>38,300	>36,350	95% certainty	MSA I (1 -37)	GX-1396
38	>31,200	>29,250	95% certainty	MSA I (1 -38)	GX-1382
39	>31,200	>29,250	95% certainty	MSA I (1B-6)	GX-1383
40	>33,500	>31,550	95% certainty	MSA I (1B-8)	GX-1384
41	>31,500	>29,550	95% certainty	MSA I (1B-10)	GX-1385
42	26,300	24,350	4300/2800	MSA I (1B-12)	GX-1386
43	>38,300	>36,250	95% certainty	MSA I (1B-12)	GX-1387
44	>32,700	>30,750	95% certainty	MSA I (1B-12)	GX-1388
45	>33,600	>31,650	95% certainty	MSA I (1B-12)	GX-1389
51	2285	335	105	LSA (5 -1)	GX-1397
34	4110	2160	160	Hearth in sand above MSA (5 -4)	GX-1378

All samples of charcoal except those of (a) shell (nos. 2b, 43, 44, 45, 51), (b) bone (no. 18), (c) carbonaceous soil (no. 20).

of published radiocarbon dates in the last two decades, it does seem that whereas there is generally good agreement for dates extending back about 20,000 years, it is difficult to regard those in excess of this with much confidence.

Table 14.1 gives all the dates obtained from Geochron; a few samples of ash submitted, and one of bone, failed to produce sufficient carbon for measuring. The number shown on the left of the table is the site sample number. Those which were collected but not submitted are not included. Dates B.C. are calculated from 1950 as agreed at the Cambridge Conference in 1962. The Geochron Laboratory advises that the dates are based upon the Libby half-life (5,570) years for ^{14}C and that the error stated is one standard deviation as judged by the analytical data alone, and also that their modern standard is 95 percent of the activity of NBS Oxalic Acid (see also comment by Butzer, chap. 4).

Independent radiocarbon dating was also carried out for us by J. C. Vogel, National Physical Research Laboratory, Pre-

toria, South Africa, with the following results: (a) Pta-1767: Geochron specimen GX-1390(46), which is from the Howieson's Poort 1A-17: > 50,000 years B.P.; (b) Pta-1765: Geochron specimen GX-1392(48), which is from Howieson's Poort 1A-18: > 40,000 years B.P.; (c) Pta-1856: Geochron specimen GX-1373(28), which is from MSA III 1A-6: > 45,200 years B.P. The following comments concern the above dates in relation to the stratigraphy at the site and also to other radiocarbon-dated MSA sites in South Africa (see especially Deacon 1966, 1968) and to the list and discussion by Klein (1974).

Later Stone Age

Excavation suggested that there were two main periods of midden accumulation in Cave 1, and the four dates obtained substantiate this: 575 and 845 B.C., both ±85, for the Upper Midden (LSA II), and 2805 ± 95 B.C. and 2745 ± 180 B.C. for the

Lower Midden (LSA I). Radiocarbon dates for a Wilton Industry in layer C at Matjes River is 3450 ± 250 B.C. No Wilton Industry was found at KRM. It is also significant that the LSA industry in Cave 5 which was similar to LSA II of Cave 1 had a similar date, 335 ± 105 B.C. This date comes from a sample of shell in the same layer as that which produced a painted stone. An underlying hearth was dated to 2160 ± 160 B.C.

MSA III

There are only two dates for this phase, both totally different and the lower one the more recent. The older one, 25,450 ± 3300/2300 B.C., exceeds two of the dates for the MSA II stage but nevertheless fits fairly well on the Howieson's Poort dates below. The younger one, 9735 ± 450 B.C., would make this stage nearly contemporary with the LSA Smithfield A at Matjes River and, coupled with the long series of events that took place at KRM after the deposition of the layers from which these samples came, is most unlikely to be correct. Its dismissal does not necessarily confirm the older date.

Vogel's date of >45,200 B.P. is significantly greater than the Geochron dates and is more in line with current concepts of the MSA.

The only comparable site with a radiocarbon date is the Holley Shelter, Wartburg, Natal (Cramb 1952). Sampson (unpublished thesis) considers the industry at this shelter in the same phase (his Phase 5) as MSA III at KRM, mainly on grounds of tool typology. Here, also, it is interesting to note that two dates were obtained from hearths close to each other vertically and horizontally, yet there is a difference of 14,000 years between them: 16,250 ± 500 B.C. (BM-30) and 2540 ± 150 B.C. (BM-34). The younger date must be discounted (Sampson 1974), and the older agrees better with the younger one from KRM. However, Sampson (1974) doubts the usefulness of this sample because of the uncertain typology.

Inskeep (1976) corrects a date listed in 1970 by Vogel, stating that the "date (GrN-5803) of 43200 + 2000 − 1500" refers to shells from a raised beach at Melkbos near Cape Town "underlying late Middle Stone Age artefacts."

Howieson's Poort Stage

There are 10 positive Geochron dates for this stage at KRM, and seven of them form a fairly consistent block between >30,000 and >36,000 B.C. Two others are around 26,000 and 27,000, and only the last one is radically different, 16,450 ± 650 B.C., and oddly enough comes from the bottom of the sequence. The inference is that the older dates are more likely to be correct. Once again, Vogel's dates appear to be significantly older than the Geochron dates, but both groups really indicate dates beyond the range of the technique. Vogel (personal communication) notes that "in a case like this the oldest date of the level is the most reliable one from a physical point of view. We must therefore, conclude that the 'Howieson's Poort' industry at Klasies is, at least in part, older than 50,000 years."

The only other sites in South Africa where the Howieson's Poort Industry has been radiocarbon dated are the type site, Montagu Cave, and Border Cave. At Howieson's Poort itself there is a date of 16,190 ± 320 B.C. (Sampson 1974), which fits well with the one, odd younger date at KRM. At Montagu Cave there are conflicting dates, 21,250 ± 180 B.C. (Grn-4726) and 17,150 ± 110 B.C., at one end of the scale and 48,850 B.C., 36,050 B.C., and 43,950 ± 210 B.C. at the other end (Keller 1973). Keller is confident that the charcoal has not been

derived from earlier, underlying Acheulian levels in the Montagu Cave but, then unaware of the KRM dates, was inclined to reject the early dates. The more recent dates probably relate to the industry found in the upper levels which are devoid of crescents and backed blades (Keller 1973, p. 40) and could be post–Howieson's Poort. Border Cave has given a date of >46,300 B.C. (Vogel and Beaumont 1972).

Pertinent dates from the Rose Cottage Cave, near Ladybrand in the Orange Free State, for the Upper Magosian layers (Pta-213, SR-116) are earlier than 48,000 B.C. (Vogel and Beaumont 1972).

In Rhodesia, the top of the Magosian levels at Pomongwe is dated to 13,850 ± 200 B.C. (SR-11) (Cooke 1963). The Magosian and Howieson's Poort Industries are very similar technologically.

There are thus a series of dates between about 14,000 to 21,000 B.C. for this industry from various sites, and another series of more than 30,000 years B.C. Both series are unlikely to be correct, at least not at KRM and Montagu Cave, which have yielded dates from both ends of the scale, and not in any logical, stratified sequence. On the evidence of the radiocarbon dating alone, all that can be said of the Howieson's Poort at KRM is that there are more earlier dates than later ones and that Vogel's date is probably the more likely.

MSA I and II

Fifteen dates have been obtained from layers containing these stages, and they range from 23,000 B.C. to >36,350 B.C., with no order in relation to the stratigraphical succession. They thus cover a similar range in time to the dates of the overlying Howieson's Poort stage, although it must be stressed that nearly all these dates are minimum dates.

There are several South African MSA sites with radiocarbon dates within this range and some others that are more recent, such as those from the Cave of Hearths. The latter were obtained in 1954 by unsophisticated techniques and are thus suspect. Although there are only five dates from Florisbad, they form a logical progression of increasing age downward through the succession of peats. The lowest peat, Peat I, which is recorded as the level of the Florisbad skull, has three minimum dates of 33,000, 39,000, and 42,000 B.C. Peat II above contains an industry which Sampson (unpublished thesis) would relate to the upper part of MSA II at KRM and is dated at 26,500 ± 2,200 B.C. (L271C). However, Sampson (1974) states that this sample is not directly associated with the cultural horizon which, supposedly, is below Peat II. This date agrees well with the dates from layers 15 and 16 of Cave 1. However, there is reason to believe that the Florisbad samples were not collected under the strictest conditions, and precise location of the skull is not known.

There is a date of 34,050 ± 2,400 B.C. from Skildergat, Fish Hoek (near Cape Town), seemingly related to the industry below the "Lower Stillbay" (B. Anthony, personal communication) which Sampson tentatively places in his MSA Phase 2 and would correlate with MSA I–II at Klasies River Mouth.

An important series of dates have been recovered from the Border Cave, Ingwavuma District, KwaZulu (in Natal). Vogel and Beaumont (1972) report a date >46,300 B.C. (Pta-459 Ingw.) for "a final MSA" of Epi-Pietersburg type (= Howieson's Poort) that overlies the "full MSA." De Villiers (1976) describes a human mandible "from the intact Third White Ash, M.S.A. stratum, dated to 80–100,000 B.P."

An early date of >39,000 B.C. (Pta-354) from the Rose Cottage Cave near Ladybrand (Vogel and Beaumont 1972) is probably associated with a similar MSA industry, as are two dates from Witkrans, Taung, of 29,050 B.C. and 31,200 B.C.

Another date from an industry which Sampson would relate to the upper part of the MSA II stage at KRM is the one of >23,050 B.C. from Olieboompoort (BM-39). This, again, agrees well with 1-15, but another date from the same level at Olieboompoort (BM-?) is >31,000 B.C.

Dates of 20,330 ± 400 B.C. and 26,180 ± 260 B.C. from the Lion Cavern, Ngwenya, west Swaziland (Dart and Beaumont 1967) are associated with an MSA industry that may relate to MSA II at KRM. The Sibebe Shelter, just northeast of Mbabane, Swaziland, provides a date (GrN-5314) of 20,900 ± 160 B.C. for the "Middle Stone Age stratum" (Sampson 1974).

There are two other radiocarbon dates from South Africa in this time range, although neither is connected with a stone industry. At Aloes, near Port Elizabeth, W. Gess recovered a concentration of faunal remains, mainly horse, in calcareous vlei deposits and obtained a radiocarbon date of 36,050 B.C. from associated shells of *Achatina zebra* (Gess 1969). At Nahoon, East London, calcrete with possible human foot impressions are dated to about 27,000 B.C. (Deacon 1966; Beater 1967).

The overall impression given by all these radiocarbon dates, both from KRM and the sites named above, of Middle Stone Age industries preceding the Howieson's Poort and the Howieson's Poort Industry itself, is that they all lie beyond the dating range of the radiocarbon method. Having reached this impasse, it is necessary to consider other lines of dating evidence.

Bada and Deems (1975) have discussed the accuracy of dates beyond the ^{14}C dating limit using the aspartic acid racemization reaction. Their results support the contention that all the radiocarbon dates for the MSA in KRM Cave 1 are beyond the ^{14}C dating limit (table 14.2). The date of 110,000 years for layer 38 is in close agreement with the presently accepted dating of the Last Interglacial period to which, on other lines of evidence, this layer corresponds.

Rate of Accumulation of Occupational Deposits

Any assessment of the time taken for occupational soils to accumulate is clearly beset with a variety of speculations, and estimates will vary accordingly, but it is still worth considering. It is impossible to regard some 22 m of accumulated soil

and litter as seen at KRM and consider their subsequent erosion without sensing the passage of a very long period of time. Some of the aspects of the accumulations are considered briefly here, in the hope that the phrase "a very long period" might be seen in terms of calendar years, however broad.

Excluding rubble accumulations as found in Cave 1, the true occupational deposits (i.e., those formed underfoot or as intentional mounds of refuse) vary greatly in the MSA, Howieson's Poort, and LSA levels; in fact there is a marked connection between the type of deposit and the type of industry. The MSA deposits are mainly sandy soils with laminations of darker soil with or without carbonaceous matter every few centimeters, or thick accumulations of bedded but otherwise almost featureless gray soil such as 1-15. The lower soils are much sandier as they were nearer the beach, but the overall similarity in the type of deposit, whether belonging to MSA I, II, or III, is remarkable. In contrast, the deposits connected with the Howieson's Poort stage are intensely black and contain a multitude of thick ash hearths superimposed on and overlapping each other. There are far fewer sandy divisions and no sandy soils comparable to those in Cave 1. Further, the massive shell accumulations of the LSA middens are distinctive. Shells occur in numbers throughout all the MSA and Howieson's Poort layers, but never do they form mounds: they always lie along the general bedding plane of the layer.

It cannot be coincidence that these three types of occupation deposits relate directly to three different industries. It shows conclusively that there were three different human activity patterns, and it might not be unreasonable to define these as cultural stages. The inference is that the MSA culture involved relatively small numbers of people, grouped perhaps in bands, one or more of which would generally be at the site. For long periods occupation may have been permanent, as the more uniform soils suggest. To judge by calcitic formations and the cementation of deposits within Cave 1, at no time can the site have been abandoned for more than a few hundred years. The cementation of the topsoil over the Upper Midden in Cave 1 is marked, and this has apparently taken place during about 2,000 years. The Howieson's Poort levels indicate much greater activity on the site of a permanent or semipermanent nature. A larger community would mean a faster accumulation of deposits, so the 1.5 m of Howieson's Poort levels may represent far less time than a corresponding thickness of the MSA levels either above or below. Lastly, the shell middens of the LSA

Table 14.2. Aspartic Acid Racemization Results for KRM Caves (modified from Bada and Deems 1975)

Stratigraphic Unit	Depth below Surface (m)	DL Aspartic Acid	[14]C Age (yr)	Aspartic Acid Age* (yr)
				$k_{asp} = 4.92 \times 10^{-6} \, yr^{-1}$
1-13	1.5	.370	>30,000	65,000
1-16	1.75	.467	>30,000	89,000
1-18[†]	2.75	.474	>30,000	90,000
1-19[†]	3.0	.548	>30,000	110,000

*See Bada and Protsch (1973).

[†]Layers 18, 19 = 37, 38, respectively (see chap. 3).

represent a Strandloper existence for which there is historical account. On the basis of the radiocarbon dates, each midden probably took about two centuries to form.

It is the MSA levels which constitute the major part of the enormous buildup from Cave 1 to beneath Shelter 1A, and it is these deposits which are thought to have accumulated slowest. A possible guide to the rate of accumulation of soils beneath occupants with this type of hunting culture might be obtained from examining rock shelter or cave sites elsewhere in the world where a similar culture stage is represented. In many respects the Mousterian of Europe and North Africa and the Levalloiso-Mousterian of the Near East bear the closest similarities to the MSA of South Africa; the range of stone tools indicate similar activities, although it would be easy to cite particular differences. A further difficulty is finding other sites with a known time range.

At the Haua Fteah in Cyrenaica there are 13 m of occupational deposits, with Levailloiso-Mousterian, Dabba, and other industries, with an inferred time span of 75,000 to 100,000 years (McBurney 1967). Hypothetically, this could mean an average of .17 to .13 m per 1,000 years, or 1.7 to 1.3 mm per 10 years. At Shanidar in Iraq, 13.4 m of deposits in a cave with mainly Mousterian occupation is thought to span about 55,000 years (Reed and Braidwood 1960), and this could mean an average of .24 m per 1,000 years, or 2.4 mm per 10 years. A rock shelter with a shorter, but unlikely to be more accurately assessed, time span is the Abri Pataud in France. Here the occupation is of Upper Paleolithic culture and thus perhaps more intense with a resulting increase in the rate of buildup. According to radiocarbon dating (Movius 1966), 9.25 m of deposits would appear to span some 16,000 years. This could mean an average of .58 m per 1,000 years, or 5.8 mm per 10 years.

The rate of buildup within the confines of post-Paleolithic urban development, with its increased population and use of imperishables, especially for building, would presumably be much faster. Assessments from Jericho and London substantiate this and, surprisingly, give similar time rates. Seventeen meters of deposits at Jericho, covering occupation from Late Mesolithic to the Bronze Age, is thought to span some 7,000 years. This could mean an average of 2.4 m per 1,000 years, or 2.4 cm per 10 years. Roman London is an average of 5 m below present road level, so in 1,900 years this could mean an average of 2.6 m per 1,000 years, or 2.4 cm per 10 years. the following summarizes the above assessments:

the figure was consistent with the rate of urban buildup, the time span inferred would be more suspect.

Another method to assess the time span involved might be to speculate in more detail on the rate of buildup, possible periods of nonoccupation, and time required for the amount of subaerial erosion since the accumulation. The following tabulation allows a greater rate of accumulation for the Howieson's Poort levels than the MSA ones on account of the type of deposit which appears to indicate more intensive settlement for the former.

If, then, a growth of 1 cm per 10 years is reckoned for the MSA levels and 1.5 cm per 10 years for the Howieson's Poort, the following would result:

MSA I and II

Depth of deposits	15 m
At 1 cm per 10 years	15,000 years
Plus factor of .5 to account	
for periods of nonoccupation	7,500 years
TOTAL PERIOD	22,500 years

Howieson's Poort

Depth of deposits	1.5 m
At 1.5 cm per 10 years	1,000 years
Plus factor of .25 to account	
for periods of nonoccupation	250 years
TOTAL PERIOD	1,250 years

MSA III

Depth of deposit extant	2 m
Depth of deposit eroded away	6 m
TOTAL DEPTH OF DEPOSIT	8 m
At 1 cm per 10 years	8,000 years
Plus factor of .5 to account	
for periods of nonoccupation	4,000 years
TOTAL PERIOD	12,000 years
Estimated minimum time for the erosion of 6 m of MSA III deposits by normal subaerial processes to its present profile, at 1 cm of deposit removed every 10 years	6,000 years

This makes a grand total of 41,750 years, and, as all the estimates are thought to be on the conservative side and no provision has been made for periods of time not represented in the section, this, perhaps, could be regarded as a minimum date. If it were multiplied by two, it would still be realistic in terms of the general observations on occupational buildups discussed above. To multiply it by three would seem unduly slow,

Site	Culture	Thickness of Buildup (m)	Inferred Time Span (yr)	Rate per 10 Years (cm)
London	Urban	5	1,900	2.6
Jericho	Urban	17	7,000	2.4
Abri Pautad	Upper Paleolithic	9.25	16,000	0.6
Haua Fteah	Middle Paleolithic	13	If 75,000	0.2
			If 100,000	0.1
Shanidar	Middle Paleolithic	13.4	55,000	0.2

If the inferred date for the initial occupation at KRM, from the correlated date of the 6–8 m sea, is taken as 75,000 and the higher radiocarbon date for the MSA III levels at the top of the sequence as 25,000, then there is a time span of 50,000 years. In 22 m of deposits this could mean an average of .4 cm per 10 years, that is, midway between the above figures for Middle and Upper Paleolithic sites, so a time span of 50,000 years could at least be regarded as a reasonable one. Conversely, if

and evidence of abnormally long periods of nonoccupation would show as unconformability on earlier eroded deposits or thicker, weathered soils.

Speculative as these calculations are, they do support a date of between about 40,000 and 84,000 years for the time taken for the sequence of occupation at KRM. It seems most unlikely that it was less than 40,000 years, and a date toward the older end of the scale is correspondingly more likely.

Conclusions

Three methods of dating have been considered so far in this chapter: sea levels, radiocarbon, and postulated rate of accumulation of the deposits. There is also the negative evidence of the mammalian fauna, for the lack of a significant number of species usually belonging to the Middle Pleistocene period proves that the sequence is unlikely to extend back as far as that. None of these methods are conclusive, but apart from the irregularity of the radiocarbon dates, they are not contradictory. If the tentative results from each method are balanced against each other, the result will be as near to the truth as present knowledge permits.

The LSA occupations in Cave 1 are quite convincingly dated by radiocarbon, especially as there is good agreement between the dating of the Upper Midden in Cave 1 and the midden in Cave 5, which have typological similarities. The LSA occupation beneath Shelter 1D must represent the most recent phase, for the presence of pottery indicates it is very unlikely to be older than c. A.D. 1500 (Rudner 1968).

At the other end of the scale, the earliest occupation (MSA I) at KRM was on the sand of the 6–8 m beach and apparently contemporary with the sea at this level. Correlations with similar sea levels in North Africa, radioactivity dated, suggest a date of no less than 75,000 years for this initial occupation. This is not an unreasonable date for most of the MSA sequence. Typologically, it can be noted that the KRM MSA I stage is not the earliest MSA industry in South Africa, but followed one with a concentration on the production of very long flake-blades, best represented at the Cave of Hearths, Bed 4, where it directly overlies an Acheulian Industry. Apart from isolated handaxes, which were probably regarded as curiosities, and one rolled handax in the beach gravel itself, there is no element of the Acheulian in KRM MSA I. The Cave of Hearths basal MSA is not dated, but its proximity to Acheulian levels makes a date prior to 75,000 very likely.

Radiocarbon does little to help assess the dates of MSA II, the Howieson's Poort, and MSA III. The cluster of dates, however, within the >30,000 to >40,000 year range for the Howieson's Poort Industry cannot be ignored. Apart from the anomalous date from layer 19 they are so consistent (i.e., for dates of such antiquity) that the possibility is that they are beyond the range of accurate measurability, as are the underlying MSA dates. It has been seen that there are conflicting dates for the Howieson's Poort from Montagu Cave; in fact three of the five dates from that site are in the 36,000 to 49,000 years B.C. range. There is only one date from Howieson's Poort of about 17,000 B.C.; so, taking KRM dates into account, the balance of evidence from radiocarbon dating is on the side of the earlier dates (especially in view of Vogel's dates) and possibly >50,000. This would be so much earlier for the Howieson's Poort than is generally considered that it is difficult to concede: it also puts a leptolithic industry into southern Africa which, if the dating is correct, is probably the earliest known anywhere (except possibly the Amudian Industry of North Africa and the Middle East). To accept these early dates invalidates the radiocarbon dates from the underlying MSA industries, for the stratigraphical evidence is sufficient to show that they must be older, and those at the base considerably so. It also suggests that dates from similar industries in South Africa are also much too recent.

The alternative is to reject the evidence for MSA I being contemporary with the 6–8 m sea and explain the interdigitation of hearths and beach sand as the result of very high seas of a 3–4 m sea. This could perhaps tie in with a mid-Würm

transgression that could well fit in with the radiocarbon dates for MSA I of 30,000 to 40,000 years. The MSA II radiocarbon dates vary, but four of six cover the 20,000 to 30,000 year period. This would make the one date of 16,450 B.C. from layer 19 of the Howieson's Poort acceptable and invalidate the other nine. One of the two dates for MSA III, of about 10,000 B.C., would continue this sequence. This is unlikely to leave sufficient time for the subaerial erosion of the deposits beneath Shelter 1A to their present profile.

A serious objection to the latter, shorter sequence is that MSA IV has to fit in the 10,000 odd years B.C. and that it was thought that the sand containing this industry was blown into the cave at a period of low sea level, when KRM was an inland site. This might have been expected to be earlier than 10,000 B.C., but there could, of course, be other origins for the sand. Perhaps a more serious objection to the shorter sequence is that an attempt to estimate the time necessary for the accumulation of 23 m of occupational deposits and the subaerial erosion of 6 m of it afterward suggested that about 40,000 years was the very minimum time in which it was possible, and that half again or double this period was likely.

The balance is in favor of the longer sequence, which is substantiated by the following report by Shackleton (see also chap. 4).

Stratigraphy and Chronology of the KRM Deposits: Oxygen Isotope Evidence
N. J. Shackleton*
Introduction

Oxygen isotope analysis of marine shells was initiated in the late 1940s following the suggestion of Urey (1947) that paleotemperatures in the geological past could be estimated by making use of the temperature dependence of the equilibrium isotopic fractionation between water and calcite. The technique was first applied to Pleistocene materials by Emiliani, who worked both with microfossils from deep-sea cores (Emiliani 1955, 1966) and with molluscs from archeological deposits and elsewhere (Emiliani et al. 1964).

At first, application to Pleistocene materials was primarily for the purpose of estimating paleotemperatures, but it is now known that sea surface temperatures can be estimated far more reliably by other means (Imbrie, van Donk, and Kipp 1973). This is because the oxygen isotope record is dominated by a quite separate effect: by changes in the oxygen isotopic composition of the whole ocean water mass, which arise from the storage of isotopically light ice in continental ice sheets during the Pleistocene glaciations (Shackleton 1967). Since the oceans are well mixed in less than 1,000 years, the oxygen isotope record is an exceptionally useful tool for stratigraphic correlation (Shackleton and Opdyke 1973).

The true record of fluctuations in ocean oxygen isotopic composition is being elucidated in ever more detail as superior deep-sea cores are analyzed and as the effects of postdepositional activity by currents or burrowing organisms are isolated. In principle an even better record might be obtained from the isotopic analysis of shell-midden deposits, since the shells would have experienced the same changes in ocean isotopic composition as did the microfossils found in deep-sea cores. Unfortunately, however, during most of the Pleistocene there were at least small ice sheets in the Northern Hemisphere, and the sea level lay below its present level, so that many shell-

* N. J. Shackleton is with the Sub-department of Quaternary Research, University of Cambridge, England.

Table 14.3. Oxygen Isotope Data for LSA Shells

KRM 1D-1, Bag 2345	KRM 1D-5, Bag 2353
+1.15	+1.35
1.21	1.59
1.04	1.55
1.18	1.25
.79	1.48
.77	1.05
.93	.58
1.46	.44
1.50	.31
1.64	.83
1.54	.95
1.28	1.24
1.19	1.19
.57	1.35
.84	1.51
1.13	
1.11	
.97	

Note. The data are expressed as $\delta\ ^{18}O$ per mil to the P.D.B. standard. δ is defined by the following:

$$\delta = 1,000\ \frac{^{18}O/^{16}O\ \text{shell} - {^{18}O/^{16}O}\ \text{standard}}{^{18}O/^{16}O\ \text{standard}}$$

midden deposits must lie below sea level on the continental shelf, and large periods of time are therefore inaccessible to study.

What we can do, and attempt in this paper, is to compare the fragmentary oxygen isotope record contained in a shell-midden sequence with the continuous record obtained from deep-sea cores, and hence correlate the first with the second. Since the dating of the oxygen isotope record in deep-sea cores is now secure throughout the past million years, this enables us to date the shell-midden deposits.

The oxygen isotopic composition of the oceans has varied more or less cyclically during the Pleistocene, so that an isolated isotope value could in principle be correlated with one of a number of different episodes, and some additional information is needed to make the method reliable. At KRM, we are dealing with middens associated with MSA artifacts. As recently as 1970 it was possible to make a case for equating the MSA of Africa with the Upper Paleolithic of Europe (Klein 1970), perhaps 35,000 to 10,000 years B.P. Although there are a few sites in which the later part of this time interval does seem to be filled by a succession of well-dated cultural entities, it is now accepted that a great many "MSA" sites are outside this time range and indeed outside the range of ^{14}C dating (Vogel 1969a; Carter and Vogel 1974).

Experimental Methods and Results

Study of shells from the deposits of the Nelson Bay Cave on the South African south coast disclosed two species that were par-

ticularly suitable for oxygen isotope studies: *Patella tabularis* and *Turbo sarmaticus* (Shackleton 1973). Both live permanently immersed in the water, and both grow sufficiently rapidly to permit sampling of discrete growth increments representing less than one month. In the Nelson Bay Cave attention was concentrated on *P. tabularis*, which yielded good information for seasonality studies. *T. sarmaticus* grows rather slowly when adult (or at least, the operculum does), and the season of death can usually not be resolved. Unfortunately, *P. tabularis* is much rarer at KRM (see chap. 13), so we have analyzed the *T. sarmaticus* operculum exclusively in this study.

After cleaning the surface physically, samples are taken using a $^{1}/_{16}$ in. drill (pl. 72). A sample spacing of about 2 mm generally provides about 10 samples through a year's growth. Maxima and minima in the measurements may be refined by closer sampling. About .3 mg carbonate is taken for each analysis. The organic contaminants are removed by roasting *in vacuo* at 450° C for 30 minutes, and carbon dioxide released by the action of 100 percent orthophosphoric acid at 50° C is collected for mass spectrometric analysis. Isotopic analysis is performed in a VG Micromass 602C mass spectrometer; analytical precision is ± .05 per mil, and analyses are referred to the P.D.B. standard (Epstein et al. 1953).

Analytical results, expressed as deviation per mil from the P.D.B. standard, are given in tables 14.3–14.6. Most of the shells yielded results in which the seasonal pattern is easily discernible. In figure 14.3, results are plotted for a representative specimen from each deposit.

Table 14.4. Oxygen Isotope Data
for Howieson's Poort Level

KRM 1A-20, Bag 2128

+2.40	+1.34
1.74	1.47
1.60	1.48
1.52	1.25
2.32	1.57
2.14	1.26
1.20	1.78
1.29	2.03
1.88	1.83

Note. The two columns refer to two
different parts of the same shell
with a gap between them.

Discussion

Figure 14.4 shows an oxygen isotope record from a deep-sea core in the southern Indian Ocean and the stages into which it is formally divided. Substage 5e is probably correlative with the Eemian Interglacial of Europe (Shackleton 1969) and is the only known part of the Pleistocene during which the sea was isotopically slightly lighter than it is today (the difference was probably only about .1 per mil). This difference is probably due to melting of the West Antarctic ice during the Eemian, which would also explain sea level having been higher then than now.

In Figure 14.5, all the measurements from each of the stratigraphically separated midden deposits have been plotted together in histograms. In each histogram, the scatter of measurements is a rough indication of the distribution of shell growth through the seasons (not analytical scatter), as may be seen from the plots through individual shells in figure 14.3. The difference between the histograms for various middens (of different ages) is due to the fact that the oxygen isotopic composition of the ocean was different during the deposition of each midden, as is indicated by the continuous record (for a

deep-sea core) illustrated in figure 14.4. Since we know that the MSA deposits are older than 30,000 years at least, it is evident that the MSA I midden, from which the histograms of oxygen isotope analyses are very similar to that for LSA shells that lived during the last few thousand years, can only have formed during isotope substage 5e, the last time the sea was isotopically as light as it is today. This is illustrated in figure 14.5 in which the histogram for this midden is plotted opposite the appropriate section of the oxygen isotope record from the deep-sea core.

The fact that beach deposits of two different altitudes are apparently associated with these MSA I middens might at first sight be thought to imply widely different ages for the deposits in KRM 1 and KRM 5. However, the detailed sequence within the 10,000 years or so of substage 5e has yet to be resolved, and the formation of two discrete beaches during that time span is not unlikely. It is possible, for instance, that the West Antarctic ice sheet melted only for a brief part of the interglacial. Thus the 6–8 m beach in KRM 1 and the 18 m beach in KRM 5 may only be separated by a few thousand years. Certainly our interpretation of the data from the isotopic analysis is that the shells in these two deposits are that close together in age.

A number of shells from an MSA II horizon (KRM 1-15, table 14.5) were analyzed. The analyses are plotted in histogram form in figure 14.5 along with those discussed above. It seems likely on the basis of this comparison that their marine correlative is either substage 5c or 5a. There is no way of choosing between these alternatives on the basis of the isotope data. It should be remarked that if the oxygen isotope data were the only information available, these deposits could equally well be much older; however, knowing that they are stratigraphically younger than the MSA I discussed above, we can state confidently that they correspond to either 5c or 5a.

The shells from the Howieson's Poort cultural stage were in poorer condition than those from the MSA I and II, and we were only able to analyze one unrecrystallized specimen (table 14.4). The values (fig. 14.5) would be consistent with deposition within stage 3, although a cooler part of stage 5 cannot be excluded.

Dating

The dating of oxygen isotope stage boundaries has been discussed by Shackleton (1969) and Shackleton and Opdyke

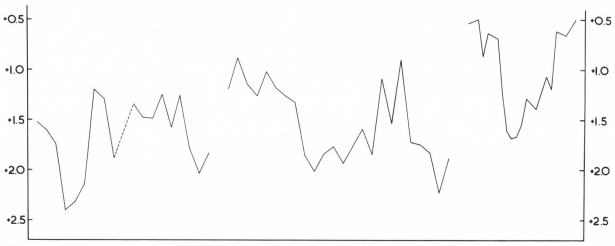

Fig. 14.3. Point-by-point oxygen isotope analyses through three of the shells analyzed from the KRM deposits. *Left,* a specimen from the Howieson's Poort levels. The broken line represents a gap in sampling where the shell was broken. *Center,* a specimen from an MSA II level, analyzed continuously through two years of growth. *Right,* a specimen

from an MSA I level, analyzed continuously from one summer to the next. Note that it was not possible to analyze any of these specimens (operculae from the large gastropod *Turbo sarmaticus*) right to the growing edge, so that the season of death is not recorded.

Table 14.5. Oxygen Isotope Data for MSA II Shells, All from KRM 1-15   197

Shell 1	2	3	4	5	6	7
+1.83	+2.24	+1.71	+2.30	+1.54	+1.19	+ .37
	1.99	1.22	1.19	1.33	.88	.36
	1.58	1.29	1.90	1.19	1.14	.77
	1.31	.99	1.61	1.40	1.26	1.99
	1.35	1.02	1.87	1.76	1.02	1.59
	1.97	1.25	2.06	1.91	1.18	1.32
	1.89	1.08	1.30	1.73	1.26	1.30
	1.37	1.61	1.39	1.20	1.32	.66
	1.70	1.43	1.02	1.06	1.85	1.36
	1.41	1.53	1.83	1.27	2.01	1.48
	1.11	1.63	2.01	1.11	1.84	1.30
	1.27	1.60	2.03	.89	1.76	1.45
	1.43	1.44	1.99	1.03	1.93	1.22
	1.47	1.44	1.61	1.28	1.75	1.65
		1.49	1.24	1.83	1.59	2.00
		1.48	1.05	1.97	1.84	1.79
		1.35	1.05	.91	1.09	1.83
		1.35	1.30	1.24	1.53	
		1.08	1.16	1.15	.90	
					1.72	
					1.74	
					1.82	
					2.22	
					1.88	

Table 14.6. Oxygen Isotope Data for MSA I

KRM 5-6, Bag 2110			KRM 1B-12, Bag 2086	KRM 1-38, Bag 1746
Shell 1	Shell 2	Shell 3		
+ .58	+ .99	+1.43	+1.28	+ .54
1.06	1.11	1.27	.78	.50
.32	1.42	1.25	1.04	.87
.84	1.32	.84	1.16	.64
.77	.82	.77	.83	.69
1.09	.58	.49	1.09	1.22
1.37	.93	.69	1.27	1.61
1.47	1.32	.80	1.84	1.68
1.43	1.69	.53	1.91	1.67
				1.55
				1.29
				1.39
				1.07
				1.19
				.62
				.81
				.66
				.50

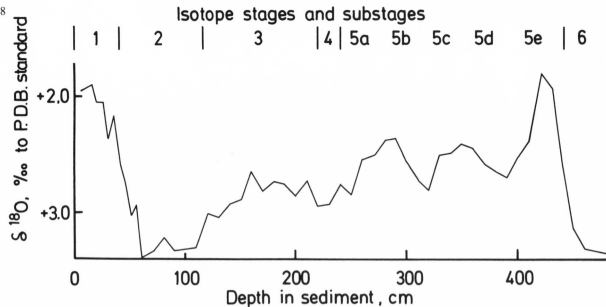

FIG. 14.4. Record of oxygen isotopic composition of planktonic foraminifera (*Globigerina bulloides*) in core RC11-120 (43°31′S, 79°52′E). The section illustrated spans about 140,000 years (from Hays et al. 1976).

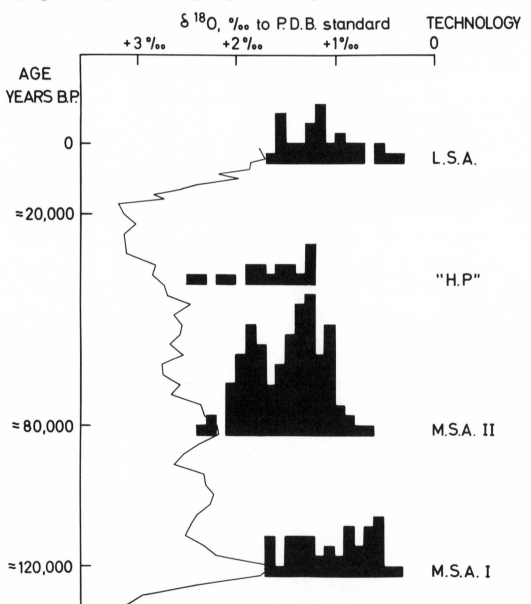

FIG. 14.5. Histogram of all the oxygen isotope analyses in each cultural group. The waters near Klasies River Mouth have experienced the same changes in oxygen isotopic composition as did the ocean at the site of core RC11-120, so the histograms have been placed beside the stratigraphic record of the core (*to left*).

(1973). Although some of the dating is still a matter of heated dispute, it is now accepted with considerable confidence that substage 5e is represented by the high sea level event that has been very widely dated at about 120,000 years. This correlation is confirmed by analyses, analogous to those reported here, of molluscs from the marine deposits on Barbados from which many of the ^{230}Th/^{234}U dates have been obtained (Shackleton and Matthews 1977). It is interesting to notice (as was drawn to my attention by Charles Stearns) that in the careful dating of coral terraces in Hawaii (Ku et at. 1974) two deposits of slightly different age may be represented. If so, these may be equivalent to the two substage 5e beaches that we postulate at KRM, and the older may be a little over 130,000 years old. The MSA I deposits may therefore span an interval from a little over 130,000 to a little over 120,000 years ago on the ^{230}Th/^{234}U time scale.

The MSA II deposits may be near either 100,000 or 80,000 years old depending on whether the age is correlated with substage 5c or 5a; we have no means of discriminating between these alternatives. The Howieson's Poort would lie in the range 50,000 to 30,000 years if the speculative correlation with stage 3 is correct; again, other evidence should be sought for the proposed correlation.

Conclusions

Over 200 oxygen isotope analyses have been made in well-preserved molluscs which represent food refuse left by the MSA inhabitants of the KRM caves. These analyses permit oxygen isotope stratigraphic correlation to be proposed between these deposits and the securely dated deep-sea sediment cores which have been analyzed and dated in many ways around the world. MSA I levels are almost certainly of substage 5e age, about 120,000 to 130,000 years B.P. MSA II levels may be correlative either with 5c (about 100,000 years B.P.) or with 5a (about 80,000 years B.P.). Howieson's Poort levels may be speculatively correlated with stage 3, in the age range 30,000 to 50,000 years B.P.

Acknowledgments

Oxygen isotope analyses were supported by National Environmental Research Council grant GR3/1762. I am grateful to Ronald Singer and John Wymer for the opportunity to undertake this study, and to Richard Klein for drawing my attention to this site as well as for his attempt (foiled by flood conditions) to show me the site of Klasies River Mouth. Elizabeth Voigt kindly made her analysis of the molluscan food remains available to me before publication.

15   KRM in Relation to Other MSA Sites in South Africa

When work commenced at KRM in 1966, 11 other MSA sites had been excavated in South Africa:

        Fish Hoek (Skildergat and Tunnel Caves)
        Florisbad
        Howieson's Poort
        Rose Cottage
        Kalk Bay (Trappies Kop)
        Makapansgat (Cave of Hearths)
        Montagu Cave
        Mossel Bay (Cape St. Blaize Cave)
        Mwulu's Cave
        Olieboompoort
        Holley Shelter

As stressed in chapter 2, none of these sites had been published in any detail. Skildergat and Mossel Bay were the only Cape sites spanning lengthy periods of occupation. At the end of work at KRM in 1967 it was impossible to make useful comparisons or correlations on anything but a broad typological basis. However, there was surprisingly little material from Mossel Bay in the South African Museum, and that from Skildergat was not available. Howieson's Poort was a selected sample. There seemed little purpose in relating KRM to such unsatisfactory evidence. It was only possible to do the reverse, i.e., relate what was known to KRM. This report was intended as an account of the investigations undertaken at KRM, a statement of what was done, what was found, and how we have interpreted the results. It was never the intention that the report should also be a review of the archeology of the MSA in South Africa. Nor is it now, but things in the 1980s are very different: 11 further sites have been excavated and the majority published in a very satisfactory manner, together with a wealth of ecological and dating evidence. The sites are

        Boomplaas
        Border Cave
        Bushman Rock Shelter
        Elands Kloof
        Die Kelders
        Duinefontein, Melkbosstrand
        Moshebi's Shelter
        Orangia 1
        Nelson Bay Cave
        Sibebe
        Zeekoegat 27

Montagu Cave has also been published. Klein has assessed the problems of the Middle Stone Age (Klein 1970), published general surveys (Klein 1974, 1977, 1978), and published the mammalian fauna of KRM (Klein 1976a). Butzer has published the sediment stratigraphy for KRM (Butzer 1978), and Voigt some preliminary notes on the shell analyses for KRM (Voigt 1973a, b).

The situation has also changed radically since 1966 with regard to the state of knowledge of the Later Stone Age, with several well-excavated and well-documented sites, apart from numerous review articles, reassessments of existing material, or reinvestigations of known sites. H. J. Deacon (1972) has given a valuable survey of the post-Pleistocene in South Africa, and J. Deacon (1972) has reassessed the Wilton Industry. H. J. Deacon has also produced a detailed study of Holocene Stone Age people in the Eastern Cape (Deacon 1976). The date of cave art has been put back by over 20,000 years by some remarkable discoveries in the Apollo 11 Cave in South West Africa (Wendt 1976).

The new LSA sites that are most relevant to KRM are

Bonteberg (Grindley 1967; Maggs and Speed 1967; Grindley, Speed, and Maggs 1970)
Boomplaas (Deacon, Deacon, and Brooker 1976; Deacon 1979)
Buffelskloof (Opperman 1978)
Byneskranskop (Schweitzer and Wilson 1978)
Glen Eliot (Sampson 1967a)
Gordon's Bay (Noten 1974)
Heuningsneskrans, Ohrigstad (Vogel and Beaumont 1972; Beaumont and Boshier 1972)
Nelson Bay (Klein 1972a)
Zaayfontein (Sampson 1967b)
Zeekoegat 13 (Sampson 1967c)

Terminology has changed, although much less in practice than recommended by the Dakar conference in 1967. "First" and "Second Intermediate" have disappeared, but "ESA," "MSA," and "LSA" remain. J. Deacon (1976a) states that "the dropping of the widely used terms Earlier, Middle and Later Stone Age has proved relatively painless," but this is not so. In the same publication, she has herself used the term "Middle Stone Age" to describe Duinefontein (1976b), although it is in quotes. By 1979, referring to the earliest industries in the Boomplaas Cave (Deacon 1979), she is using "Middle Stone Age" without quotes. Other authors in the *South African Archaeological Bulletin* and elsewhere have continued to use both "Middle Stone Age" and "Later Stone Age." We mention this only to emphasize the necessity for some all-embracing term to cover the complex of industries which fall so readily under the rubric "MSA" or "LSA."

This problem of terminology was very apparent to Sampson when he published his survey of the Stone Age industries of the Orange River Scheme and South Africa (Sampson 1972), and his more general work on the *Stone Age Archaeology of Southern Africa* (Sampson 1974). Terminology of Sampson (1972):

Middle Stone Age

Phase 1	Includes Pietersburg Industry
Phase 2	Includes Pietersburg Industry
Phase 3	Includes Bambata Industry
Phase 4	Includes Howieson's Poort Industry
Phase 5	Includes KRM Stage IV

Later Stone Age

Phase 1	Previously Smithfield A
Phase 2	Previously Smithfield A and Wilton
Phase 3	Previously Wilton
Phase 4	Previously evolved Wilton
Phase 5	Previously evolved Wilton and pottery
Phase 6	Previously Smithfield B and C

This scheme was used as "Tentative Proposals for a New Terminology" and the basis for a somewhat modified version in Sampson (1974):

LSA Phase 2

Cave 1	575 B.C. ± 85 (GX-0969)
	845 B.C. ± 85 (GX-0971)
Cave 5	335 B.C. ± 105 (GX-1397)

LSA Phase 3

Shelter 1D Ceramic

There are non-Wilton stone industries with all the phases and are thus included by Sampson in his Coastal Complex, generally referred to as "Strandloper" sites. The relationship of the KRM LSA to other sites in the region is discussed in chapter 9.

Mossel Bay

The first MSA site to consider is the one with the greatest similarities, in spite of a dearth of objective information on the stone industries and stratigraphy of the actual site, i.e., Mossel Bay (Goodwin 1933; Dreyer 1934; Goodwin and Malan 1935; Keller 1969). Five subdivisions were made by Goodwin and Malan of the "black earth" which was designated layer C

Complex	Industry	Phase
Pietersburg	Pietersburg, Orangian, Mossel Bay	Early and Late
Bambata	Bambata, Mwulu, Florisbad, Stillbay?	. . .
?	Howieson's Poort, Umguzan	. . .
Oakhurst	Oakhurst, Lockshoek, Pomongwan	Early and Late
Wilton	Coastal and Interior Wilton, Matopan, Pfupian, Zambian Wilton, Nachikufan	Early—Classic—Developed—Ceramic
Smithfield	?	Preceramic and Ceramic
Coastal	Sandy Bay	Preceramic and Ceramic

The merits and demerits of these schemes are ably reviewed by Sampson himself (especially 1972, pp. 60–70, 212–14, and 1974, pp. 8–9) and more critically by J. Deacon (1976a).

Particularly relevant to KRM is the identification of a stone industry at Nelson Bay Cave which seems to fill part of the gap in the KRM sequence between MSA IV and the earliest LSA in Cave 1. This industry has been termed the Robberg Industry (Klein 1974) and has become accepted nomenclature for South African prehistory. It is not the intention of this book to criticize these schemes or propose any alternatives on the basis of the KRM evidence. The main concern is to establish that the terminology used in this brief survey does not produce confusions or misunderstandings. What does seem fortunate is that the use of such terms as "MSA" and "LSA," if suitably qualified, should not do this, in spite of the fears that have frequently been expressed because of their temporal connotations.

"MSA" is therefore used in this report in the general sense as applied by Goodwin (1928, 1929). At KRM, MSA I and MSA II are equivalent to the industry found at Mossel Bay. In terms of Sampson (1974), this is the Mossel Bay Industry of the Pietersburg Complex. MSA III and MSA IV at KRM are not strictly comparable with anything, either typologically or temporally. Sampson described them as post–Howieson's Poort blade industries. These are discussed further below.

There are at least three phases of the LSA represented at KRM:

LSA Phase 1

Cave 1	¹⁴C 2745 B.C. ± 180 (GX-0973)
	2805 B.C. ± 95 (GX-0970)
Cave 5	2160 B.C. ± 60 (GX-1378)

below disturbed and undisturbed midden material, layers A and B. The latter two are LSA, while it is C which produced the Mossel Bay Industry. Layer C was subdivided into C, C1, C2, C3, and C4. The extremely rich industry in C2 was considered comparable to the Howieson's Poort and thus seen as intrusive between layers containing the industry described as Mossel Bay MSA. Keller could find only 286 artifacts from this layer C2 in the South African Museum collections, and there were no crescents or trapezes. One neat unifacial point of quartzite and an oblique angle graver are present, but the most likely diagnostic piece is a small flake-blade of chert obliquely blunted to form an angle (Keller 1969, p. 134, fig. 1G). Two others were also found, but these, unfortunately, like the previous one, came from "undifferentiated layer C." Although it cannot be substantiated by the collections, there seems little reason to doubt the original conclusion. Thus, the vertical succession at KRM is a repetition of that at Mossel Bay, viz., MSA–Howieson's Poort–MSA. The characteristic tool from Mossel Bay has been described as a triangular flake or flake-blade with prepared striking platform, not removed by secondary trimming. Keller has shown that this was by no means the commonest artifact and that parallel-sided flakes (i.e., flake-blades) are more common than triangular ones (i.e., pointed flake-blades). This has been demonstrated at KRM in all the MSA industries there. Keller also tabulates tool classes through the five subdivisions of layer C, all of which can be paralleled by classes from KRM. At Mossel Bay it is interesting that radial cores predominate over single and double platform ones, although the samples are so small that it would be unwise to press comparisons. Many of these would probably have been classified as irregular and/or undeveloped cores at KRM. Keller's category of struck cores would be termed tortoise cores by us. The only one he records and illustrates from Mossel Bay is from layer C2, the Howieson's Poort horizon. No such large, quartzite tortoise cores were found at KRM in the Howieson's Poort layers, although there were several small cores or microcores, mainly in fine-grained nonlocal rock.

An examination of the flake-blades from Mossel Bay in the South African Museum showed that at least four had small, carefully prepared striking platforms with battered edges, a feature found to be almost restricted to the MSA I stage at KRM. Goodwin and Malan (1935) also concluded that the industry, presumably the lower part, was contemporary or older than the 20 ft. (6–8 m) raised beach. Subject to reexamination of this site, if practicable, it would seem that occupation commenced at the same time as KRM and that later people with a Howieson's Poort Industry took over the cave, to be superseded by people with an industry similar to that below the Howieson's Poort. This would repeat the KRM sequence, although it is unlikely that occupation was so continuous or intense at Mossel Bay.

Cave of Hearths, Makapansgat

The finest excavated sequence of MSA industries in the Transvaal is at the Cave of Hearths, Makapansgat. The sequence has been described as follows:

Mason (1962)	Sampson (1972)	Sampson (1974)
Bed 9 Upper Pietersburg	Industry of Bambata(?) Complex. MSA Phase 4	Umguzan Industry of (?) Complex
Bed 8 Upper Pietersburg	Industry of Bambata Complex. MSA Phase 3	Mwulu Industry of Bambata Complex
Bed 7 Upper Pietersburg	Same as above	Same as above
Bed 6 Upper Pietersburg	Same as above	Same as above
Bed 5 Middle Pietersburg	Industry of Pietersburg Complex. MSA Phase 2	Pietersburg Industry of Pietersburg Complex
Bed 4 Lower Pietersburg	Industry of Pietersburg Complex. MSA Phase 1	Same as above

In Sampson's Phase 1 there is little Levallois technique, and none at all in his Phase 2. In the latter (within Bed 5 of Mason's stratigraphy) there is a general decrease in artifact size, and in the slenderness and length of blades. The number of utilized flakes and the use of fine-grained rock increase. There is also a decrease in the quantity of flake-blades produced; pointed flake-blades increase at sites in the northern Transvaal and the southern Cape coast, where also gravers and worked points occur for the first time. (He cites examples of this stage from Mwulu's Cave [Bed 1], Kalkbank, Aasvoëlkop, Border Cave [basal industry], Rose Cottage [basal industry], Zeekoegat 27a, Elandskloof, Orangia 1, Mossel Bay, KRM, and Skildergat [lower industry].) Sampson (1972) is disinclined to accept the sharp subdivision of Mason's Lower and Middle Pietersburg, as he argues that there is no definite stratigraphical break between Beds 4 and 5, and thinks that the combined beds constitute one continuous sequence. Mainly on the basis of the greater length of flake-blades at the Cave of Hearths in Bed 4, Sampson concludes that KRM MSA I and the lower part of KRM MSA II correlate with the upper part of his MSA Phase 1 and his Phase 2, i.e., that part of the Cave of Hearths sequence covering the upper part of Bed 4 and the whole of Bed 5.

Worked points, borers, and gravers do not appear in the Cave of Hearths sequence until Bed 6, after a near sterile layer

about 30 cm thick. This is Sampson's MSA Phase 3. Yet at KRM worked points and gravers constitute a fair proportion of the tool forms (see bar diagram, fig. 7.1). Comparison of the cores is difficult, as different criteria have been used at KRM and the Cave of Hearths. However, KRM double platform cores are equivalent to Cave of Hearths opposed platform cores, and whereas there are none in Bed 5 of the Cave of Hearths, they occur throughout KRM MSA I and II. Discoid cores are not a feature of the KRM MSA, whereas they are at the Cave of Hearths. There is no reason why there should be these differences as far as the raw material is concerned, for the quartzite in general use at both of these sites is of similar quality and therefore of similar knapping propensities. On typological grounds it would certainly seem that the two industries are dissimilar sufficiently to warrant being placed into separate industries (Pietersburg and Mossel Bay). However, the general level of technology is the same, and it is reasonable to place them under the same industrial complex, viz., the Pietersburg Complex.

Continuing the Cave of Hearths sequence upward, Beds 6–8 contain Mason's Upper Pietersburg Industry. The worked points, borers, gravers, scrapers, and outils écaillés are common to these levels and MSA I–III at KRM, as is Levallois technique in the form of preparing striking platforms. However, it is impossible to make precise comparisons as the Cave of Hearths Beds 6–9 include another industry, which Sampson (1972) has termed the Umguzan and has related to Bed 9. Also, there is no industry at KRM which would fit Sampson's (1974) description of his Bambata Complex Industries, which are more refined that all the KRM MSA stages (excluding the Howieson's Poort) and contain backed crescents, trapezes, fine borers, and grindstones. Such industries seem genuinely transitional between the MSA industries based on flake-blade production and the leptolithic industries variously referred to as Magosian, Howieson's Poort, or Umguzan. Most significant is the appearance at both KRM and the Cave of Hearths of a leptolithic industry in the upper part of the sequence; at the former site it is referred to as Howieson's Poort and is succeeded by MSA III and IV. It appears suddenly, and there is no transitional industry beneath it. At the latter site, it succeeds a transitional industry. Being at the top of the sequence, it is not known what may have followed it.

Skildergat Cave

Returning to the Cape, after Mossel Bay the most important site to yield a succession of Late Pleistocene stone industries is Skildergat Cave, Fish Hoek. First excavated by the Peers family in 1927, later by Jolly in 1947 (Jolly 1947) and by Anthony in c. 1965, the cave has a sad history of inadequate publication.

The situation is best described by Sampson (1972). Peers interpreted the sequence as

Wilton
Coarse Stillbay
Howieson's Poort
Stillbay

Jolly (1948) saw no evidence for the Coarse Stillbay but argued for a development from the near-microlithic Howieson's Poort to the truly microlithic LSA Wilton. Sampson does not accept this but believes Peers did find the "Coarse Stillbay" above the Howieson's Poort. If so, this is a further site in the Cape after KRM and Mossel Bay to yield an MSA-type industry after the Howieson's Poort. Barbara Anthony is considered to have dug an "earlier and less advanced industry," probably a Mossel Bay industry. The status of the Stillbay and Coarse Stillbay Industries is problematical in view of the insufficient data available, but it is possibly a facies of the Mossel Bay Industry. Other caves and shelters in the Fish Hoek–Kalk Bay area have produced good evidence of occupation. Howieson's Poort Industries are known from Peers' Shelter, Trappies Kop (Goodwin and Peers 1953), Skildergat Kop (Malan 1955), and Tunnel Cave (Malan 1955). These sites do not add anything to an elucidation of the local sequence, but they emphasize the relatively intense occupation of the Cape Peninsula at that time of the Late Pleistocene.

Montagu Cave

The next site to consider is Montagu Cave. There, the Howieson's Poort Industry is in layer 2 (Keller 1973), which varied in thickness from .23 m on one side of the cave to about 1.52 m on the other. Seven surfaces were meticulously excavated. There were no crescents above Surface IV and only two obliquely truncated blades on and in Surface III. The Howieson's Poort Industry at Montagu does not overlie a Mossel Bay Industry, as stated erroneously by Sampson (1974, p. 241, and see comment by Deacon 1976a), but, on the contrary, the published evidence could be read as indicating that, as at KRM and Mossel Bay, and also probably Skildergat, the Howieson's Poort was overlain by an industry of MSA type. The radiocarbon dates for layer 2 in Montagu Cave are inconsistent, but three of five dates are greater than 38,000. The excavator takes the view that these are too old and that the younger ones around 19,000 and 23,000 B. P. are more likely to be correct, especially as they are more in harmony with the radiocarbon date from Howieson's Poort itself (18,740 ± 320 B. P.) However, as seen in the section on radiocarbon dating (chap. 14) the KRM dates are also inconsistent but mainly old. There are also very early dates from Howieson's Poort levels from the Border Cave in Zululand, indicating an age in excess of 47,000 B.C. (Beaumont and Boshier 1972).

Other Sites

The industry at the Howieson's Poort type site adds nothing further to the position of this industry in the South African Late Pleistocene sequence. Although it is a considerable distance from the Cape, the Howieson's Poort Industry at Rose Cottage Cave, Ladybrand (the Magosian of Malan 1952), is beyond the range of radiocarbon dating. It is also at the base of the sequence at Boomplaas (Deacon 1979), but details have not yet been published.

MSA discoveries made during the Orange River Scheme (Sampson 1968, 1972) included 27 sites of which 7 were in sealed contexts, but only 2 of these were in primary contexts: Orangia 1 and Zeekoegat 27. Elands Kloof was of particular importance, as the earliest MSA of the area (Sampson's MSA Phase 1) was recovered from within the body of a thick (c. 10 m) accumulation of fluviatile silt and sand which covered a surface with an Acheulian industry with Levallois cores but no cleavers. This Phase 1 MSA, on the basis of typology (long blades with coarsely prepared striking platforms, prismatic cores, rare pointed flake-blades, no points or gravers), is probably earlier than anything at KRM. Nearby , however, was a gully with Sampson's MSA Phase 2 stratified within sediments above Acheulian. This phase may equate with the earliest MSA at KRM.

The great interest of the MSA sites at Orangia 1 and Zeekoegat 27 is the presence of boulder structures. At Orangia 1 there were several semicircular or elliptical arrangements of stones, and "sleeping hollows." At Zeekoegat 27 was a large boulder circle c. 11 m diameter. Both sites were associated with an MSA industry which could equate with KRM I–II, and in this respect it is very interesting to note that at KRM there were no traces whatsoever of any boulder structures, in spite of the large numbers of beach cobbles and broken rocks which abounded. In no place had any attempt been made to make walls and improve the natural protection given by the cave, or delimit horizontal areas of occupation as found in a few caves in Europe occupied by Acheulian hunters (e.g., Lazaret, France).

Three caves which may be usefully compared with KRM are Die Kelders, Nelson Bay, and Boomplaas. The first two are sea caves along the Cape Coast in a very similar geographical context to KRM. Boomplaas, also in the Cape, near Oudtshoorn, is 75 km inland, in the foothills of the Swartberg Range. In this respect it is particularly interesting that the first evidence for occupation in the Boomplaas Cave is after the equivalent of MSA I and II at KRM, assuming that the Howieson's Poort Industry at Boomplaas is contemporary with that at KRM (Deacon 1979). Although the industries following the Howieson's Poort at Boomplaas have not yet been published, there is a reversion, as at KRM, to an MSA–type industry with pointed flake-blades and a later MSA which has been compared with that from Cradock. The former is probably to be equated with KRM MSA III, and the latter not represented at KRM.

The industry from Die Kelders has also not yet been published, but there are several preliminary reports (Schweitzer 1970; Tankard and Schweitzer 1974; Tankard 1974; Klein 1975b). The initial occupation is on beach boulders at about 2 m above present sea level, and is considered to be "after the onset of high latitude glaciation." If so, this would suggest that the earlier phase of the MSA, as represented by stage I and part of II, is not present at Die Kelders. Dune sand blocked the cave until it was reopened by the recovery of the sea level: a history similar to that of KRM. However, at the Nelson Bay Cave near Plettenberg, on the Robberg Peninsula, there is a long sequence of MSA which, on radiocarbon dating, is greater than 50,000 years and commences at a period probably relating to oxygen isotope stage 5e, i.e., the same as the initial occupation of KRM. Preliminary details have been published for the Nelson Bay Cave (Klein 1972a, b), and the MSA lithic material will probably prove very similar to that from KRM Stages I and II.

Further away, in Lesotho, the same sequence of a leptolithic industry ("Magosian") above one of MSA type has been excavated from Moshebi's Shelter (Carter 1969). The MSA there contains worked points, scrapers, and gravers and best equates with KRM I or II. The industry from Sibebe Shelter in Swaziland has not yet been published, but Vogel (1970) reports an MSA stratum 1.20 m thick with "well-flaked bifacial points" and a transitional phase between MSA and "second intermediate." The latter is lacking at KRM.

It has already been noted above that there is mounting evidence, both from radiocarbon dating and lithostratigraphy, to place the Howieson's Poort Industry at a very early date: 50,000 years at least and more likely c. 95,000 years. This, of course, puts any underlying MSA industry to even much earlier dates. The excavation of KRM in 1966–68, with its long record of near-continuous occupation until MSA IV, then the evidence for major erosion of the occupational sediments that had accumulated, indicated a long time sequence. This was echoed in the results of the excavation of the Bushman Rock Shelter, Ohrigstad District, by Louw (1969). About a meter of MSA deposits was excavated under the shelter, covered by 1.5 m of LSA. Bedrock was not reached. The MSA industry contains bifacially worked points and various scrapers. Tentatively, it might equate with KRM I or II. It also included, as at KRM, a couple of handaxes which the excavator concluded had been found somewhere and brought in. There are also a couple of "bone points," but to judge from the illustrations, these look doubtful as artifacts. The main interest of the site was the obtaining from the MSA levels of two radiocarbon dates which prompted the conclusion that "MSA cultures were existing before 51,000 BC" in the Transvaal (Vogel 1969b). The significance of this was commented upon by Mason (1969). Since 1969, a wealth of evidence, including that from KRM, has pushed the appearance of MSA industries in South Africa back to the equivalent of the Last Interglacial of the Northern Hemisphere (equated with oxygen isotope stage 5e) and even earlier (Butzer 1978). Border Cave is particularly relevant in this respect. The site has a long history of investigation and is well known for its human infant burial (MSA "Pietersburg"), an adult cranium (MSA "Pietersburg"), and a mandible ("Epi-Pietersburg" = Howieson's Poort) (Beaumont and Boshier 1972; Beaumont 1973a, 1979). The industrial material has not yet been published, but there is an industry above the "Epi-Pietersburg" (= Howieson's Poort) which may equate with KRM MSA III. This is succeeded by an "Early" LSA which is radiocarbon dated to about 38,000 B. P. Butzer, Beaumont, and Vogel (1978) have assessed the evidence from the lithostratigraphy and concluded that the earliest MSA at the Border Cave is "substantially older than the Last Interglacial, dating back to the beginning of the Penultimate Glacial," i.e., c. 195,000 years.

Further support for this very early chronology comes from the site of Duinefontein, Melkbosstrand, 80 km north of Cape Town (Klein 1976b). An analysis of the sparse stone artifacts can do little more than attribute them to MSA technology, but Butzer considers that they predate the Last Interglacial near shore dunes. It would seem that the earliest MSA of the southern and eastern Cape is not represented at KRM.

The distribution of known occurrences of MSA artifacts has been mapped by Clark (1967) under the term "Stillbay/Pietersburg Complex." There are nearly 200 sites spread over most of South Africa except for northern Natal and the Karroo. Coastal sites are very sparse along the Atlantic coast north of Saldanha Bay, which is to be expected considering the inhospitable terrain. Few of these sites are more than surface scatters of artifacts considered diagnostic of MSA industries, and there is, of course, a very long time span involved. As yet, it is not possible to know which particular regions may have been favored at particular times in the Late Pleistocene. However, it

does show that people of this period were able to adapt to a variety of very different environments without changing the basic technology of their stone equipment.

Clark (1967) has also mapped "Late Upper Paleolithic" industries of the "Second Intermediate Period," including the Howieson's Poort Industry, under the term "Magosian." For South Africa, 17 such sites are shown, mainly restricted to the coastal fringe from Bokbaai in Table Bay to the Natal coast, and along the Orange River. KRM is not included on either map, as it was unknown at the time of the map's production. It is very likely that many other sites exist along the Indian Ocean coastline. However, although Howieson's Poort itself is only some 40 km inland, Montagu (not mapped by Clark for the same reason as KRM) is 112 km.

The early dating for the whole KRM sequence implies a considerable hiatus between the final MSA (Stage IV) and the next evidence for occupation in the immediate area in the third millennium B.C. Shackleton suggests that the Howieson's Poort Industry at KRM lies in the range of 50,000 to 30,000 years (see chap. 14). There is nothing to indicate a time interval between the Howieson's Poort and MSA III, but a long time must be allowed for the vast accumulation of the MSA III occupational deposits which, on the evidence of tabular calcite still attached to the roof of Shelter 1A, eventually reached to that height. Time must also be allowed (a) for the great mass of Howieson's Poort and MSA III deposits in Cave 2 and under Shelter 1A to be eroded back to their present angle of rest (note the truncation of the layers particularly in the drawn section for Side Cutting A, fig. 3.7) and (b) for the accumulation of eolian sand which partly filled Cave 1. This sand must be post–MSA III because nowhere is it included in the occupational deposits of this stage or earlier. There are many unknown factors, but it would seem less surprising if the date for the Howieson's Poort were nearer 50,000 years, or even earlier, rather than 30,000. In this respect it should be noted that Butzer (1978) places the Howieson's Poort at KRM into oxygen isotope stage 5b, dated to c. 95,000 B.P., and the accumulation of the eolian sand (1-13) into stage 4, c. 70,000 years B.P. This would mean a hiatus of c. 65,000 years between the final MSA of KRM and the earliest LSA there. Alternatively, if the eolian sand accumulated during the period of very low world sea level at the end of the Pleistocene (c. 20,000 years B.P.), that leaves a gap of only 18,000 years. From what has emerged in the last very active decade of archeological studies in South Africa, 18,000 years does not seem long enough, and one of the longer chronologies is preferred.

The term "LSA" has usually been considered to denote stone industries of Holocene or Recent date. It is now clear that some of the industries so described go back some way into the Late Pleistocene. This is on the basis of radiocarbon dating and revised chronologies first published by Vogel and Beaumont (1972). The base of the "Early LSA" of Heuningneskrans Shelter was estimated at about 32,000 B.C., and the "Pre-Wilton" at Rose Cottage to "well before 27,500 B.C." At Nelson Bay Cave, Klein (1972a, b, 1974) had identified two industries between the MSA and Wilton. Radiocarbon dates suggest a span of about 18,000 to 12,000 years for the earlier Robberg Industry, and 12,000 to 8,000 years for the Albany Industry. Although not yet published, it would seem that both industries are composed mainly of nonformal tools, but the Robberg Industry has small, steep scrapers and a few small, backed pieces, whereas the Albany Industry has large scrapers. Previously, these industries would probably have been classified as Smithfield. Sampson (1974), with his experience of the Orange River sites and his attempt to create a more work-

Table 15.1. A Tentative Correlation between the KRM Stages and Selected South African Sites

Shackleton (O isotope stages) Years BP (This volume)	KRM Butzer (1978 and this volume)	Mossel Bay	Howieson's Poort	Nelson Bay Cave	Boomplaas	Die Kelders	Skildergat	Montagu Cave	Border Cave (Butzer 1978)	Cave of Hearths (Sampson 1974)
				Albany / Robberg	Albany / Robberg				"Early LSA"	
	MSA IV 70,000 (4)									
	MSA III 80,000 (5a)	MSA		MSA	MSA	? MSA	MSA	MSA	Late MSA (80,000-50,000)	
30,000 - 50,000 (3)	HP c. 95,000 (5b)	HP	HP		HP	HP	HP	HP	HP (95,000 -80,000)	Umguzan
80,000 (5a) or 100,000 (5c)	MSA II 105,000 (5c) 110,000 (5c) 115,000 (5d)	MSA		MSA		or MSA	MSA		MSA	Bambata (Mwulu Ind.) .... Pietersburg
120,000 (5e(i)) 130,000 (5e(ii))	MSA I c. 120,000 (5e-5d)	MSA		MSA					(195,000- 95,000) Early MSA	Pietersburg

Note. Dotted lines indicate a hiatus in the sequence.

able terminology, had already abandoned the term "Smithfield A" for his Oakhurst Complex.

Robberg and Albany Industries have been identified at Melkhoutboom (Deacon 1976) within the same radiocarbon time range, and an Albany Industry has been identified at Buffelskloof (Opperman 1978). There is nothing at KRM to represent any human activity during this time, but it could exist in the unexcavated Caves 3 and 4.

The correlation chart displayed as table 15.1 is a tentative one, based on a few fairly definite associations and an assumption that the Howieson's Poort Industry is confined to a particular time span. In reality, there must have been overlap between these various units.

To summarize, there is ample evidence to show that South Africa was occupied throughout a long period, at least from the beginning of the Last Interglacial to the first half of the Last Glaciation in terms of the climate sequence of the Northern Hemisphere, by a resourceful, adaptable *Homo sapiens* population with an MSA industrial technology and who exploited a variety of environments. The evidence from Klasies River Mouth proves that the economy could be so successful that a stability was achieved comparable to or in excess of anything else known elsewhere in the world at this time. The Transvaal and the Cape were the most favored areas, and it has been suggested (Willcox 1974) that such apparently suitable areas for occupation as the Natal Drakensberg were too thickly forested during most of this period for both hunters and most game animals. Consistent evidence from KRM and Die Kelders alone shows that cooler conditions prevailed during the later period of the MSA, and the sum of the geological data can be interpreted only as implying a retreat of the coastline. At KRM this was thought to have receded so far by the time of the MSA IV stage that the occupants ceased to live there.

The Howieson's Poort Industry appears to reflect a considerable change in the activity pattern, and as yet, it is not understood how much this was a response to changed circumstances or genuine cultural evolution. At some sites, such as KRM and the type site, the industry is in such marked contrast to the traditional MSA that quite separate populations might be considered. Elsewhere, e.g., Nelson Bay Cave and perhaps Mossel Bay, it would seem more like the adaptation of a few new ideas with little overall change. The Howieson's Poort Industry as seen in its fully developed form implies several specialized activities normally unknown or of very much lesser importance in the MSA. Apart from hunting equipment (crescents, trapezes, projectile points), the use of microgravers, many neat small scrapers, outils écaillés (= chisels?), and notched or strangulated scrapers points to several technical innovations. Microblades were fashioned in the thousands, presumably as knives for delicate work such as on bone, wood, and leather. This general trend in specialized technology is the basic theme of human cultural evolution in the latter part of the Pleistocene period throughout much of Africa and the rest of the world. It culminates in the so-called Upper Paleolithic or leptolithic industries of the Old World. The very early dates for the Howieson's Poort at KRM, supported by dates from other Howieson's Poort sites in South Africa, show that such cultural development was evident in this region several tens of thousands of years before it appeared in Europe. It is also apparently earlier than the leptolithic industries of North Africa and the Near East.

The last MSA occupation at KRM may have been 65,000 years ago. There is a hiatus between that time and when the cave was reoccupied by LSA Strandlopers about 5,000 years ago.

16   Subsistence and Change at KRM during the MSA

During the long sequence of occupation at Klasies River Mouth, changes in the local fauna, both terrestrial and marine, may reflect gradual alterations in the climate and vegetation. On the other hand, changes in the terrestrial faunal distribution, as reflected in human deposits, may reflect, inter alia, either changing hunting preferences or migrational patterns of animals (for whatever reasons), as opposed to postulated extinctions. Changing sea levels had their effect upon the availability of marine food, but the very existence of the vast midden in and around the cave complex emphasizes that this was a highly favored living site for a long period in spite of this. It seems to have been so until eventually the sea receded so far that it became impracticable to exploit the food resources of the coastline and constantly travel the distances involved.

While the sea was close, the attractions of the site were numerous: an almost unlimited supply of shellfish; large and small mammals available for hunting in the immediate hinterland and at the watering places along the adjacent river; abundant fresh water; seals, dolphins, and fishes from the sea; marine birds to be caught easily on the beach; natural caves and rock shelters for protection; and an unlimited supply of good quality siliceous quartzite for making tools and weapons. It is thus not surprising that the archeological record infers a continuous or near-continuous occupation of the area for many hundreds of generations. It seems irrefutable that the MSA populations had achieved an ecological balance with the available resources and possessed a suitable social order to allow them to maintain it.

Other sites along the coastline of the eastern Cape were probably as favorable, and there are indications of numerous settlements of MSA date close to KRM and further away. With the exception of Nelson Bay Cave and Die Kelders, no other coastal sites have yet been systematically investigated and, as yet, nothing of the magnitude of KRM is known. However, there are no inland sites of this period which suggest the same duration and intensity of occupation. Yet, inland, there were many favorable areas with fresh water, abundant game, suitable toolmaking raw material, and natural shelters. There are numerous MSA sites to show that these advantages were enjoyed, but nowhere is there any great buildup of occupational soils remotely comparable to KRM. Some factors must have been lacking, and the one environmental factor at KRM which is present there and not inland is the ocean. The exploitation of marine food resources must be the key to the success and stability of the economy of this particular MSA population.

This utilization of marine resources is evident in the earliest MSA occupation of Stage I, and this is the earliest evidence for such activity in southern Africa, if not the world. There are no records of any Acheulian sites with shellfish food remains, but so marked have been the geomorphological changes since the Middle Pleistocene that erosion and chemical dissolution may have destroyed the evidence. It is only the fortunate circumstances of preservation at KRM that have allowed these interpretations.

Although they may have been rapid in geological terms, the changes in climate and sea levels, with their whole effect upon the environment, would hardly have been noticeable from one generation to another. Yet changes there were, but until the coastline retreated too far, none were so drastic as to cause any major change or breakdown in the economy; the population made minor adaptations in diet, and only in one phase, that of the Howieson's Poort, is there a suggestion of some radical change in at least some activities. This is discussed below. Each MSA stage is considered in turn, from the aspect of these economic and environmental changes.

MSA Stage I

The initial occupation was at a time of high sea level, probably 6–7 m above present sea level, but just below the level of the floor of Cave 1. Conditions were similar to those at present, with mixed forest and grassland in the vicinity. Eland and buffalo (both the Cape and the Giant Buffalo) predominated in the meat supply, and Klein (1976a) has demonstrated that the overwhelming majority of eland brought to the site were adult animals, but a fairly high proportion of the buffalo were very young. He believes this difference to have been caused by the danger involved in hunting adult buffalo, noted for their cunning and ferocity. Pregnant cows or calves were easier prey. Elephant and rhino are virtually absent from the faunal list probably for the same reasons, or because their habitats were distant and there would be problems in transportation over the adjacent mountainous area. They may have been eaten at distant kill sites. Hippopotamus, bushpig, and several antelopes (grysbok/steenbok, reedbuck, bloubok, hartebeest, bushbuck, kudu) were all successfully hunted.

The stone-tipped spear was presumably the weapon used for hunting these large terrestrial mammals, and the pointed flake-blades and worked points are identified as such weapons.

These must have been combined with numerous ingenious devices that have left no trace in the archeological record (pits, traps, fire, etc.).

Cape fur seals, dolphins, and penguins were also hunted in numbers, presumably with spears and clubs, unless they were found dead on the beach. Fish are poorly represented throughout the entire MSA sequence at KRM, and it can only be concluded that fishing (with hooks and lines or nets or traps) was not practiced. The few fish remains found are the vertebrae of quite large (1–4 kg) fish, and these could well have been picked up along the shore when stranded after a high tide.

Shellfish supplemented the meat diet, mainly limpets, small periwinkles, Turbo, and brown mussels. The preference was for limpets and mussels. All these shells could have been collected at normal low tides with a minimum of wading (see chap. 13).

This diet of meats and shellfish was made even more varied with the addition of marine birds, mainly cormorants and black-backed gulls. Any vegetable addition can only be guessed, as there is no evidence for it. No grindstones or rubbers were found in any of the MSA levels, so there can have been no regular grinding of fruits or seeds, if there was any at all.

The limited evidence from the human dental remains indicates a meaty or fibrous diet (devoid of grit or sand) in both MSA I and MSA II. In the LSA, one specimen (43110) reflects a "sticky," more cereal diet, while another (614) demonstrates the effects of shellfish food—an abrasive reaction to gritty food and sandy substances so typically observed in the skeletons from coastal midden deposits and later Bush-Hottentot individuals.

Butzer (chap. 4) agrees that the sea level during this phase of the MSA was at about the present level or lower. It is difficult to assess the time span involved, but at least 3 m of occupational deposits built up outside the cave mouth, and this seems more likely to have happened in thousands rather than hundreds of years. The interdigitation of occupational material and clean beach sand in the lower levels of layer 39 prompts us to conclude that the sea was very close to the 6–8 m level at the beginning of the MSA I stage but may well have dropped to about the present level by the end of the phase. Abundant angular rock fragments in layer 37 may indicate a general lowering of temperature by this time with some frost, but Butzer does not regard it as incontrovertible roof spall.

MSA Stage II

During this exceedingly long stage, Cave 1 was blocked up with refuse and at least 9 m of occupational soils built up outside in the lee of the cliff face and Shelter 1A. Eboulis horizons throughout the whole stage probably indicate lower temperatures than at present, with occasional frost. A moist climate is still implied by the continued formation of dripstone, and the faunal assemblage is regarded by Klein as indicative of Forest Bush Cover, in contrast to the previously more open country. There is a significant decrease in alcelaphine antelope, and an increase in bushbuck and kudu. Eland, buffalo, and hippopotamus remained a major source of the meat supply, but there was a gradual increase in the numbers of grysbok-steenbok, bushbuck, and blue antelope (bloubok) brought back to the site. The Cape fur seal was now hunted intensively, possibly as much for its fur as its meat. Colder winters called for some protective, warm clothing, but the manufacture of garments cannot be substantiated by the archeological evidence; nothing was found in the way of needles, awls, or fastenings, but this does not mean that some form of simple body covering could not have been made, or used as "blankets" or simple "drapes" (as used by modern populations), especially during cold nights.

Marine birds, occasional dolphins, and even whales still feature in the diet, and shellfish throughout in quantity. There are distinct changes in the proportions of molluscan species from the earlier MSA I, and these are just as likely to reflect environmental changes as dietary preferences. Voigt (chap. 13) has drawn attention to the increase of the limpet, *Patella granatina,* in this stage. This limpet is now a cold water (West Coast) species with a limited distribution east of Cape Agulhas and is thus strongly suggestive of a general lowering of sea temperature. Either the brown mussel (*Perna perna*) had been overexploited or preferences had changed or its numbers had decreased for environmental reasons, for this animal became less common in the diet, and over half the shellfish consumed were limpets. The large gastropod, aurikreukel (*Turbo sarmaticus*), constituted nearly a quarter of the other species collected.

It is clear that the sea was still very close to the site, probably no further away than it is now. Butzer has identified beach sand in 1-14 and 15.

KRM 1-15 is a true midden of occupational soil, although it seems to have suffered some distortion through compaction or dissolution of much of its shell content (see chap. 3) since it formed. It represents the last occupation in the mouth of the cave during this stage, for by this time refuse had piled up so high and close to the cave roof that the actual cave was difficult to enter, and was dark and unpleasant. There is no way of stratigraphically relating the MSA II levels outside Cave 1 under Shelter 1A with those actually in Cave 1 (i.e., 1-14 to 17 with 1A-22 to 36), but it would seem safe to assume that the upper layers outside the cave are more recent than those within it. It is difficult to reconstruct the exact topography of the site during the latter part of this stage, yet it is clear that occupation was strongly attached to the same place. By the end of this stage the occupants were living on an artificial platform of their ancestors' rubbish at least 14 m above natural ground level. The attraction was presumably the shelter provided by the cliff from cold westerly winds.

Howieson's Poort Stage

Many changes are reflected in this stage, in both the climate and the living patterns of the occupants. There are large rockfalls associated with the upper MSA II levels beneath Shelter 1A, and it may be significant that occupational levels above this height rise upward instead of sloping down. Various interpretations are implied. There may have been a considerable temporal hiatus between the MSA II and the Howieson's Poort accumulations with some erosion of the earlier deposits in between, but it is impossible to demonstrate it. A puzzling feature is that the residual layers of MSA II cemented to the cliff wall show that the occupational buildup was originally as high as the floor of Cave 2, yet there was nothing to indicate any use of the cave in that period. In the small area investigated, Howieson's Poort levels lay directly on top of the bedrock, and the same could be seen where the levels were naturally exposed by erosion in the front of the cave.

Angular rock spalls and the continued presence of *Patella granatina* testify to the continued relatively colder climate. Klein (1976*a*) sees the increase in alcelaphines and quagga as suggesting open habitat conditions. Decalcification as opposed to the formation of dripstone is interpreted by Butzer as denoting wet conditions.

Eland and buffalo still figure strongly in the diet, but there is now a marked increase in the numbers of grysbok/steenbok, reedbuck, bloubok, and bontebok. Butzer notes the lack of any eolian beach sands in these levels and concludes a regresssion of the sea is implied. Even so, the sea was unlikely to have retreated far, as seafood continued to be an important element of subsistence. Cape fur seals were still hunted and shellfish collected. A major difference is that *Turbo* was the most popular food, and mussels usually predominated over limpets.

There are two differences which suggest that this stage may represent an influx into the district of people with different traditions and habits: layer after layer of small hearths superimposed on one another contrast with the more even spreads of ash within sandier levels in the preceding MSA stages, and the stone industry is in marked contrast to that immediately below it. The stone industry is also very different from the succeeding MSA III stage. It is unfortunate that no human remains were recovered from this stage to compare with those, albeit sparse, from layers above and below the Howieson's Poort, and the few remains above and below do not permit analysis of change (i.e., admixture of new physical elements). There is certainly nothing to suggest that the Howieson's Poort stage at KRM evolved from the preceding MSA industry of Stage II. It is tempting to see this radical change in equipment reflecting new hunting methods devised to cope with the hunting of smaller, fleeter game in the more open landscape. The feasible explanation of the numerous crescents and trapezes is that they were the barbs inset into wooden spears. Some of them are so small that they may have tipped arrows, implying the possible invention of the bow. Poison could have been applied to these barbs. Such sophisticated hunting techniques, on the evidence of the material remains, spread worldwide during the Late Pleistocene, and the European replacement of the Mousterian by the Upper Paleolithic is a fair parallel. Just how and where these innovations developed in southern Africa is beyond the scope of this report, but a reasonable model would be the adaptation or invention of these new hunting methods by an ''MSA population'' somewhere where survival might depend upon it. This is unlikely to have been in a coastal environment such as KRM, where the successful exploitation of marine resources would have greatly reduced any urgent necessity for change.

It is not only the hunting aspect of the Howieson's Poort equipment which differs from the preceding MSA, but a whole range of tools that are not to be found in the earlier levels: outils écaillés, microgravers, small scrapers, strangulated scrapers, and other small, delicately backed blades. Whatever activities these represent, presumably of a domestic nature, they suggest something quite different from the preceding communities. The technical equipment brought or developed by the Howieson's Poort people may have influenced their hunting preferences, as reflected in the above-mentioned shifts in the relative amounts of faunal remains in the various deposits.

The local quartzite, to be found in unlimited quantities as beach pebbles or blocks of fallen cliff, is siliceous and relatively fine grained compared with some outcrops of Table Mountain sandstone. With skill, it could be knapped into thin, elegant blades. These were produced in large numbers in the Howieson's Poort Industry, and many were made into crescents and trapezes. However, the thinner the barb the easier it would have been to fix to the spear shaft, and the more effective it would have been in use, but the thinner the quartzite blade the more brittle it became. The problem was overcome by the use

of fine-grained rocks. Pebbles of such rocks (silcretes, indurated shales, chalcedony, quartz crystals) were to be found occasionally on the beach or along the beds of the local Klasies and Tzitzikama Rivers. There are several instances in the MSA I and II of occasional pebbles having been brought back to the site and used as knapping material. The small size of the pebbles and the fine nature of the rock induced the production of several small flakes and blades in marked contrast to the more massive flake-blades produced from the local quartzite. There does not appear to have been any great demand for such pieces, but this situation altered completely with the advent of the Howieson's Poort. There was now a wholesale search for every available piece, and it is intriguing to see this recorded so plainly in the stratigraphic record. The finest material to be found in any quantity was a red silcrete, and this predominates in the lower levels. As it became more and more difficult to find pebbles of this rock, so there is a mixture of whatever was available. Finally, when virtually nothing else could be found, the people resorted to quartz. This could be located plentifully within veins of the local sandstone of the cliffs, but it was usually thin, friable, and quite unsuitable for conventional knapping. The technique adopted was just to smash the pieces of quartz into a jumble of shattered fragments and select those which were thin and had at least one sharp edge. This was very evident in the Howieson's Poort levels of Cave 2.

It is impossible to gauge the original extent of the area occupied during this phase because so much has since been eroded away, but nothing was found other than within Cave 2 or under Shelter 1A. Both sites, although they were then almost certainly one contiguous occupied platform, would have been at least 20 m above the contemporary sea level, and this meant a laborious climb up and down the slope many times a day by the inhabitants. It was also the most sheltered part of the whole site with the best protection from the cold and rain, and this would explain their otherwise needless expenditure of effort. It fits well with the climatic interpretations given by Butzer. As with other stages of the MSA, there may have been a wider spread of the populations in nearby and distant caves. This raises the whole question of successful (or otherwise) social interactions, distribution of labor, food, etc., which cannot be answered by the present archeological evidence.

MSA Stage III

There are no reasons to suggest that the climate and environment of this phase were any different from that of the Howieson's Poort stage preceding it: wet with cold spells (Butzer, chap. 4, does not record the presence of frost spalls) and an open landscape. This is supported by the occupants remaining in the most protected part of the site. The occupation was of a very long duration, probably equivalent to that of MSA II, for, although less than 2 m of buildup was present in the area excavated, residual layers on the cliff wall show that a thickness of at least 6 m originally existed. Tabular dripstone remains beneath the actual overhang of this shelter, and this must have formed on the surface of the youngest layers before they were eroded away. Cave 2 was probably choked with refuse from the Howieson's Poort stage and Cave 1 completely obscured or otherwise uninhabitable.

As very little of this period was investigated, the faunal samples are small and thus less reliable as indicators of availability or preference. However, there is a list of game animals similar to that in the Howieson's Poort stage: eland and buffalo supplemented by several species of antelope normally found in open country. This is particularly interesting, as it was mentioned above that the new industrial equipment of the Howieson's Poort may have reflected new hunting techniques specifically designed for the purpose of killing the smaller game of the open country. Such equipment is lacking in this phase of the MSA. The few crescents found are more easily explained as intrusive pieces derived from earlier layers. The whole MSA III stage has its industrial traditions in the earlier MSA I and II stages, although there are signs of some change, with a general reduction in the size of flake-blades and an increase in the number of small unifacial points. The long occupation emphasizes the success of the people's economy and presumably their ability to hunt small game by traditional methods. If this is the correct interpretation, it supports the idea that the Howieson's Poort originated in a different environment and came fully developed into the district, but readily made use of the marine resources. If so, some territorial infringement may be implied, but considerably more sites in South Africa will have to be investigated on a large scale before this can be assessed.

The Cape fur seal continued to be hunted during MSA III. Shell-collecting habits were more in keeping with the earlier MSA stages, especially MSA II, the only essential difference being a reduction in the numbers of brown mussels brought to the site. Various limpets again constituted over half of the shellfish diet.

MSA Stage IV

A long period separates this final phase of the MSA at KRM from the top level of the MSA III stage investigated beneath Shelter 1A. Sufficient time was required in the intervening period for the buildup of the occupational soils, now only remaining in part, cemented to the cliff walls. Time was also needed for the erosion of enough of the vast accumulation in order to once again expose part of the mouth of Cave 1. This period may constitute a major portion of the Last Glaciation in European terms. Butzer interprets the sand which blew into Cave 1 as a true regressional eolianite. The sea must have receded far from the site, and it was no longer a favorable place to live, especially in view of the prevalence of blowing sand. It is therefore not surprising that the archeological material for this period is sparse. There was certainly no occupation of any duration sufficient to produce any spreads of ash, soil, and other refuse. The artifacts and few bones and shells found within the body of the eolian sand, in spite of the long time interval inferred, are still of MSA tradition, although little can be said of them save that they show a considerable reduction in the size of the flakes and flake-blades, but this may merely reflect the now greater distance away from the sea coast and source of raw material. Limpets total nearly three-quarters of the shellfish brought into the cave. Cape fur seal, bloubok, rock hyrax, and Cape buffalo are the only animals represented by the bones of more than single individuals. This material is interpreted as the litter from casual visits by wandering hunters and does little to explain the general economy or subsistence of the population at that time.

A very long period of time, possibly in the order of 50,000 years, was to elapse before LSA Strandlopers were to occupy Cave 1.

General

There are several aspects of this sequence at Klasies River Mouth which are unique for both African and world prehistory. It may represent the longest continuous occupation of one site ever known. The only comparable site is Haua Fteah, also in Africa but at the other end of the continent, and also spanning a long period of the Late Pleistocene and also probably involving people at a similar cultural level.

The evidence for the KRM food economy is, in archeological terms, good, but there is virtually nothing to suggest what spiritual activities were involved. It has already been speculated above that the long continuous occupation would have necessitated the implementation of a firm social order, and it is frustrating to find nothing that hints at what this may have been. Customs, codes, and classes must have existed. The discovery of red ocher pigment in nearly all levels shows some preoccupation with coloring, and it was much hoped that traces of paintings might be found on the smoother walls of the caves, especially Cave 1C, where conditions would have been ideal for their preservation. In this latter cave, rendered inaccessible some time during MSA II by the blocking of its entrance, there were wide, light-colored rock surfaces, which had never been buried by an accumulation of occupational soils, but nowhere could be seen the slightest trace of any pigment adhering to them, nor were there any signs of scratchings or engravings. Similarly, nothing was seen on the rock walls behind any deposits removed during the course of excavation, yet there can be no doubt that the pieces of ocher which were found had been used somehow; several pieces had well-rubbed edges or surfaces and may even have been shaped for more convenient handling. The conclusion is that the people were using the pigment to decorate their artifacts or themselves. Although featured so scantily in the archeological record, these implied activities may have been of considerable social importance, and in this respect, it is worth recalling the surprising evidence for the actual mining of ocher in Swaziland (Dart and Beaumont 1967, 1968, 1971) during a Middle Stone Age phase with radiocarbon dates on the order of 22,000 and 28,000 years, and another at about 41,000 B.C. Beaumont (1973b) argues for the exploitation of such materials being already in progress at 120,000 years ago.

There is nothing in the whole vast collection of stone artifacts that need have anything but a functional interpretation. There is no sign of sculpture in spite of the mass of bone. Two pieces of rib with serrated edges and a bone with some faint parallel scratches are the only pieces which might be described as bonework in the MSA stages. It is tempting to consider these pieces as possible "tallies," as Marshack (1972) has been able to demonstrate so convincingly from European Upper Paleolithic sites, but the inference remains inconclusive.

Whatever bound the MSA societies together so successfully must remain a matter for speculation. Most significant is the correlation of such a long period of occupation, to be measured in thousands and not hundreds of years, with little if anything to show in any change in subsistence and economy. That this apparent stability failed to lead to any major changes must have important implications for the manner in which human society developed during the latter part of the Pleistocene period.

Appendix: *Catalog numbers of artifacts figured*

	Cat. No.	Cave or Shelter	Layer
FIG. 5.2			
1	25106	1A	19
2	4470	1	13
3	1109	1A	6
4	1108	"	"
5	25074	"	19
6	25100	"	"
7	4466	1	13
8	4467	"	"
9	4465	1A	19
10	25103	"	"
11	25081	"	"
12	25111	"	"
FIG. 5.3			
1	4626	1	13
2	4538	"	"
3	4654	"	"
4	4494	"	"
5	4679	"	"
6	4533	"	"
7	4529	"	"
8	4534	"	"
9	4532	"	"
10	4671	"	"
11	290	"	"
12	4704	"	"
13	4100	"	"
14	4631	"	"
15	4647	"	"
16	4633	"	"
17	4694	"	"
18	4618	"	"
19	4695	"	"
20	4622	"	"
21	4612	"	"
22	4613	"	"
23	4688	"	"
24	4610	"	"

	Cat. No.	Cave or Shelter	Layer
FIG. 5.4			
1	1206	1A	6
2	1209	''	''
3	1233	''	''
4	1210	''	''
5	1260	''	''
6	1255	''	''
7	1119	''	''
8	1110	''	''
9	1173 and	''	''
	1157	''	''
10	813	''	3
11	814	''	''
12	1172	''	6
13	1179	''	''
14	1177	''	''
15	1178	''	''
16	1149	''	''
17	1143	''	''
18	1216	''	''
19	1128	''	''
20	1127	''	''
21	1129	''	''
22	1130	''	''
FIG.5.5			
1	25038	1A	32-34
2	21403	''	28
3	21344	''	''
4	10797	1	15
5	21441	1A	28
6	21396	''	''
7	21559	''	''
8	21451	''	''
9	25046	''	32-34
10	12374	1	15
11	12500	''	''
12	13398	''	''
13	11752	''	''
14	10811	''	''
15	10725	''	''
16	10724	''	''
17	10268	''	''
18	10267	''	''
FIG. 5.6			
1	24036	1	38
2	24173	''	''
3	24253	''	''
4	20457	''	''
5	24266	''	''
6	24028	''	''
7	24046	''	''
8	24090	''	''
9	24274	''	''
10	27679	''	''
11	24280	''	''

	Cat. No.	Cave or Shelter	Layer
12	24270	''	''
13	24283	''	''
14	27680	''	''
FIG. 5.7			
1	21108	1A	26
2	21038	''	25
3	21036	''	''
4	21026	''	''
5	21050	''	''
6	21035	''	''
7	21048	''	''
8	21573	''	28
9	25044	''	33
10	25042	''	''
11	21474	''	28
12	6748	1	14
13	12258	''	15
14	12023	''	''
15	6743	''	14
16	11922	''	15
17	6727	''	14
18	6739	''	''
19	6725	''	''
FIG. 5.8			
1	816	1A	3
2	815	''	''
3	818	''	''
4	27932	''	1-3
5	27933	''	''
6	27950	''	''
7	27949	''	''
8	27951	''	''
9	28017	''	4
10	28018	''	''
11	928	''	''
12	929	''	''
13	28076	''	5
14	1081	''	''
15	28075	''	''
16	28122	''	6
17	28123	''	''
18	1244	''	''
19	1246	''	''
20	1250	''	''
21	1245	''	''
22	1251	''	''
23	28124	''	''
FIG. 5.9			
1	1931	1A	7-9
2	1936	''	''
3	1933	''	''
4	1930	''	''
5	28196	''	7
6	28197	''	''

	Cat. No.	Cave or Shelter	Layer
7	28198	"	"
8	1942	"	9 resting on 10
9	28195	"	7
10	28193	"	"
11	28194	"	"

FIG. 5.10

	Cat. No.	Cave or Shelter	Layer
1	10158	1A	23-24
2	10160	"	"
3	21133	"	25
4	31208	"	23
5	30000	"	36
6	22384	1	17
7	22365	"	"
8	30888	"	16
9	27488	"	14
10	22368	"	17
11	26737	"	17b
12	16135	"	16
13	26084	"	14
14	24726	"	"
15	21590	1A	28-29
16	29990	"	36
17	10156	"	23-24
18	30885	1	16
19	10155	1A	23-24
20	10124	"	"
21	27482	1	14

FIG. 5.11

	Cat. No.	Cave or Shelter	Layer
1	27847	1B	4
2	27844	"	"
3	27845	"	"
4	27850	"	"
5	27840	"	"
6	27841	"	"
7	27846	"	"
8	27851	"	"
9	27862	"	5
10	27820	"	3
11	27823	"	"
12	27779	"	2
13	27780	"	"
14	27861	"	5
15	27860	"	"

FIG. 5.12

	Cat. No.	Cave or Shelter	Layer
1	26081	1	14
2	24311	"	38
3	10120	1A	23-24
4	9393	1	14
5	16109	"	16
6	24305	"	38
7	11866	"	15
8	11894	"	"

	Cat. No.	Cave or Shelter	Layer
9	1941	''	10 top of
10	10138	''	23-24
11	10135	''	''
12	23394	1	37
13	10123	1A	23-24

FIG. 5.13

1	27536	1	13
2	305	''	''
3	28017	1A	4
4	28229	''	9
5	27099	1	15
6	8308	''	14
7	26761	''	17b
8	16115	''	16
9	31265	1A	24
10	9397	1	14
11	16127	''	16
12	10127	1A	23-24
13	16121	1	16
14	31266	1A	24
15	30867	''	36
16	27796	1B	3
17	27793	''	''
18	27222	1	37
19	27776	1B	3
20	27794	''	''

FIG. 5.14

1	27471	1	14
2	27470	''	''
3	27761	''	37
4	27048	''	14
5	4733	''	13
6	27792	1B	3
7	26709	1	17a
8	27468	''	14
9	27537	''	13
10	28205	1A	7
11	28143	''	6
12	28142	''	''
13	27469	1	14
14	26708	''	17a

FIG. 5.15

1	10162	1A	23-24
2	31203	''	23
3	22374	1	17a-b
4	12516	''	15
5	16215	''	16
6	12398	''	15
7	12344	''	''
8	12372	''	''
9	12448	''	''
10	12500	''	''
11	12309	''	''

	Cat. No.	Cave or Shelter	Layer
12	31293	1A	25
FIG. 5.16			
1	28698	1A	12
2	31818	1	37
3	26734	"	40
FIG. 5.17			
1	4750	1	14
2	12741	"	16
FIG. 6.3			
1	30687	1A	18
2	4289	"	17-21
3	31420	"	20
4	28166	"	10
5	4292	"	17-21
6	28361	"	10
7	28354	"	"
8	30689	"	18
9	30236	"	17
10	4295	"	17-21
11	30091	"	17
12	31620	"	20
13	30123	"	17
14	30688	"	18
15	31623	"	20
16	29955	"	16
17	31622	"	20
18	4353	"	17-21
19	31353	"	20
20	31428	"	"
21	30329	"	17
22	31422	"	20
23	30322	"	17
24	31619	"	20
25	31618	"	"
26	31434	"	"
27	31421	"	"
28	28855	"	11
29	28856	"	"
30	28857	"	"
31	4302	"	17-21
32	4300	"	"
33	4306	"	"
34	4288	"	"
35	4294	"	"
36	31435	"	20
37	31433	"	"
38	31628	"	"
39	31432	"	"
40	31627	"	"
41	28942	"	12
42	30093	"	17
43	30325	"	"
44	30691	"	18
45	31413	"	20

	Cat. No.	Cave or Shelter	Layer
FIG. 6.4			
1	4308	1A	17-21
2	4314	"	"
3	4313	"	"
4	4312	"	"
5	4315	"	"
6	4311	"	"
7	4317	"	"
8	30096	"	17
9	30353	"	"
10	3316	"	17-21
11	30097	"	17
12	29725	"	15
13	30327	"	17
14	29796	"	15
15	30354	"	17
16	30328	"	"
17	4309	"	17-21
18	4349	"	"
19	4310	"	"
20	29724	"	15
21	29864	"	16
22	30355	"	17
23	29792	"	16
24	28585	"	11
25	28586	"	"
26	4321	"	17-21
27	29698	"	15-16
28	28375	"	10
29	29727	"	15
30	30704	"	18
31	4345	"	17-21
32	4301	"	"
33	4325	"	"
34	4323	"	"
35	4327	"	"
36	4320	"	"
37	30100	"	17
38	30697	"	18
39	4322	"	17-21
40	30107	"	17
41	31584	"	20
42	4323	"	17-21
43	28167	"	10
44	28164	"	6
FIG. 6.5			
1	2801	1A	17-21
2	31588	"	20
3	28454	"	10
4	30115	"	17
5	28241	"	9+
6	31469	"	20
7	28230	"	9
8	31461	"	20
9	30815	"	19
10	30722	"	18

	Cat. No.	Cave or Shelter	Layer
11	30723	''	''
12	4351	''	17-21
13	30128	''	17
14	30129	''	''
15	30282	''	''
16	29849	''	16
17	31114	''	21
18	31657	''	20
19	31973	''	''
20	31586	''	''
21	31113	''	21
22	31176	''	''
23	29954	''	16
24	31656	''	20
25	31972	''	''
26	31112	''	21
27	31655	''	20
FIG. 6.6			
1	29038	1A	12
2	28409	''	10
3	4348	''	17-21
4	29920	''	16
5	29702	''	15-16
6	29041	''	12
7	29841	''	16
8	29043	''	12
9	29764	''	15
10	29612	''	14
11	29042	''	12
12	29949	''	16
13	29918	''	''
14	29950	''	''
15	29040	''	12
16	29763	''	15
17	29728	''	''
18	29794	''	16
19	31975	''	20
20	29795	''	16
21	30536	''	17
22	29953	''	16
23	31463	''	20
24	30262	''	17
25	29848	''	16
26	29925	''	''
27	30263	''	17
28	29700	''	15-16
29	29916	''	16
30	29703	''	15-16
31	29951	''	16
32	29948	''	''
33	29734	''	15
34	30279	''	17
FIG. 6.7			
1	31654	1A	20

	Cat. No.	Cave or Shelter	Layer
2	27055	"	On scree slope
3	31652	"	20
4	16417	2	Cemented to cave wall
5	31974	1A	20
6	30416	"	17
7	19532	2	Surface of cave floor

FIG. 9.4

	Cat. No.	Cave or Shelter	Layer
1	443	1	1-3
2	418	"	7
3	410	"	"
4	—	"	"
5	435	"	5
6	2	"	1-4
7	—	"	7
8	808	"	11
9	448	"	1-3
10	558	"	5-7
11	27039	"	4

FIG. 9.5

	Cat. No.	Cave or Shelter	Layer
1	932	1	8
2	2236	"	1-6
3	676	"	11
4	1625	"	7-11
5	612	"	5
6	23622	3	Surface
7	27504	1	7-12
8	669	"	8
9	613 a/b	"	5-7
10	675	"	9
11	27785	"	8-14
12	673	"	9
13	1	"	1-4

FIG. 9.6

	Cat. No.	Cave or Shelter	Layer
1	670	1	8
2	30183	4	Surface
3	1623	"	8 top of
4	611	"	6-7
5	24462	"	Disturbed surface layer W. Cutting G
6	27791	"	7-12 Rear chamber South trench
7	1629	"	6-7
8	29569	5	3
9	29570	"	"

FIG. 10.3

	Cat. No.	Cave or Shelter	Layer
1	29347	5	1
2	29356	"	Wall B

	Cat. No.	Cave or Shelter	Layer
3	29372	"	2
4	29373	"	"
5	29472	"	2a
6	29471	"	"
7	29349	"	1
8	29367	"	2

FIG. 10.4

1	——	——	——
2	30005	5	5
3	30008	"	"
4	30015	"	"
5	30014	"	"
6	——	——	——
7	——	——	——
8	——	——	——
9	——	——	——
10	——	——	——
11	——	——	——

PLATE 29

1-7	——	1	17b
8	5072	"	14
9	5070	"	"
10	5067	"	"

PLATE 31

1	5149	1	14
2	5156	"	"
3	5146	"	"
4	5143	"	"
5	5140	"	"

PLATE 32

1	5106	1	14
2	5105	"	"
3	5104	"	"
4	17377	"	17

PLATE 33

1	7197	1	14
2	7200	"	"
3	7205	"	"
4	7162	"	"
5	7171	"	"
6	7184	"	"
7	7124	"	"
8	7136	"	"
9	7142	"	"

PLATE 34

1	4433	1	13
2	——	"	"
3	4661	"	"
4	4445	"	"
5	4441	"	"
6	4452	"	"

	Cat. No.	Cave or Shelter	Layer
7	4457	''	''
8	4461	''	''
9	4444	''	''
PLATE 35			
1	1104	1A	6
2	12370	1	15
3	12375	''	''
4	1103	1A	6
5	1107	''	''
6	12445	1	15
7	1106	1A	6
8	1102	''	''
9	12444	1	15
PLATE 36			
1	20962	1A	25
2	25060	''	32-33
3	25061	''	''
4	21060	''	26
5	20965	''	25
6	21061	''	26
7	25070	''	32-33
8	21071	''	26
9	21064	''	''
PLATE 37			
1	30901	1B	12
2	32216	1	38
3	32219	''	''
4	32214	''	''
5	32222	''	''
6	32201	''	''
7	32211	''	''
8	32200	''	''
9	32210	''	''
PLATE 38			
1	29675	1A	15-16
2	30193	''	17
3	29680	''	15-16
4	30192	''	17
5	30215	''	''
6	28518	''	11
7	28550	''	''
8	30202	''	17
9	1970	''	10-12
10	1983	''	''
11	1984	''	''
12	28598	''	11
13	30208	''	17
14	30677	''	18
15	30206	''	17
16	28596	''	11
17	28551	''	''

PLATE 39

1	1956	1A	10-12
2	2796	"	18-21
3	1965	"	10-12
4	2791	"	18-21
5	1990	"	10-12
6	1945	"	"
7	1959	"	"
8	1949	"	"
9	2798	"	18-21
10	30211	"	17

Bibliography

Abel, W. 1933. Zahne und kiefer in ihren Wechselbezicheingen bei Buschmänner, Hottentotten, Negern, und deren Bastarden. *Zeitschrift für Morphologie und Anthropologie* 31: 314–61.

Acocks, J. P. H. 1975. Veld types of South Africa. *Botanical Survey of South Africa, Memoir* 40: 1–128.

Bada, J. L., and L. Deems. 1975. Accuracy of dates beyond the ^{14}C dating limit using the aspartic acid racemization reaction. *Nature* 255: 218–19.

Bada, J. L., and R. Protsch. 1973. Racemization reaction of aspartic acid and its use in dating fossil bones. *Proceedings of the National Academy of Sciences, U.S.A.* 70: 1331–34.

Bakker, E. M. van Z., and K. W. Butzer. 1973. Quaternary environmental changes in southern Africa. *Soil Science* 116: 236–48.

Beater, B. E. 1967. Middle Stone Age implements on Aeolianite at Isipingo Beach, Natal. *South African Archaeological Bulletin* 22: 59.

Beaumont, P. B. 1973a. Border Cave—a progress report. *South African Journal of Science* 69: 41–46.

———. 1973b. The ancient pigment mines of southern Africa. *South African Journal of Science* 69: 140–46.

———. 1979. Comment on Rightmire, G. P. 1979. Implications of Border Cave skeletal remains for later Pleistocene human evolution. *Current Anthropology* 20: 26–27.

Beaumont, P. B., and A. K. Boshier. 1972. Some comments on recent findings at Border Cave, Northern Natal. *South African Journal of Science* 68: 22–24.

Beaumont, P. B., and J. C. Vogel. 1972. On a new radiocarbon chronology for Africa south of the equator. *African Studies* 31: 65–89, 155–82.

Biberson, P. 1966. Review of *Environment and Archaeology*, by K. W. Butzer. *Current Anthropology* 7: 502.

Bigalke, E. 1973. The exploitation of shellfish by coastal tribesmen of the Transkei. *Annals of the Cape Provincial Museums (Natural History)* 9: 159–75.

Bigalke, E., and E. A. Voigt. 1973. The interdisciplinary aspect of a study of shellfish exploitation by indigenous coastal communities. *South African Museums Association Bulletin* 10: 256–61.

Bordes, F. 1961. *Typologie du paléolithique ancien et moyen*. Publications de l'Institut Préhistorique, Université de Bordeaux. Mem. 1 (2 vols.). Bordeaux.

Bordes, F., and D. Crabtree. 1969. The Corbiac blade technique and other experiments. *Tebiwa* 12: 1–21.

Brabant, H. 1965. Observations sur la denture des Pygmées de l'Afrique Centrale. *Bulletin de Groupement Européen pour la Recherche Scientifique en Stomatologie et Odontologie* 8: 27–49.

Brabant, H., and F. Twiesselmann. 1964. Observations sur l'evolution de la denture permanente humaine en Europe Occidentale. *Bulletin de Groupement Européen pour la Recherche Scientifique en Stomatologie et Odontologie* 7: 11–84.

Brain, C. K. 1969. Faunal remains from Bushman Rock Shelter, eastern Transvaal. *South African Archaeological Bulletin* 24: 52–55.

———. 1974. Some suggested procedures in the analysis of bone accumulations from southern African Quaternary sites. *Annals of the Transvaal Museum* 29: 1–8.

Branch, G. M. 1974. The ecology of *Patella* Linnaeus from the Cape Peninsula, South Africa. 3. Growth-rates. *Transactions of the Royal Society of South Africa* 41: 161–94.

Brothwell, D. R. 1963. *Digging up bones*. London: British Museum (Natural History).

Buchanan, W. F.; Hall, S. L.; Henderson, J.; Olivier, A.; Pettigrew, J. M.; Parkington, J. E.; and P. T. Robertshaw. 1978. Coastal shell middens in the Paternoster area, south-western Cape. *South African Archaeological Bulletin* 33: 89–93.

Butzer, K. W. 1971. *Environment and archaeology: An ecological approach to prehistory*. Chicago: Aldine, and London: Methuen.

———. 1973a. Geology of Nelson Bay Cave, Robberg, South Africa. *South African Archaeological Bulletin* 28: 97–110.

———. 1973b. Pleistocene "periglacial" phenomena in southern Africa. *Boreas* 2: 1–12.

———. 1975. Pleistocene littoral-sedimentary cycles of the Mediterranean Basin: A Mallorquin view. In K. W. Butzer and G. L. Isaac, eds., *After the australopithecines: Stratigraphy, ecology, and culture change in the Middle Pleistocene*. Chicago: Aldine, and The Hague: Mouton, pp. 25–71.

———. 1976. Pleistocene climates. *Geoscience and Man* 13: 27–44.

———. 1978. Sediment stratigraphy of the Middle Stone Age sequence at Klasies River Mouth, Tsitsikama Coast, South Africa. *South African Archaeological Bulletin* 33: 141–51.

Butzer, K. W.; Beaumont, P. B.; and J. C. Vogel. 1978. Lithostratigraphy of Border Cave, KwaZulu, South Africa: A Middle Stone Age sequence beginning *c*. 195,000 B.P. *Journal of Archaeological Science* 5: 317–41.

Butzer, K. W., and D. M. Helgren. 1972. Late Cenozoic evolution of the Cape Coast between Knysna and Cape St. Francis, South Africa. *Quaternary Research* 2: 143–69.

Carter, P. L. 1969. Moshebi's Shelter: Excavation and exploitation in eastern Lesotho. *Lesotho* 8: 1–11.

Carter, P. L., and Vogel, J. C. 1974. The dating of industrial assemblages from stratified sites in eastern Lesotho. *Man* (n.s.) 9: 557–70.

Clark, J. D. 1957. A re-examination of the industry from the type site of Magosi, Uganda. In J. D. Clark, ed., *Proceedings of the Third Pan-African Congress on Prehistory, Livingstone, 1955*. London: Chatto & Windus, pp. 228–41.

———. 1959. *The prehistory of southern Africa*. London: Pelican Books.

———. 1967. *Atlas of African prehistory*. Chicago: University of Chicago Press.

Clark, J. D.; Cole, G. H.; Isaac, G. L.; and M. R. Kleindienst. 1966. Precision and definition in African archaeology. *South African Archaeological Bulletin* 21: 114–21.

Climate of South Africa. 1954. Part 1. *Climate statistics*. Pretoria: South African Weather Bureau.

———. 1954. Part 2. *Rainfall statistics*. Pretoria: South African Weather Bureau.

Connolly, M. 1939. A monographic survey of South African non-marine mollusca. *Annals of the South African Museum* 33.

Cooke, C. K. 1963. Report on excavations at Pomongwe and Tshangula caves, Matopo Hills, Southern Rhodesia. *South African Archaeological Bulletin* 18: 75–151.

Cramb, G. 1952. A Middle Stone Age industry from a Natal rock shelter. *South African Journal of Science* 48: 181–86.

Dart, R. A., and P. B. Beaumont. 1967. Amazing antiquity of mining in southern Africa. *Nature* 216: 407–8.

———. 1968. Ratification and retrocession of earlier Swaziland iron ore mining radiocarbon datings. *South African Journal of Science* 64: 241–46.

———. 1971. On a further radiocarbon date for ancient mining in southern Africa. *South African Journal of Science* 67: 10–11.

Davies, O. 1951. The early beaches of Natal. *South African Archaeological Bulletin* 6: 107–12.

———. 1967. The dates of the Late Pleistocene sea-levels. *South African Archaeological Bulletin* 22: 31.

———. 1969. The Quaternary beaches of South Africa—with special reference to the 200 ft. beach in Natal and the Eastern Province. *South African Archaeological Bulletin* 24: 125–126.

———. 1971. Pleistocene shorelines in the southern and southeastern Cape Province, part 1. *Annals of the Natal Museum* 21: 183–223.

———. 1972. Pleistocene shorelines in the southern and southeastern Cape Province, part 2. *Annals of the Natal Museum* 22: 255–279.

Day, J. H. 1969. *A guide to marine life on South African shores*. Cape Town: Balkema.

Deacon, H. J. 1965. Cultural material from the Gamtoos Valley shelters (Andrieskraal). *South African Archaeological Bulletin* 20: 193–200.

———. 1966. An annotated list of radiocarbon dates for sub-Saharan Africa. *Annals of the Cape Provincial Museums* 5: 5–84.

———. 1968. Supplementary list and index to "An annotated list of radiocarbon dates for sub-Saharan Africa." *Supplement to Annals of the Cape Provincial Museums* 5: 1–24.

———. 1969. Melkhoutboom Cave, Alexandria District, Cape Province: A report on the 1967 investigation. *Annals of the Cape Provincial Museums (Natural History)* 6: 141–69.

———. 1972. A review of the post-Pleistocene in South Africa. *South African Archaeological Society Goodwin Series* 1: 26–45.

———. 1976. *Where hunters gathered*. South African Archaeological Society Monograph Series no. 1.

———. 1979. Excavations at Boomplaas Cave— a sequence through the Upper Pleistocene and Holocene in South Africa. *World Archaeology* 10: 241–57.

Deacon, H. J., and M. Brooker. 1976. The Holocene and Upper Pleistocene sequence in the southern Cape. *Annals of the South African Museum* 71: 203–14.

Deacon, H. J.; Deacon, J.; and M. Brooker. 1976. Four painted stones from Boomplaas Cave, Oudtshoorn district. *South African Archaeological Bulletin* 31: 141–45.

Deacon, J. 1972. Wilton: An assessment after 50 years. *South African Archaeological Bulletin* 27: 10–48.

———. 1974. Patterning in the radiocarbon dates for the Wilton/Smithfield complex in Southern Africa. *South African Archaeological Bulletin* 29: 3–18.

———. 1976a. Review of *The Stone Age archaeology of southern Africa,* by C. G. Sampson. *South African Archaeological Bulletin* 31: 58–63.

———. 1976b. Report on stone artifacts from Duinefontein 2, Melkbosstrand. *South African Archaeological Bulletin* 31: 21–25.

———. 1978. Changing patterns in the Late Pleistocene/Early Holocene prehistory of southern Africa as seen from the Nelson Bay Cave stone artifact sequence. *Quaternary Research* 10: 84–111.

De Villiers, H. 1973. Human skeletal remains from Border Cave, Ingwavuma District, KwaZulu, South Africa. *Annals of the Transvaal Museum* 28: 229–56.

———. 1976. A second adult human mandible from Border Cave, Ingwavuma District, KwaZulu, South Africa. *South African Journal of Science* 72: 212–15.

Dingle, R. V., and J. Rogers. 1972. Pleistocene palaeogeography of the Agulhas Bank. *Transactions of the Royal Society of South Africa* 40: 155–65.

Drennan, M. R. 1929. The dentition of a Bushman tribe. *Annals of South African Museum* 24: 61–88.

Dreyer, T. F. 1933. Archaeology of the Matjes River Rock Shelter. *Transactions of the Royal Society of South Africa* 21: 187–209.

———. 1934. The stratification of the superficial deposits at Mossel Bay, and the age of the Mossel Bay and other lithic industries. *Transactions of the Royal Society of South Africa* 22: 165–69.

Emiliani, C. 1955. Pleistocene temperatures. *Journal of Geology* 63: 538–78.

———. 1966. Palaeotemperature analysis of Caribbean cores P 6304-8 and P 6304-9 and a generalized temperature curve for the last 425,000 years. *Journal of Geology* 74: 109–26.

Emiliani, C.; Cardini, L.; Mayeda, T.; McBurney, C. B. M.; and E. Tongiorgi. 1964. Palaeotemperature analysis of fossil shells of marine mollusks (food refuse) from the Arene Candide Cave, Italy, and the Haua Fteah Cave, Cyrenaica. In H. Craig, S. L. Miller, and G. J. Wasserburg, eds., *Isotopic and cosmic chemistry*. Amsterdam: North-Holland, pp. 133–60.

Epstein, S.; Buchsbaum, R.; Lowenstam, H. A.; and H. C. Urey. 1953. Revised carbonate-water isotopic temperature scale. *Geological Society of America Bulletin* 64: 1315–26.

Fagan, B. M. 1960. The Glentyre Shelter and Oakhurst re-examined. *South African Archaeological Bulletin* 59: 80–94.

FitzSimons, F. W. 1921. The cliff dwellers of Zitzikama. *Illustrated London News*, 24 Dec., p. 880.

———. 1923. The cliff dwellers of Zitzikama. *South African Journal of Science* 20: 541–44.

———. 1926. Cliff dwellers of Zitzikama: Results of recent excavations. *South African Journal of Science* 23: 813–17.

Folk, R. L. 1966. A review of grain-size parameters. *Sedimentology* 6: 73–93.

Gatehouse, R. P. 1955. The prehistoric site at Cape Hangklip. *Transactions of the Royal Society of South Africa* 34: 335–44.

Gear, H. S. 1926. A further report on the Boskopoid remains from Zitzikama. *South African Journal of Science* 23: 923–34.

Gess, W. H. K. 1969. Excavation of a Pleistocene bone deposit at Aloes near Port Elizabeth. *South African Archaeological Bulletin* 24: 31–32.

Goodwin, A. J. H. 1928. An introduction to the Middle Stone Age of South Africa. *South African Journal of Science* 25: 410–18.

———. 1929. The Middle Stone Age. *Annals of the South African Museum* 27: 95–145.

———. 1933. The Cape Flats complex. *South African Journal of Science* 30: 515–23.

Goodwin, A. J. H., and B. D. Malan. 1935. Archaeology of the Cape St. Blaize Cave and Raised Beach, Mossel Bay. *Annals of the South African Museum* 24: 111–40.

Goodwin, A. J. H., and B. Peers. 1953. Two caves at Kalk Bay, Cape Peninsula. 1. Nero's Cave (C/103); 2. Peer's Shelter B/102. *South African Archaeological Bulletin* 8: 59–77.

Greene, D. L.; Ewing, G. H.; and G. J. Armelagos. 1967. Dentition of a Mesolithic population from Wadi Halfa, Sudan. *American Journal of Physical Anthropology* 27: 41–56.

Grindley, J. R. 1967. The Cape rock lobster *Jasus lalandii* from the Bonteberg excavation. *South African Archaeological Bulletin* 22: 94–102.

Grindley, J. R.; Speed, E.; and T. Maggs. 1970. The age of the Bonteberg Shelter deposits, Cape Peninsula. *South African Archaeological Bulletin* 25: 24.

Hays, J. D.; Lozano, J.; Shackleton, N.; and G. Irving. 1976. Reconstruction of the Atlantic Ocean and western Indian Ocean sectors of the 18,000 B.P. Antarctic Ocean. In R. M. Cline and J. D. Hays, eds., *Investigation of Late Quaternary paleoceanography and paleoclimatology*. Geological Society of America Memoir, no. 145, pp. 337–72.

Helgren, D. M., and K. W. Butzer. 1977. Paleosols of the southern Cape Coast, South Africa: Implications for laterite definition, genesis, and age. *Geographical Review* 67: 430–45.

Hendey, Q. B., and H. J. Deacon. 1977. Studies in palaeontology and archaeology in the Saldanha region. *Transactions of the Royal Society of South Africa* 42: 371–81.

Hoffman, A. C. 1967. Archaeological research of the National Museum in Bloemfontein during 1965. In E. M. van Zinderen Bakker, ed., *Palaeoecology of Africa (1964–1965)*, vol. 2. Cape Town: A. A. Balkema, pp. 55, 56.

Howell, F. C., and J. D. Clark. 1963. Acheulian hunter-gatherers of sub-Saharan Africa. In F. C. Howell and F. Bourlière, eds., *African ecology and human evolution*. Chicago: Aldine.

Imbrie, J.; van Donk, J.; and N. G. Kipp. 1973. Paleoclimatic investigation of a Late Pleistocene Caribbean deep-sea core: Comparison of isotopic and faunal methods. *Quaternary Research* 3: 10–38.

Inskeep, R. R. 1961. Review of *Prehistory of the Matjes River Rock Shelter*, by J. T. Louw. *South African Archaeological Bulletin* 16: 30–31.

———. 1976. A note on the Melkbos and Hout Bay raised beaches and the Middle Stone Age. *South African Archaeological Bulletin* 31: 26–28.

Jennings, J. E., and A. B. A. Brink. 1961. A guide to soil profiling for civil engineering purposes in South Africa. *Transactions of the South African Institute of Civil Engineers*, vol. 3, no. 8.

Jolly, K. 1947. Preliminary note on new excavations at Skildergat, Fish Hoek. *South African Archaeological Bulletin* 2: 11–12.

———. 1948. The development of the Cape Middle Stone Age in the Skildergat Cave, Fish Hoek. *South African Archaeological Bulletin* 3: 106–7.

Keller, C. M. 1969. Mossel Bay: A redescription. *South African Archaeological Bulletin* 23: 131–40.

———. 1973. Montagu Cave in prehistoy: A descriptive analysis. *Anthropological Records*, vol. 28. Berkeley: University of California Press, pp. 1–98.

Kingston, H. D. R. 1900. Notes on some caves in Tzitzikama or Outeniqua District, near Knysna, South Africa, and the objects found therein. *Journal of the Royal Anthropological Institute* 30: 45–49.

Klein, R. G. 1970. Problems in the study of the Middle Stone Age of South Africa. *South African Archaeological Bulletin* 25: 127–35.

———. 1972a. Preliminary report on the July through September, 1970, excavations at Nelson Bay Cave, Plettenberg Bay (Cape Province, South Africa). In E. M. van Zinderen Bakker, ed., *Palaeoecology of Africa, 1969–1971*, vol. 6. Cape Town: A. A. Balkema, pp. 177–208.

———. 1972b. The Late Quaternary mammalian fauna of Nelson Bay Cave (Cape Province, South Africa): Its implications for megafaunal extinctions and environmental and cultural change. *Quaternary Research* 2: 135–42.

———. 1974. Environment and subsistence of prehistoric man in the southern Cape Province, South Africa. *World Archaeology* 5: 249–84.

———. 1975a. Ecology of Stone Age man at the southern tip of Africa. *Archaeology* 28: 238–47.

———. 1975b. Middle Stone Age man-animal relationships in southern Africa: Evidence from Die Kelders and Klasies River Mouth. *Science* 190: 265–67.

———. 1976a. The mammalian fauna of the Klasies River Mouth sites, southern Cape Province, South Africa. *South African Archaeological Bulletin* 31: 75–98.

———. 1976b. A preliminary report on the "Middle Stone Age" open-air site of Duinefontein 2 (Melkbosstrand, southwestern Cape Province, South Africa). *South African Archaeological Bulletin* 31: 12–20.

———. 1977. The ecology of early man in southern Africa. *Science* 197: 115–26.

———. 1978. Stone Age predation on large African bovids. *Journal of Archaeological Science* 5: 195–217.

Kleindienst, M. R. 1967. Questions of terminology in regard to the study of Stone Age industries in eastern Africa: "Cultural stratigraphic units." In W. W. Bishop and J. D. Clark, eds., *Background to evolution in Africa*. Chicago: University of Chicago Press, pp. 821–59.

Koch, J. H. 1949. A review of the South African representatives of the genus *Patella* Linnaeus. *Annals of the Natal Museum* 11: 487–517.

Krige, A. V. 1927. An examination of the Tertiary and Quaternary changes of sea level in South Africa. *Annals of the University of Stellenbosch* A-5: 1–81.

Ku, T.-L.; Kimmel, M. A.; Easton, W. H.; and T. J. O'Neil. 1974. Eustatic sea level 120,000 years ago on Oahu, Hawaii. *Science* 183: 959–62.

Kukla, G. J. 1975. Loess stratigraphy of central Europe. In K. W. Butzer and G. L. Isaac, eds., *After the australopithecines: stratigraphy, ecology, and culture change in the Middle Pleistocene*. Chicago: Aldine, and The Hague: Mouton, pp. 99–188.

Laidler, P. W. 1947. The evolution of Middle Palaeolithic technique at Geelhout, near Kareedouw in the southern Cape. *Transactions of the Royal Society of South Africa* 31: 283–313.

Link, A. G. 1966. Textural classification of sediments. *Sedimentology* 7: 249–54.

Louw. A. W. 1969. Bushman Rock Shelter, Ohrigstad, eastern Transvaal: A preliminary investigation, 1965. *South African Archaeological Bulletin* 24: 39–51.

Louw, J. T. 1960. *Prehistory of the Matjes River Rock Shelter. National Museum, Bloemfontein Memoir,* no. 1, pp. 1–143.

Mabbutt, J. A. 1955. Cape Hangklip—a study in coastal geomorphology. *Transactions of the Royal Society of South Africa* 34: 17–24.

McBurney, C. B. M. 1967. *The Haua Fteah (Cyrenaica) and the Stone Age of the south-east Mediterranean.* Cambridge: Cambridge University Press.

Maggs, T., and E. Speed. 1967. Bonteberg Shelter. *South African Archaeological Bulletin* 22: 80–93.

Malan, B. D. 1949. Magosian and Howieson's Poort. *South African Archaeological Bulletin* 4: 34–35.

———. 1952. The final phase of the Middle Stone Age in South Africa. *Proceedings of the First Pan-African Congress on Prehistory, Nairobi, 1947.* Oxford: Blackwell, pp. 188–94.

———. 1955. The archaeology of the Tunnel Cave and Skildergat Kop, Fish Hoek. *South African Archaeological Bulletin* 10: 3–9.

———. 1957. The term "Middle Stone Age." In J. D. Clark, ed., *Proceedings of the Third Pan-African Congress on Prehistory, Livingstone, 1955.* London: Chatto & Windus, pp. 223–27.

Marshack, A. 1972. Cognitive aspects of Upper Palaeolithic engraving. *Current Anthropology* 13: 445–77.

Martin, A. R. H. 1968. Pollen analysis of Groenvlei lake sediments, Knysna. *Review of Palaeobotany and Palynology* 7: 107–44.

Mason, R. J. 1962. *Prehistory of the Transvaal.* Johannesburg: Witwatersrand University Press.

———. 1969. Tentative interpretations of new radiocarbon dates for stone artefact assemblages from Rose Cottage Cave, O.F.S., and Bushman Rock Shelter, Tvl. *South African Archaeological Bulletin* 24: 57–59.

Mason, R. J.; Dart, R. A.; and J. W. Kitching. 1958. Bone tools at the Kalkbank Middle Stone Age site and the Makapansgat australopithecine locality, central Transvaal. *South African Archaeological Bulletin* 13: 85–116.

Moffett, R. O., and H. J. Deacon. 1977. The flora and vegetation in the surrounds of Boomplaas Cave: Cango valley. *South African Archaeological Bulletin* 32: 127–45.

Mörner, N. A. 1975. Ocean paleotemperature and continental glaciations. In *Les méthodes quantitatives d'étude des variations du climat au cours du Pléistocène.* Colloques Internationaux du CNRS (Paris), no. 219, pp. 43–49.

Movius, H. L. 1966. The hearths of the Upper Périgordian and Aurignacian horizons at the Abri Pataud, Les Eyzies (Dordogne), and their possible significance. *American Anthropologist* 68: 296–325.

Noten, F. L. V. 1974. Excavations at the Gordons Bay shell midden, southwestern Cape. *South African Archaeological Bulletin* 29: 122–42.

Opperman, H. 1978. Excavations in the Buffelskloof Rock Shelter near Calitzdorp, southern Cape. *South African Archaeological Bulletin* 33: 18–38.

Parkington, J. E. 1976. Coastal settlements between the mouths of the Berg and Olifants Rivers, Cape Province. *South African Archaeological Bulletin* 31: 127–40.

Paterson, W. S. B.; Koerner, R. M.; Fisher, D.; Johnsen, S. J.; Clausen, H. B.; Dansgaard, W.; Bucher, P.; and H. Oeschger. 1977. An oxygen-isotope climatic record from the Devon Island ice cap, arctic Canada. *Nature* 266: 508–11.

Peringuey, L. 1911. The Stone Ages of South Africa as represented in the collection of the South African Museum. *Annals of the South African Museum* 8: 1–218.

Phillipson, D. W. 1969. The prehistoric sequence at Nakapapula rockshelter, Zambia. *Proceedings of the Prehistoric Society* 35: 172–202.

Reed, C. A., and R. J. Braidwood. 1960. Towards the reconstruction of the environmental sequence of northeastern Iraq. *Studies in Ancient Oriental Civilisation* 31: 163–74.

Rightmire, G. P. 1976. Relationships of Middle and Upper Pleistocene hominids from sub-Saharan Africa. *Nature* 260: 238–40.

———. 1978. Human skeletal remains from the southern Cape Province and their bearing on the Stone Age prehistory of South Africa. *Quaternary Research* 9: 219–30.

———. 1979. Implications of Border Cave skeletal remains for later Pleistocene human evolution. *Current Anthropology* 20: 23–35.

Robertshaw, P. T. 1977. Excavations at Paternoster, southwestern Cape. *South African Archaeological Bulletin* 32: 63–73.

Rowland, M. J. 1976. *Cellana denticulata* in middens on the Coromandel Coast, New Zealand: Possibilities for a temporal horizon. *Journal of the Royal Society of New Zealand* 6: 1–15.

Rudner, J. 1968. Strandloper pottery from South and South West Africa. *Annals of the South African Museum* 49: 441–663.

———. 1971. Painted burial stones from the Cape. *South African Journal of Science,* Special Issue no. 2, pp. 54–61.

Rudner, J., and I. Rudner. 1973. A note on early excavations at Robberg. *South African Archaeological Bulletin* 28: 94–96.

Salmons, J. E. 1925. The Bush and Bantu mandibles. *South African Journal of Science* 22: 470–79.

Sampson, C. G. 1962. The Cape Hangklip main site. *Journal of the Science Society, University of Cape Town* 5: 14–31.

———. 1967a. Excavations at Glen Elliot Shelter, Colesberg District, northern Cape. *Researches of the National Museum, Bloemfontein* 2, nos. 5–6: 125–209.

———. 1967b. Excavations at Zaayfontein Shelter, Norvalspont, northern Cape. *Researches of the National Museum, Bloemfontein* 2, no. 4: 41–119.

———. 1967c. Zeekoegat 13: A Later Stone Age open-site near Venterstad, Cape. *Researches of the National Museum, Bloemfontein* 2, nos. 5–6: 211–37.

———. 1968. *The Middle Stone Age industries of the Orange River Scheme area.* National Museum, Bloemfontein Memoir, no. 4, pp. 1–111.

———. 1972. *The Stone Age industries of the Orange River Scheme and South Africa.* National Museum, Bloemfontein Memoir, no. 6, pp. 1–288.

———. 1974. *The Stone Age archaeology of southern Africa.* New York and London: Academic Press.

Schauder, D. E. 1963. The anthropological work of F. W. FitzSimons in the eastern Cape. *South African Archaeological Bulletin* 18: 52–59.

Schepers, G. W. H. 1935. A fossilised human mandible from Kopje Enkel. *South African Journal of Science* 32: 587–95.

———. 1941. The mandible of the Transvaal fossil human skeleton from Springbok Flats. *Annals of the Transvaal Museum* 20: 3.

Schweitzer, F. R. 1970. A preliminary report of excavations of a cave at Die Kelders. *South African Archaeological Bulletin* 25: 136–38.

Schweitzer, F. R., and M. L. Wilson. 1978. A preliminary report on excavations at Byneskranskop, Bredasdorp District, Cape. *South African Archaeological Bulletin* 33: 134–40.

Shackleton, N. J. 1967. Oxygen isotope analyses and Pleistocene temperatures re-assessed. *Nature* 215: 15–17.

———. 1969. The last interglacial in the marine and terrestrial records. *Proceedings of the Royal Society (London)* B174: 135–54.

———. 1973. Oxygen isotope analysis as a means of determining season of occupation of prehistoric midden sites. *Archaeometry* 15: 133–41.

———. 1975. The stratigraphic record of deep-sea cores and its implications for the assessment of glacials, interglacials, stadials, and interstadials in the mid-Pleistocene. In K. W. Butzer and G. I. Isaac, eds., *After the australopithecines: Stratigraphy, ecology, and culture change in the Middle Pleistocene*. Chicago: Aldine, and The Hague: Mouton, pp. 1–24.

Shackleton, N. J., and R. K. Matthews. 1977. Oxygen isotope stratigraphy of Late Pleistocene coral terraces in Barbados. *Nature* 268: 618–20.

Shackleton, N. J., and N. D. Opdyke. 1973. Oxygen isotope and palaeomagnetic stratigraphy of Equatorial Pacific core V28-238: Oxygen isotope temperatures and ice volumes on a 10^5 year and 10^6 year scale. *Quaternary Research* 3: 39–55.

Shaw, J. C. M. 1931. *The teeth, the bony palate, and the mandible in the Bantu races of South Africa*. London: John Bale & Sons.

Singer, R. 1959. Rejoinder to Dart. *American Anthropologist* 61: 114–15.

———. 1961. Review of *Prehistory of the Matjes River Rock Shelter*, by J. T. Louw. *South African Archaeological Bulletin* 16: 29–30.

Singer, R., and Fuller, A. O. 1962. The geology and descriptions of a fossiliferous deposit near Zwartklip in False Bay. *Transactions of the Royal Society of South Africa* 36: 205–11.

Singer, R., and P. G. Heltne. 1966. Further notes on a bone assemblage from Hopefield, South Africa. *Actas del V Congreso Panafricano de Prehistoria y de Estudio del Cuaternario* 2. Museo Arqueológico de Tenerife publicaciones del S.I.A. del Excmo. Cabildo Insular, no. 6, Santa Cruz de Tenerife, Islas Canarias, pp. 261–64.

Singer, R., and P. Smith. 1969. Some human remains associated with the Middle Stone Age deposits at Klasies River, South Africa. *American Journal of Physical Anthropology* 31: 256.

Singer, R., and J. S. Weiner. 1963. Biological aspects of some indigenous African populations. *Southwestern Journal of Anthropology* 19: 168–76.

Singer, R., and J. J. Wymer. 1968. Archaeological investigations at the Saldanha Skull site in South Africa. *South African Archaeological Bulletin* 23: 63–74.

———. 1969. Radiocarbon date for two painted stones from a coastal cave in South Africa. *Nature* 224: 508–10.

Slater, R. A. 1970. *Geomorphology and Cainozoic geology of the Continental Shelf between Cape Seal and Cape St. Francis*. South African National Committee for Oceanographic Research, Marine Geology Programme Technical Report, no. 2 (progress reports for June 1968 to December 1969), pp. 28–32.

Speed, E. 1969. Prehistoric shell collectors. *South African Archaeological Bulletin* 24: 193–96.

Stapleton, P., and J. Hewitt. 1927. Stone implements from a rock shelter at Howieson's Poort, near Grahamstown. *South African Journal of Science* 24: 574–87.

———. 1928. Stone implements from Howieson's Poort, near Grahamstown. *South African Journal of Science* 25: 399–409.

Stephenson, T. A. 1944. The constitution of the Intertidal fauna and flora of South Africa. Part 2. *Annals of the Natal Museum* 10: 261–358.

Tankard, A. J. 1974. Surface textures of detrital grains: An application of electron microscopy to archaeology. *South African Archaeological Society Goodwin Series* 2: 46–54.

Tankard, A. J., and F. R. Schweitzer. 1974. The geology of Die Kelders Cave and environs: A palaeoenvironmental study. *South African Journal of Science* 70: 365–69.

———. 1976. Textural analysis of cave sediments: Die Kelders, Cape Province, South Africa. In D. Davidson, and M. Shackley, eds., *Geoarchaeology: Earth science and the past*. London: Duckworth.

Tobias, P. V. 1967. The hominid skeletal remains of Haua Fteah. In C. B. M. McBurney, ed., *The Haua Fteah (Cyrenaica) and the Stone Age of the south-east Mediterranean*. Cambridge: Cambridge University Press, pp. 338–52.

———. 1971. Human skeletal remains from the Cave of Hearths, Makapansgat, northern Transvaal. *American Journal of Physical Anthropology* 34: 335–68.

Turner, M. 1970. A search for the Tsitsikamma Shelters. *South African Archaeological Bulletin* 25: 67–70.

Urey, H. C. 1947. The thermodynamic properties of isotopic substances. *Journal of the Chemical Society:* 562–81.

Vallois, H. V. 1951. La mandibule humaine fossile de la Grotte du Porc-épic près Dire-Daoua (Abyssinie). *L'Anthropologie* 55: 231–38.

Vogel, J. C. 1969a. The radiocarbon time-scale. *South African Archaeological Bulletin* 24: 83–87.

———. 1969b. Radiocarbon dating of Bushman Rock Shelter, Ohrigstad District. *South African Archaeological Bulletin* 24: 56.

———. 1970. Groningen radiocarbon dates IX. *Radiocarbon* 12: 444–71.

Vogel, J. C., and Beaumont, P. B. 1972. Revised radiocarbon chronology for the Stone Age in South Africa. *Nature* 237: 50–51.

Voigt, E. A. 1973a. Stone Age molluscan utilization at Klasies River Mouth Caves. *South African Journal of Science* 69: 306–9.

———. 1973b. Klasies River Mouth: An exercise in shell analysis. *Bulletin of the Transvaal Museum*, No. 14, pp. 14–15.

———. 1975. Studies of marine mollusca from archaeological sites: Dietary preferences, environmental reconstructions, and ethnological parallels. In A. Clason, ed., *Archaeozoological studies*. Amsterdam: North-Holland, pp. 87–98.

Volman, T. P. 1978. Early archaeological evidence for shellfish collecting. *Science* 201: 911–13.

Wells, L. H. 1952. Human crania of the Middle Stone Age in South Africa. *Proceedings of the First Pan-African Congress on Prehistory, Nairobi, 1947*, pp. 125–33.

———. 1957. The place of the Broken Hill Skull among human types. In J. D. Clark, ed., *Proceedings of the Third Pan-African Congress on Prehistory, Livingstone, 1955*. London: Chatto & Windus, pp. 172–74.

Wendt, W. E. 1976. "Art mobilier" from the Apollo 11 Cave, South West Africa: Africa's oldest dated works of art. *South African Archaeological Bulletin* 31: 5–11.

Whitworth, T. 1966. A fossil hominid from Rudolf. *South African Archaeological Bulletin* 21: 138–50.

Willcox, A. R. 1974. Reasons for the non-occurrence of Middle Stone Age material in the Natal Drakensberg. *South African Journal of Science* 70: 273–74.

World Nautical Chart No. 3838. 1963. U.S. Naval Oceanographic Office.

Zeuner, F. E. 1959. *Dating the past*. 4th ed. London: Methuen.

Author Index

General Index

230